Social Democracy
in Latin America

Social Democracy in Latin America

Prospects for Change

EDITED BY

Menno Vellinga

Westview Press

BOULDER • SAN FRANCISCO • OXFORD

Copyright © 1993 by Westview Press, Inc.

Published in 1993 in the United States of America by Westview Press, Inc., 5500 Central Avenue, Boulder, Colorado 80301-2877, and in the United Kingdom by Westview Press, 36 Lonsdale Road, Summertown, Oxford OX2 7EW

Library of Congress Cataloging-in-Publication Data
Social democracy in Latin America : prospects for change / edited by
    Menno Vellinga.
      p. cm.
    Includes index.
    ISBN 0-8133-8216-5
    1. Socialism—Latin America.
HX110.5.S65   1993
320.5'315'098—dc20   93-3009
                                                                         CIP

Printed and bound in the United States of America

10   9   8   7   6   5   4   3   2   1

For Bram

Contents

Preface

This volume includes fifteen contributions by leading European and Latin American social scientists. They reflect on a critical issue in the present debate on possible ways out of the economic and political crisis that continues to punish the South American continent. As editor I want to extend my heartfelt gratitude to all the contributors. They have been extraordinarily diligent, resourceful and patient. My invitation to them to participate in the project was met by an immediate and enthusiastic response. The chapters reflect their honest scholarship, as well as their high levels of personal commitment to a political future for Latin America that would bring equality, social justice and civil and human rights within the context of a process of *social* democratization. The book renews one's idealism without, however, losing a keen awareness of the possibilities and impossibilities of realizing such a development.

Latin Americans often look with envy upon the European welfare states—styled by social democracy—where economic growth, combined with distributive action by the state, led to a reasonable degree of equality and social justice. However, they often lack a clear knowledge about the economic, political and ideological significance of the social democratic alternative. The label "social democratic" is often used without sufficient awareness of the extent to which structural transformation and reform—leading to income distribution, production for basic needs provision and access to these basic goods and services for the poor majorities of the Latin American population—could form a part of social democratic policies in specific countries. In this context, it is useful to discuss the European experience with social democracy and to indicate whether it contains a model of development that suits a Latin American reality characterized by the demise of populism, fragile processes of democratization and an uncertain economic future that likely has only narrow margins for reformist policies.

I owe Paula Duivenvoorde, Petra Nesselaar and Jan Withagen a debt of gratitude for their help in preparing the manuscript. I would like to thank Thomas and Francis Gibbons for their cooperation in

ix

making the necessary translations. The University of Florida's Center for Latin American Studies offered me hospitality when I was a visiting professor there during the second half of 1990 and enabled me to work on the manuscript. The University of Utrecht's Center for Caribbean and Latin American Studies has been extremely supportive of my research endeavors. I am very grateful for the space they have given me to pursue these interests.

I dedicate this book to Dr. Bram Peper, mayor of the city of Rotterdam, a superb intellectual, a most stimulating analyst of the social democratic movement and—above all—my dearest old friend.

Menno Vellinga
University of Utrecht

PART ONE

Introduction

1

The Internationalization of Politics and Local Response: Social Democracy in Latin America

Menno Vellinga

To suggest social democracy as a viable source of inspiration while trying to find a solution to the present economic and political crisis in Latin America may seem rather unrealistic. The model has been so identified with the Western and Northern European welfare states that its application to poverty-stricken Latin America will probably not be among the first thoughts that occur to foreign analysts. Yet, in Latin America itself, the possibilities and limitations of developments styled along social democratic lines and accompanying democratization are being widely discussed. The term *tercera via*, third road, which originally referred to a position between East European *socialism* and *capitalism* and which had lost its significance after the events in Eastern Europe, was reactivated and applied to the Latin American situation. Here it was used to refer to a position between neoliberal policies and the traditional national populist approaches. It came to stand for a strategy that would allow for a restructuring of the economy and society "with a human face." This is contrary to the recipes of the International Monetary Fund (IMF)—which show an ugly, unrestrained free market capitalism, according to many Latin American observers—and contrary to a restoration of national-populist practices that would represent a return to a path that has brought disaster in the past.

Until recently, the term *social democrat* was not viewed very positively in Latin America, but this has changed. Several factors have contributed to the reevaluation of a strategy that is more reformist and less revolutionary, more pragmatic and less ideological,

more capitalist and less Socialist than the radical political elites in
the 1960s could stomach. First, the radical political options defended
by these elites fared badly in subsequent years. In many countries,
entire political generations were killed off, exiled or neutralized in
other ways. The extreme repression practiced by the military-
authoritarian regimes brought a new appreciation of liberties and
human rights that previously had been discounted as liberal-bourgeois
tricks diverting attention from the need to fulfill more basic
socioeconomic needs. Second, these regimes' efforts to restructure the
economy at great social cost, together with a complete disregard for
the considerable increase in social inequality, forced many to
reconsider their past rejections of social reformism.

The (social democratic) Socialist International (SI) actively
opposed the military-authoritarian regimes, the repression they
unleashed against the civilian population and the economic policies
they had put into practice. SI's record in this area has been
impeccable, which has enhanced the image of the social democratic
movement among Latin American intellectuals. In addition, a number
of events in Europe reduced the traditional antagonism between
Communists and social democrats. Within the Euro-Communist
movement, a parliamentary and reformist approach was emphasized
that did not exclude coalitions with social democracy. In several
Southern European countries (Spain, Portugal, France, Greece, Italy),
social democrats took power, giving considerable prestige to the
movement as a whole. Meanwhile, Marxist theory had entered into a
deep crisis. Even among strong supporters, its severe limitations in
providing a methodology for the organization of a national economy
and society and an explanation of the dynamics of the international
economy had to be acknowledged. Slowly it became clear that the
market mechanism had to be given a place in the organization of an
economy. That was not very different from the role given to it by the
social democrats in the so-called mixed economies of Northern and
Western Europe. The collapse of the East European economies and the
complete discrediting of their political systems finally convinced
those who had still been wavering. The interest in social democratic
political and economic strategies rapidly increased. At one point,
there was even a considerable struggle going on among old and new
parties in Eastern Europe to use the label "social democratic."

Parallel to the changes in social democracy's image in Latin
America, the interest in the region among European social democrats
increased. This occurred in response to the developments in Latin
America mentioned above. It was also motivated, however, by an
independent missionary zeal within the European social democratic

parties that emerged in the 1970s. How did this come about? What was being proposed and why? In this period, politics became increasingly internationalized. This trend also influenced the European Christian democrats and the liberals. What were the motives behind such development as far as the social democrats are concerned? The internationalization of politics first emerged as a distinct phenomenon during the transition toward democracy in Southern Europe in the 1970s. More recently it showed its power again during the developments in Eastern Europe. Latin America was no exception.

Background and Motives

In Western Europe in the 1960s, the welfare state was built up. The period of reconstruction after World War II had ended. International development cooperation emerged in the course of the 1960s as an almost natural extension of the social services within the welfare state. At first, it extended to the former colonial areas in Africa and Asia, but later on it was also directed to Latin America. Other countries in Northern and Western Europe without a strong colonial tradition also initiated development cooperation programs that included Latin America. In many of these countries during those years, social democrats were in power and controlled the ministries of international development cooperation. Would it be too simple to assume that the actions of European social democracy with regard to Latin America in those years were initiated as a sequel to the growth of development cooperation activities in an area with a considerable cultural proximity to Europe—an area that was experiencing political events that had created a strong response in the mass media? Most of the contacts were new. The concrete relationships with Latin America in this period were few in number. The social democratic movement had ties with a few Latin American parties, although—admittedly— these were not strong. The Latin American section of the SI had been founded in Montevideo in 1955 and in that period united few parties— Acción Democrática (AD) in Venezuela, Partido Liberación Nacional (PLN) in Costa Rica, Partido Radical (PR) in Chile, People's National Party in Jamaica and People's National Movement (PNM) in Trinidad-Tobago. The entire SI came together on Latin American soil for the first time in Santiago, Chile, in February 1973, shortly before the September coup.[1]

Among the Europeans, German social democracy (through the Sozialdemokratische Partei Deutschland, SPD) had been particularly active in developing relations with Latin America. It had a foothold in the region since 1966 when its Friedrich Ebert Foundation founded the Latin American Institute for Social Research (ILDIS) in Santiago. Active political involvement in Latin America, however, did not start before 1976, when Carlos Andrés Pérez played host in Caracas to the leading European social democrat and Socialist leaders (Willy Brandt, Olof Palme, Bruno Kreisky, Mano Soares, Felipe González and others). They met with a wide range of Latin American political groups. The major objective of the meeting was to take a stand against the repression and the trampling of human rights by the military regimes in the region. It had a strong follow-up. In subsequent years a flow of conferences, meetings, missions, declarations and the like were produced. Meetings were mostly held in Latin America as regional meetings in which European sister parties participated. But in 1986, the SI held its 17th Congress in Lima. For the first time, an SI congress was held on Latin American soil. Leading topics were the process of democratization in the area, the peace process in Central America and the debt crisis. The SI deals with these general activities. The organizational and financial support to the affiliated parties in Latin America is handled at the bilateral level and involves contacts between individual parties and movements. The Germans, again, have been particularly active in this field. The Friedrich Ebert Foundation —present in most Latin American countries—was used as a most effective instrument to structure these activities. These comprised seminars, grants and technical assistance in the fields of trade union organization, adult education, mass communications, agrarian reform, financial institutions and general planning, as well as direct organizational and financial assistance to political parties and movements. They had a wide political scope, for example, they were not specifically or exclusively directed toward those parties associated with the SI. The clientele of "friends and associates" consisted of a varied assortment of guerrilla organizations, Marxist movements, parliamentary Socialists, populists, liberal-conservatives and movements of a strong personalist nature. All took advantage of the opportunity to deepen their ties with Europe and to internationalize their political links through contacts with a movement that at the very least had an impeccable record of opposition against the oppressive military regimes and of struggle for political freedom and human rights. At the same time, the social democratic parties represented one of the few international links giving material help and providing political "know-how."

The intensity of the German effort in the 1970s has raised some questions about deeper motives besides the more general ones mentioned previously. In his chapter, Tilman Evers has evaluated systematically the various hypotheses that have been posed. Most of these focus on material interests the Europeans supposedly were furthering. After all, one does not need to be a full-fledged Marxist to acknowledge that few people do something for nothing. Evers's analysis, however, lends little support to these theses. Neither the idea of the social democratic offensive being a political complement to the extension of Western capital nor the thesis of a social democracy creating markets overseas for Western industrial exports appear to have been a strong motive. Kenneth Hermele suggests that initially these factors played a role in the Swedish case. The results for Swedish capital, however, have been small. It is indicative that the social democratic effort was most concentrated in countries where industrial development was weak (Central America, Cuba, the Dominican Republic). Political interest appears to have been the real driving force. But even this seems not to have formed part of a conscious strategy to provide an acceptable alternative to bourgeois domination while maintaining the basic logic of the capitalist order, a strategy that was pursued in the post-1974 situation in Portugal. Rather, the real motive must have been a very simple one: the building of networks of political contacts, often of a strong personal nature, in an area in which they did not exist.[2] Often this had to do with an effort to help political elites survive in situations of strong repression and difficult economic times and with an elite's consciousness of its own weaknesses and reduced alternatives for potential allies. Sometimes the elites were of social democratic persuasion, but more often they were not. As such, this strategy is not much different from the one practised by the Ford Foundation in Brazil after 1964. It preserves the possibility of an influence in future political developments. International development cooperation projects organized by several Western countries (The Netherlands, Sweden) have practised a similar strategy.[3]

In the course of the 1970s, the interest in Latin America was heightened by the discussion about the economic relations between the Western industrialized nations and the Third World as part of the so-called North-South debate. This movement was led by people like Brandt and Palme, who at the same time dominated policymaking within the SI. The ideological orientation of the North-South debate and the one shared by the Western social democratic parties united in the SI ran parallel, and this accounted for the debate's progressive image. Central elements of the social democratic creed, such as defense of worker organizations, support for an improvement in wages and working conditions, a belief in the effectiveness of the parliamentary system, free elections and the responsibility of the state for the creation of conditions of equality and social justice, may have become part of the status quo in the West European situation. In Latin America, however, these challenge the existing models of development and in doing so form an appealing political alternative for reformist-oriented participants.

After having reviewed the motives behind the activities of European social democracy in Latin America, the question arises: What can it really offer as a model of development, beyond the more general elements mentioned above? One may assume that the opportunity to participate in international political networks is not the only factor determining its present popularity among Latin American intellectuals and politicians. What are the real possibilities for a social democratization of politics? Does it offer a way out of the present economic and political crisis? What are the factors limiting the possibility of such a strategy being realized?

Social Democracy in Latin America

The European Model

Social democracy in Europe and in Latin America originated in differing sociohistorical contexts, and, subsequently, it has developed differently. The strong European influence is a recent phenomenon. European social democracy, as Alain Touraine notes in his chapter, has been characterized by the dominance of social categories over political ones. In Latin America, however, political categories have always prevailed over social ones. This is an important difference. Of course, there is not *one* brand of European social democracy. Considerable differences exist between the Scandinavian, German and Dutch types on the one hand and the French, Italian and Spanish types on the other, with the British and Belgians somewhere in between.[4] All share, however, strong roots in the labor movement and emphasize the role of the state in achieving conditions of general welfare and equality. Socialism in its pure form was left by all at an early stage and exchanged for a more pragmatic, reformist position. Socialism has always been a political, rather than a social, force. In practice the workers opted for short-term material gains, and all through the history of the labor movement, it has been difficult to mobilize the rank and file for long-term projects of massive socioeconomic transformation. Those political parties or movements that tried suffered disastrous defeats at the polls and fell into decline. The reformist approach of the social democratic movement has developed within the context of dynamic capitalist development. Strong economic growth made it possible to honor demands for wage increases, to improve working conditions and to finance social welfare policies while still giving the capitalist a superior part of the economic surplus. Pluralist political structures, run by a parliamentary system based on general and free elections, made it very worthwhile to try to gain influence and power over the state. This became even more relevant because the state had assumed important functions in the mobilization of resources—especially with regard to the distribution and allocation of capital and labor. Since the 1930s the state role has increasingly been characterized by Keynesian economics. In the reconstruction years following World War II, the commitment to create a welfare state emerged. The basic provisions of such a welfare state were accepted as part of a broad national consensus, and the consensus remained, even under governments in which social democracy had no presence.

This shift within the social democratic movement from the goals of the radical transformation of society to the very pragmatic course of piecemeal reformism is viewed by Adam Przeworski as an inevitable development.[5] In his opinion, no radical mass movement in a situation governed by liberal democratic freedoms will be able to resist the enticement of short-term material gains. The transition toward socialism in any society will be viewed as too costly a process, one that is loaded with sacrifices for an ideal that present generations will not live to see put into practice. The case of Cuba appears to refute this thesis. It can be argued, however, that this case is highly atypical, and, viewing Cuba's present problems, a social democratic alternative may be the only one that is indicated in order to preserve the provisions for basic needs and social welfare that the Cuban Revolution installed.

One can debate whether the development, as outlined by Przeworski, is one of "free" choice or one "forced" by the mechanisms of the capitalist system that leave little alternative. Paul Cammack—while discussing Przeworski's ideas—argues in defense of the latter position, but regardless of whether the decision for reformism is negative or positive, it is hard to deny that Przeworski's analysis is appealing in light of what has happened historically. For European social democracy there always has been little separation between the logic behind the functioning of the economy and that behind the course political action has taken. This explains its pragmatism. It depends on one's own political stand whether this is viewed as a negative or a positive element. Social democracy has its origins in the labor movement, but, once installed, it de-emphasized class identities and in political practice provided a context for a wide constituency situated left of the center of the political spectrum. The challenge to capitalism and the free market economy was replaced by an emphasis on the responsibility of the state to provide regulations that would prevent excesses and repair nasty consequences. Where necessary the state should take an active entrepreneurial role itself and establish a mixed economy. These elements, added to a considerable flexibility and capacity to adapt to changing circumstances—in the absence of a well-developed ideological framework with prescriptive powers—appeal to political strategists not only in Latin America but also in other regions that are suffering a severe economic and political crisis, such as Eastern Europe.

Ironically, this discussion about social democracy as an attractive and viable option between state socialism and free market capitalism or between neoliberalism and national populism is taking place at a time when, in Western Europe itself, the social democratic movement has entered into a deep crisis. Its political base of support in society underwent a dramatic change under the influence of alterations in the economic structure. The traditional industrial proletariat has substantially decreased in size. The expanded populations in the new tertiary and "quaternary" sectors feel less attracted to the social democratic movement. It has become increasingly difficult to build the coalition that in the past had been so effective: the one between the "haves" and the "have-nots," between the bottom layers of society and the intellectual elite. Several of social democracy's problems are in fact the result of past successes in the emancipation of the working class. Its original objectives in the areas of social security and protection against the consequences of illness, old age or unemployment were achieved. The state has expanded its responsibilities to virtually all areas that involve a medical, social or economic risk. All this led to a decrease in the mobilizing power of the social democratic movement. In addition, the policies the movement had inspired created problems of their own. In all Northern and West European nations, the state came to absorb more than half of the gross national product (GNP). An elaborate bureaucracy was created to manage the state-run or state-subsidized programs. Bureaucratic excesses, the demands made on the state when so many individual problems were made part of a collective responsibility, critically high levels of payments for taxes and social security and the strong redistributive actions of the state that limited the capacity for accumulation among the well-to-do all fed the neoconservative criticism of the welfare state, even in social democracy's stronghold, Sweden. In several countries, social democracy lost to Center-Right governments. In the political opposition, an often painful process of evaluation and redefinition of objectives and strategy began. The social democratic movement never had a well worked out and consistent theoretical perspective. Action has always been inspired by no more than a few rather general principles. The dynamic relationship between these principles and new developments in society were the main source of inspiration and creativity. Again, paradoxically, this has been one of the movement's weaknesses and at the same time one of its strengths.

To map out a new course has become a complicated affair. The discussion has centered around the following issues:[6]

- the definition of rights and duties of the civilian subjects in relation to those of the state;
- the kind of care to be extended to those who, against their will, have fallen into a situation of economic dependence—an issue of solidarity also motivated by the insight that in order to keep society from disintegrating, the existence of neglected sectors cannot be tolerated in an open democratic system in which socioeconomic welfare has been fairly generalized;
- the realization of essential human and civil rights;
- the relationship between economic growth and ecological considerations;
- the necessity to build new North-South relationships that include a solution to the debt problem;
- the integration of these social, ecological and economic objectives in a consistent strategy.

The recognition of the importance of the market system and the need to support a competitive, efficient and innovative business sector has been essential throughout these discussions. This has gained, so it appears, priority over the objective of full employment that has dominated the social democratic action programs since the world crisis in the 1930s. Past vitriolic criticisms of capitalism have subsided. This has meant a change from positions that were taken in the 1970s when the emphasis was on the distributive, rather than the productive, side of the economy. Fernando Cardoso makes clear in his contribution to this volume that this element has also emerged in the discussion within Latin American social democracy.

The Latin American Tradition

The social democratic movement in Latin America does not have very strong roots. In Europe, the movement's growth has run parallel to the development of an industrial structure. It was—in the first instance—a worker movement. In Latin America, the political discussion on the Left—from the end of the nineteenth century on—had great problems finding its way to the spheres of organization and action in defense of consistent, long-term emancipatory objectives. The Second International initially maintained Marxist theory as its source of inspiration and had the creation of socialism as its primary objective. In the selection of means, though—free elections and parliamentary procedures, gradual change, liberal-democratic rules of the game—a strategy was chosen in political practice that created a considerable distance from the more radical sectors on the Left. This gap increased in subsequent decades when Marxism continued to inspire the political discourse among social democrats. It remained, however, on the level of phraseology and lost any prescriptive power over the course of the movement.

Sociohistorically, Latin America does not seem to be the most ideal breeding ground for politics styled along social democratic lines. The heritage of Iberian bureaucratic patrimonialism in Latin America left phenomena like a strong presidentialism, political centralism, authoritarianism, corporatism, clientelism and personalism, none of which—in combination with a weak industrial capitalist development in most countries—is associated with the emergence of independent social democratic mass organizations in which the working class might be integrated. In the more industrialized countries of Latin America, the labor movement rapidly became a part of corporatist structures, through which it lost its autonomy, integrity and identity as a class organization. Following the populist political formula, its leadership was co-opted into official political networks, while its members were bought off through small improvements in working and living conditions that set them off as a privileged minority against those not forming part of the unionized urban-industrial world. Those bargaining structures through which social democracy was able to cash in on the expansion of its base of support among workers, intellectuals and part of the middle classes have very much remained a European phenomenon.

Cammack points to the lack of maturity in capitalism, resulting in an absence of bourgeois hegemony, as the main explanatory factor. This is a much-discussed issue in Latin America—and with reason. Obviously, it takes two to tango. A process of class formation among the working population entailing organization, the development of an ideology and engagement in action in defense of its own interests requires the presence of a bourgeoisie to define itself against. This presence, however, does not always guarantee capitalist maturity in all spheres, which also depends on the form the bourgeoisie will take as far as its identity and sense of mission is concerned. In several regions of Latin America a bourgeoisie has developed. Monterrey/ México, Medellín/Colombia and Arequipa/Perú are cases in point.[7] Their behaviour in the economic sphere conforms to classical capitalist criteria. The actions in the social and political spheres, however, are governed by rules that are totally different. In the industrial city of Monterrey, the bourgeoisie maintains industrial relations with a strong paternalist element, represses autonomous labor organizations and shows deep hostility toward any form of political reformism seeking more than insignificantly small changes. The insistence among the bourgeoisie on following archaic patterns of labor-management relations is completely opposed to an institutionalization of class conflict through an emphasis on cooperation, compromise and bargaining with an independent labor movement. This last-mentioned development is what one would expect given the degree of maturity in capitalist development in Monterrey.[8]

Viewing the social democratic heritage in the various countries, it becomes clear that in many cases it has been tied up in the populist regimes of the 1930s, 1940s and 1950s, characterized by *caudillismo,* the ample use of clientelism as a mechanism of class control and the integration of labor into corporatist structures. There are few exceptions. The Socialist movement in Chile and the Alianza Popular Revolucionaria Americana (APRA) of Perú could be mentioned. Their nonconformity to the pattern, however, probably has more to do with the lack of access to government power than with anything else. The formal membership of the social democratic movement was small. When the Latin American section of the SI was founded in 1955, it counted only three Latin American members and two from the Caribbean. This total number had increased to only eight in 1971. But in the following decades the section experienced an explosive growth. A great number of parties in Latin America and the Caribbean defining themselves as social democratic organizations joined the SI, either as full members or with observer status.[9]

Those with full membership status in Latin America are Partido Democrático Trabalhista (PDT) (Brazil), Partido Radical (PR) (Chile), Partido Liberación Nacional (PLN) (Costa Rica), Partido Revolucionario Dominicano (PRD) (Dominican Republic), Izquierda Democrática (ID) (Ecuador), Movimiento Nacional Revolucionario (MNR) (El Salvador), Partido Socialista Democrático (PSD) (Guatemala), Partido Revolucionario Febrerista (PRF) (Paraguay) and Acción Democrática (AD) (Venezuela). Those with observer states are Movimiento de Izquierda Revolucionaria (MIR) (Bolivia), Partido Aprista Peruano (APRA) (Perú), Movimiento Electoral del Pueblo

(MEP) (Venezuela), Partido Independentista Puertoriqueño (PIP) (Puerto Rico) and until 1988 the Partido Revolucionario Democrático (PRD) (Panamá).

In the Caribbean the SI counts as full members Barbados Labor Party (BLP) (Barbados), Movemientu Antiyas Nobo (MAN) (Curaçao), People's National Party (PNP) (Jamaica) and until 1983 the New Jewel Movement (NJM) (Grenada). Those with observer status are Movimiento Electoral di Pueblo (MEP) (Aruba), Working People's Alliance (WPA) (Guyana), Parti Nationaliste Progressiste Revolutionaire (PANAPRA) (Haiti), Progressive Labor Party (PLP) (St. Lucia) and Labor Party SVG (St. Vincent and the Grenadines).

The membership of the SI in Latin America is continuously expanding, and it has come to organize parties and movements of some variety: traditional parties with considerable experience in the center of the political spectrum, like APRA, AD and PLN and on the other hand those with a strong anti-imperialist and anticapitalist tradition like MNR and the New Jewel Movement. This pattern has continued. In the beginning of the 1980s the Liberal Party of Colombia, as well as the insurgent movement M-19, courted the SI. The Partido Revolucionario Institucional (PRI) (México) and the Frente Sandinista de Liberación Nacional (FSLN) (Nicaragua) did the same thing. And at one moment even the Montoneros of Argentina and the Ejército Guerrillero de los Pobres (EGP) of Guatemala knocked at the door of the SI to ask for support.

Perspectives

The failure of social democracy to develop a strong power position in Latin American politics during the period of successful capitalist industrialization after World War II is as striking as its success in Europe during the same period. I indicated a few of the more important factors that may explain this phenomenon. Some of these still count, and from their presence one could easily conclude that any social democratically inspired solution to the present economic and political crisis in Latin America is impossible. Various countries suffered long years of a ruthless brand of authoritarianism. Others carry a suffocating heritage of populist rule. The processes of democratization in these countries are fragile and vulnerable. Social democracy implies—as Pablo González Casanova explains in this volume—*social* democracy, that is, the establishment of a system of government that guarantees pluralist political participation with full political and civil liberties in order to level out economic, social and cultural inequalities; its success in doing so is a necessary condition to reproduce this system. One does not need much imagination to see the problems involved. At the same time it is obvious—as most chapters in this volume show—that old solutions to Latin America's economic and political problems have worn out. The populist formula cannot be revitalized. The model of a paternalist, distributive state, which is constantly undermining the autonomy of the social sectors through their integration into centrally controlled corporatist structures with a strong input of authoritarianism, has been exhausted. It no longer offers a way out of the present chaos, if only because the continuing economic crisis will prevent its implementation, and that is not even the most important limiting factor. The military-bureaucratic authoritarian option is also one that is worn out. It has been thoroughly discredited nationally and internationally and is not likely to be resurrected. The present chaos is pressuring most countries down a road of neoliberal policy options. All of them deepen existing inequalities, erode the social responsibilities of the state and emphasize its identification with the interests of the upper layers of society. Paradoxically enough, if one continues this course of action, the state may come to resemble the bourgeoisie's executive committee of the traditional Marxist analyses after all, more than in any period since the time of the old oligarchical republics. Deep contradictions exist between the trend toward democratization, generating claims from previously unrepresented and/or repressed segments of society, and the trend toward state reform, in practice consisting of shock measures that cut deep into the state-run or state-subsidized programs that would have to respond to these claims. These contradictions surface in riots and revolts, as we have seen in Argentina, Brazil, Venezuela, Perú and other countries.[10]

So where does one go from here? The authors contributing to this volume take differing positions, exhibiting varying degrees of optimism or pessimism with regard to the possibility of a social democratically inspired solution to the present economic and political crisis. I mentioned earlier Cammack's thesis that the lack of capitalist hegemony is the main factor that will impede such a solution. Full capitalist development, one can assume, indeed would bring about distributional and structural reforms, creating an opening. The present economic crisis, though, would present a major obstacle to the realization of such a development. Cardoso and Touraine are less pessimistic. Touraine agrees with Cammack that the most logical way to establish social democracy would be through a victory of capitalism, the formation of an entrepreneurial class and the organization of a worker movement that would force state intervention on behalf of workers' interests and establish an industrial democracy. This is the Western model, and there is at the moment only one country that appears to be moving in this direction: Chile. This observation is supported by Alex Fernández Jilberto in his chapter on this country. Marcelo Cavarozzi seconds this opinion, mentioning the Chilean case as an example of what he calls "the renewed Left." In order to speed up the process, however, labor would need to operate from a position of greater strength and consciousness, giving it greater independence vis-à-vis the employers or the state and making it more complicated for either one of those to control it. A reduction of pressures on the labor market would help here, but that is not going to be achieved very soon. Class conflict would have to be institutionalized—following the classic social democratic recipe—through an emphasis on cooperation, compromise and bargaining with a labor movement structuring the greater part of its concrete activities around an economism that would change the distribution of income and power but would leave the basic elements of a capitalist, free market system intact.

In countries other than Chile, this development is still far away, and neoliberal strategies and politics prevail. Touraine rightfully notes that all new political strategies, whether populist, antiliberal or social democratic, will have their end (and their point of departure) in neoliberal policies because these represent a very basic way of running an economy. Awareness of the unworkability of past political formulas, Touraine notes, should produce an effort to combine these economic strategies with an advanced social policy, however strange bedfellows they may seem to be. This would be the starting point for a Latin American brand of social democracy and one of the few ways to ward off the combined phenomenon of the impoverishment of the middle classes and the increased exclusion of the lower classes. Cardoso sees this process of social democratization happening more as a result of a "serendipity effect," an unexpected course of action with even more unexpected consequences, than as the outcome of a consciously planned strategy of social reform. His position on the essentials of social democratic policy shows some parallels with the discussion that is carried on within the European social democratic movement. He emphasizes the need to give proper attention to the productive side of the economy and then to the distributive side, which always has been social democracy's main interest. But this emphasis on economic growth and consequently the recognition of the international dimensions involved has to be reconciled with the rational medium-term interests and claims of various social groups. This balance between support for redistributive policies aimed at social equality and the maintenance of those elements in the economy that will motivate individual groups to move ahead is a very delicate one. The state will have to play a role here. There is no institution capable of taking its place in this area. In almost all Latin American countries, the neoliberal offensive pushes toward the creation of a "minimal" state, but it is obvious that this entity will not be able to take on the responsibilities envisioned in the social democratic conceptions of the socially necessary state. To steer between these neoliberal conceptions and the heritage of a populist-corporatist state is one of the main challenges for the social democratic movement in Latin America.

A major source of inspiration in the 1980s has been the way in which the Spanish social democratic party (Partido Socialista Obrero Español, PSOE) has engineered the change from an authoritarian state with strong corporatist features to a state that has withdrawn from many areas and practices a very selective intervention in the economy and society as a part of a strategy combining basically neoliberal measures with "social protectionism." Social democracy here employs a methodology rather than a model of development. It has a number of basic objectives—social justice, a certain degree of socioeconomic equality, the reduction of social tensions while maintaining a limited free market economy—and means that are basically those of an open, pluralist and democratic parliamentary system. In the Spanish case, social democracy's flexibility in adapting to local circumstances proved again to be its strength. The Iberian heritage has often been pointed out as being responsible for the political backwardness of Latin America. But the developments in Spain after the Franco regime show that it is not an invincible stumbling block on the road toward the creation of a *social* democracy.

The internationalization of politics has become a phenomenon as inevitable as the internationalization of the economy. It is as difficult to close oneself off from external influences in the political sphere as it is in the economic sphere. The discussion of "native" solutions to the political crisis ignore the influences that are already present—through the SI, the Christian democrats, the European liberals and the U.S. conservatives. These have a heavy impact on local discussions of political strategies. The appeal of the PSOE is a case in point. In the past fifteen years, the internationalization of politics entailed a considerable transfer of funds to local parties. In some cases these have become very dependent upon financial and political aid from abroad. U.S. aid to conservative parties during election time in Central America (Nicaragua, El Salvador, Panamá) and South America (Perú) has often been quite voluminous. But the European internationals have also become heavily involved. This is a drawback to the extent that it may reenforce the established party structures to the disadvantage of competing social movements. In this way it may hamper full democratization, instead of furthering it.

Most of the contacts that include concrete aid and assistance are part of bilateral relations between individual European social democratic parties and their Latin American sister parties within the SI. A more general and more diversified package of relations with the European Economic Community (EEC) is still far from becoming a reality. The social democratic majority in the European parliament has not been able to produce EEC policies that respond in a satisfactory way to the Latin American quest for closer relations in the economic, cultural and political spheres. This has generated a considerable amount of frustration. For Latin Americans it has often been difficult to distinguish between the positions taken by individual parties or the SI and those assumed by social democratic governments and the EEC. The former tend to be more programmatic and often are different from those taken by governments or the EEC.[11]

The economic relations between Europe and Latin America have not been intense, as I mentioned earlier. The prospects for a strong autonomous growth in the near future are not very bright. Trade relations do grow—but at a rather slow pace. An important historical reason has to do with Latin America's traditional relations with North America. The composition of the Latin American export package, however, is also part of the problem. Several agricultural products are produced by the EEC countries themselves and in abundant quantities. Other products can be imported more cheaply from other areas. The import of products manufactured in Latin America (for example, textiles) suffers from European protectionism. Exports from Western Europe to Latin America are less important than those to other areas, and they are dominated by big enterprises and multinational corporations. At the moment, growth is very slow. Restrictive import policies, as a result of the indebtedness of most Latin American countries, create little room for expansion.

Since Spain and Portugal joined EEC, the discussion about a redefinition of the economic relations between Europe and Latin America has intensified. In the last few years, the European parliament has discussed, several times, the need for a new trade agreement that would create more opportunities for Latin American products in the European market. The need to support the creation of stable democracies is mentioned as a major motive. As of now, this has not resulted in an expansion of the so-called Lomé agreements that regulate the relations between the EEC and a large number of nations with which individual EEC countries have or had a "special" relationship, mostly through former colonial ties. The recent developments in Eastern Europe have drawn attention away from almost all other issues and have given the necessary changes in the relationship with Latin America a low priority on the political agenda.

The EEC has a general program for development aid to Asia and Latin America, in addition to the various bilateral programs maintained by the member states. Also, it has special programs for the Andean region and the Central American countries, but the total volume of aid is not impressive. On the multilateral level, the various EEC countries are involved in international financial institutions, such as the World Bank, the IMF and the Interamerican Development Bank (IDB)—institutions that have not succeeded in building a reputation for social reform-minded policy recommendations.

European social democracy has long disputed U.S. domination in Latin America, but in recent years its policy of confrontation has been replaced by a low-profile policy. One wonders whether the actions of the United States in the Caribbean (Grenada) and in Panamá introduce a new period of U.S. hegemony in the region with political consequences that—considering the history of U.S. economic and political involvement—may not be conducive to reform. Apart from this external development, a considerable number of other factors could be mentioned that limit the prospects of reforms inspired by social democracy. Most of these played a role in the Iberian situation in the 1970s and 1980s. Reform strategies are difficult to accomplish. They often fall short of expectations because they must satisfy so many diverse goals: those of justice, equality and growth. In addition, these goals—given their abstract nature—can be put into operation in many different ways. In the Iberian situation, one would not have expected a process of social democratization. Cardoso's prediction of such a development eventually coming about in Latin America as the result of a "serendipity effect" may not appear to be so far-fetched after all.[12]

Notes

1. For an account of the activities of the SI in Latin America in the 1970s and early 1980s, see Uwe Koppsch, *Die Rolle und Aktivitäten der Sozialistischen Internationale und Ihrer Mitgliedsorganisationen in Latein Amerika seit 1976* (Hamburg: Ibero-Amerikanisches Institut, 1982).

2. The experience in the Dutch case supports this point.

3. At one time in Perú, these elites employed by research institutes financed through Dutch development aid were called "the Juliana boys," after Queen Juliana of The Netherlands.

4. Menno Vellinga, "Reestructuración Económica, Mercado de Trabajo y

Relaciones Laborales: Experiencias de Europa Occidental," in *Investigación Económica*, vol. 46, no. 180, 1987, pp. 111–124.

5. Adam Przeworski, *Capitalism and Social Democracy* (Cambridge: Cambridge University Press, 1985).

6. These issues played a role in almost all European social democratic parties; see Martin Sommer and Eric van Venetie, *Socialisme in Spagaat* (Amsterdam: De Volkskrant, 1988).

7. Mario Cerutti and Menno Vellinga, eds., *Burguesía e Industria en América Latina y Europa Meridional* (Madrid: Editorial Alianza, 1988).

8. Menno Vellinga, *Industrialización, Burguesía y Clase Obrera en México* (México, D.F.: Siglo XXI, 1989), 3d ed.

9. Koppsch, *Die Rolle und Aktivitäten der Sozialistischen Internationale*, passim.

10. John Walton, "Debt, Protest and the State in Latin America," in Susan Eckstein, ed., *Power and Popular Protest: Latin American Social Movements* (Berkeley: University of California Press, 1989), pp. 299–328.

11. For the relations between the EEC and Latin America, see: Juan Pablo de Laiglesia, "Las Relaciones Entre la Europa de los Doce y América Latina: Un Proceso de Cambio Acelerado," in *Pensamiento Iberoamericano*, no. 13, 1988, pp. 137–151; Klaus Bodemer, *El Margen de Maniobra de la Comunidad Europea Hacia América Latina* (Madrid: IRELA, 1987); and Alberto van Klaveren, "Europa Occidental y América Latina: Expectatives, Logros y Problemas," paper presented at XV LASA International Congress, Miami, Fla., December 1989.

12. See also Jorge G. Castañeda, "América Latina y la Socialdemocracia," in *Nexos*, no. 173, 1992, pp. 55–59.

PART TWO

The European Experience with Social Democracy and Its Relevance for Latin America

2

European Social Democracy in Latin America: The Early History with Emphasis on the Role of Germany

Tilman Evers

Although international social democracy is a new arrival on the Latin American political scene, it has established itself firmly. For several years now, it has not been possible to engage in—or think about—politics in the Latin American context without taking it into consideration. However, since Latin American social democracy seems to build connections in almost every direction at the same time, it is extremely difficult to assess the possibilities and limitations of its presence in the region and éven to determine its interests and objectives.

Its first presence in the region—as explained in the previous chapter—dates from the mid-1950s. German social democracy (SDP) began its activities ten years later, through its Friedrich Ebert Foundation. The famous Caracas meeting of 1976 initiated a period in which the Socialist International devoted an increasing part of its efforts to Latin American politics.[1] Willy Brandt, the former German chancellor, president of the SDP and since 1976 also president of the SI, was very active in opening roads toward Latin America through both organizations. Social democracy energetically stated its position in several countries by defending human rights and democratic liberties, aiding member parties in elections and even supporting national liberation movements in their armed struggles and in their conflicts with the United States. In October 1979, the SI ended its historical Eurocentrism when it created a Socialist International Committee for Latin America and the Caribbean under the presidency of the Dominican José Francisco Peña Gómez. In November 1980, it created a committee in defense of the Nicaraguan Revolution under the presidency of Felipe González.

However, at the time, one could not speak of a *single* Latin American policy of the Socialist International. Rather, the organization functioned as a gathering of autonomous parties that shared some common concerns but were at variance with each other and even in conflict at times. Within this spectrum, German social democracy played the most influential role since it had the greatest political, organizational and financial weight. But other member parties (for example, the Scandinavians, the Dutch, the Austrians, the Spanish and the Portuguese) also made important contributions.

The most concrete financial and organizational support, however, has always been organized at a bilateral level, party to party. At this level, the most effective instrument was and still is the Friedrich Ebert Foundation, a multifunctional institution in the hands of the SPD, not controlled by the party activists, parliament, the government, or the general public. Like other, less prominent, party foundations, it received vast state funds through the Ministry of Economic Cooperation, which required little accountability. Precisely because of its nonofficial and "apolitical" form the foundation could play an active political role in the respective host countries that would be prohibited to any official foreign representation. No other capitalist power had an institution comparable to this "parallel" service for foreign relations.

The kinds of activities that European social democracy developed were many and diverse and, besides the organizational and financial help for political parties, usually included projects within the context of development cooperation. In organizing these activities, the Socialist International did not associate only with parties of a similar ideological or organizational character, nor did it make recruitment of new members its prime objective.

The success of the Socialist International in Latin America could not have been so rapid if a large number of political forces within the region had not been receptive to it. Undoubtedly the political, economic and social conjuncture in Latin America in the second half of the 1970s played an important role in this. Just a few years earlier, it was unthinkable that the Latin American Left would make any contact with European social democracy since it was considered nothing more than an extension of North American imperialism.

The situation had changed dramatically. The era of the big anticapitalist movements and of guerrilla movements was closed. At the same time, the undisputed hegemony of the United States in the capitalist world ended with the Vietnam War, and East-West relations had entered a phase of relative calm. Events in Venezuela were a good illustration of this dramatic change. In 1966 the Socialist International supported the Venezuelan government in its repression of guerrillas. Twelve years later, surviving guerrillas were members of parliament for the Movimiento al Socialismo (MAS) and Movimiento de Izquierda Revolucionaria (MIR) parties and attended meetings of the Socialist International together with Carlos Andrés Pérez who, as minister of the interior, had been responsible for wiping out the guerrillas. Moreover, Pérez was now president and was giving both moral and material aid to the Sandinista guerrillas in Nicaragua. Obviously the Socialist International was not the same, but neither was the Latin American Left.

I will not attempt an in-depth analysis of Latin America's attraction toward social democracy. It is a subject that should be examined primarily by Latin Americans themselves. Nevertheless, it does constitute the other side of the coin, without which an analysis of the backgrounds of the social democratic offensive would not be complete. To give a provisional idea, I will sum up a few of the arguments that have been put forward on this subject.

1. The Socialist International offered the Latin American elites an opportunity to strengthen their economic and political ties with Europe, thus lessening their dependence on the United States. The crisis of U.S. supremacy after Vietnam and Watergate provided a favorable moment for stressing the "European option."

2. The internationalization of the world economy meant that any party aspiring to government also had to internationalize its political links in order to gain access to international centers of decisionmaking. Among the few available alternatives, the social democratic connection had the advantage of conceding a high degree of autonomy without presenting an openly imperialist image. European social democracy presented the traditional populist parties with an acceptable cover for collaborating with multinational capital without openly betraying their anti-imperialist traditions.

3. The Latin American Left had experienced several failures in its bids for political power. To recover, it was required to collaborate with other groups, such as the social democrats, with which it shares objectives, such as obtaining human rights, basic social needs and political freedom. This collaboration offered an opportunity to consolidate *tactical* alliances without losing *strategic* autonomy. There were also organizations of the Left that, lacking a political project of their own, were attracted to the social democratic

proposition of a "third way," either as a transitional or as a definitive project. These organizations were also induced toward change by the obvious inadequacy of their previous ideology in the face of new mass movements that did not fit into the classist or populist molds of the past.

4. The Socialist International was almost the only organization that could offer political and material help to those leftist groups operating under conditions of illegality and repression or to groups engaged in armed struggle. The link with the Socialist International granted all groups a Western, non-Communist legitimacy and gave those working under military dictatorships protection against repression.

5. Even to some sectors of the Latin American Right, the military dictatorships did not seem very reliable or permanent. The Socialist International therefore appeared as an acceptable agent of controlled transition.

6. Rapid industrialization in various countries created complex social structures to which individualist and amorphous party organizations had not yet adapted themselves. European social democracy seemed therefore to have the knowledge necessary to modernize political methods and structures. In this respect there was greater affinity for European concepts than for Anglo-Saxon ones since the former are based on a historical experience that is comparable to that of Latin America concerning the more active role of the state.

These are strong reasons for thinking that the social democratic offensive in Latin America was as much a "Noah's ark" for the most varied Latin American political forces as it was a "Trojan horse" for European interests. It is no coincidence that at the same time that SI was gaining force other groups emerged with their own proposals aimed at political and ideological internationalization. Thus, the Christian Democrat Organization of America (ODCA) reactivated its international links. In the United States some liberals in the State Department during the Carter administration sought to relegitimize U.S. hegemony, using the theme of human rights. In October 1979, a Permanent Conference of Latin American Political Parties (COPPAL) was founded. It was similar in composition and focus to the Latin American wing of the Socialist International, but it was led by the Mexican PRI.

Although international social democracy worked mainly in a rhetorical and ideological way, its presence had important practical effects in a number of instances. In 1978 it helped its member party in the Dominican Republic, the PRD, to win the election and to force the armed forces loyal to Joaquín Balaguer to accept this result. The most important case is without doubt that of Nicaragua. SI gave the FSLN material support and, even more important, gained international recognition for it at the end of 1978.

As the commitment of social democracy in Latin America became more concrete and conflictive, the question arose as to which interests the Socialist International was pursuing. This was also the key issue for the different forces of the Latin American Left who had established contact with international social democracy and were eager to reach a realistic assessment of the possibilities and limitations of this contact.

In my analysis of the operations of European social democracy in Latin America I shall emphasize the case of German social democracy, which has played a central role. Such an analysis raises a number of problems. In the first place, we know relatively little, in concrete terms, about the contacts between European social democrats and their Latin American colleagues. The major part of existing documentation is confidential, and the most significant contacts may have been on a personal level, where they remained undocumented.

In the second place, social democracy's diffuse activities and attitudes gave the impression of pure pragmatism and empiricism. Its connection to underlying causes or ideas remained vague. The actors themselves put forward no theory for their actions and even suggested that the absence of theory is in itself one of the prerequisites for practical success. There was no coherent ideological discourse except for a general antidictatorial posture (an area where ethics and interest coincide for those organizations that can only gain power through elections) and support for a political and "social" democracy. There was no definition of the level of combativeness required to achieve this end, nor was there any definition of the common reference point of democratic socialism. In practice, what was understood to be socialism usually did not go beyond a very general conception of Keynesian economic policies and a verbal commitment to a welfare state. Democracy was understood to be a system of representation that used bureaucratic and hierarchical mechanisms to grant moderate legitimacy to the masses while—again in practice—a political class with strong ties to the structures of the bourgeois state retained a monopoly on decisionmaking.

A Political Complement to an Economic Offensive?

At first sight the social democratic offensive in Latin America after 1976 would seem to be a political complement to the expansion of German capital. The volume of trade and the importance of German investments in Latin America in the 1950s and 1960s was not congruent with the relative lack of political interest. This lack of interest was in fact only apparent. It meant an acceptance of the status quo and of the hemispheric dominance of the United States. However, with the rise of German capital to the stature of a serious competitor to U.S. capital, German interests would have to start building their own political connections in the region. The nuclear deal with Brazil in 1975 was the first definite step in the direction of overt competition with the United States. Germany entered into serious conflict with the United States for the first time, winning a $5 billion order for its strategic nuclear industry.

This explanation, linking political and economic interests, is the one most commonly accepted by political analysts of all sides. This is reflected in the remarks of one North American, one Latin American and one German. "German social democracy is involved in Latin America so that it can create a political base for German capital. . . . It is difficult to escape the conclusion that the pink flag of social democracy will give way to the green light for German capital." "The loss of competitiveness of the United States strategic industry, the increasingly apparent capacity of European economies to compete with it for markets, also allows the 'export' of European policy." "The attempt to transform economic power into world political ascendancy increasingly characterizes the basic feature of official German policy, as much in relation to its Western 'allies' (including the United States) as to the countries of the Third World."[2]

This argument is supported by the statements of the politicians responsible for German policy in the 1970s. Helmut Schmidt, for instance, said: "We have now gained world economic importance, a relevance which demands that we prove ourselves equal to the task. In effect we are making a real effort in that direction and we believe that until now we have managed to cope honorably with this responsibility."[3]

There is also a strong basis for this explanation of the social democratic offensive in the economic data. At the time, the German Federal Republic was the second largest exporter in the world, slightly behind the United States. In 1977, for example, it exported almost as much as France and Great Britain together. This commercial ascendancy was achieved during the years of prolonged world capitalist prosperity and after World War II until the mid-1970s.

This sharing of trade dominance by the United States and Germany was not new. It had existed since 1959. But the difference between the volumes exported by them had been diminishing. The closing of the gap was connected with the composition of German exports.

Machinery, vehicles and chemical and electrical products accounted for more than half of the export package. In other words, the Federal Republic specialized in the production of those goods whose worldwide demand was bound to grow in the postwar phase of capital expansion and that involved the use of the most advanced technology. The Federal Republic occupied first place as world exporter of manufactured products, having surpassed the United States by the end of the 1960s. Germany's trade surplus resulted in constant pressure to revalue the deutsche mark, which went up spectacularly in relation to the U.S. dollar and other currencies and became the dominant currency of Western Europe.

The commercial power of Germany was and is without doubt impressive. But was there a direct relation between this and the Latin American political context that interests us? In the first place, there were no sharp changes in global trends in the first half of the 1970s that could explain the emergence of a new political strategy. In the second place, looking at the distribution of German foreign trade by regions at the time, the relation with the developing countries was clearly secondary to trade with industrialized countries and especially with other members of the EEC. Exports to the Third World represented only 14.3 percent of Germany's total in 1979, and Latin America took last place after Asia and Africa, with only 3.1 percent. The tendency for Latin America and for all developing countries was one of decrease in its relative position despite a constant increase in absolute terms.[4]

However, Third World markets are considered "markets of the future." Their raw materials continue to represent a vital interest that is not reflected in the quantitative relations of the world market. The composition of German trade with the developing countries (excluding the Organization of Petroleum Exporting Countries, OPEC) showed the classic pattern: manufactured products in exchange for raw materials and foodstuffs.

The drastic rise in the price of various raw materials, particularly oil, after 1973 brought a significant change in the commercial relations between the Third World and Germany. To what extent did Latin America participate? Statistics from the "critical years" 1973–1976 show that the increase in value of Latin American exports to Germany was modest and was due in part to products such as copper and sugar whose rise in 1973–1974 was short lived. In fact, the increase in trade during those years with Latin America was less than in other regions. The largest increase—as one would expect—was with the oil-exporting countries. The relative participation of Latin America in the external trade of the Federal Republic tended to decrease throughout the 1970s despite an increase in absolute terms. No Latin American country accounted for even 1 percent of the imports or exports of Germany. Some Latin American imports did signify important inputs for some sectors of the German economy. Coffee and bananas came entirely from Latin America.[5] There was also an important Latin American contribution in copper (Chile), tin (Bolivia, Perú), some special metals (Brazil) and cotton (Guatemala, Colombia).

On the Latin American side, trade with Germany took either first, second or third place. Therefore, from the Latin American point of view, there was a reason for a growing interest in closer relations. But from the German perspective there was no new aspect to trade relations that could have explained the sudden "discovery" of Latin America by the Socialist International.

With respect to *direct investment* a different picture emerges. The continuing rise in the external value of the mark increased the price of Germany's exports but facilitated the export of capital. Annual external investment increased constantly from the 1950s to the 1980s. From a net importer of capital, the Federal Republic became an exporter. It has been estimated that in 1980 the total amount of accumulated German investment abroad surpassed, for the first time, the amount of foreign investment in Germany.[6]

In fact, there was an important advance in the Federal Republic, but it was not yet enough to challenge the clear leadership of U.S. and British capital. Compared to these nations the Federal Republic was a "giant in exports and a dwarf in investments." The external production of U.S. multinational affiliates is more than four times the value of U.S. exports, and in the case of Britain the relationship is double, but the German economy produces scarcely a third of the value of its exports outside the Federal Republic. In relation to Latin America, German trade is worth more every year than the total value of the investments made since 1952.[7]

German investment presents a picture very similar to that of its exports: Chemicals, banking, insurance, electrical engineering, iron and steel metallurgy, machinery and cars are at the top of the list. This also reflects the high degree of concentration in these strategic sectors of the German economy, with a few giant enterprises dominating exports as well as foreign investment.

The regional distribution of this investment clearly favored the industrialized countries. This explains why within the Third World, Latin America was the favored destination of German capital, with 12.3 percent of total German foreign investments. This is due primarily to the importance of Brazil, which alone took 9.1 percent of foreign investment and was the fourth largest recipient after the United

States, Belgium/Luxembourg and France in 1978. The importance of Brazil reflected the preference of German investors for the industrial sector. Investments in mining and agriculture were minuscule. German investments in Brazil were higher than those in Africa and Asia together, including OPEC countries. In fact, they nearly equaled investments in the rest of the Third World and perhaps even surpassed them since many of the investments processed through Curaçao and Panamá end up in Brazil.[8]

These facts correct the impression that Latin America was of minor importance for Germany in the field of trade. As by far the most industrialized and "wealthy" (in terms of gross per capita product) region of the Third World, Latin America's economic relations with Germany were not only through trade but also largely through direct industrial investment, which demands a developed internal market and an extensive material and social infrastructure. This is also expressed in the structure of foreign employment by German capital, 20 percent of which was concentrated in Latin America. In Brazil alone, German capital employed more people than it did in the United States (16 and 14 percent, respectively, in 1978).[9]

However, we see once more that despite an increase in absolute terms, the relative weight of German capital invested in Latin America decreased in the 1960s and only remained more or less stable during the 1970s. But these statistics do not show with sufficient clarity the significant change in the direction of outflows during the critical years under discussion.

Regarding direct investments, there was a clear increase of interest in Latin America during the time that the SI launched its political incursion into the region. But is this sufficient explanation for the offensive? Was the economic expansion of German capital in Latin America during the 1970s so dramatic that it can explain the simultaneous export of a new political strategy? If this is the case, why were the social democrats especially active in small countries such as Nicaragua and the Dominican Republic, where the interests of German capital were negligible?

But more important, how do we explain the social democratic character of this strategy? Why did they not simply intensify the political expedients already available to German capital, such as government-to-government contacts, the chambers of commerce or the public relations offices of the multinationals themselves?

In effect, all of these were resorted to and were expanded during the 1970s. We must not allow ourselves to be deceived by the resonant publicity that accompanied the emergence of international social democracy. During the 1970s its practical contribution to German business interests was minimal (with the exception, perhaps, of Venezuela). It was as a governing party that social democracy gave direct support to German interests. Did German capital need international social democracy to establish a political link? It seems instead that the opposite was true. The volume of trade and German investments in the region constituted the bases for German political activity. In this sense, capital supported the social democratic offensive after 1976, rather than the other way around.

To sum up, the interpretation of the social democratic offensive as the political complement to European economic interests, especially those of Germany, has an element of truth if we go from the supposition that there should be some relationship between those interests. However, this does not explain (or show the political significance of) what it is that gave this political position its specifically social democratic character and distinguished it from a straightforwardly imperialist policy. We must conclude that the relationship is more complex.

A Strategy to Expand Internal Markets?

The mistake that, from my point of view, leads to simplification lies in identifying social democracy directly and exclusively with the safeguarding of the long-term interests of capital. Yet the historical roots of German social democracy in the workers' movement still affect its practice today, even if to a much lesser degree. Its political existence is not identified with capital but rather with the relationship between capital and labor and with certain methods of resolving conflicts within the relationship. Could it be that in Latin America this particular quality was needed to further the advance of German interests in the region? In effect, one of the explanations given for the social democratic offensive departs from the fact that, in several parts of the subcontinent, economic development produced a relatively mature industrial culture, calling for the utilization of political formulas of social integration and negotiated methods of distribution and solution of conflicts.[10] The argument is that in the industrialized zones where German interests are concentrated, there would be an industrial proletariat too broad and experienced to remain controlled —in the workplace or in the political arena—by purely repressive measures. Nor could the extreme forms of poverty be tolerated since they could lead to massive social eruptions.

But apart from preparing the social climate for Germany-based multinational companies, there would also be a very concrete economic rationale for the social democratic presence. With its concentration in the production of manufactured goods for local consumption, German capital could only benefit from a gradual improvement of the purchasing power of the wage-earning class and from the integration of the masses (supposedly) marginalized from the capitalist market. The model of accumulation based on the production of durable consumers goods is hampered by the structural limitations of internal markets, originating in the social organization of income with (also supposedly) precapitalist characteristics. According to this interpretation, a strategy to enlarge internal markets for German capital was hidden behind the rhetoric of *social* democracy, stressing the defense of union rights and programs for basic needs.

To sum up, according to this argument, the political project of international social democracy had as its goal the formation of a social bloc for associated industrialization, which would support a subsequent stage of industrial development directed toward the internal market. Such an expansion would interest all the social agents of the process of industrialization in Latin America, including multinational capital that would inevitably exercise hegemony within such a bloc. As an inexplicit consequence, this interpretation visualized the social democrat project as a historic, updated recurrence of the class alliances that constituted the populism of the 1940s. The political implications of such an interpretation are no less one-dimensional than those of the previous explanation; they just give the opposite result. Instead of appearing as European imperialism, social democracy appears now as the legitimate heir of Latin American populism and, as a result, as a strategic ally of the Latin American Left.

There is also some economic basis for this argument. At the end of the 1970s, Latin America had a gross national product per capita of $1,775—two-and-a-half times the average of all the countries on the capitalist periphery, and it also superseded the apparently newly rich oil-exporting countries.[11] Among the ten developing countries with the largest absolute gross product, four were Latin American countries (Brazil, México, Argentina and Venezuela). In the list of the newly industrializing countries (NICs) were twelve Latin American countries. In the eyes of the German investor, this meant that Latin America "had risen to be a kind of middle class."[12]

The regional and sectoral concentration of German external investments showed clearly that they were mostly oriented toward existing and future internal markets. Social democratic discourse with respect to North-South relations constantly reiterated that the German economy had no interest in perpetuating underdevelopment in the countries of Africa, Asia and Latin America. In 1969 then Minister of Economic Cooperation Erhard Eppler said:

We will still export less to the whole of Africa than to Switzerland. Certainly not because our machinery would not be of use in Africa, but because it can't pay for it. The more developed a trading partner is, and the more purchasing power it has, the more interesting it is to us.[13]

It seems certain that the degree of industrial development reached in various Latin American countries, with their corresponding relations of production based on a wage-earning and relatively well-organized labor force, produced a social substratum without which European social democracy could not have become an interlocutor sought after by a variety of Latin American political forces. It also seems certain that in the long term there is a correlation between the expansion of internal industrial markets and the social democratic types of politics. But this does not mean that there is an economic rationale on the basis of which multinational capital virtually demanded the intervention of social democracy in Latin America in the mid-1970s.

In the first place, it would be necessary to make much more specific the general proposition that the industrialization of the Third World benefits the German economy. What kind of industrialization in which group of countries in the periphery would today benefit which sectors of German multinational capital? How does this kind of industrialization affect the relations of production and distribution of each respective country? Only on the basis of this information can an analysis be constructed to determine whether the external interests of German capital are compatible with a social democratic methodology.

We cannot enter into a detailed analysis by country here, but on the basis of the general information at our disposal, our hypothesis would be falsified. The economic principle underlying any social democratic policy concerns an evolution of real wages allowing the market price of the labor commodity to be perceived as a "fair wage." This is a precondition for regarding the relationship between labor and capital as not necessarily antagonistic. This demands a context of relatively integrated reproduction within which the bulk of wages reappears in the market as demand, fueling the circulation of capital all the way up to its most advanced sectors.

In Latin America, on the contrary, an "associated" model of industrial accumulation has predominated for some time already, the dynamic of which is based on the purchasing power of the higher-income sectors. For the foreseeable future it is not likely that there would be a profound restructuring of the income distribution that would allow the demand for mass consumer goods to displace the production of consumer durables as the most dynamic sector. This leads us to the first conclusion, that an ostensible broadening of the internal market in a social democratic project would be oriented exclusively toward those class factions integrated into the urban-industrial sphere. It would have little or nothing to offer economically to the majority of the population, involved in subsistence activities in the rural and urban environment.

However, it seems unlikely that the transnational model of accumulation is really running up against a serious bottleneck in the internal market. The system has the capacity to continue growing upwards through the introduction of new products or their exportation to other countries of the periphery or even to developed nations. The fact that this could lead to a process of deindustrialization in other Latin American countries (e.g., Chile) does not invalidate the argument. The dynamic of capital accumulation takes place in geographic areas not identical with national boundaries.

In strictly economic terms, the margin for social democratic reformism has been rather limited, and it is heavily dependent on the ability of national and international capital to improve their rates of accumulation by expanding their markets downward so as to include the top layer of the poor. In this there are great differences among the countries of Latin America. There are poles of industrial growth where the market for manufactured products already has reached an appreciable degree of diversification and saturation and where the purchasing power of wages, as much in their level as in their total volume, already represents a reasonable proportion of the existing market. The most typical region in this respect is the industrialized triangle of Brazil (São Paulo-Rio-Belo Horizonte). Here the incorporation of wage earners in the consumption of durable goods (radios, televisions, refrigerators and so forth) has taken place through a system of consumer credits. These were introduced in Brazil at the time of the economic miracle, when political repression was at its height, and without any "push" by social democratic forces. In 1978 the wage increases won by the metalworkers of São Paulo, through their strikes, effectively led to an additional growth in sales of simple consumer goods by about 5 percent. But these strikes were organized without any support from international social democracy, and during the strikes in the following years the businesspeople of São Paulo—far from considering any benefits from the increase in demand—mobilized all their repressive resources to reduce real wages, once again.[14]

Naturally, the resistance of the dominant classes themselves does not in itself invalidate the argument. German social democrats still remember from their own historical experience that capitalists are never voluntarily convinced of the need to increase wages. So in Germany, too, the rise of real wages, which ended up benefiting industrial accumulation, was the result of hard social struggles.

It would therefore be necessary to strengthen the protest potential of the lower classes by supporting their ability to organize parties and unions sufficiently strong to wring wage concessions from the capitalists. But it would also be necessary to organize other "victims of underdevelopment"—mainly agricultural workers and the subproletariat or marginal masses—in order for them to gain access to the market. Given their diffuse and precarious economic situation, this would require, as an intermediate strategy, programs aimed at meeting basic needs with the participation of those affected. German social democracy has never been alarmed at the possibility that such a social mobilization might endanger the existing regimes in some countries. It accepted the necessity of exchanging temporary instability for stability in the long term.

These other social and political repercussions of a strategy aimed at expanding the market were in fact discussed among German social democrats under the apparently innocuous title of "dynamization of structures." In 1970 Minister of Economic Cooperation Eppler said:

> We must start with a flexible, pluralistic, perhaps even consciously contradictory approach, appealing for example to the future vision of dominant forces such as young and pragmatic managerial groups, at the same time as encouraging and supporting groups with reformist tendencies and continuing to talk to revolutionary elements. The decisive factor is the chance to dynamize structures effectively.

In the same vein, then Vice Minister Hans Matthoefer stated one year later:

> It is a task of social democratic parties and the most lucid forces in the United States, first to organize the foundation and continuous support of democratic socialist parties and effective trade unions, so that they can institute a program of radical structural transformation and reforms. . . . Secondly, it is necessary to give massive support, through development aid programs, to reformist movements as they become governments.[15]

Once again, if this strategy was aimed at encouraging the interests of German capitalists, they did not perceive it in this way. In Latin America, the German multinationals have been as much or more opposed to the activities of trade unions as their counterparts in other developed countries. Faced with the danger of social disruption by the "marginalized masses," their perspective has been to consider such disruption a police question, and they certainly do not view these masses as structures to be dynamized. The most flexible position has been a willingness to tolerate the existence of unions and to coexist with them, as long as they do not have any real influence in managing the company or in wage policies. Limited to the function of being mere sounding boards for the consideration of labor problems, these unions would operate as a system of advanced alert for the social climate inside and outside the companies.

Any ulterior economic or political demand would have found German capital strongly allied with the other dominant local forces in a common front of resistance. Consequently, this type of demand could not have been easily proposed through the programs of a social democratic policy, even if they are no more than reformist in their content.

Is this just a failure to see the multinationals' objective interests? If our economic argument was correct, we would have to concede that there is a considerable degree of realism in the fear of the multinationals that, in the foreseeable future, higher wages would mean reduced profits rather than greater ones. As for the marginal masses, sufficient has been said and written to believe that they are in fact integrated into existing markets in the only (and for this reason the "best") way compatible with the actual form of accumulation and that the basic needs programs proposed by the World Bank and assumed by the official German agencies tend to stabilize—also politically—this type of marginal integration in the market rather than change it.

Logically, as long as there is no real economic improvement to offer, any political mobilization of the masses would be counterproductive. A mobilization of social pressures on behalf of other interests (e.g., in elections) could rebound on the promoters within a short period, with all the weight of frustrated expectations. It is precisely this type of situation that has brought the downfall of all the reformist governments in the region since the end of the 1950s, including governments led by member parties of the SI. As a result, in the actual practice of these parties, we find little or nothing to suggest that they have been organizing or mobilizing a trade union movement among urban or rural workers. On the contrary, where such party unions remained from previous years, the present party leadership collaborated in their demobilization. None of the Latin American parties belonging to the Socialist International was historically rooted in the workers' movement in its country (as is the case with the German SPD), and today few have the characteristics of a workers' party.

But neither did the policy of the German SPD with respect to the Latin American parties and trade unions bear much resemblance to the proposal for "radical structural changes" put forward by Matthoefer in 1969. It is no accident that the proposal for "dynamizing structures" was presented in the initial phase of the social democrat government under Willy Brandt, which was marked by reformist euphoria. Soon after, there was a return to the discourse of the pragmatism of "mutual interests." Thus, at the end of the 1970s, the Friedrich Ebert Foundation in Latin America defined its own role as

> social policy assisting relevant social groups such as trade unions and parties to moderate and channel their conflicts. This also means maintaining these societies in a socially tolerable, if precarious equilibrium, and finding viable compromise solutions to pressing social problems.[16]

Certainly this static conception does not cover all aspects of social democratic policy in Latin America. But neither does the idealistic vision of a social bloc for associated industrialization capable of stimulating internal markets. All the indications are that, for the foreseeable future, the process of industrialization in Latin America will continue to be based more easily on authoritarian and repressive political structures than on class conciliation.

Of course it is possible that a detailed, country-by-country analysis would be able to establish the margins for expansion in existing internal markets. A practical policy ought to try to take advantage of these margins, however limited they may be. However, whether there would be a sufficient margin to serve as a socioeconomic support for a social democratic type of class conciliation is to be doubted.

I do not mean to discount as mere ideology the objective of broadening internal markets, so dear to social democracy on both sides of the Atlantic. Does the Latin American Left have economic programs that are less illusory to offer? In a sense the objective of broadening internal markets is a historically necessary utopia expressing a national aspiration and as impossible to carry out as it is to abandon at the present time. If this is so, the significance of the social democratic alternative today must be found not in economic issues but in the political, ideological and symbolical spheres.

In conclusion, the degree of Latin American industrial development, which is relatively advanced in various countries, constitutes, without doubt, a precondition for social democratic formulations. In this sense it helps to explain the warm reception given to international social democracy in Latin America since 1976. But the actual contents, geographic emphases and timing of its Latin American policy are not explained by the thesis of the extension of internal markets. The disappointing experience of member parties of the SI in government demonstrates that their democratic socialism—useful as it may have been as a common meeting ground for heterogeneous opposition forces— did not have a model of development to offer that was suited to Latin American reality.

A Project for Change in Bourgeois Domination?

In the absence of a direct economic rationale to link the penetration of Latin American markets by German capital with the proliferation of activities by social democracy, we must seek a more truly political explanation. Various interpretations identify social democracy as an alternative project for bourgeois domination in Latin America.[17] Some emphasize an immediate counterrevolutionary objective; others see a role with regard to a more long-term social and political stabilization. A third version expands on this latter interpretation and considers the social democratic alternative as a strategy of co-opting elites in the long term.

A Counterrevolutionary Device?

According to this argument, European social democracy entered the Latin American scene to preempt radical protest movements that were emerging there in response to military authoritarianism. The United States was seen as incapable of performing this function because it was completely identified with the dictatorships themselves and its imperialistic image would have exacerbated the opposing forces rather than placated them. The economic competition between the United States and Germany would be subordinate to their common interest in stabilizing the region. Rather than rivalry, there would be a division of labor.[18]

The model for this experience is Portugal. German social democracy played a key role in reversing a social process that, for a time, had real anticapitalist perspectives. Through a party of its creation, the Portuguese Socialist Party led by Mario Soares, social democracy managed to capitalize electorally on the legitimacy of the armed forces movement of 1974 and to use it as part of an anti-Communist strategy.

Understandably, this interpretation finds wide acceptance among representatives of the more orthodox Left. But can the Portuguese case be transposed to the Latin American situation? Was there an urgent need to "save capitalism" from mass anticapitalist movements in

1976? In fact, the year 1976 was the culmination of the defeat of such movements throughout the South American continent. None of the dictatorships appeared seriously threatened, and in some countries the counterrevolutionary offensive was still in full ascendancy (Argentina, Perú, Colombia).

When Willy Brandt brought together the Latin American political leaders in Caracas, Venezuela was like a liberal democracy marooned by the tide of military authoritarianism. Though there was repudiation of all types of dictatorships, the political impetus of the meeting was directed against rightist regimes. Since then, the rhetoric as well as the practice of international social democracy in Latin America has been openly antidictatorial and not openly anti-Communist. In its Latin American relations, German social democracy made no attempt to avoid contact with those organizations of the Left that in Germany itself would have been decried as "extremist" and "terrorist."

After the 1979 revolution in Nicaragua, international social democracy had good cause to identify an alternative anticapitalist power in the region. Its response was to support the *tercerista* faction of the FSLN and to create a special committee within SI whose most important function was to defend the Nicaraguan process against the international Right but also, by implication, to control the internal "pluralistic" process. At the time the Marxist Left had not been reconstituted after its defeats in any other Latin American country, nor did it have a revolutionary project capable of bringing together a material force with a possibility of gaining power.

A Project to Reinstitutionalize Bourgeois Domination?

This interpretation was based on the prediction of possible social disruptions if the military governments of the 1970s would fail to become "civilized" and to give way to more institutionalized bourgeois alternatives with a broader social base. After fulfilling their main objective of repression and demobilization of the forces that threatened capitalism, the dictatorships would have no means of stabilizing their rule. Their permanence in government would become unnecessary and even counterproductive as they offered too obvious an image of the social enemy, capable of uniting all the opposition forces. This would apply to situations where they have succeeded in strengthening capitalist economic development (Brazil) as much as to situations where their economic and social projects have failed (Perú, for example). A parliamentary system with parties and elections was to be reestablished, to give state power a certain legitimacy and to make the relations of social domination more anonymous and less open to attack. The degree of institutional liberalization would be adapted to the relationship among the political forces in each country, and it could result in a "relative" or "restricted" democracy. This change of image would also facilitate international economic and political relations with the metropolitan capitalist countries that are organized politically according to these bourgeois, "civilized" norms. For reasons of internal politics, the European and U.S. governments are uncomfortable dealing with "Fascist-style" regimes.[19] Counter-revolutionary and anti-Communist intentions were not absent from this variant of the argument, but they operated more as preventative measures and at the level of ideological struggle.

This perspective includes an ambiguous relationship of cooperation and competition between the United States and Europe. In principle, it was a transformation supported and pursued by "liberal" sectors within the United States that temporarily gained governmental positions during the Carter administration. The European social democratic presence was required to "flank" U.S. interests. While the United States was to calm the military regimes and even put moderate pressure on them through the rhetoric of human rights, the Europeans were to establish contacts with the opposition political parties that, because of their anti-U.S. traditions and rhetoric, would be prevented from having direct relations with the United States. At the same time, social democracy would be the guarantee that the political transition would not exceed the limits of the transnational economic model and that liberalization would not lead to uncontrollable social eruptions.

A united operation of this type was effectively carried out in 1978 during the Balaguer/Guzmán transfer of power in the Dominican Republic, where there was the simultaneous presence of the Organization of American States (OAS) and the SI. Elements of this joint strategy appeared in a less clear-cut fashion in other cases of bourgeois-democratic reinstitutionalization (for example, Ecuador in 1978). But subsequently there has been a sharpening of the competitive elements between the capitalist powers, which coincided with the conservative turn of the Carter government after 1979. By then, the United States was no longer prepared to accede to any interference from the SI voluntarily. In Nicaragua a confrontation was avoided only because both countries lost control of the situation and were at a loss for alternatives. In all the elections from mid-1978 onward more pro-U.S. candidates were opposed by candidates supported by the SI (in Costa Rica, Venezuela, Perú, Jamaica). Finally, in El Salvador after 1980, the two international strategies ended in public confrontation. This culminated in the action taken by the French

Socialist government together with México in August 1981, recognizing the legitimacy of the Salvadorian armed opposition. The United States ended up by giving priority, in these critical moments, to the stability of the status quo while neglecting human rights. In this type of situation, with the North Americans busy trying to maintain their imperial control over the continent, social democracy boasted antidictatorial and progressive positions whose radicalism was irreconcilable with North American interests.

Retrospectively, it seems that this interpretation only fits into a limited time scale. It begins in 1977 with the resurgence of massive popular protest (Perú, Brazil, Chile, Bolivia, Guatemala, Nicaragua) and ends in 1979 when the United States departed from the project of a change in bourgeois domination in order to give priority once again to its imperial role. For that time, I believe that this interpretation accurately points out some key elements of the political climate from which the international impulse of social democracy emerged in Europe (Portugal, Spain) and that also had a temporary impact in Latin America. The interpretation, however, does not account for the starting point of the Caracas offensive, nor for the situation of conflict between the United States and the SI after 1980.

But even for this interval of expectations for "redemocratization," it does not offer an explanation of the German interests in the process. The interest of the Latin American forces in gaining allies for their endeavor of trying to reestablish a framework of democratic bourgeois action is understandable, and so is the interest of the United States in maintaining the "liberalization" of authoritarian governments within controllable bounds. But what could have been the specific interest of German social democracy in approaching these two actors? Moreover, the increasing success of the Christian democratic parties in the region since 1978 demonstrated that a democratic-bourgeois return could occur through other formulas and without the specific methodology of social democracy.

To sum up, although initially European social democracy played a role in the sense of proposing and implementing strategies for a change in bourgeois domination, it does not seem to have been an essential actor either for the capitalist system in itself or as a safeguard of the economic and political interests of Germany in the region.

The Assimilation of Political Elites

Until now I have not found that German social democracy had an immediate interest of its own that might have explained its offensive in Latin America. Instead I have found various objective and subjective conditions that from the Latin American perspective have facilitated its acceptance. Can it be that there was no such immediate interest with respect to Latin America but rather a sense of seizing the opportunity to occupy the political spaces as they presented themselves, for some future use?

If this is the case, the activities would have had more of a preliminary function aimed at establishing relations with present or future political leaders, in order to form personal acquaintances and to create loyalties. A change in bourgeois domination in several countries would not then have been the focus of attention but would rather have characterized a conjuncture in which the formation of new elites was the order of the day. In a long-term perspective, it would mean forming political allies and party structures oriented toward Germany that would guarantee access to the centers of political and economic decisionmaking in the respective countries in the future. The optimum result would be having these political leaders in government positions. However, even as the legal opposition they would be useful intermediaries.

This interpretation was suggested by one of the most perceptive observers of social democracy in Latin America, Daniel Waksman Schinka. In an article published shortly before his untimely death,[20] he compared the first phase of social democratic penetration in Latin America with the "opening gambit" in chess. It was not yet a question of engaging in battle but of occupying the best strategic and tactical positions for any future contingency. In my judgment, this interpretation has not received the attention it deserves among political observers. This is not a situation as crude as "buying off" leaders with grants, travel to Europe, and funds for their party activities (although these things are also done). Nor is it a question of ideologically indoctrinating them with a defined social democratic ideology. This political assimilation operates in much more subtle ways. It works at the level of nonverbal behavior, which I would call the political unconscious (and indeed it is probable that many of the representatives of German social democracy have only a vague consciousness of their own modus operandi). This political unconscious is characterized by: the personalization of politics around leaders who are increasingly professionalized and detached from their base; the practice of seeking political support on a personal basis from among other leaders and not at the initiative of the party; thinking in terms of "factors of power" and not forces, interests and social processes; the notion of politics as a transaction between elites arbitrating interests and conflicts that are not their own; perspectives for change that do not question the social relations of domination in themselves, by excluding from their field of vision all the "microstructure" of power in daily life and by putting forward the state as the only place and agent of transformation; a detached and technocratic discourse that prevents the immediate representation of interests; the conception of political organizations as hierarchical apparatuses and the unquestioned hierarchical practice among the leaders themselves. In other words, it is not a question of directly inculcating a specific political content but of transmitting a bureaucratic political style. By this indirect and often unperceived means, the political content becomes part of the attitudes even of those forces that believe they can "use" social democracy with no danger to their own distinct political identity.

A long-term strategy does not need a complete economic and social project designed for the present time. On the contrary, any premature definition would only limit the options of the future. Besides, an element of ambiguity and inconsistency forms part of the "offer," maintaining a kind of neutrality in the open forum that is being presented to the Latin American interlocutors. For the moment all that is required is the image of having a distinct development project—the critical issue is knowing up to what point you can tolerate ambiguity without losing "credibility," a favorite expression of Willy Brandt's. From this perspective, it was not lack of sincerity but part of an impeccable logic that led German social democracy to knock on several doors at the same time, for example, supporting a friendly governing party while at the same time keeping up contact with opposition groups either of the Left or of the Right.

With this interpretation it is already easier to understand why the activities of German social democracy did not necessarily concentrate in the same Latin American countries as German capital. If it is a question of co-opting elites, the symbolic value of these activities is of greater importance than the practical in the initial phase. Consequently, social democracy had to locate itself in those areas where struggle symbolizes the conflicts and aspirations of the leaders with whom it wishes to establish relations—which without doubt during those years have been the countries of Central America and the Caribbean, including the two subregional powers of México and Venezuela.

Without an imminent danger to capitalism, the United States had no interest in the Germans building up their "own" political network in the region. Instead, there was clear competition between the two countries that was visible in the final phase of the Carter administration and definitely under Ronald Reagan.

We see that with this interpretation we can understand many of the questions and contradictions of the social democratic offensive. But some doubts remain. If it was just an opportune moment for co-opting elites, why was such a sudden thrust required? A gradual and discrete increase of presence would have been a better tactic. The explosive character of social democratic activities in Latin America had to be motivated by a stronger impulse, more directly linked to essential interests. Also, it cannot be denied that the Willy Brandt team took certain risks in entering into conflict with the United States and in allowing the SI to be flooded by the nationalist or even anti-imperialist tendencies. These are risks that politicians are not used to taking without being forced to do so in some way. We need to continue our search for an explanation in other contexts.

Germany and North-South Relations

Even when we consider the argument settled that the rationale of the social democratic offensive was concerned exclusively with economic relations between Europe and Latin America, we should not exclude from our possible explanations the dramatic developments in other areas that shook the world capitalist economy in the first half of the 1970s. I do not believe we can understand the revitalization of the SI without situating it in the broader context of the "North-South conflict" that became more acute at that time. This conflict contributed to the determination of the German government to explore margins of compromise within this conflict over reordering the structures of exchange and decisionmaking in the world economy and to project a conciliatory image of Germany before the demands of the Third World.

In this broader context there were many threatening indicators for the German economy, such as a fall in the real value of exports, an increase in inflation and an alarming unemployment rate. The favorable trend in the terms of trade with the developing countries was reversed with the spectacular increase in the price of oil and other raw materials. As a consequence, the expenses for importing products from developing countries increased considerably, especially in regard to OPEC countries.

The crisis highlighted the fact that the other side to the German economy's strength in exports was its extreme dependence on these exports and, as a result, its vulnerability to any disturbance in the capitalist world market. There were few industrialized countries in which external trade was this vital for a healthy economy. In fact, all the dynamics of the German economy and a good proportion of jobs in Germany depended on its privileged position in the world market.

As a result, with the 1973–1974 crisis, the German ruling elites saw the only salvation in securing and even accentuating the exporting base of the German economy. This strategy was made explicit in 1975 in a book by two leading SPD economists. The authors proposed a policy of "active structural adaptation" to the "critical modifications of the national and international economic context."[21] There would be conscious reinforcement of the advantages of German industry in the capital goods sectors through multimillion-dollar state subsidies, and there would be increased specialization in "intelligent products" that involved the most advanced technology (research, automation, nuclear and solar energy, recycling, communications, transport, military technology and so forth). Internally this strategy demanded a strengthened process of rationalization, automation and concentration. It would be necessary to tolerate and even stimulate the transfer of less competitive industries with a higher labor coefficient to countries on the periphery, although this meant sacrificing jobs in Germany. This was exactly what happened, and the policy effectively enabled the German economy not only to survive the crisis with less damage than occurred in other economies but even to obtain the highest trading surplus in its history.

The political presupposition of this strategy was that the world capitalist system should basically be maintained as a system of open markets, with free access to the sources of energy and raw materials and without excessive national protection. However, throughout the 1970s, threats to this system kept the economists and politicians of the Western industrialized nations awake at night.

At the end of the 1960s, under the inspiration of Latin American nationalism, the countries of the periphery had come to dominate international forums such as the United Nations and United Nations Conference on Trade and Development (UNCTAD), with their demands for a "new international economic order" (NIEO). In 1974 the Charter of Economic Rights and Duties of Nations was approved in the UN with 130 votes in favor, 10 abstentions and 6 votes against, among them those of the United States and Germany.

. The collapse of Portuguese colonialism in Africa paved the way for the revolution of 1974 in Portugal and also for the eventual arrival of Soviet and Cuban military personnel and advisers in several African countries. The "nonaligned" movement reached its closest approximation to the positions of the Soviet camp with the election of Fidel Castro as president of its conference in Havana in 1979. Higher oil prices sharpened economic problems and social conflicts in countries of the periphery, creating "ungovernability" that in turn gave encouragement to tendencies toward Fascist or Communist dictatorships.[22] In addition, there were various specific problems with countries of the periphery, such as the extension of maritime sovereignty to 200 miles and the problem of the migrant workers of Southern Europe and Turkey in the countries of the European Economic Community.

As for the developed countries, U.S. hegemony was in crisis as a result of the defeat in Vietnam, a weak dollar and the loss of internal consensus after Watergate. In Europe, with the rise of "Eurocommunism," the Italian and French Communist parties seemed one step away from participating in their respective governments. After initial confusion, the response of the capitalist powers to these threats to free trade was a strong resistance to any substantial modification of the existing world economic order but at the same time a show of willingness to engage in dialogue on mutual concessions on secondary points. Basically, the central countries were willing to concede either what already suited them or what they could not avoid, such as accelerated industrialization by some of the more advanced countries of the Third World, greater participation by the new financial powers of the Middle East in international bodies such as the IMF and more stable prices for certain raw materials. These concessions would have to be matched by guarantees from the countries of the periphery to keep their markets as well as their resources of energy and raw materials open to multinational capital. The central countries opposed the polemic Latin American concept of dependency with the North American one of interdependence, suggesting to the countries in the periphery—not without a threatening tone—that their interests were inexorably linked to the unhindered forward march of accumulation in the metropolitan economies (which is true, within the parameters of the present model of development and international trade).

In essence, the strategies of confrontation and dialogue with which the industrialized countries resisted the demands of an NIEO are one and the same thing. This is reflected in the differentiated but complementary roles assumed throughout the 1970s by the twin institutions of the IMF and the World Bank. Nevertheless, the dialectical tension between the strategies of dialogue and confrontation meant that the two were represented in distinct international institutions and competing political currents. In Germany, the SPD was the receptacle, through its ideological discourse, for the line of mutual interests, while the Christian democrat opposition party became the mouthpiece for a defense of legitimate self-interest against unfounded demands. The policy of the liberal-social democrat coalition government under Schmidt was a combination of both responses.

A point of conceptual reference for these policies is found in the historical trajectory of German social democracy within the German labor movement, which it transposes to the present international context. In the words of Willy Brandt:

> Perhaps a part of what is happening today is explained by looking back at the process undergone by some of today's industrialized countries in the nineteenth and beginning of the twentieth centuries. A long and difficult process of apprenticeship was necessary until it was understood that higher wages for workers contribute to a massive increase in purchasing power which is sufficient to give impetus to the entire economy.[23]

The idea is completed by quoting from Egon Bahr, a close collaborator of Brandt's:

> Today we find ourselves in the same process on a global scale, with the difference that all of us, the entire Federal Republic, belong to the minority of the rich. We would be denying our history and conviction if we didn't encourage at a world level the process through which we ourselves have come. . . . Whoever denies evolution encourages revolution.[24]

Interestingly, the comparison of the countries of the periphery to the workers of German history assigns to the former a role similar to that of the great social democratic union confederations in the Federal Republic. Ideologically, politically and legally integrated into a corporative system of *Sozialpartnerschaft* (social partnership), the union confederations are considered "co-responsible" for economic prosperity and social welfare. As such they have considerable power in negotiating labor demands as long as they subordinate them to the capitalist imperative of a "satisfactory" rate of profit. The "offer" that is implied in the conceptual transposition of this model of North-South relations is clear. Material concessions and even certain political co-responsibility are granted in exchange for not pursuing any modifications in the world economic system that the dominant countries find incompatible with their own interests. It is not by chance that after 1980 a tendency emerged to replace the term "new international economic order" with "international development strategy."

The conceptual transposition of internal social relations to external ones reveals much about the social democratic mode of thought, which is classically liberal in the sense of going by the outward appearance of freedom and equality in the market. By moving conceptually in the sphere of circulation while ignoring underlying material differences between the agents of production, the antagonism between capital and labor seems just a divergence of interests based on a gradual asymmetry of the power of negotiation of the parties. With the international transposition of this "circulationist" ideology, class relations disappeared completely from sight. The most genuine expression of this line of thought and action was the North-South Commission. It was initiated by Robert MacNamara in 1977, was chaired by Willy Brandt, had a bourgeois composition and, predictably, yielded results that reassert the essence of the existing international economic order.

The conciliatory German position encompassed various other nonexplicit messages:

- to the countries exporting raw materials, that "fair" prices could be obtained without creating cartels like OPEC;
- to African countries, that in their confrontation with South Africa they had no need to take on an anti-West or antiwhite posture;
- to the countries of the Third World in general, that economic development was to be synonymous with rapid industrialization, which at the same time was the best method for absorbing internal social conflicts—and Germany was willing to cooperate in this effort with its machinery and experience of social integration; and
- there was no economic partner more respectful of political autonomy than Germany.

Let us examine this last point in more detail.

Faced with the threats to the developed countries during the 1970s, the Federal Republic showed its total solidarity with the Western world in the defense of the free market.[25] Nevertheless, the world economic crisis also sharpened competition between the different capitalist powers. In the midst of joint efforts to resist the demands for an NIEO, the first open conflict between the United States and Germany occurred over the nuclear agreement with Brazil in 1975.

Of course, both competitors made use of their respective political resources. The position of Germany during the 1970s was marked by a strange inconsistency between its rapidly rising real influence and its image of international political modesty, created during the previous two decades. In the words of a well-known journalist: "Vitally interested in the stability of its irreplaceable raw material supplies, (the Federal Republic) is about to take some of the political responsibilities which until now it left entirely to its allies . . . the innocence of the economic giant dressed as a political dwarf has gone for ever."[26]

However, the reputation of "political innocence" seems to have remained throughout the 1970s. As a result, during the second half of the 1970s German social democracy was in the comfortable situation of being able to make use—in government policy—of all the real weight of the Federal Republic in international matters and at the same time—in its party diplomacy—deny that Germany had pretensions or even the capacity to assert itself as a world power.

This useful disparity between reality and appearance originates in the peculiar historical situation of the defeated Germany of the postwar period that forced it to give up the traditional political-military expansionism. As opposed to its competitors in the West—and despite the fact that it had become the fifth largest exporter of arms in the world—it was unthinkable that the Federal Republic would use military force to "defend" its economic interests in the Third World, at least at the present moment. Due to this, the representatives of German capital could rely on greater credibility when they presented themselves to the leaders of countries in the periphery as honest tradespeople, respectful of contracts and laws, defenders of a capitalism with a human face, noninterventionist, nonplundering, even antiracist (with some effort). For lack of any other alternative but also due to self-interest, Germany became the defender of the principle of free trade both in the sense of opposing protectionism and in the sense of keeping up the appearance of the liberty and equality of all parts of the market. In this, it counted on the advantage that its colonial past has been forgotten.

To a certain extent, the Federal Republic took advantage of the political-military control that the United States (and to a lesser degree France and Great Britain) exercised over the countries of the capitalist periphery in order to promote its own economic interests in competition with the United States, without bearing the burden of the financial and political costs of this control. The widespread anti-Yankeeism in many parts of the Third World was not matched by similar anti-German feelings. From the 1973 crisis onward, it seems that these symbolic advantages—until then unpremeditated—were discovered as a possible public relations element within an active export strategy.

In short, the conciliatory posture chosen by German social democracy toward the Third World derived from two distinct but related interests: first, from the need to dialogue within a double strategy of channeling the demands for an NIEO into secondary points compatible with its own interests and second, from the behavior adopted by German capital in the postwar period. Both interests converge in the idea that North-South relations must be organized as contractual market relations, in which the different national economies participate as sovereign, free and equal. As Willy Brandt wrote in the prologue of the report of the North-South Commission, "We must aspire to a world community founded on contracts rather than hierarchy, on consensus rather than coercion." The advantages of such neoliberalism "with a human face" over unrestricted neoliberalism are undeniable. But it is also undeniable that this neoliberalism falsifies the historical and material differences between North and South, ignores the relations of domination and leaves out the underlying structural inequalities.

The specifically social democrat ingredient in this neoliberal projection consists of accepting certain reforms of these inequalities and distrusting market forces as the only guarantee of free trade and capitalist growth. As Brandt had said in 1976: "Following the policy of protecting the weak, that proved successful in our own country," supervising and regulating institutions should be founded that could become international arbitration organizations in the future. Accordingly, the Caracas document affirms, "In order to enforce the ideals of justice and solidarity, the parties of Europe and Latin America must engage in concerted action."[27] This is a clear call for international regulating organizations, of which the SI would be one.

The revitalization of the SI after 1976 took shape, then, as a materialization of this conciliatory conception of North-South relations. That this concept is a concrete reference point for the social democratic offensive is suggested by the fact that the central and most extensive paragraph of the declaration of Caracas is dedicated to the theme of the NIEO. The incorporation of parties and movements of the Third World as new associates of the SI also meant a first step toward their integration into a nonantagonistic method of resolving this conflict. In this sense the international conferences of the SI also symbolized a style of participating in international politics that it wanted to project. The signals were sent out not only to Latin America but also to the Third World in general—or more specifically, to all those countries on the periphery that represent some special interest or danger for German interests (the most industrialized countries, OPEC, national liberation movements, Southern Europe, and so forth). The importance of Latin America derived more from attractive factors within the region than from the actual designs of European social democracy. These were factors having to do as much with the political conjuncture as with the region's more "mature" and familiar social preconditions in comparison with the majority of African and Asian countries. For many of these, Latin America was an example of industrialization and relative progress. As a result, SI's assistance to various Latin American movements struggling for radical social transformation created a progressive image not only among antidictatorial forces in Latin America[28] but also among reformist movements throughout the world.

Without doubt, the progressive behavior of the SI in Latin America also raised distrust. Nevertheless, it worked as a sign of "non-imperialism," attractive for nationalism of all types. A greater national self-determination and more industrialization ("progress") also interests right-wing governments. This is precisely what unites them with those of the Left in their demands for an NIEO and what gives us a hint of the margin of possible concessions by developed countries.

It is clear then that the progressive posture and practice of international social democracy in Latin America did not reflect the official European policy but just the ideological projection of a conciliatory posture. The restricted range of real concessions is more authentically expressed in the Brandt Report. As to the official policy of the government—not to speak of direct representatives of German capital—its basic orientation continues to be to grant only inevitable concessions, while doing whatever is needed to defend the present international economic order. As a top official of the Friedrich Ebert Foundation and protagonist of its Latin American relations has said, the trick consists in "discerning correctly between such distinct things as the SI, bilateral party relations, and government policy."[29]

Implied in this is a division of roles that reflects the intrinsic ambiguity of German social democracy. Until now, I have treated it as if its own interests were identical with those of German capital, which it promotes with its international policy. Nevertheless, the SPD does not consider itself the direct political representative of German capital, nor does the latter accept it as such. There may be identification but not identity. The difference seems minimal, but nevertheless, it is only this nonidentity that creates the political space that allowed social democracy in Latin America to be transformed into a political force of its own and even into an ally of the Left. Politically, then, all depends on a correct evaluation of capital and the particular interests of the SPD.

The Erosion of the "German Model"

In discussing German social democracy, we must not lose sight of the fact that its historical roots are in the labor movement. The party's origin continues to be detectable in its internal operations, its discourse and even in elements of its practical politics. We can understand social democracy better if we consider it not as a political expression of the dominant class but as an expression of working-class acceptance of that domination. This is what defines its character as a "party of the people" in Germany today.

But even in its other identity as a party of the state, it directly represents a relationship of social forces, not the interests of capital. This "statist" character comes from a long conceptual tradition that, since the origins of the party in the nineteenth century, pinned all hopes of emancipation on the regulatory and redistributive action of the state, conceived of as a neutral agent that can be transformed into an instrument of liberation and social justice in the hands of a workers' party. Thus the whole history of German social democracy could be seen as a gradual rise from the status of slave to that of master in regard to the traditional goal of creating a society free of exploitation. The most important theoretical steps toward this were:

- to consider socialism to be the same as "centralized economic planning";
- to see "organized capital" as the stage supposedly preceding socialism, still capitalist but already centrally regulated;
- to have social welfare within a "social market economy";
- to accept the state's demand for fluid capital accumulation as a prerequisite for redistributive measures and social peace.

With the transformation of its former communitarian motivation into functions of the state, being in government became virtually a substitute for a program. To continue in government, even at the price of carrying out policies that were no longer recognizable as social democratic, appeared almost as a historical mandate. Every decision, then, was shaped by the principle of remaining in power. With this, social democracy's central leadership was transformed into a state personnel par excellence. In order not to put its governments in danger, it tried to provide administrative solutions to social conflicts and to balance the existing relation of forces but not to modify it.

Nevertheless, although the dominant interests within this relationship are logically those of capital, they are not the only ones. The interests of the subordinate classes, which social democracy cannot ignore in its balancing act, are also present, especially those of the main trade union organizations and the party's own salaried electoral base.

It is my thesis that this always precarious capacity to balance the different social forces is due to the specific conditions of German society in a phase of its history that we can call the "post-postwar."

The resignation of Willy Brandt as head of government in 1974 was the first symptom of crisis in the preconditions of social democratic government. The international activity of the SPD was, to a considerable degree, an external expression of its efforts to halt the collapse of these social preconditions internally.

The SPD referred implicitly to these preconditions when it coined the slogan "the German model" for its 1972 electoral campaign. In a drive to gain the votes of the right, it appealed to nationalist pride by extolling the German way of life and contrasting it favorably with that of other nations. The SPD, according to this propaganda, would be, if not the creator, at least the best guarantor of this "German model" whose main features were sustained economic growth accompanied by a proportional growth of real wages, full employment, a welfare state and social peace.

With the ascension of Willy Brandt to the government (1969–1974), the way was clear for a period of overdue reforms. Doors were opened to increased trade with the countries of the East, and collective consumption was expanded. More attention to education gave greater advancement opportunities to the middle classes and preempted the storm of student revolt in 1968–1969.

The crisis of 1973–1974 marked the end of the material and financial basis for such Keynesian reforms. In this sense, it was not accidental that Willy Brandt resigned as head of the government in 1974 and that the "pragmatic" Schmidt took over. In subsequent years, the SPD no longer dedicated itself to reforms but to easing and administering the crisis. Its efforts to preserve the "German model" were increasingly reduced to an attempt to shore up its two principal pillars: international competitiveness and the level of wages and employment within the central nucleus of the working class, at the expense of the weaker sectors. It has already been shown that the privileged world position of German exports has its counterpart in a high vulnerability of the economy as a whole in terms of its external sector. In its strategy for survival, the SPD saw no alternative other than a complete identification of its economic policy with the interests of large-scale German capital. The revitalization of the SI after 1976 can be placed, as I see it, within this context. Everything that has been discussed so far, in relation to its flexible posture on the North-South conflict as a strategy of goodwill for German exports, must be complemented by this internal political background. The forward flight in the economic sector was complemented by a forward flight in the realm of the political and ideological. Thus, the German social democratic offensive in Latin America was, in good part, the expression of a defensive internal policy.

It is in the defense of the internal status quo that we find the connection between the foreign policy of the SPD and its traditional working-class roots. But there is no direct link between this working-class tradition and its support for forces of the Left in Latin America, except at the level of mutual ideological predispositions. The material link takes a long detour. It starts off from the determination to remain in power, goes through the preoccupation with the wage and employment levels of its organizational support and its identification with the exporting interests of the German industry and ends up in the propagation of strategies for "associated" industrial development, the projection of a positive image for the Federal Republic and the assimilation of modernizing elites.

Finally, the spectacular international progressive stance also played the important role of balancing the different political wings within the SPD. It served as a field of action and a receptacle for the popular and reformist element in the party that had been removed from the tasks of government as a consequence of the crisis. Similarly, it was able to satisfy, albeit symbolically, the aspirations of the left-wing currents of its electorate within and outside the party, who were very sensitive on (some) Latin American subjects since the Chilean coup in 1973. Later, as the divergences between the German foreign policy and that of the United States under Jimmy Carter and Ronald Reagan increased, the policy of the social democrats toward the Central American conflicts was definitively established as a subject of internal controversy, becoming an indicator of the degree of independence from or servitude to the United States.

In general terms this flight forward succeeded during the years 1975–1979. Exports soon recovered their upward rhythm. The loss of jobs in key sectors of industry was kept at a minimum at the cost of enormous unemployment in the peripheral sectors. The stability of the Schmidt administration was maintained, and in 1980, he was able to defeat without any problems the candidate from the Right. This coincided with the expansionist phase of the SI in Latin America.

However, in 1980–1981 the symptoms of the crisis began to sharpen once more, threatening the basic consensus of the "German model." The new doubling of the price of oil in 1978–1979 led, for the first time in the history of the German economy, to a negative balance of payments. Unemployment reached its highest levels since 1954, surpassing 7 percent at the end of 1981. The massive process of marginalization of labor threatened to go beyond the social democratic government's ability to finance social integration. The astronomic cost of unemployment subsidies created a permanent drain on the federal budget that was already, for other reasons, in full fiscal crisis. In order to finance the growing fiscal deficit, the state resorted to borrowing beyond any level of Keynesian rationality. In mid-1981, the government decided to implement cuts even in politically sensitive areas such as unemployment subsidies and housing.

In this situation the SPD was retreating before a conservative ideological offensive that proposed to solve the crisis in accordance with the ultra-neoliberal formulas of Milton Friedman, demanding that the welfare state give way to the forces of the market. Such a strategy would have led to increasing marginalization and social polarization and would definitively have ended the "German model," with the exception of the hegemony of the export sector.

However, on the Left as well, there were groups that openly renounced the consensus that is the basis of the "German model." Unlike the student movement of 1968, these new social movements no longer based their expectations on the state. The features that transcended the many differences of the diverse ecological, pacifist, neighborhood, feminist, youth, "alternative" lifestyle and spiritual movements were their grass-roots democratic structures and the demand for autonomous control. This latter implied a rejection of the bureaucratic forms of social democracy and made their integration into the existing corporative system impossible.

Given the severe deepening of the crisis, a renewed forward flight would have been as useful and urgent as after the 1973–1974 crisis. Nevertheless, the SPD's economic and political space had been reduced.

This time, the flight was backward, leading almost inevitably to the government's downfall and its replacement by a Christian democrat-liberal coalition. The social democrats have been in the opposition ever since. Here they suffered the dual pressure of its defensive internal position and of the renewed and aggressive hegemonic ambitions of the Reagan and Bush administrations. The social democrats ostensibly lowered the tone of the Latin American sorties after 1981. In the interest of a favorable climate in its relationship with Washington over the central question of arms limitation, parts of the SPD and of the government at one point seemed disposed to abandon the international resistance to the U.S. policy of repression and intervention, sacrificing basic principles of SPD's Latin American policy that they had defended until then.

Political Perspectives

What then are the consequences and perspectives that can be derived from this argument for the Left in Latin America in its contacts with social democracy? Is it fair to define the activities of the social democratic movement in Latin America as the "smiling face" of Western imperialism?

In my view, the progressive image of the social democratic policies in Latin America is not a mere fantasy. As part of an historical legacy, the social democratic credo contains some of the essential principles of the workers' movement, such as the defense of the right of workers to organize in trade unions, the demand for a fair wage, the belief in the parliamentary system and in free elections and the responsibility of the state for securing the common good.

While in Europe this set of principles has been converted into a basis for social appeasement and maintenance of the status quo, in the present Latin American context it has taken on a very different coloring. It represents a direct challenge to the dominant model of capitalist development in the region, and it is a common platform for all opposition forces. In other words, European social democracy, at one and the same time, has been promoting the multinationalization of the Latin American economies and supporting political forces that struggle against the effects of this associated development!

In essence, we find here the contradiction at the heart of social democracy, which is that it wants to be the defender of the working class without questioning bourgeois domination—a contradiction that, in the Latin American political arena, shaken as it is by its extreme social conflicts, is seen in all its inherent crudeness.

But as long as it can avoid clearly defining itself, the political space will remain in which the Socialist International can offer itself as the projection screen for very diverse interests and objectives. Did the Latin American Left deceive itself when it got in touch with European social democracy? On the contrary, it is my impression that it made realistic use of the space for a limited and temporary cooperation, in view of its own weaknesses and of the reduced alternatives regarding possible allies. However, there may have been certain illusive expectations in some of the sectors of the Left, and the price of these illusions could be a loss of identity.

In conclusion, both sides have been consciously playing a game of "who uses whom." Perhaps the basic rule of the game can be summed up as follows: Give me opportunities to think that I am using you, and I will give you opportunities to think that you are using me.

Notes

This is a revised version of a contribution to a publication of the Latin American Bureau: *The European Challenge* (London, 1982); parts used with permission. Throughout the chapter, "Germany" refers to the former West Germany.

1. The conceptual birth of this initiative is documented in the conversations and correspondence of Willy Brandt, Bruno Kreisky and Olof Palme between 1973 and 1975, published in the book *La Alternativa Social Democrata* (Barcelona: Blume, 1977); see also the account of Daniel Waksman Schinka, "América Latina y la Crisis Europea: Rol de la Socialdemocracia Europea," Permanent Seminar on Latin America, México, August 4, 1977, mimeo, and by the same author, "La IS en América Latina," a series of four articles in *El Dia*, México, April 8–11, 1980.

2. See James Petras, "La Social-Democratie en Amerique Latine," in *Le Monde Diplomatique*, June 8–11, 1980, pp. 15–17; Irma Bucher, "La Socialdemocracia ¿Alternativa Política para América Latina?" in *Uno Mas Uno*, November 27, 1979; Dieter Boris, Dietrich Busch and Rainer Falk, "Dritte Welt-Expansion der BRD," in *Antiimperialistisches Solidaritätsbulletin*, no. 10, 1978, pp. 6–10.

3. SPD, *Modernisierung der Wirtschaft-Sichere Arbeitsplätze* (Bonn: Sozialdemokratische Fachkonferenz, 1976), p. 20.

4. See *Monatsberichte der Deutchen Bundesbank*, January 1981, p. 71; *Journalisten Handbuch* (Bonn: Bundesministerium für Wirtschaftliche Zusammenarbeit, 1980), p. 176.

5. Data are taken from *Politik der Partner* (Bonn: Bundesministerium für Wirtschaftliche Zusammenarbeit, 1977), p. 36.

6. Data were provided by Bundesministerium für Wirtschaft, 1981.

7. Reiner Frenkel, "Die Deutsche Herausforderung," in *Die Zeit*, March 23, 1979.

8. Cf. *Monatsberichte der Deutschen Bundesbank*, January 1981, p. 39.

9. Ibid.

10. Stefan Saarbach, "Einige Aspekte der Aktuellen Lateinamerika Politik der Sozialdemokratie," in *Lateinamerika-Analysen und Berichte* (Berlin: Olle & Wolter, 1980), vol. 4, pp. 120–160.

11. *World Development Report 1980* (Washington D.C.: World Bank, 1981), p. 11.

12. "Bundesministerium für Wirtschaft," in *Frankfurter Rundschau*, April 25, 1978.

13. Erhard Eppler, "Generalformel zur Entwicklungspolitik," in *Die Zeit*, April 4, 1961.

14. Cf. Tilman Evers, Thomas Hurtienne and Urs Müller-Plantenberg, "Länderbericht Brasilien," in *Lateinamerika-Analysen und Berichte* (Berlin: Olle & Wolter, 1979), vol. 3, pp. 222–239, 225.

15. Erhard Eppler, "Entwicklungspolitik und ihr Beitrag zum Strukturwandel," in *Mitteilungen, Bundesministerium für Wirtschaftliche Zusammenarbeit*, vol. 4, April 1970, p. 26. Hans Matthoefer, *Frankfurter Rundschau*, June 11, 1969.

16. Gunter Grünwald, "Einige Grundsätzliche Uberlegungen und Anregungen der FES zur Lateinamerika-Politik," in *Friedrich Ebert Stiftung Informiert*, no. 5, September, 1980, p. 3.

17. Luis Maira, "Fuerzas Internacionales y Proyectos de Recambio en América Latina," in J. C. Portanteiro, L. Maira, Lliana de Riz et al., *Proyectos de Recambio y Fuerzas Internacionales en los 80* (México: Edicol, México, 1980), pp. 21–66; D. Wahl, "Zur Rolle Sozialdemokratischer Entwicklungskonzeptionen in der Neokolonialistchen Strategie des Imperialismus Gegenuber den Entwicklungsländern unter Besonderer Berücksichtigung Lateinamerikas," in *Lateinamerika* (Rostock: Wilhelm-Pieck-Universität, 1978), pp. 5–40; Saarbach, "Einige Aspekte der Aktuellen Lateinamerika Politik," p. 120; Heinz Dieterich, "Die Sozialistische Internationale und die Amerikanische Revolution," in *Links*, no. 132, March 1981, pp. 11–12.

18. "Increased German effort in Latin America also suits Washington's interests, because historical resentment toward the USA means that it is not best qualified to win sympathy for the West in that continent." *Frankfurter Allgemeine Zeitung*, April 4, 1979.

19. See Petras, "La Social-Democratie en Amerique Latine," p. 16, and for general views, see Maira, "Fuerzas Internacionales," pp. 21–66.

20. Waksman Schinka, "La IS en América Latina," passim.

21. Volker Hauf and F. W. Scharpf, *Modernisierung der Volkswirtschaft: Technologiepolitik als Strukturpolitik* (Frankfurt: Europäische Verlagsanstalt, 1975), p. 28.

22. Ibid.

23. This quote is taken from Brandt's comments about the results of the North-South Commission prepared during his administration, in: *Brandt Report, or Das Uberleben Sichern: Bericht der Nord-Sud Kommision* (Köln: Kiepenheuer & Witsch, 1980), p. 29. This idea was already present in his speech in Caracas.

24. Egon Bahr, cited in Wahl, "Zur Rolle Sozialdemokratischer Entwicklungkonzeptionen," p. 19.

25. This assertion is based on the restrictive position taken by the Federal Republic in all international conferences that have been held on the subject: a negative vote on the Charter of Economic Rights and Duties of States in the United Nations in 1974; at the Conference on International Economic Cooperation in Paris in 1975–1977; at the UNCTAD Conference in Nairobi (1976) and Manila (1979); and at special conferences, such as the 9th Special General Assembly of the United Nations in New York, 1980, and others.

26. Kurt Becker, "Kein Zwerg Mehr: Bonn Wird International Gefordert," in *Die Zeit*, June 9, 1978.

27. Final Declaration, Conference of European and Latin American Leaders for International Democratic Solidarity (Caracas, May 23–25, 1976).

28. "The reaction of the international and national social democratic forces to the *Sandinista* revolution and the revolutionary popular state in Nicaragua will be a thermometer indicating the true nature and project of social democracy. . . . Our attitude toward social democracy will, in these circumstances, be conditioned by the attitude it takes toward the *Sandinista* revolution"—

Declaration of the Guerrilla Army of the Poor (EGP-Guatemala), in *Nueva Sociedad*, no. 45, November–December 1979. pp. 300–316.

    29. *Der Spiegel*, August 4, 1980.

3

The End of a Road:
Swedish Social Democracy
and Third World Solidarity

Kenneth Hermele

In 1975 Olof Palme visited Cuba. In preparing the public for Palme's visit, Cuban press and television presented a picture of Sweden as an egalitarian, almost Socialist country with strong policies of solidarity with the Third World. At the time this idealization of the Swedish model was not uncommon in Latin America. Less obvious then was the fact that Palme's visit to Cuba fitted into an overall strategy to wed Swedish long-term strategic interests to a growing role for the Third World.

Since then, 15 years have passed, and Sweden has undergone a change from social democratic to bourgeois rule, then back again to social democracy, and after the 1991 elections to a new political conjuncture. Simultaneously, Swedish Third World policy has undergone great changes, and the importance of the Third World to Sweden and to Swedish economic interests has dwindled. What appeared as a strategic factor—the importance of the Third World to Sweden—was only a conjunctural phenomenon. In the light of this development, Swedish Third World policy also changed. These alterations are primarily related to long-term strategic considerations of Swedish capitalism, considerations that carry much more weight than the political stand of the party or parties in power.

The Swedish social democratic party Sveriges Socialdemokratiska Arbetareparti gained control of the government in 1932. It would not relinquish that hold until 1976, 44 years later, when the government was taken over by a three-party bourgeois coalition. For two consecutive election periods, 1976–1979 and 1979–1982, social democracy remained in opposition until it regained power in the elections of 1982, only to lose it again in 1991.

Swedish Third World policy is intimately linked to social democracy's hold on power. In fact, because Sweden has (almost) no colonial history,[1] there was no need to elaborate a specific Swedish Third World policy until after World War II, when the decolonization of Asia and Africa began. But even before that, a Swedish presence had existed in the Third World as Swedish capital—first merchant and later industrial—began to penetrate distant markets. Swedish firms began investing in Latin America in the early decades of the twentieth century, with a great upsurge after World War II.

Nevertheless, it was in the late 1950s that a Third World policy began to be formulated. It grew out of a mixture of specific experiences, and curiously enough none of them was primarily related to Swedish commercial interests. Rather, the policy that emerged took as its point of departure the Swedish missionary tradition in countries such as Ethiopia and the growing concern over the "population bomb" coupled with a wish to alleviate absolute poverty, focusing Swedish attention on countries such as Pakistan and India.

Thus, Swedish Third World policy came to be directed toward Africa and Asia, whereas Latin America was relegated to a secondary importance as religious and social concerns blended to impress their mark on the first stages of that policy. Also contributing to this development was the fact that Swedish capital at the time did not exert a great deal of pressure to have a Third World policy tailored to its needs. In fact, Swedish capital was much more concerned with the social democratic domestic economic policy. Therefore, a few words must be said about the basic political alliance that has had a dominating influence over political and economic developments in Sweden.

The Swedish Model and Third World Solidarity

Swedish social democracy and its Third World policy should be seen against the background of the basic political alliance that has underpinned the political dominance of social democracy in Sweden. In essence, this alliance has been constituted between *monopoly* capital and *organized* labor. It should be noted here that it is not only an alliance between capital and labor but also a more limited alliance that has left important sectors of Swedish society by the wayside.

On the side of capital, minor enterprises, small-scale ventures and so forth have been disfavored through a policy of giving support to big capital. Through the tax system, expanding and investing firms have been subsidized at the expense of smaller undertakings.[2] The outcome has been a strong tendency toward concentration and monopolization of the Swedish economy.

Similarly, on the side of labor, *organized* labor was seen as the group to benefit. Later this was interpreted as relating particularly to the metalworkers, in essence to the permanently employed staff of the Swedish transnational companies. Unorganized workers, part-time workers (especially women) and the personnel of less successful industries, such as textiles, were left behind. In the 1980s, this led to a segregated labor market.

This economic and political alliance—the essence of the Swedish model—has led to an unusual concentration of economic power in the hands of a small number of private owners, a concentration that has grown ever stronger over the years. It has enabled a small number of firms to establish themselves as crucial for what is normally called Sweden's economic interests. By way of example, the richest 2 percent of households own 62 percent of the shares on the Stockholm stock exchange, and the top twenty industrial transnational corporations (TNCs) account for almost half of Sweden's total exports and two-thirds of its industrial exports, pay for 60 percent of global industrial outlays on research and development and employ 85 percent of all people employed by Swedish TNCs outside Sweden. It is therefore not surprising that social democracy, especially in the 1980s, has conducted its political line in parliament with the support of different and varying bourgeois parties, often allying themselves with the conservative party, Moderaterna. This alliance has aptly been coined the "alliance of concrete" (Betongalliansen).

Although Sweden may be special in terms of how far the monopolization and concentration of power and influence has advanced, similar (although somewhat less extreme) situations exist in many of the core countries of the capitalist system. Still, Sweden's Third World policy has been outstanding in a number of respects, which has earned the nation a reputation as a spokesman for the Third World and a friend of the poor countries. This reputation is based on two foundations: the Third World policies of Sweden and the deviation of these policies from the "norm"—i.e., the average policies of other core capitalist countries. This anomaly is basically related to the anticolonial position of Swedish social democracy, coupled with an old tradition of international solidarity that has been with Swedish social democracy since the beginning of the labor movement in the late nineteenth century. As we will see shortly, an unequivocal anticolonialist position was by no means a hallmark of Sweden in the

1950s. Nevertheless, by the late 1960s, Sweden had come to support anticolonialist and anti-imperialist struggles in Angola, Mozambique and Guinea-Bissau as well as in Vietnam. These were the major areas of struggle receiving growing political and material support from Sweden. To begin with, the material support was perhaps not of any major scope in terms of its quantity, but it was nevertheless important in that it signified the first breaches in a common position of the capitalist countries up to that time. Of perhaps greater importance was the political and diplomatic recognition that Sweden awarded the liberation movements, which were allowed to open "information offices" with semidiplomatic status in Sweden. Later, this position was carried further when Sweden was the first Western country to recognize North Vietnam.

As far as Latin America is concerned, the Swedish involvement has been more restricted, but at least two positions helped to strengthen Sweden's reputation as a spokesman for the Third World: first, the political and economic support of Chile during the three years of Unidad Popular and the termination of that support after the coup d'état and the killing of President Salvador Allende and second, the support of the Cuban Revolution and the close contacts with Fidel Castro. Until May 1976, Cuba was a main recipient of Swedish development assistance. A few years later, after the liberation from the dictatorship of Anastasio Somoza, Nicaragua was to be accepted as a main cooperation country, thus maintaining the image in Latin America of Sweden as a friendly, anti-imperialist country. This image was also bolstered by the generous terms and conditions under which tens of thousands of Latin American refugees in the 1970s were received in Sweden and given political asylum and possibilities to begin a new life.

As I have argued, these aspects of Sweden's relationship with the Third World constitute an anomaly, which needs to be explained: Why did Sweden behave differently than similar capitalist countries? And why did the interests of Swedish transnational firms appear to play such a secondary role? Or, put differently, why is it that economic and ideological interests could be kept separate? Why did not business objectives influence Sweden's Third World policy more?

The factors that spring to mind in explaining this phase of Swedish Third World policy focus upon the fact that Sweden did not have any major economic interests to defend in the Third World in the 1960s. In the absence of a colonial position and with Swedish capital expanding primarily in Western Europe, it can be argued that a political space was created that could be taken advantage of by radical forces, within as well as outside the social democratic movement. And for some sectors of Swedish capitalism, the radical Swedish departure from the norm was seen as positive, a way to take advantage of Sweden's reputation and turn it into a weapon in the competition with capital from other, more traditional capitalist powers. Hence, solidarity held out the promise of becoming profitable in economic terms. As decolonization and the anti-imperialist liberation struggle gained strength, promising new markets were created in the Third World.

But this anomaly was in fact only one aspect of Swedish Third World policy—and not the most important one at that. The truth is that during this whole period, Sweden practised quite a contradictory policy. For example, it allowed for a condemnation of U.S. aggression against Vietnam, while at the same time supporting its economic policies, including the international monopoly position of the U.S. dollar. The liberation struggle in Portugal's colonies was aided while Sweden cooperated with that country within the European Free Trade Association (EFTA). As I hinted earlier, in the 1950s Sweden was in no way a defender of unilateral decolonization. Quite the contrary was true: Sweden defended the position of the colonial powers—that colonies should be given independence *when the colonial power thought it appropriate*. In the United Nations, Sweden advocated resolutions known to be acceptable to the colonial powers. Hence, Sweden's real role was one of arbitrator, and the real difficulty encountered by Sweden in the United Nations was to get the concurrence of the militantly anticolonial Third World. The colonial powers, on the other hand, were normally much more pleased with the Swedish initiatives.[3]

As we will see shortly, this double standard was to be repeated later, when the United Nations resolution on the new international economic order was approved in 1974. For the time being it is enough to stress that in the 1960s and early 1970s, the two faces of Sweden coexisted without problems, and the progressive aspects continued to attract admiration and applause from the Third World.

In fact, the progressive aspects of social democratic policy in relation to the liberation struggle were growing stronger, and hence the Swedish stance was also becoming more important as a political support for the liberation movements. This position was, however, often mistaken for a dedication to Socialist principles or for a support of noncapitalist development paths. But it was actually an extension of the principle of anticolonialism, opposing the bullying of small countries by the big powers and defending the right of every country to choose its own development strategies in a hostile world, dominated by the two superpowers. Furthermore, what counts in politics is often not the absolute merits or faults of a policy but its relative benefits as compared to those offered by the policies of other countries. Hence, the image of Sweden shone ever brighter.

It can surely be questioned whether the term *image* really does justice to this phase of Sweden's Third World policy; many would argue that the policy in fact did contain a great deal of real solidarity and political courage. Still, one reason for sticking to this somewhat derogatory expression is that in many other respects Swedish international policy was firmly based in the mainstream of the political mix of the dominant capitalist countries. Thus, seen from a Swedish horizon, what was most remarkable about this period is not only the fact that social democracy had a progressive face but also that at the same time it managed to wear two faces that appeared to be completely at odds with each other.

By the middle of the 1970s, this peaceful coexistence between the two faces of Swedish social democracy was being threatened. Until then it had been possible to live comfortably with both; from then on, growing pressures were exerted on the social democrats to choose sides. Two major developments prompted this situation. First, in the 1970s the Third World began to carry a greater weight for Swedish capital. Exports to and direct investments in the Third World became of growing importance. Second, the interpretation of this growing weight of the Third World has to be understood in the context of a series of developments on a global scale that gave this tendency increased importance in the eyes of Swedish social democracy. Overall, the mid-1970s was a period when the balance of power appeared to be changing in favor of the Third World. This trend was set off in 1973, when the OPEC countries doubled the price of oil on the world market. It was given further impetus when the nonaligned countries, led by Algeria, called a special United Nations session in 1974 on a new international economic order. Although these alterations in the international balance of power today may appear insignificant in comparison with later reversals and defeats—I am thinking especially of the debt crisis of the 1980s—it should not be overlooked that the mid-1970s to many governments and transnationals alike heralded the dawn of a new balance of economic power. The Third World now offered great promises of growing markets and interesting direct investment opportunities.

In Sweden, these perceived changes gave rise to new demands on its Third World policy. No longer could capital let this area of Sweden's economic policy be left to the judgment of progressive social forces. Rather, representatives of Swedish capital required that the Third

World policy should be streamlined to conform to the overall economic interest of Swedish transnational capital. But this alteration did not immediately imply that business interests should take precedence over aid; rather, Swedish firms wanted to be the executors of the Swedish aid policy, hence bridging the separation of trade and aid—a separation that until then had been said to be a matter of principle to Swedish social democracy.[4]

The offensive launched by capital against the progressive face of Swedish Third World policy is dressed in the attractive gown of a "coordinated Third World policy" (*samordnad u-landspolitik*). In the future, the argument went, development aid and general economic policy could not be allowed to work independently of each other. Instead, they would be coordinated to work for the same goal. The real question was of course what that goal was to be: Was it to be the overall interests of Swedish capital to have free access to as great a part of the world market as possible, or was it rather the needs of the Third World that would be supported, along the lines of a new economic order?

Representatives of capital formulated their demands in unequivocal terms. The changed international conditions required that Sweden support its firms in the markets of the Third World. This meant two things: Aid should be transformed into commercial credits, and the Third World policy should stop giving priority to Africa and instead begin to focus upon Latin America and Southeast Asia. In this way, Swedish transnational firms would be given an opportunity to compete with other firms on equal terms through a new credit scheme and in the markets where they saw the greatest potential for expansion. This, clearly, constituted a fundamental change in Swedish Third World policy.

The procapital position also gained support from the trade union congress Lands Organisationen (LO). By arguing that Swedish taxpayers' money should be spent to generate employment in Sweden and not elsewhere, the LO sided with capital to defend a tying of aid to the purchase of Swedish goods and services. Only in this way, the LO maintained, could the labor movement's support of a generous aid allocation be maintained.[5]

Against this, the adherents of Sweden's progressive tradition, inside and outside of the social democratic party, argued in favor of a policy in line with Sweden's support of the NIEO and the programme of action adopted by the United Nations General Assembly in 1975. This would entail establishing new trade and financial links between the industrialized countries and the Third World, support for raw materials producer organizations to bolster the negotiating power of the Third World, a restriction of the power of the transnational corporations and a transfer of industrial production capacity to the Third World.

These two lines faced each other in Sweden during the mid-1970s. It was easy to see, or so it appeared at that time, that the double nature of Sweden's relations to the Third World would soon be a thing of the past. Now it was necessary to choose either the progressive tradition of anticolonialism and independence or the commercial interests and the claim to subordinate Swedish Third World policy to the needs of capital—or as the choice was phrased in a book title of the time, either solidarity or imperialism. But social democracy could no longer have it both ways.

The Palme Doctrine: Its Rise and Demise

However, the social democrats refused to make the choice. It was unnecessary, so they said, since there was in fact no contradiction between what was good for Sweden and what was good for the Third World. In Sweden this line of reasoning is called the Palme Doctrine, or the Small States Doctrine. It is quite similar in its approach to the strategy put forward by the Brandt Commission a few years later (which should not surprise us since Palme was a member of the commission).

The Palme Doctrine maintained that a community of interests existed between all small states of the world. The term *small states* was further defined as comprising most Third World countries and the minor industrialized countries, with Sweden of course being a prime example of the latter category. There were three reasons for the shared interests assumed to exist between the small states of the world:

1. A common interest in peace and the peaceful settlements of conflicts. This led to the conclusion that small states should avoid choosing between either of the power blocks: Neither the North Atlantic Treaty Organization (NATO) nor the Warsaw Pact was to be preferred, and there should be no alliance with either of the two superpowers.
2. A shift in the balance of power in favor of the Third World, symbolized by OPEC, the declaration of an NIEO and the growth of the nonaligned movement (where Sweden has observer status). As economic and political power moved from the North to the South, it made good sense to redirect the priorities of small states in the North in the same direction.
3. An increase in the development of Swedish transnational firms

in the Third World. By the mid-1970s the Third World counted as heavily as some of the traditionally most important regions for Swedish transnationals. Measured in terms of markets, the Third World equaled the combined weight of North America, Japan and Australia. Measured in terms of Swedish transnational corporations employees abroad, the Third World equaled the United States and the Nordic countries taken together.

Hence, the Palme Doctrine argued that it made sense for all small states—and especially for Sweden—to involve themselves in a *strategically* new area: the establishment of new economic links between the North and the South, without being part of any colonial or superpower "sphere of interest." Just as in the Brandt Commission, a solution to the crisis in the North and in the South is seen as complementary and not contradictory. As Willy Brandt has said:

> North and South have more interests in common on a medium- and long-term basis than many have so far been able to recognize. . . . We are becoming more aware that a quickened pace of development in the South also serves people in the North.[6]

But what was the real meaning of the Palme Doctrine? Was it to be a coordinated Third World policy, based on the principles of the NIEO—as so frequently and eloquently given verbal support by Sweden? Or was it to signify a turnaround in the established tradition of separation between business and aid interests, heralding their complete amalgamation?

During the six years of bourgeois rule, 1976–1982, some important changes were introduced in Swedish Third World policy. They were not all of a conservative nature, but they all reflected a closer integration between commercial and Third World interests, with the lead given to the former. Let me illustrate this with two cases from Latin America.

To begin with, Sweden's close cooperation with Cuba was terminated. The decision had already been made in May 1976 by drawing lots, a procedure that was sometimes necessary since the Swedish parliament at that time contained an equal number of seats. The bourgeois parties clearly wanted to punish Cuba for the military support that it was giving to the besieged Angola—irrespective of the fact that Angola also was a preferred recipient of Swedish development aid and that a firm antiapartheid policy was one of the hallmarks of Swedish foreign policy, embraced by all the parties (except the conservatives).

The actual termination of Sweden's special relationship with Cuba took place in 1980. By then, another basic change in Sweden's presence in Latin America had also occurred, when Sweden joined the Interamerican Development Bank in 1977. The decision to join in what was a difficult conjuncture for Latin America—only a few years after the coup in Chile—caused a great deal of domestic political debate, with the social democrats opposing the decision, despite the fact that in the preceding year they had been involved in preparing it. The concern to give Swedish transnational firms "equal opportunities" in the Third World was the overriding argument at this point. At times Sweden even defended lending by the IDB that was contested by the United States during the period of President Carter's human rights offensive in Latin America.[7]

The change of government in 1976 also brought a change in Sweden's policy vis-à-vis the South African apartheid regime—but not of the kind that was to be expected. One month earlier, before the social democratic election defeat, Olof Palme had advocated, for the first time, unilateral Swedish actions against South Africa—a marked departure from the traditional social democratic stance that no unilateral move would be undertaken in the absence of a decision by the United Nations Security Council. It was left to a bourgeois government, however, to introduce a law restricting (although not putting an end to) the presence of Swedish transnationals in South Africa. The considerations were rather pragmatic. The new Swedish law was seen as a strong argument in favor of Swedish firms, a move that would open up new markets in Africa and perhaps in other countries of the Third World as well and avoid economic sanctions from African countries, especially from oil-exporting Nigeria.

Although the changing of the guard in 1976 thus meant a stronger and more open integration of Swedish commercial and aid objectives, some of the alterations can be seen to have been to the advantage of the anti-imperialist struggle, at least in Southern Africa. This may seem contradictory, and perhaps it is. But it becomes a little less confusing if we analyze the position of Swedish social democracy with regard to the NIEO.

The 1970s, as I have argued, carried a contradiction between two aspects of social democracy's Third World policy. On the one hand, the Swedish strand of international solidarity was radical and far reaching in that it supported the major anti-imperialist movements engaged in armed struggles against the United States and Portugal. On the other hand, Swedish social democracy embraced a traditional procapitalist policy that went out of its way to defend free trade, the free flow of capital and the urgency to maintain a capitalist world system under the leadership of the United States, including the crucial role of the dollar.

The social democratic support of the NIEO in no way changed this. In fact, the Swedish support of NIEO was a piece of make-believe, for two reasons. First, it was a support in words much more than in deeds. And second, even this verbal support was qualified by serious limitations and reservations—irrespective of the fact that Sweden officially had embraced the principles as they were laid out in the United Nations declarations of 1974 and 1975. In its votes at the same United Nations sessions, Sweden explained that there were certain parts of the NIEO that it could not accept. These turned out to encompass crucial aspects of the NIEO: Sweden refused to agree to a price indexation to guarantee the terms of trade for Third World exports; organizations of raw materials exporters (e.g., OPEC) should not only defend the interests of their members but should likewise cater to the needs of the consuming countries; and any conflicts between a "host" government and a transnational company should be settled by international court—not, as the NIEO had wished, according to national law (i.e., the law of the Third World "host" country).

Here we can clearly see the limitations of the progressive facet of the Swedish social democratic stance: The much talked about support of an NIEO turned out to be mainly a policy declaration that, from its inception, was so circumscribed by exceptions that its objective must have been primarily to bolster Sweden's image as a progressive country. Perhaps the Swedish position was a necessary complement to the Palme Doctrine in order to hold out the prospects of a qualitatively different economic relationship between the "small" country Sweden and its intended partners in the Third World.

In 1982, the social democratic party returned to power. Sweden seemed to return to the double-faced Third World policy of the 1970s. It meant a turn for the better. Sweden once more climbed the barricades, defending Third World countries' rights and interests. This was particularly clear in the Development Assistance Committee of the OECD, the coordinating body for the aid policies of the industrialized capitalist countries.

With the beginning of the Reagan era in 1980, an effort was made by the United States to streamline development assistance under the leadership of the IMF and the World Bank. This meant a growing influence for the United States. Through its 18 percent share of the votes it had a dominant position in both of these international bodies. The Reagan offensive took the form of advocating "aid coordination," a positive-sounding concept to which few could object. However, in this context "coordination" meant subordination to the policies and concepts that ruled the IMF and the World Bank through the application of a common set of terms and conditions that would force the developing countries to follow a liberal, antistatist, export-led strategy, giving the right of way to transnational firms and to the dominance of the world market. This is a policy that we now know quite well, almost a decade after the beginning of the debt crisis, with most countries in Latin America and in Africa south of the Sahara having gone through consecutive programmes of "structural adjustment" precisely designed by the World Bank and the IMF.

But in the early 1980s, the issue was still a hot one among the industrialized countries, and the alignment that was to follow was not yet quite complete. Here Swedish social democracy, faithful to its proud spokesman traditions, took a firm stand against the policy of coordination/subordination. In 1983, the under secretary of state for international development cooperation wrote that he felt ashamed to have to remind his Swedish audience that:

> It is contrary to all the principles of sovereignty and non-interference that drastic policy decisions in one country should be dictated by an alien power, and furthermore by staff [of the IMF and World Bank] who do not even respond to their own parliaments for the steps taken.[8]

A year later, in an official memorandum from the Swedish Ministry of Foreign Affairs, a principle was tabled:

> Aid coordination cannot for our part lead to a situation where Swedish development assistance is tied to the carrying out of macro-economic reforms, e.g., the conclusion of macro-economic stand-by agreements with the IMF. . . . The primary aim of coordination must not be to try and unilaterally impose changes in the national development policy by using aid leverage.[9]

Thus, Sweden's position seemed quite firm, and as usual Sweden reaped goodwill as being one of the few industrialized countries opposing the "ganging up" against the Third World. In reality, however, and during the very same period, the Swedish policy was undergoing the very changes that the rhetoric condemned. Also Sweden de facto embraced aid coordination and a strengthening of the IMF and the World Bank as watchdogs of the international system. A few years later, a former under secretary for development cooperation confirmed that during these years Sweden entered into a new phase of "policy dialogue" with its collaborating Third World countries, but he maintained that this was done "reluctantly" and "without directly linking [macroeconomic policy matters] to Nordic aid flows." Hence, Sweden carried out a policy dialogue without "any conditions related to aid transfers."[10] However, in reality Sweden and the other Nordic countries exerted pressure in favor of IMF formulas, particularly in Africa, on several occasions.

Hence, after its return to power, Swedish social democracy went back to mainstream Third World politics—and this in an area where sharply contradicting positions between the North and the South were evident and where a Swedish moderating position could have been expected, if everything had gone back to normal. But everything did not return to the way it used to be, and it soon became evident that the social democrats now had other and more urgent preoccupations than maintaining an image as spokespeople for the Third World.

Even in the areas where the social democrats in opposition had voiced their harshest criticisms of the bourgeois government, their return to power failed to mean that the policy was changed. The membership in the IDB was not terminated, nor was Cuba reinstated as a main recipient of aid, although these had been standard demands of the social democrats in opposition.[11] Nor was the social democratic proposal that Sweden should lower its financial contributions to the World Bank and the IMF confirmed once the party was in a position to carry out its policy. Quite the contrary was true: Whereas the party in opposition had once required that the contributions to the World Bank should be reduced, ten years later wanted it to see them increased. And whereas the party in opposition had questioned the advisability of the dominating position of the World Bank and the IMF, once back in power it found that these very institutions were clearly beneficial to the Third World.[12] Moreover, in opposition, the social democrats had demanded a democratization of the IMF, but once back in power they refuted the very same demand when put forward by the Communist and the green parties.[13] Sweden's relationship with Cuba was not even reconsidered in the late 1980s when it became evident that the Cuban military effort in Angola had been decisive in bringing about the South African withdrawal from Namibia—in addition to its key role in defending Angola against repeated South African invasions.

Here, in the case of Cuba, Sweden has avoided giving continuity to its role of "matchmaker" and arbitrator, which is all the more surprising since it has played exactly this part in the case of Nicaragua. To overcome the U.S. blockade against Nicaragua and the attempt to block Nicaragua's access to the customary flows of credits and debt renegotiations, Sweden intervened and stepped into the shoes of the World Bank and the IMF: It contracted a team of economists who elaborated a structural adjustment plan that, after the agreement with the Sandinista government, was utilized to convene a donor conference in Stockholm. Thus, additional resources were made available to Nicaragua through the effort of Sweden, whereas Cuba was left out in the cold.

Now, it may seem that these are harsh judgments that fail to take into account the fact that the world has changed since the euphoria of the mid-1970s. And indeed, this is the line of argument that social democrats like to put forward when countering the critique that they have deserted the Third World. Yes, the world has changed in the 1980s—and changed in such a way that the basic premises for the Palme Doctrine no longer are valid.

First, the superpower competition in the Third World subsided gradually, beginning in the early 1980s when the Soviet Union started to limit its involvement to a restricted number of countries (Cuba, Vietnam, Afghanistan, Ethiopia). In return, the United States—and the financial institutions it dominated—gained ever-increasing room for maneuver as the "destabilization" policy and the "low-intensity" wars began to take their grim toll in Nicaragua, Angola and Mozambique.

Second, the economic and political support that had appeared behind the NIEO disappeared and was substituted by the ever-deepening debt crisis. Hence, instead of a shift in the balance of power to the advantage of the Third World, heralded by the NIEO, we have witnessed during the 1980s an increasing marginalization (especially of Africa) to the world system.

Third and as a reflection of the development mentioned earlier, Swedish firms concentrated on the growth poles of the capitalist world economy—especially Western Europe and the United States—and accorded the Third World less importance in their strategic considerations. Swedish capital has become one of the most active investors in the European Economic Community during the last few years. During the latter half of the 1980s, total direct investments virtually exploded, reaching 70 billion Swedish crowns ($12 to 14 billion dollars) in 1989. Fifty percent of these involved real estate and portfolio investments of a speculative nature and centred upon London and Brussels. Investments in the Third World, on the other hand, have dwindled into insignificance, also in absolute current figures. In 1989, they accounted for a mere 1 percent of the total flow of direct investments.[14]

When the world changed, so did the role and importance of Swedish Third World policy. The need for a small-state doctrine vanished, and the Palme Doctrine became obsolete. Since then, the strategic aim of the Swedish transnational firms as well as of the social democratic party has been to achieve a full-scale and permanent integration with the dynamic and capitalist project of growth and expansion, especially within the framework of the European Common Market. Instead of advocating the principle of free trade for all—in itself a dubious argument as far as Third World countries are concerned—Swedish social democracy now adheres to the limited and restricted freedom of the Common Market, in essence a protectionist bloc with its point directed against the outer, non-European world. Instead of adopting the Palme Doctrine, which opted for a third road and refused to make a choice between the United States and the Soviet Union, Swedish social democracy has now chosen the European road, allying itself with the European superpower in the making against the United States and Japan.

As far as Swedish transnationals are concerned, they not only perceive their long-term interest to be firmly rooted in Europe and North America but also have come to consider the advantage of being identified with a progressive country as rather dubious or at best of marginal interest. This lesson was brought home quite forcefully in Zimbabwe, where after independence was declared in 1980 transnationals from Britain and Germany gained the contracts, whereas their Swedish competitors—in spite of the Swedish policy of support for the liberation struggle—lost out. Political goodwill turned out to be of little value when it boiled down to a matter of interest rates and export credits.

Into the 1990s

As we enter the mid-1990s, Swedish social democracy has turned out to be capable of creatively squeezing aid money from the budget and putting it to uses for which it was not intended. This began in the 1970s when aid was tied to the purchase of Swedish goods and services. And it went on with the creation of special "soft" credits, enabling Swedish firms to compete on the markets of the Third World. With the developments in Eastern Europe and the avalanche of goodwill toward the emerging but heavily indebted democracies, aid money was increasingly put at the disposal of non–Third World countries. Sweden in fact pioneered the policy in the OECD that the Eastern European countries should be supported via the aid budget. In addition, development cooperation funds will be diverted to sustain refugees from the Third World in Sweden.

And so it continues: The fact that Sweden's contribution of $20 million to the IDB led to Swedish exports for a total value of $120 million to IDB-financed projects was presented as evidence of the wisdom of increasing Swedish participation in IDB. However, when the IDB entered into structural adjustment lending in collaboration with the World Bank, the social democrats considered that the IDB contributions should pass as aid and therefore decided to finance IDB from the aid budget starting in 1990–1991 and not as before from the trade budget.

Another such contribution was made to the World Bank–sponsored Multilateral Investment Guarantee Agency (MGA). This agency insures transnational firms against commercial and noncommercial— i.e., political—risks. Although the Swedish contribution is small— only six million Swedish crowns or $1 million—it constitutes a marked change from the position of strengthening the host countries and not the already-mighty transnationals, apart from the fact that the aid budget ought to be reserved for the Third World.

In fact and on a more general level, the decreased importance—or growing marginality—of the Third World to Swedish capital has meant that no strategic considerations are present as far as the relationship between Sweden and the Third World is concerned. Thus, while the Palme Doctrine took as its point of departure a changed balance of power on a global scale, the present Swedish policy simply considers the Third World as an object of aid. All the talk in the 1970s—especially during the social democratic opposition—of an NIEO, of the need for reform of the International Monetary Fund and the World Bank, of limiting the power of the transnational firms by introducing social clauses and codes of conducts has now been reduced to a simple lamentation of the debt crisis and the state of the Third World in general. The only cure that Swedish social democracy is offering these days is some aid and the advice to the Third World to consent to the policies imposed by the creditor countries through the IMF and the World Bank.

In spite of the recognition that the debt crisis is the most pressing problem for most countries in Latin America and Africa, Sweden continues to advocate that new loans create the necessary conditions for development in the future—albeit on "soft" terms. Hence, Sweden has been increasing its support through the aid budget to the World Bank and to the African, Latin American and Asian development banks. In the years 1990–1991, 10 percent (1.2 billion Swedish crowns or $220 million) of the Swedish aid budget went to these undemocratic international lending institutions in order to facilitate their extended lending. The fact that these banking institutions are so-called preferred creditors and that the indebted countries in principle cannot default on such loans means that the debt burden in the long run may become considerably more problematic.

The limitations of the social democratic position can clearly be seen from the attempt to define a specific Swedish strategy for Latin America. In the 1991–1992 government bill on foreign policy, this strategy is presented as the fruit of hard intellectual labor. Sweden's ambition is to promote four out of the five basic objectives of Swedish development aid: economic growth, social and economic equity, democratization and an ecologically sustainable development. The only principle left out was the one that concerns strengthening self-reliance, a sign that the social democrats now feel that Latin America ought to be "integrated" rather than made strong and independent.

The Swedish strategy goes on to present an interesting division of labor in order to fulfill these objectives: The "hard" goal of promoting economic growth is delegated to the World Bank and the IMF, and Sweden's function is to channel financial support through these institutions that supposedly know best how to achieve growth and create a climate of business confidence. The "softer" goals, like equity, democracy and sustainability, however, are considered to be the areas where Sweden should assume a direct responsibility. Thus, social democracy here continues the traditional division of labor between the hard-liners and the softhearted, the latter category normally encompassing the Scandinavian and other "like-minded" countries.

This division of labor is problematic for two reasons. First, it implies that Sweden hides its economic and political support of the austerity programmes imposed by the World Bank and the IMF. The international financial institutions thus will be held responsible for a policy that in fact has been agreed to by all the creditor countries, including Sweden. And second, the inherent contradiction between the different components of Sweden's policies is swept under the carpet. In real life, the consequences of the austerity programmes that with Sweden's concordance are imposed by the World Bank and the IMF conflict with the other, "softer" objectives of Sweden's own policy.

One example is the overexploitation of the forest resources of Latin America, which obviously runs against an ecologically sustainable development strategy. But what is less clear is that this exploitation has been created by two pressures that are produced by the strategy imposed by the World Bank and the IMF. These pressures have to do with the need to increase export earnings through the exploitation of raw materials valued on the world market and the need for poor farmers and other marginalized people to open new farm land or look for gold as an alternative to the social exploitation that the austerity has spelled in urban and rural areas of Latin America.

Conclusion

The death of the Palme Doctrine is more than a shift in policy emphasis; it also should be understood at a conceptual level. Basically, the Palme Doctrine maintained the absence of conflicts of interest between the North and the South. In this respect it was a faithful replica of the domestic social democratic dictum that what is good for big business is also good for the people.[15]

When the social democratic party regained government power in 1982, a contradiction was acknowledged, for the first time, between the interests of capital and those of the people, at least in the short run: In order to promote private investment and keep the firms "believing in Sweden,"[16] companies were offered satisfactory conditions in terms of profit margins. To keep capital happy was an explicit objective of social democratic economic policy during the 1980s. The party also acknowledged the price that was to be paid in terms of growing social inequalities but reasoned that it was worth it since it assured full employment—and this in a context of European mass unemployment at an average of perhaps 8 or 9 percent, with many countries having two-digit rates.

The social democratic party called this turnabout in economic policy the "third road." The common choice for a country to get out of an economic imbalance is either to grow out of the crisis or to save in order to correct the imbalance. The social democrats refused to make that choice. Instead, they opted for an "ambitious" target, summed up in the party's own proposal for a programme for the 1990s:

> We wanted to re-establish the balance in our economy and at the same time to stimulate the private actors. We wanted to fight unemployment while simultaneously suppressing inflation. We told ourselves that we could work *and* save ourselves out of the crisis.[17]

This third road of the Swedish social democrats of the 1980s was, however, a completely different road than the one discussed in this book's introduction. There, the third road implies an option between raw capitalism and Stalinistic socialism, bringing most of the goodies without the disadvantages of either of the "models." The Swedish third road, however, brought increasing social differentiation and a growing concentration of economic power in the hands of a few (Swedish) transnational firms, while the ambition to carry out a Swedish development model was lost, symbolized by the successive liberalizations of Sweden's control over its own transnational firms through the termination of the system of control over direct investments and transfer of resources.

The social democratic government announced in October 1990 that Sweden would apply for membership in the European Common Market. What was impossible and unthinkable only one month earlier—at the 31st Social Democratic Congress in September 1990, where a Swedish membership in the EEC was refuted with reference to Swedish foreign policy and neutrality—was now considered reasonable, social democratic policy. A more definite end to the Palme Doctrine is difficult to imagine. It started as a third road and an alternative to the superpower rivalry and ended lining up with the European super-power in a protectionist bloc.

This is one of the reasons why the international seminar on the relevance of the Swedish model to Latin America—held in Chile in May 1989—seemed somewhat out of place.[18] The Swedish social democrats complimented themselves extensively on the achievements of the Swedish model, from the eradication of social injustices, via international solidarity and foreign policy, to the advantages of the Swedish bureaucratic setup. It was left to Latin American participants to present a few critical analyses of the Swedish experience, which helped to show the relative merits and demerits of the Swedish development path. Rather ironically, the seminar in fact coincided with the dismantling of the Swedish model. The specific traits of this model and of Sweden's Third World policy belong to history.

On the domestic political scene, the special position of social democracy in Swedish political life has come to an end. In the polls of 1989 and 1990, the party was receiving ever-decreasing shares of the votes, and in the 1991 elections, it captured only a little over one-third of the electorate. This end to the period of social democratic hegemony will by necessity lead to new political alliances, as social democracy tries to survive in a changing political and social context. Whereas the Swedish model was based on an alliance between organized labor and monopoly capital, today the social democratic party is deserting its old political base and is leaning ever more heavily on bourgeois parties. This came out clearly at the 1990 congress, where no policy guidelines were tabled but where the party leadership received a carte blanche to arrange for "broad" solutions for all the pressing issues of the time: nuclear energy, transport systems, European integration and sustainable development. In reality, what the congress did was authorize the party to ally itself with the bourgeois parties and to seek compromise solutions with any group that could guarantee it would retain government power.

Simultaneously and while both the trade unions and the social democratic party are losing members, the resistance against this version of the third road is growing from below. This opposition is still rather weak and quite fragmented, and it will probably take decades before a new social force to be reckoned with will emerge. But it is here, in opposition to the *present* social democratic policy, that a real alternative—a real third road—may emerge.

Notes

1. The only four exceptions are brief spells of a colonial presence in today's Ghana (until 1663), in Delaware (until 1655) and in the Caribbean islands of Guadalupe (1813–1814) and San Bartolomé (1784–1808).

2. For instance, although the official tax rate for capital is 52 percent on net profits, the firms on the Stockholm stock exchange rarely paid more than 30 percent during the 1980s, due to favorable rules that, through investment funds, permit expanding firms to postpone the payment of taxes "indefinitely" (i.e., as long as they go on expanding).

3. B. Huldt, *Sverige och Förenta Nationerna—Historia och Framtidsperspektiv* (Stockholm: Sekretariatet för Framtidsstudier, 1976).

4. R. Jacoby, "Idealism Versus Economics: Swedish Aid and Commercial Interests," in P. Frühling, ed., *Swedish Development Aid in Perspective: Policies, Problems and Results Since 1952* (Stockholm: Almqvist and Wiksell, 1986); C. Brundenius, K. Hermele and M. Palmberg, *Gränslösa affärer: Om Svenska Företag î Tredje Världen* (Stockholm: Liber Förlag, 1980); K. Hermele and K. A. Larsson, *Solidaritet Eller Imperialism: Om Sverige, Världsordningen och Tredje Världen* (Stockholm: Liber Förlag, 1980).

5. The tying of aid to purchases in Sweden did in fact increase until in 1975–1976 and 1976–1977 it reached 29–30 percent of the bilateral aid allocations. Since the real "return flow," i.e., the share that is actually spent on Swedish goods and services, in most years greatly exceeds this tied share—an average figure is 40–50 percent of the bilateral allocation—the tying of aid has become a nonissue, and the formally tied section of the aid budget has also been decreasing. See Jacoby, "Idealism Versus Economics," and K. Hermele, *Sweden and the Third World: Development Aid and Capital Involvement*, AKUT 11, Uppsala University, 1981.

6. W. Brandt, "A Plea for Change: Peace, Justice, Jobs," in the Brandt Commission report, *North-South: A Programme for Survival* (London: Pan Books, 1980), p. 20.

7. P. Schori, *I Orkanens Öga: Om den Kommande Revolutionen i Centralamerika* (Stockholm: Tiden, 1981).

8. G. Edgren, "Om Biståndets Villkor" in C. Anderson, L. Heikensten and S. de Vylder, eds., *Bistånd i Kris: En Bok om Svensk Biståndspolitik* (Stockholm: Liber Förlag, 1984), p. 47.

9. "Memorandum on Aid Coordination from the Under Secretary of State for International Cooperation," Ministry of Foreign Affairs, Stockholm, March 2, 1984.

10. G. Edgren, "Changing Terms: Procedures and Relationships in Swedish Development Assistance," in Frühling, *Swedish Development Aid*, p. 56.

11. See social democratic (opposition) motions to parliament, *Motion med Anledning av Proposition* 1977–1978: 135 *om Rinktlinjer för Internationellt Utvecklingssamarbete mm,* Motions 1977–1978: 1912, and 1978–1979: 1771, by Olof Palme, Ingvar Carlsson et al.

12. Compare ibid., p. 20, with social democratic (government) bill 1988–1989, p. 44.

13. Compare social democratic (government) bill 1988–1989, pp. 20-21, with *Utrikesutskottets utlåtande UU* 1987–1988: 20, pp. 60–61. This position was confirmed by the Social Democratic 31st Congress in 1990, where the need for reform of the IMF and the World Bank was refuted.

14. B. Swedenborg, Johansson-Grahn and M. Kinnwall, *Den Svenska Industrins Utlandsinvesteringar 1960–1986* (Stockholm: Industriens Utrednings-institut, 1988).

15. This Swedification of the well-known saying about General Motors and the United States is credited to the former social democratic minister of finance, Gunnar Sträng.

16. I borrow this expression from a book title by the leading Swedish capitalist and strategic thinker, Volvo president P. G. Gyllenhammar, *Jag tror på Sverige* (Stockholm: Askild & Kärnekull, 1973); also see Ministry of Industry, *Svensk Industry och Industripolitik* (Stockholm, 1989).

17. Social Democratic Party of Sweden, "Motioner (Häfte Mu) och Partistyrelsens Utlätande (Häfte U4) om Internationelle frägor," in *Socialdemokraternas 31a Kongress,* Stockholm, 1990, p. 236; also Social Democratic Party of Sweden, "90-talsprogrammet," in *En Debattbok om Arbetarrörelsens Viktigaste Frågor Under 90-talet* (Stockholm: Tidens Förlag, 1990).

18. J. Goñi, *Democracia, Desarrollo y Equidad: La Experiencia de Suecia, Reflexiones para Lationoamericanos* (Caracas: AIC/Editorial Nueva Sociedad, 1990).

4

Latin American Social Democracy in British Perspective

Paul Cammack

The purpose of this chapter is to assess the prospects for social democracy in Latin America through (1) a critical analysis of Adam Przeworski's account of social democracy as a form of class compromise and (2) a comparison, from a structural-historical perspective, of the British and Latin American experiences of social democracy. Without a theoretical investigation of the kind undertaken by Przeworski, cross-national comparisons are impossible. I argue, however, that Przeworski's own analysis is defective in a number of ways. It can only lead to valid conclusions if faults in its internal logic are corrected and if it is supplemented by a structural-historical analysis capable of identifying regional variations in patterns of class formation and structure, conflict and compromise. The social democratic traditions in Europe and Latin America spring from profoundly different social-historical contexts. Within the broad contrast that this difference in context suggests, the British case is of particular interest. It provides, in the specific case of the Labour Party, an example of an early and sustained, if only intermittently successful, strategy of reformism within the confines of the capitalist system. I approach the British case through Stein Rokkan's analysis of the process of party formation in Western Europe, drawing attention to the emergence of the British Labour Party *after* bourgeois parties in Britain had begun to develop a broad social base and to reshape themselves as modern mass parties. I then apply a Rokkan-style analysis to Latin America, arguing that whatever the differences from case to case, one can observe, as a general pattern, that there was no such early development of modern mass parties of the bourgeoisie. As a consequence of this different historical pattern of institutional development, the political capacity of the dominant classes of Latin America was significantly weakened by the depression, and since that time they have not been able to compete successfully in mass democratic politics. On the basis of this analysis, I conclude that the major obstacles to successful social democracy in Latin America are to be found in the long-run political and institutional weakness of the economically dominant classes, rather than in the severe economic problems currently besetting the region.

Class Compromise and Social Democracy

According to Przeworski, initially radical social democratic movements are bound either to abandon their revolutionary goals and shift to reformism or to lose influence and disappear. This is so for four related reasons: Wage earners and others can improve their material conditions within the confines of capitalism; the state can make a difference in allocating resources and distributing incomes, so that partisan control over it matters and must be sought; the opportunity inherent in democracy forces mass movements to orient their strategies toward short-run improvements and to de-emphasize class identities; and major social transformations, such as the transition to socialism, are costly and will not be attempted by movements powerful under capitalism.[1] Two conditions have to be met for the "class compromise" at the heart of reformist social democracy to be achieved. First, profits have to be high enough to allow the reproduction of capital, and wages must be high enough to convince workers they have a stake in the system. Second, the bourgeoisie has to be willing to accept compromises over distribution and to acquiesce in the construction of a state over which it is not guaranteed direct control.[2] For Przeworski, this explains the shift toward reformism in European social democracy: The availability of material gains within the capitalist order and the remoteness of the prospect that capitalism could be overthrown led workers to opt for available gains within the system. Parties that persisted in holding out for an unrealizable alternative and rejected the strategy of settling for short-run gains were punished by the withdrawal of support and fell into decline.

Przeworski's analysis is useful because it defines the conditions for successful social democracy under capitalism—the generation of a sufficient surplus to allow distribution to workers without threatening the process of accumulation, together with the willingness of capitalists to give up a part of the surplus and relinquish direct political power. This provides a starting point for comparative analysis. However, his analysis has three serious weaknesses, with direct implications for the comparison between British and Latin American social democracy. Firstly, as the conditions noted earlier suggest, it takes an extremely optimistic view of the economic potential of capitalism and of the willingness of capitalists to allow policies of redistribution to be carried out. Secondly, despite the illustrative use made of historical examples, the case is made at the level of formal argument and demonstration. For these reasons, it is not easy to apply the analysis directly to real-world situations. Thirdly, and most significantly, its internal logic is defective. Przeworski argues that material gains are available and that parties must pursue them on behalf of their followers or be deserted. But his formulation of the model of class compromise is deficient. In his account of the "material bases of consent," he reaches the conclusion that "given the past history of profits *there must exist at any time a level of wage increases which is minimally necessary to reproduce consent.*"[3] Here consent is defined as cognitive and behavioural—choosing particular courses of action and following them in practice. Workers "consent" in this sense to capitalist relations when they enter them, by working for a wage. The error in the argument is that, despite Przeworski's claim to the contrary, workers do not need to view capitalism as a positive-sum game, to receive or expect wage increases, in order to consent to it in this way. It is simply necessary, as he himself argues extensively elsewhere and as my summary of his views above shows, that they see no better alternative. Workers may "consent," as workers or as citizens, while regarding the game as zero- or negative-sum but as less costly than any imaginable alternative. If so, the iron law that pushes social democracy toward reformism rests more upon the ability of capitalists and their allies to impose capitalist relations and make the cost of achieving socialism prohibitive than upon the conviction that positive gains are always available for workers under capitalism. It follows that the primary inducement for social democratic parties to adopt reformist policies is negative rather than positive.

This leads us back to a line of analysis that Przeworski goes to great lengths to resist. The social democratic parties he describes are committed unconditionally to capitalism, whether workers gain in the short run or not. As he argues, such parties are unlikely to bring socialism about. But this is precisely because they press for class compromise in times of *crisis*, rather than openly in the good times when short-run gains are available: It is this that provides the key to their role in capitalist society. Social democracy is a source of political support for capitalism in times of crisis because of the energy with which its adherents insist that there is no alternative. It deters workers from the consistent pursuit of material gains under capitalism and from the active consideration of revolutionary alternatives. By adopting a one-sided view of the economic potential of capitalism in his formal model, relegating his critique of it to an accompanying moral commentary and failing to characterize it as inherently subject to periodic crises whatever the behaviour of workers, Przeworski manages to present the compulsion to which workers are subject under capitalist relations as a positive advantage and to pass off as a scientific discovery the undefended and highly ideological assertion that there is no alternative.[4]

It is not surprising, in the light of this analysis, that he draws very conservative conclusions from the application of his ideas to Latin America. After describing the schematic form of class compromise in capitalist society and identifying Keynesianism—with its "combination of private property, redistribution of income, and a strong state"—as its ideal economic project, he immediately goes on to deliver a very different message from that contained in his confident advocacy of the potential for material advances for all within capitalism:

> Keynesian projects may be more appealing from the point of view of building a democratic coalition than they are auspicious for establishing a stable democratic regime: a good net to catch allies, but one highly vulnerable to anyone with sharp teeth. It seems as if an almost complete docility and patience on the part of organized workers are needed for a democratic transformation to succeed. Here again it may be worth noting that the democratic system was solidified in Belgium, Sweden, France and Great Britain only after organized workers were badly defeated in mass strikes and adopted a docile posture as a result. . . . We cannot avoid the possibility that a transition to democracy can be made only at the cost of leaving economic relations intact, not only the structure of production but even the distribution of income.[5]

Here Przeworski contradicts himself, by arguing for democracy *without* any material basis for consent. He also passes in silence over the fact that Latin American workers have already suffered their share of defeats and that in the European cases he cites, the workers who adopted a docile posture after their defeat in mass strikes *were* subsequently material beneficiaries of class compromise along Keynesian lines. Finally, he confirms his own commitment to a conservative position: Where material gain is not possible under capitalism, workers must learn to do without. The kindest and the most likely explanation for this conclusion, which denies large parts of his theoretical work, is that he believes either that Latin American capitalism lacks the capacity to provide workers with a

flow of material benefits or that Latin American capitalists lack the
will to do so and that if workers press their case within the system or
seek to overthrow it, they will be defeated. If so, the conclusion must
be that there is room in Latin America today for neither social
democracy nor socialism. Let us see, through an examination of British
social democracy's implications for Latin America, whether this is
necessarily so. To do so, we must examine British and Latin American
social democracy alike in historical context, rather than in terms of
formal abstraction.

British Social Democracy

Social democracy in Britain has certainly been resolutely reformist
virtually since its inception. The extension of suffrage to incorporate
the bulk of the working class began in earnest with the Second Reform
Act of 1867, with which "Britain, alone among large European nations,
peacefully adjusted her institutions to meet the emergence of a
powerful working class."[6] This step followed upon the defeat of the
radical initiatives espoused by the Chartists in the 1830s and 1840s,
and throughout the nineteenth century the expansion of suffrage and
incorporation of a minority of the working class into electoral politics
remained under the control of the Liberal and Conservative parties.
From 1867 onward these parties were actively engaged in recruiting
and mobilizing working-class supporters, while limiting the pace of
expansion and seeking to avoid the "political combination of the lower
classes, as such and for their own objects" that Walter Bagehot,
writing in 1872, regarded as "an evil of the first magnitude."[7]

Against this background, the first working-class members of
parliament (MPs) were elected with the support of the Liberal Party,
and it was only in 1893 that the Independent Labour Party came into
being. This was followed in 1900 by the founding of the Labour
Representation Committee, with Keir Hardie describing labourism as
"the theory and practice which accepted the possibility of social
change within the existing framework of society."[8] From small
beginnings and a secret pact with the Liberal Party in 1903, this
committee became the Labour Party in 1906, winning 29 seats in that
year and raising its total to 191 in 1923, displacing the Liberal Party in
the process. It briefly formed a minority government in 1924, and in the
wake of the general strike of 1926, which its leaders conspicuously
failed to support, it settled into "a broad acceptance of the existing
economic system and an optimism about its potential for reform," based
upon a Fabian belief in gradualism, class cooperation and the
neutrality of the state.[9] The consequence of this orientation, which

represented the majority view of leaders and trade union activists from the first days of the existence of the Labour Party, was the second minority government of 1929–1931, which saw Labour leaders in office applying orthodox economic measures to combat the slump and ended with Prime Minister Ramsay MacDonald and Chancellor Philip Snowdon leading a break with the party to head the national government coalition founded in the latter year. In the 1931 election Labour Party representation fell back from 287 seats (in May 1929) to 51. The party did not return to power until 1945, with a majority for the first time. In power, it implemented a classic reformist social democratic package of welfare legislation and limited nationalization, establishing a commitment to the mixed economy and the welfare state that was to endure, virtually across the whole of the political spectrum, until the end of the 1970s. The party narrowly retained power in 1950, but it was defeated by the Conservatives in 1951. Thirteen years of Conservative rule followed, with Labour returning to office again from 1964 to 1970 and from 1974 to 1979.

In all, then, the Labour Party has governed Britain for seventeen years since its departure from office in 1931, attempting to base its practice while in office on policies on the welfare state and the mixed economy borrowed from two liberals, William Beveridge and John Maynard Keynes, respectively, and in matters of foreign policy and internal security (in relation to the cold war on the one hand and the nationalist challenge in Northern Ireland on the other) keeping to a broad consensus shared with the Conservative Party.

If the first period of majority Labour government (1945–1951) fits the image of positive-sum class compromise that Przeworski describes, the same cannot be said either of Labour's earlier periods of minority rule or of its return to power in the 1960s and the 1970s. As a minority party in 1924 and between 1929 and 1931 it sought to establish its credentials as an alternative party of government by eschewing unorthodoxy. And by the 1960s the poor performance of the British economy was already making it difficult to combine continued accumulation with redistribution; far from presiding over further successful reformism, the Labour governments of the 1960s and 1970s tended to sacrifice the aspirations of their electorate in the face of worsening economic crisis, beginning the downward pressure on public spending that was to accelerate after Margaret Thatcher's election victory in 1979. In Colin Leys's apt words, the 1960s saw "the paralysis of social democracy."[10] The following decades saw its decline and defeat. Of all the cases of European social democracy, the British case is the one that most clearly illustrates the obvious fact that capitalism cannot be guaranteed to produce the material resources needed for the class compromise at the heart of his model to be endlessly sustained.

A central feature of the record of British social democracy arises from the fact that the British Labour Party found itself competing from the start with bourgeois parties that had developed an institutional capacity to build support within the working class. Doctrines of class compromise were first articulated in the late nineteenth century by Conservative and Liberal politicians, and both parties reorganized themselves in order to compete for the working-class vote before the Labour Party came into being. The politics of class compromise were sustained through the first decades of independent Labour Party activity by the economic fruits of early industrialism and imperialism and the ideological hegemony they made possible. But those same politics continued to be preached most ardently by Labour leaders, in periods of economic crisis in particular. Regarding the Trade Union Congress (TUC) in the wake of the general strike of 1926, Harold Laski remarked that "its chief purpose seemed to be the repression of any militant policy among the unemployed lest this be taken as an index to sympathy for Communist ideas";[11] Ralph Miliband noted that there is "no record of any Labour Party leaders ever having used their commanding position to press more radical policies on reluctant activists: the trend has always and uniformly been the other way."[12] Doctrines of class compromise have been far more insistently preached in times of crisis than in times of plenty, while the thinking that Przeworski ascribes to the rational worker has been more characteristic of reformist leaders than of workers themselves. Commenting on the 1960s, Leys contrasted Prime Minister Harold Wilson's claim that "capitalism could provide affluence for the working class while at the same time preserving the gains of the well-to-do" with the record of disaffection and militancy in the period and a social situation characterized by "on the one hand, a class of capital still deeply attached to many pre-capitalist values, and on the other, an organized working class deeply sceptical of any suggestion that any advantage they might concede to the employers would actually advance their own long-term interests."[13]

British social democracy, in the institutional form of the Labour Party, took shape in a period of British supremacy in the capitalist world order, and it was contained in its formative years by the ideological hegemony of capital. It was able to preside after World War II over an implementation of social and economic policies of class compromise within limits respectful of the needs of capitalist accumulation, but it has been most notably occupied, before and since, with the discovery and enforcement of those limits. As David Coates remarked, "It is not simply that Labour politics never challenge the interconnections between the state machine and the capitalist order. It is rather that the Labour Party in power invariably *strengthens* those inter-connections."[14] For this reason it has been able to offer neither a *radical* nor a *reformist* alternative to Thatcher's attack upon the postwar social democratic consensus on Keynesian economic policy and the steady expansion of the welfare state.

There are, then, significant and interrelated elements to British social democracy as a historical phenomenon: its emergence in the wake of the successful organization of modern mass parties of capital; its development in circumstances of capitalist expansion and hegemony; its intermittent success in extending material gains to its adherents; and its enforcement in office of the limits set by crises of accumulation. We may now consider how the Latin American experience compares.

Latin American Social Democracy
as a Historical Phenomenon

I shall develop in this section a contrast between Britain and Latin America derived from a consideration of Latin America in the light of Stein Rokkan's work on the development of party systems in Western Europe. This work contains a powerful political economy orientation whose comparative potential has not been fully exploited. In turn, a development of its comparative potential reveals some of the problems that arise from Przeworski's attempt to generalize on the basis of the European experience of social democracy. Rokkan's classic essay on the origins of European party systems, jointly authored with Seymour Lipset in 1967, was a pioneering historical-structural analysis of party and party system formation. At its core was a focus on the timing, character and effects of successive national and industrial revolutions and the interactions between them. Its authors traced varied conflicts and alliances arising out of basic confrontations between centre and periphery, church and state, agriculture and industry, and workers and employers. They contended that outcomes in each of the first three conflicts at successive critical historical moments led to different contexts within which the class struggles of the industrial era were faced and different, enduring systems of political incorporation. Thus

> the crucial differences among the party systems emerged in the early phases of competitive politics, before the final phase of mass mobilization. They reflected basic contrasts in the conditions and sequences of nation-building

and in the structure of the economy at the point of take-off toward sustained growth.[15]

Lipset and Rokkan argued that the choices made at the crucial historical junctures dominated successively by centre-periphery, church-state and land-industry conflicts explain the variety in party systems and the different outcomes in each case from the similar impact of class conflicts between owners and workers. Finally, they attached particular importance to the issue of whether mass organizations had been developed by Conservatives and Liberals before the final thrust to full suffrage took place:

> Where the challenge of the emerging working-class parties had been met by concerted efforts of countermobilization through nationwide mass organizations on the liberal and the conservative fronts, the leeway for new party formations was particularly small; this was the case whether the threshold of representation was low, as in Scandinavia, or quite high, as in Britain. Correspondingly the "post-democratic" party systems proved markedly more fragile and open to newcomers in the countries where the privileged strata had relied on their local power resources rather than on nationwide mass organizations in their efforts of mobilization.[16]

The message here is clear. Where Liberal and Conservative mobilization had provided modern party organizations before the full extension of suffrage to the working class (as in Britain), it proved possible to preserve democratic continuity. Where such mobilization had not done so (as in Italy, France, Spain and Germany), it proved impossible to maintain this continuity. The distinctive feature of the argument is that it moves from an initial broad but historically situated focus (upon national and industrial revolutions) to an understanding of particular party systems in Europe as they stood in the 1960s; it is close in style to Barrington Moore's historical essay on the origins of democracy and dictatorship or to Charles Tilly's historical sociology and quite different from the more abstract analysis pursued by Przeworski. Furthermore, its focus on varied national combinations and configurations on "common" issues rejects the possibility of meaningful correlations between abstracted socioeconomic indicators and any particular political events. And its specific focus upon the emergence of party systems (and of enduring democracies) in Western Europe, in specific historical conditions not reproduced elsewhere (the Reformation and the Industrial Revolution), argues against any direct reading from the European cases to other times and places. In other words, it invites scholars of other regions to consider what a similar exercise might suggest, rather than to draw hasty conclusions based upon generalizations derived from the European experience. In particular, by suggesting that issues of class organization, capacity and conflict may be decisive in every case while rejecting the naive imposition of identical outcomes across different cases, it points the way to a systematic comparative analysis of politics from a class perspective in which a single logic is applied to all historical cases and different outcomes are explained by theoretically significant differences in historical context. Let us consider how the record and prospects of social democracy in Latin American might be approached in the same style.

From the perspective of comparative historical sociology, the "national" and "industrial" revolutions that Lipset and Rokkan took as their starting point may be seen as European expressions of two related global processes, one of the emergence of a system of nation-states, the other of the coming into being of a global capitalist economy. Both processes have a history in which the European experience, though central, has been part of a greater whole. A first step toward an approach to Latin American in a comparative framework derived from the Lipset-Rokkan exercise would be to identify the distinctive forms that these "national" and "industrial" revolutions took in the region and to assess the consequences by looking for key conflicts that might have played the shaping roles that Lipset and Rokkan attributed to successive core-periphery, church-state, land-industry and owner-worker conflicts in Europe. It is necessary to identify the specific form of the national and industrial revolutions or, more precisely, the character in Latin America of the process of emergence of nation-states and the spread of the international capitalist economy. It will then be necessary to identify conflicts constituting key cleavage structures and the various patterns that emerged from country to country within the region. This is too large a research project to permit a comprehensive account here, but some broad outlines can be suggested as a point of departure.

On the two dimensions identified, Latin America has a distinctive regional history. Practically all the Latin American nations, formerly colonies of Catholic Spain or Portugal (in the case of Brazil), came to independence in a brief period between 1810 and 1830, in large part as a consequence of the impact upon Spain and Portugal of the Napoleonic Wars in Europe. They share a common history of *early political independence*. In addition they were all drawn into the emerging global capitalist economy in a role that complemented the Industrial Revolution already gathering strength in Europe but at the same time reflected the different circumstances prevailing in Latin America's distant, sparsely populated and relatively undeveloped new states.

Virtually without exception, the Latin American states were drawn
into the Europe-centred world economy as suppliers of raw materials
and importers of manufactured goods. The process was most dynamic in
the half century between 1880 and 1930, in many cases after serious
instability in the immediate period after independence as different
factions struggled for control. They thus experienced a process of
internal economic change, complementary to the Industrial Revolution
in Europe but in their case based upon *export-led development*.

For Latin America the relevant parallels to national and industrial
revolutions, from the perspective of comparative historical sociology,
are early independence from Iberian rule and export-led development
from the late nineteenth century on. On this basis, three very broad
contrasts can be drawn with the European experience. Firstly, the
process of state formation arose from a single source, the breakdown of
Iberian rule. Within two decades the map of the region took on a
shape that would be readily recognizable today. The following period
was marked by sometimes intense hostility within and between states,
but Latin America did not become a focus of struggle *between* major
powers. Secondly, while major disputes often centred around church-
state conflict, the Catholic church never experienced a challenge from
the Protestant offshoots of the Reformation. Thus while conflicts were
sometimes acute and long lasting and gave rise (as in Colombia) to
significant party expression, they were never as complex as in Europe.
On the whole, where they were prominent, they tended to provide a
basis for a single cleavage between Conservatives and Liberals,
thereby reinforcing a parallel cleavage between social and economic
groupings either based on the colonial structures or provoked in the
name of free enterprise and free trade. They thus played a part in the
major changes that preceded the commitment of the region to export
orientation but seldom provided cross-cutting cleavages, and they
rarely persisted into the twentieth century. Thirdly and most
significantly, the battle between land and industry that structured so
much political exchange in Europe was never properly joined in Latin
America. Until 1930, industry took second place to export production,
either mineral or agricultural. This reinforced the dominance of
landed elites, acting directly in concert with the mostly foreign
exploiters of mineral resources.

On each of these points, variations from country to country led to
patterns of conflict and alliance as different from one another as those
depicted by Lipset and Rokkan in Europe. They were differences,
though, within a common framework provided by the sharing of
Iberian rule, Catholic dominance, early independence and export
orientation. For our limited purposes, the key to subsequent

developments is provided by the common consequences of all these various developments for the fourth Lipset-Rokkan variable—conflict between workers and owners and the consequences in terms of political incorporation. The central difference between the British and Latin American cases is this: Few opportunities or incentives existed in Latin America before 1930 for the construction of mass organizations into which the working class might be incorporated. The primary cause here was the dominance of export-oriented development. Landowners and mineowners, seeking to keep the costs of production as low as possible, had no incentive to extend citizenship to their workers; the workers themselves were often divided by distance, status and category (from peasant producers to migrant workers drawn by debt); industry was too weak to figure—or to wish to figure—as an ally of labor. As to the conflicts that arose on regional bases or between Liberals and Conservatives, where they were not resolved through the raising of temporary armies they generally gave rise to exactly those clientelistic structures or at most urban political machines whose fragility in Europe Lipset and Rokkan underlined.

The consequence of this was that prior to 1930, even where the franchise was most extensive, the working class proper had not been substantially incorporated into durable mass organizations devised or controlled by elements of the bourgeoisie. In Argentina, where the franchise had gone furthest, the working class clustered in Buenos Aires was for the most part either excluded by lack of citizenship or loyal to the Socialist Party. The Radicals had clashed with workers after World War I and relied upon a political machine based on the white-collar government employees and the middle classes of the capital. In Uruguay, the farsighted welfarism of José Batlle had a similar base. In Brazil, the question of labor had been notoriously defined by the last president of the Old Republic (1889–1930) as "a question for the police." In Perú, the dictator Augusto B. Leguia (1919–1930) had made an initial attempt to bring the working class into a populist alliance, but this broke down in 1922, leading to the emergence and banning of APRA and the Socialist Party, which directed their efforts to workers in the export sectors and the urban economy, respectively. In Colombia, Ecuador, Bolivia and Venezuela, urban industry was in its infancy, and export workers were either scattered and differentiated (as in Colombia) or isolated, few in number and subject to close control, as elsewhere.

The consequences of the failure to incorporate workers and peasants into mass organizations by 1930 were dramatically exposed by the crash of 1929 and the ensuing depression. This had a political influence across South America, far beyond its immediate economic impact, that was sometimes relatively mild and short lived. The depth and lasting consequences of its political impact, in contrast, stemmed precisely from the limited extent of political development at the time. Coming in the wake of growing social challenges to existing regimes since World War I, the crash and the depression spelled the end of export-led development as a growth strategy around which consensus could be built by the elites that had come to the fore over the previous fifty years. The existing elites lost their consensus on the "rules of the game," where they had achieved it, and their ability to organize support from their electorates. New counterelites pushed to the fore, either within existing parties or outside them, and the result was the breakdown or slow death of existing party systems in every case. In Argentina, in a classic demonstration of a major Lipset-Rokkan hypothesis, Juan Perón tapped an unworked area of the "support market" (after more than a decade of authoritarian rule following the immediate military coup of 1930), winning an unchallenged majority among the formerly immigrant and new migrant working class. The resulting dynamic led eventually to the bloody and destructive alternation of the military and the Peronists in power. In Bolivia, again after two decades of political turmoil following upon the disastrous Chaco War, successive attempts by military caudillos to launch counterelite regimes and a conservative reaction leading to the government of Mamerto Urriolagoitia, the urban middle-class opposition MNR linked up with the radicalized tin miners to put together the initially radical coalition that made the Bolivian Revolution of 1952. In Colombia, strong dissident factions arose in the Liberal Party, espousing first agrarian reform and then urban populism under the dynamic leadership of Jorge Gaitán. The strength of these currents split the party and provoked antidemocratic currents in response in the Conservative Party, leading to the breakdown of consensus, the exacerbation of local rivalries and the breakdown of political and civil society in the period of *la violencia*. In Ecuador, the excluded urban masses rallied behind the episodic populism of José Maria Velasco Ibarra, never strong enough either to impose itself politically for the longer term or to provide the social base for the kinds of economic programme pursued with greater effect in Argentina and Brazil. In Perú, a brief experiment with military populism after 1930 defeated the rival populism of APRA, and control reverted to conservative elites, only to give way successively to experimental regimes seeking an alternative way forward, the last three before long-term military intervention being the right-wing populism of General Manuel A. Odría, the mild conservatism of Manuel Prado, and the military-backed but ineffective reformism of Fernando Belaúnde.

In Uruguay, the Blanco and Colorado parties tried to keep their system going, after a very brief flurry of military interest in the 1930s, by reinforcing and extending the clientelistic range of their parties, until the system lost touch with its social roots and collapsed into military authoritarianism in the 1970s. And in Venezuela, following the long Juan Vicente Gómez dictatorship, Acción Democrática emerged after a decade as a radical challenger, only to be swiftly ousted by a broad conservative reaction. Again, military rule was the outcome.

There is a simple pattern behind the variety recorded here. The exogenous shock of the depression rendered existing ruling elites incapable of either resolving their own differences amicably or winning popular support for their programmes. In circumstances in which neither the peasantry, where it existed, nor the working class had previously been brought into politics, it proved impossible after 1930 to combine responsiveness to the needs of the dominant classes with the rallying of sufficient popular support to make democracy work. In the best cases, either traditional political forces were able to hang on, despite a steadily increasing incapacity to act effectively on behalf of the interests of dominant economic elites (as in Colombia, Perú and Uruguay), or populism took over as a "second-best" solution, based on a precarious alliance that continually threatened to tilt the balance too far toward the economic interests of workers and in the meantime stifled the sources of political opposition and potential alternates in power (as in Argentina for less than a decade, in Brazil or in a different way in Bolivia under the MNR). In Ecuador, the lack of party development and the persistence of a weak and contradictory populism led to repeated exchanges between populism and military rule. In Venezuela, the three years of democracy between 1945 and 1948, themselves ushered in by a reformist military intervention, were all the country had to show since Simón Bolívar, over a hundred years ago, had likened the challenge of postrevolutionary government to that of ploughing the sea.

Through all these episodes, each country retained the particularity of a political dynamic whose outlines had been traced during the period of export-led development. But for a generation the shared failure to incorporate the national majorities into mass-based political parties before 1930 imposed a similar dynamic on each country, giving rise to a political cycle that began with the loss of political capacity on the part of the elites in power at the time of the crash and ended in an episode of protracted military rule. One final "world event" created a further critical historical juncture in this cycle. Just as, according to Lipset and Rokkan, the Bolshevik

Revolution had a decisive effect upon the shaping of worker loyalties after 1917, the Cuban Revolution of 1958–1959 had a decisive effect on the character and organization of military rule in the final sequence of the cycle. Before 1958 (in Colombia and Venezuela) the military leaders who came to the fore eventually essayed forms of Peronist populism; in the wake of the Cuban Revolution they would back reform in those countries where national majorities awaited incorporation (in Ecuador and Perú) or reaction where they faced a mobilized working class (in Argentina, Brazil and Uruguay). In Bolivia, where the revolution had come and gone by the mid-1960s, a brief attempt was made at a genuinely popular mass-based regime under Juan-José Torres and Alfredo Ovando, before Hugo Banzer stepped in with a repressive regime far more similar to those of the Southern Cone.

Lipset and Rokkan found for Europe that "the 'centre-periphery,' the state-church and the land-industry cleavages generated national developments in divergent directions, while the owner-worker cleavage tended to bring the party systems closer to each other in their basic structure."[17] I have found that the same reading can be made of the history of party systems in Latin America. After 1930 each country followed a similar cycle of instability leading eventually to protracted military rule, and in each case the root cause was the same: The failure to incorporate national majorities into the political system before the crash of 1930 undermined the already weakened efficacy of the different systems that had arisen during the period dominated by export-led growth. As a consequence of this failure, the elites that had dominated during the period of export-led development were unable to retain their hegemony. The contrast with the development of the party system in Britain is clear. Whereas in Britain the creation of modern mass parties of capital preceded large-scale working-class enfranchisement and organization, in Latin America it did not. For a generation after 1930, no mass bourgeois party able to win competitive elections emerged in South America. As a consequence, the region proved highly unstable. Where social and economic policies reminiscent of European social democracy were pursued, they could not produce the same consequences. Frequently they were put into practice by authoritarian regimes that relied heavily on the state in its organization of political support (as in the cases of populism in Argentina and Brazil); they could not command a consensus across the greater part of the political spectrum; and they tended to spill over into radical challenges threatening the limits that European social democracy prudently observed.

The failure of social democracy in Latin America since World War

II is as striking as its success in Western Europe. In part this is because capitalist development has been far less successful in Latin America. However, I attach greater significance to the absence of bourgeois hegemony after 1930, reflected in the absence of successful mass parties of capital in the region. Neither the political nor the economic conditions existed for the implementation of the class compromise discussed by Przeworski. It is his failure to absorb the implications of this structural-historical difference that leads him to the contradictory position of urging Latin American workers to accept social democracy *without* material gains.

The Prospects for Social Democracy in Latin America Today

The question that this analysis necessarily provokes is straightforward: What are the prospects for social democracy in Latin America today? The analysis suggests that they are not good, for two reasons. The first is the *conjunctural* crisis of accumulation. The second is a deep-seated and more enduring political and institutional weakness on the part of capital. In terms of Przeworski's requirements for successful social democracy, the first—a flow of surplus sufficient to provide for accumulation and distribution—is at present particularly problematic. But I do not accept either the assertion that, even now, there is no room for substantial redistribution, in what are in many cases some of the most unequal countries in the world, or the assertion that prospects are so bleak that the access by future generations to substantial distributable surpluses can be ruled out. What is lacking is a willingness on the part of capital to cede control over a part of its inherited patrimony and continuing surplus and to accept programmes of reform that will create the basis for the practice of social democratic politics. This should not be seen as a result of greed or shortsighted folly. It reflects the absence of an essential prior condition for the emergence of a social democratic politics respecting the limits required by capital: capitalist hegemony and its organization in modern and enduring institutional forms. In its absence, there is a very substantial risk that any process of redistribution or reform will run out of control. In other words, the objective and subjective conditions of Latin American capitalism are such that any social democratic project is arguably as likely to bring Socialist transformation onto the agenda as to keep it at bay. Equally, of course (as capitalist elites across the region are perfectly aware), without some measure of social and economic incorporation of the mass of the population perennial sources of instability will not be removed. Capitalism in Latin America faces a genuine political dilemma.

It is not surprising that capitalist hegemony and modern mass parties of capital were not established in Latin America either before 1930 or in the decades that followed. However, I believe that following the retreat of the military from long-term rule over the last decade the political conditions for the construction of capitalist hegemony have existed in principle but that the opportunity has been missed. The retreat of the generals gave rise to a situation in which civilian politicians strongly committed to capitalism were able to command considerable support by virtue of their commitment to restore the rule of law and preside over the restoration of democracy. With more radical currents temporarily weakened by the earlier defeat of guerrilla movements and the fear that radicalism would prompt the return of the military, it appeared at first that the succession would be disputed between Liberals or Conservatives, on the one hand, and reformists, for the most part social democrats, on the other. A window of opportunity was opened in which decisive action might have laid the basis for enduring bourgeois hegemony. It may have already closed because the procapitalist political elites of the region have not had the courage to attempt to construct it while they had the chance. In the meantime, the proliferation of "independent" probourgeois candidates continues to testify to the institutional weakness of the dominant classes.

The first requirement for the construction of bourgeois hegemony was a commitment to redistribution, at the very least through meaningful fiscal reform. The advice offered by Przeworski and others—that redistributive reform should be avoided in the new democracies—is a counsel of despair as it perpetuates the circumstances that make bourgeois rule by consent impossible. The fact is that in Latin America today there is a widespread perception, supported by the daily reality of the lives of the majority as well as by abundant statistical evidence, that only a minority gains from capitalism and that it defends its privileges with selfish intransigence.[18] While this endures, the prospects for building capitalist hegemony are slim.

A second and equally important aspect of the missed opportunity of the 1980s relates to the failure to organize successful parties. In part this stems from the effects of economic crisis and timidity in the area of social and economy policy. But it is a consequence, too, of a failure to recognize or respect the conditions required for party institution-alization. Circumstances have varied, but in general the task of party organization has been neglected. Indeed, the general pattern has been one of determined opposition to the emergence of viable party systems.

In part this reflected the perceived need for consensus among civilian politicians during the period of negotiation over the departure of the military. This may have been justified for a time, but it hindered the development of organized political alternatives in the early period of civilian rule. In addition, the activities of new civilian rulers have tended to work against the development of parties, even of their own. Five examples must suffice. In Argentina, Raúl Alfonsin's vacillation between personalism and party government hampered the development of the Radical Party, while the promise of the emergence of a social democratic alternative within Peronism was cut off by Antonio Cafiero's failure to develop and promote a reformist programme. The consequence was a reversion to the personalism of Carlos Saúl Menem and a government above parties. In Perú, the potential for converting APRA into a social democratic party was destroyed by the extreme presidentialism of Alan García and his insistence in governing in defiance of the party rather than as its representative; the adoption of Mario Vargas Llosa as standard-bearer by the Right, followed by the sudden emergence of Alberto Fujimori as victorious contender at the head of a broad coalition of forces, confirms the extreme fragility of party development and identification. In Ecuador, León Febres Cordero persisted in an antiparty orientation that long predated his election to the presidency, abused the prerogatives of congress and sought to destabilise incipient party formation by the calculated use of official patronage. In Uruguay, the current political elites have conspired to avoid the reform of the existing list system that represents an absolute barrier to the development of coherent parties. And in Brazil, the considerable political capital accumulated as a result of the election of Neves has been entirely eroded not only by José Sarney's resolute opposition to reform but also and equally by his unprincipled personalism and his sustained vendetta against the Partido do Movimento Democrático Brasileiro (PMDB). Again, as in Perú, the result was the emergence of Fernando Collor as an entirely independent candidate of the Right, without significant party or state support. These various developments have been damaging not only to the prospects for organized social democratic alternatives in the region but also to the capacity of bourgeois politics in general.

If democracy has not been consolidated, then, it has been because of the failure either to build effective parties or to implement or accept the structural and distributional reforms that would have created the space for social democracy alongside liberal or conservative parties of the bourgeoisie. Given a historic opportunity to lay the basis for capitalist hegemony, the civilian politicians who have governed in

Latin America's new democracies over the last decade have neglected the institutional and structural tasks that might have made it possible. As a result, if Socialist transformation returns to the agenda across the region, despite the enormous costs exacted in the past where it has been attempted, these politicians will have only themselves to blame.

Conclusion

One of the most disappointing characteristics of comparative political sociology over the last ten years has been the double move away from grand theory, on the one hand, and political economy, on the other. Both are now thoroughly out of favor. While grand theory has been challenged for its penchant for heroic abstraction and given way to "middle-range" theory tightly focused on single case studies or narrow comparisons, renewed emphasis upon choice and leadership has emphasized the gap between social-structural determination and political outcomes, while doing little at the level of theory to bridge it. The years between 1967 and 1974 saw the publication not only of the pioneering work of Stein Rokkan but also of Barrington Moore's *Social Origins of Dictatorship and Democracy*, Fernando Henrique Cardoso and Enzo Faletto's *Dependency and Development in Latin America*, Perry Anderson's *Passages from Antiquity to Feudalism* and *Lineages of the Absolutist State* and Immanuel Wallerstein's *The Modern World System*. Since those days, the tradition of large-scale historical-structural comparative political economy has faltered.[19] Recent comparative studies of Latin American politics, in particular, have often shown an impressive depth of scholarship but a lack of theoretical ambition.[20] They have been characterized by a reevaluation of "the political" unaccompanied by a rethinking of the complex relationship between social-structural and political phenomena and an overly hasty abandonment of the dominant research agenda of the 1970s. And where theoretical ambition has been maintained, as in Przeworski's work, it has been under the influence of a methodological individualism that rules out of consideration in formal analysis the sociostructural and institutional factors that shape and explain choices. While it may be accepted that the most ambitious exercises in comparative political economy tended in various ways to generate somewhat reductionist accounts of the relationship between social-structural and political change, it is unfortunate that the potential they offered for a more satisfactory analysis of political phenomena has been so little explored. The comparative exercise carried out here suggests that a focus on the political in isolation from historical-structural analysis is unlikely to be of value. It also suggests that the "political" focus of much recent work on Latin America has been too narrow. In its obsession with leadership and choice, this work has failed to consider the institutional side of political analysis that has been the concern of much of classical political sociology. Finally, it suggests that while direct lessons and comparisons are difficult to draw, it is possible to identify, beyond the universal logic of social democracy if considered in the abstract, significant structural and historical contrasts between the formative contexts of European and Latin American social democracy, respectively. In the light of these, one can draw from a comparative analysis of the British experience of social democracy some valuable insights into the character and potential of social democracy in Latin America.

Notes

1. Adam Przeworski, "Class, Production and Politics: A Reply to Burawoy," in *Socialist Review*, no. 89/2, 1989, p. 89.

2. Adam Przeworski, *Capitalism and Social Democracy* (Cambridge: Cambridge University Press, 1985), pp. 136–137.

3. Ibid., p. 147; emphasis in the original.

4. For relevant critiques of Przeworski's work, see M. Burawoy, "Marxism Without Micro-Foundations," in *Socialist Review*, no. 89/2, 1989, and E. Meiksins Wood, "Rational Choice Marxism: Is the Game Worth the Candle?" in *New Left Review*, no. 177, September-October 1989, pp. 41–88. Burawoy rightly characterized Przeworski's argument as a more devastating critique of reformist social democracy than of revolutionary Marxism.

5. Adam Przeworski, "Problems in the Study of Transition to Democracy," in Guillermo O'Donnell, Philippe C. Schmitter and Laurence Whitehead, eds., *Transitions from Authoritarian Rule: Prospects for Democracy* (Baltimore, Md.: Johns Hopkins University Press, 1986), part 3, p. 63.

6. F. B. Smith, *The Making of the Second Reform Bill* (1966, p. 3), cited in Ralph Miliband, *Capitalist Democracy in Britain* (London: Oxford University Press, 1982), p. 24

7. Miliband, *Capitalist Democracy*, p. 26.

8. Cited in David Coates, *The Labour Party and the Struggle for Socialism* (Cambridge: Cambridge University Press, 1975), p. 6.

9. David Howell, *British Social Democracy* (London: Croom Helm, 1976), pp. 27, 34.

10. Colin Leys, *Politics in Britain* (London: Verso, 1983), pp. 64–77.

11. Harold Laski, *Reflections on the Constitution* (Manchester: Manchester University Press, 1951), p. 68.

12. Miliband, *Capitalist Democracy*, p. 69.

13. Leys, *Politics in Britain*, pp. 69, 71.

14. Coates, *The Labour Party*, p. 151.

15. Seymour Martin Lipset and Stein Rokkan, eds., *Party Systems and Voter Alignments* (New York: Free Press, 1967), p. 35.

16. Ibid., p. 57.

17. Ibid., p. 35.

18. For a fuller discussion of this point, see Paul Cammack, "The Politics of Democratization," in B. F. Galjart and Patricio Silva, eds., *Democratization and the State in the Southern Cone: Essays on South American Politics* (Amsterdam: CEDLA, 1989), pp. 13–34.

19. Given her beginnings and subsequent intellectual development, Theda Skocpol's *States and Social Revolutions* (Cambridge: Cambridge University Press, 1979) may be seen as marking a crucial turning point.

20. I have in mind particularly O'Donnell, Schmitter and Whitehead, eds., *Transitions from Authoritarian Rule*; Larry Diamond, Juan Linz and Seymour Martin Lipset, eds., *Democracy in Developing Countries: Latin America* (Boulder, Colo: Lynn Rienner, 1989); Enrique Baloyra, ed., *Comparing New Democracies: Transition and Consolidation in Mediterranean Europe and the Southern Cone* (Boulder, Colo.: Westview Press, 1987); and James M. Malloy and Mitchell A. Seligson, eds., *Authoritarians and Democrats: Regime Transition in Latin America* (Pittsburgh, Penn: Pittsburgh University Press, 1987).

5

Spanish Social Democracy and Latin America

Manuel Alcántara Sáez

Spanish socialism, suffering under the Franco regime from repression and exile, had developed an image of Latin America that was totally different from the one created by Franquista politics. It had been enriched by the many personal experiences in the Spanish diaspora and included a critical attitude toward existing dogmas about Latin American development. At the time it had—regrettably—little influence within Spanish society. In addition, it lacked impact in the international media, which constituted a part of the sphere of influence of the Spanish Left and failed to affect any of the principal political strategies that were debated with reference to Latin America.

The rapprochement between European social democracy and diverse Latin American political forces occurred with the first, almost simultaneous, steps of the Spanish democratic transition.[1] The relaunching of the Partido Socialista Obrero Español and of its new leaders, who were not well known internationally, went hand in hand with the consolidation of the "third position" of the Socialist International. The experience accumulated by Spanish socialism throughout the transition made it possible to transfer strategies and interpretative schemes about the dismantling of authoritarian structures and recommendations concerning more pragmatic approaches among the moderate Left to Latin America. At the same time, the young leaders of what was then the opposition party traveled through the region and established solid personal relationships with outstanding representatives of the Latin American democratic forces. Later, these informal contacts prevailed over formal and institutional relations and served as an extremely useful channel on some occasions.

In other cases, however, this type of diplomacy with the Latin American chancellors and presidents entailed serious dangers due to its connotations of *amiguismo*, or favoritism based on friendship. At those moments, the structuring of relationships through economic ties and cooperation that survives changes of government was sorely missed.[2]

The stages that Spanish socialism went through during the transition had a decisive influence on the manner in which the Latin American Left has responded to the crisis of the dictatorships.[3] During the first stage, which started in 1974, a reformist-revolutionary model was supported until 1978, when the constitution was approved with great consensus. The second stage was of a reformist-democratic nature. It began with the rejection of Marxism as the leading ideology of PSOE. This was agreed upon during the Extraordinary Congress of 1979, which was also the occasion for Felipe González's rise to leadership. This stage ended with the successful legislative elections of October 1982. The PSOE changed from an opposition to a government party. The last stage started after the electoral triumph, at a time when the various political actors considered that the transition toward democracy had ended and that the democratic system of government had to be consolidated.[4] The unsuccessful coup of February 1981 had demonstrated the weakness of the system, and now was the moment to prop it up.

The elimination of the Marxist orientation and the party's rise to power offered new coordinates for the PSOE that were framed according to the decisive adoption of a pragmatic and gradualist strategy. Above any other consideration was the fundamental priority of modernizing Spain. Its foreign policy—which had been freed from strong ideological influences—reflected the need to consolidate the democratic political system, to strengthen the political parties and to encourage their free competition for power under poliarchical forms.

All of this coincided, a bit later, with the entry of Spain and Portugal into the European Economic Community in 1986. The increase of European interest in Latin America was not hurt by the new solid international position of Felipe González and Mario Soares.[5] This leadership was also felt in the Socialist International, where it counterbalanced the influence of politicians like Willy Brandt, Olof Palme and Bruno Kreisky.

Internal Problems of the Spanish Socialist Project

The years of political transition (1976–1982) were characterized by an implicit general consent between all parties that was instrumental in the drafting and approval of the constitution, the implementation of the Statutes of Autonomy of the regions and nationalities and the consolidation of harmony in the socioeconomic realm. Later, once the PSOE was in power, the social democratic project was defined in a classical manner around the support of an ample social base organized (theoretically) in trade unions. The relationship between the PSOE and the Unión General de Trabajadores (UGT) was very harmonious until 1987. It resulted in agreement on electoral programs for 1982 and 1986 and in a complete concordance with the PSOE Congress of 1984 on economic policy. At that time, the secretary general of the UGT, Nicolás Redondo, was a member of the Executive Committee of PSOE, and it was customary to have members of the UGT representing PSOE in parliament. This situation started to deteriorate in 1987, and it reached its worst point on December 14, 1988, with the call for a general strike, the first in fifty years. The concerted action that for the previous ten years had been the basic bargaining instrument during the consolidation of the Spanish democratic regime and had contributed to the success of the policies of economic adjustment had ended.

The reasons for the changing situation can be found, on the trade union side, in a decrease in bargaining power that even affected the unions' own existence as institutions representing the workers. During the stage of concerted action, the unions had legitimized the long-standing policy of adjustment and the necessary processes of industrial restructuring. The adjustment policy hit very hard in the area of employment. In addition, the downward pressure on labor costs created a notable frustration of union demands. The UGT itself was not able to capitalize on its connection with the party in government and to increase its leverage in collective bargaining with the great companies. Next, the biggest confederation, the Communist Comisiones Obreras (CCOO), continued to gain even more membership.[6] The loss in support among the rank and file within the UGT caused its leaders to reassess the alignment with the PSOE. They tried to demonstrate a critical attitude toward its policies, keeping themselves aloof from it in order to shorten the distance that separated them from the CCOO.

Since 1986, the government has witnessed an impressive process of capital formation and a dynamic growth of the Spanish economy that was enhanced by the entry of Spain, that same year, to the European Economic Community. Nonetheless, in the opinion of the labor movement, this bonanza did not bring about distributive development. The absolute majority, revalidated in the elections of 1986, introduced something in the policy of concerted action that was alien to its definition: Labor unions did not bargain; they were simply travel companions.

During 1988, labor unrest occurred to a degree that had been unknown during the entire decade. The government's program of jobs for young people, which was one of the basic tools of its employment policy, did not have the agreement of the union movement. This prompted union leaders to call the general strike in December. The action went beyond a struggle to merely vindicate worker rights and developed into a majority protest of a civil society that took this opportunity to express its vague discontent with government policies.

In 1989, the relationship between the UGT and the PSOE cooled even further, "resulting in antagonistic points of view about essential issues."[7] In the European elections of June and in the general elections of October, for the first time in its history, the UGT did not officially support the PSOE. Instead, it encouraged its members to vote for the political group that "best represented their interests." The "fresh recovery of communism and of its labor movement [CCOO]" ran parallel to the reestablishment of social democratic reformism in view of the year 2000.[8] In this respect, communism's decisive gamble in favor of the newly formed electoral coalition Izquierda Unida (IU) forced the Communists to win over the discontented Socialist voters in order to increase the vote for IU, which had made its first electoral appearance in the elections of June 1986. The electoral setback the Communists had suffered in October 1982 was being repaired not only through a change of leadership but also through a new electoral strategy. The result of the campaign in favor of the no vote in the referendum about NATO in March 1986, which sanctioned continued membership in the organization by a vote of only 52.5 percent, convinced them of the correctness of this option. However, only ten months after the general strike, the legislative election of October 1989 reinforced the position of the Socialist government in opposition to the unions. It appeared that four out of five votes on the Left continued to go to the PSOE, in spite of the wear and tear suffered by the party in government and of the opposition or belligerent neutrality of the workers' unions.

After two years of open confrontation, the peculiar social democratic Spanish project did not take the "social turn" labor considered necessary.[9] The fact that only 13 percent of the economically active population had affiliated and that the union movement seemed incapable of translating its capacity to mobilize the masses—as shown during the general strike—into negotiating strength weighed heavily against its ability to influence official politics. The government, on the other hand, had discovered that monetarist measures were not enough when it came to correcting the imbalances threatening to devour the fruits of growth (through inflation and a deficit in the balance of trade as consequences of the uncontrolled increase of internal consumption). There was a need to develop a closer link between wages and productivity in order to make the other corrective policies effective.[10] President González's offer in his 1989 inaugural speech to engage in dialogue and the subsequent negotiations that were reopened in January 1990 were the results of this situation.

PSOE and Latin America

Any analysis of the position on Latin America held by Spanish social democracy during the last fifteen years should consider at least four elements: first, the ideological evolution that has taken place within Spanish socialism; next, the three stages the party has gone through during these years, as mentioned earlier; third, the profound confrontation that occurred within the Socialist family after 1982, when the policy of the PSOE as a party and the policy of the party as national government clashed; and finally, the changing nature of the Latin American political situation that requires responses that are conditioned by the constantly changing content of the political agenda.

The first two of these factors overlap and influence each other. It is important to remember that until the "moment of truth" of the general elections of June 1977, the Spanish Socialist forces were very fragmented. PSOE itself was split into *renovadores* and *históricos* (reformists and traditionalists), and the group led by Enrique Tierno Galván and the Socialistas Mediterráneos gathered around the Partido Socialista Popular. In addition, there were other less important groups on a regional level. In this preconstitutional era, however, all shared a position toward the Third World that consisted, with minor differences, of "the denunciation of capitalist imperialism which through the multinational companies impoverishes the countries of the Third World and deprives them of their sovereignty."[11] In their view, the struggle against international capitalism was linked to the fight against totalitarian regimes. Finally, they stated their opposition to all hegemonic powers, to the division of the world in zones of influence and to the military alliances that maintain the status quo.

Under the influence of the political sanctioning of PSOE as the main opposition party, after the elections of 1977, PSOE's ideologized, militant position on the Third World and Latin America was gradually watered down. Between 1978 and 1982 several developments took place that served to define its position toward Latin America. The first basic factor was the sympathy for the countries that gave refuge to Socialist Spanish exiles and traditionally had shown a strong anti-Franco position: México, Chile, Venezuela and Costa Rica.[12] The last two were governed by parties that were members of the Socialist International, and they were constant points of reference for the leaders of PSOE on their trips to Latin America. Also, the Venezuelan party, Acción Democrática, had provided financial assistance that was crucial for the growth of PSOE. The Chilean connection was forged by Chileans in European exile who were in constant contact with the Spanish Socialists. The second basic factor was the triumph of the Nicaraguan Revolution in July 1979, which generated lots of goodwill; "it should not surprise anybody to find out that European socialists were among the first international actors to celebrate the victory of the Sandinistas, and to offer material aid to the revolutionary government."[13] PSOE's Felipe González was nominated president of the Sandinista Revolution Support Committee formed by the SI in 1980. Interestingly enough, this line of policy was not continued during the crisis in El Salvador. This was very clear when set in contrast to the French Socialist government that was particularly active and that, in conjunction with México, produced a statement, in August 1981, regarding the civil war in El Salvador. The third basic factor was that the relationship with Cuba reached a notable level of understanding in this period, and the island was frequently visited by Spanish Socialists. The example was set by Adolfo Suárez, then president of the government and leader of Unión de Centro Democrático (UCD), with his visit to Cuba in September 1978. Lastly, there was a special relationship between Spanish socialism and Panamanian Torrijoism from 1978 to 1981. It even led to very concrete results when Omar Torrijos created the Partido Revolucionario Democrático (PRD) in 1978 after his interview with Felipe González.[14] However, the Partido Social Demócrata Panameño condemned several aspects of his visit to Panamá and stated that his support to the Torrijos project, which brought the Socialist International close to the nationalist and anti-imperialist stand of the general, was a political slip.[15]

When PSOE became the governing party in December 1982, an interesting confrontation emerged between the policies toward Latin America elaborated through the various resolutions at party congresses or through actions taken by the Socialist International and the Latin American policy that the party developed gradually as it fulfilled its governmental role. The old polemic between "party policy" and "government policy" was thereby well served. The interpretation of the results, in some cases, was that the original Socialist project was being mortgaged and that, following the logic of dependence, there was "a strange coincidence with the politics of the

Reagan administration and the North American State Department."[16] In other cases, the analysis impinged on the pragmatic position of the Socialist government in regard to Central America because it was "limited by its desire to maintain good relations with the old colonies in the area," which would lead to a reluctance to take sides in the conflict.[17] Generally, the lack of originality in the orthodox answers offered by the Spanish government to the Latin American economic problems was pointed out. The discussion of this dealt mainly with the debt problem. It ignored the contributions made by the North-South debate of the 1970s and by the rich variety of some of the *dependencia* analyses.[18] The party policy was criticized and said to repeat the traditional situation in which the Left in the metropole used the Third World as a laboratory where its ideological-theoretical constructions could be tested.[19] The need to balance this situation and to carry out studies that were less ideological and less emotional was reaffirmed.

Party Policy and Government Policy

Once Socialist parties are in power they tend to push aside the resolutions of the Socialist International in the pursuit of their own interests by following what could be termed "state policy." This does not apply only to the case of Spain. A good example was offered at the congress of the SI in 1983. At that time, the French Socialists were in the government and abstained when a vote was called on the resolutions regarding disarmament. These resolutions reflected mainly the position of other Socialist parties in the opposition.

Within the Socialist International, PSOE often proposed original lines of policy regarding Latin America. At the same time, however, and from its position in the Spanish government, it has modified them according to what seemed politically convenient at the moment. The Spanish Socialist government put its main emphasis on Central America by coordinating the actions of the Plan de Cooperación Integral. It made evident its support to the Contadora Group, awarding it the Principe de Asturias Prize in 1984 and by developing (once it became a member of the European Economic Community) the ministerial conferences dealing with political dialogue and economic cooperation (held in San José). However, these policies were notably affected by changes in both internal and foreign policies.

In Spanish internal policy the terrorism of Euskadi Ta Askatasuna (Basque Country and Freedom, ETA) was one of the most worrisome factors, and it continues to be so. When, in 1983, the alleged ETA connection with Nicaragua was discovered, the credibility of the

Sandinista revolution suffered seriously in the eyes of the González government. The fact that the presence of members of ETA in Nicaragua could not be completely verified and the categorical denial of Tomás Borge were not enough to dispel the shadow of doubt. Since then, the distancing of PSOE from the Sandinista project has been evident.

The foreign policy of the PSOE government had to redefine the relationship with the United States and with the new associates in the European Economic Community in regard to defense. The crucial element was the need to fulfill the electoral promise regarding a referendum to decide the issue of Spanish membership in NATO. The Socialist option in favor of an Atlantism that was new to the party created important tensions. Eventually it caused the first ministerial crisis and the nomination of Francisco Fernández Ordóñez to replace Fernando Morán as foreign minister. The confrontation was between the official Socialist line as directed by Felipe González and the pre-1979 tendencies of the Spanish Socialist Party that had not been completely integrated into PSOE. The exit from the political scene of a minister who had stated that he anticipated "stepping out of NATO if the United States engaged in military intervention in Central America"[20] was consistent with the type of change that was proposed. Spanish diplomacy could not continue under the direction of someone who referred to the role of the United States as "one of the main obstacles for self-determination in Central America and as one of the main reasons for the present crisis."[21] The apparent incongruence was profound in the Spanish cabinet—despite the fact that Fernando Morán himself denied being anti-NATO[22]—and a change was indicated. On the other hand, the person responsible for international relations within PSOE, Elena Flores, gained support and stature within the party. The same thing occurred with the highest political authority figure in charge of Ibero America, Luis Yañez. There, no contradictions were present.

However, the Spanish government had an interesting capacity to draft a certain autonomous policy that at the same time had received a strong injection of pragmatism. This was particularly visible in the relations with Cuba, which after 1982 combined cordiality with an argument on issues like the indemnifications owed to Spanish citizens who had lost their property as a consequence of the revolution and the reception offered to etarras. Other aspects such as the lack of political freedom in Cuba and Cuban support to guerrilla forces in Central America were also points of divergence.[23] Felipe González, while emphasizing these points of disagreement, visited the island in November 1986. He was the first leader of a NATO member country to do so. A month later, Fidel Castro referred to the president of the Spanish House of Representatives, Felix Pons, as a "fascist character."[24] This did not prevent him from being decorated by the president of the Spanish Senate, José Federico de Carvajal, two years later.

In the realm of European politics, party and government coincided regarding the need of the European Economic Community to project itself vis-à-vis Latin America. They agreed also on the diagnosis and the solutions to the most pressing problems of the region. The support for the reestablishment of democratic systems of government and for the attempts at mediation in Central America was conceived as a unique opportunity for transforming the European Economic Community into an alternative reference point to the United States and the Soviet Union. Nevertheless, there were enormous differences on how to deal with the problem of the foreign debt. Within the party voices were raised in favor of a "gradual and flexible" way of paying the debt without overburdening the debtor countries,[25] but the efforts of the government, in its domestic policy as well as in the international financial sphere, still brought no result. In a similar way, the government was failing to take assertive action to pressure for a change of the agricultural policy of the European Economic Community. An in-depth revision had been considered by the PSOE to be the key for the development of an economic cooperation with Latin America that could be beneficial to both sides.

In synthesis, PSOE was designing policies giving it a role as the critical conscience of the government. These satisfied, in some cases, even the demands of its most leftist members through various motions in foreign affairs, while the government concentrated on pragmatically carrying out a state policy.

Democracy as an Interpretative Factor

At the end of a decade of profound political changes, we recognize a strong similarity between what has occurred in Latin America and the basic objective of PSOE's strategy to contribute to the establishment of democratic systems of government. "The now commonplace that democracy has replaced revolution as the central category of political and intellectual debate is doubtlessly correct."[26] The conviction within PSOE that the Spanish democratic process was exportable was emphasized a few months after the party came to power. The gigantic Encuentro en la Democracia, organized by the Instituto de Cooperación Iberoamericana in April 1983, brought together over fifty of the most outstanding politicians and intellectuals of the region. The Caminos en la Democracia, put on by the Pablo Iglesias Foundation in June 1983, and the seminar Europa ante los Cambios en el Cono Sur de América Latina in March 1984, organized by the Instituto de Cooperación Iberoamericana, are proof of the speed with which this issue was tackled. It is not surprising then that this democratic conviction, independently of some of the other factors previously mentioned, also played a role in the gradual distancing of the Spanish government from Managua and the subsequent rapprochement with the Salvadoreño Napoleón Duarte in the years 1983–1984.

The commitment to a correct course for the democratic process, however, was already a central aspect of PSOE policy before 1982. The decisive intervention of Miguel Angel Mártinez, a PSOE representative who was sent by the SI to observe the developments surrounding the 1978 elections in the Dominican Republic, helped prevent electoral fraud and assured the triumph of the leader of Partido Revolucionario Dominicano, Antonio Guzmán.[27] This intervention was endorsed by Felipe González when he visited President Guzmán in Santo Domingo in August of the same year.

The success of the Spanish process of democratization, apart from its potential as a theoretical model to be studied and applied to Latin American countries, indicated the bankruptcy of the historical anathema that for decades influenced thinking among the Latin American elites, emphasizing the responsibility of the Spanish legacy for the failure of democratic experiences in Ibero America. The traditional pessimism regarding the Spanish influence was subverted, and there emerged instead a profound admiration for the process that had brought about a political change without trauma and had created the conditions for economic prosperity.

The main political element was "pluralist democracy," in the words of ex–Vice President Alfonso Guerra,[28] or "a democracy to which adjectives should not be applied," according to Elena Flores.[29] The concept had an elasticity, allowing pragmatic interpretations. The interests of the Spanish government, together with its limited options in political practice, destroyed the romantic vision of the concept of democracy in the era of transition. When Fernando Morán, then Spain's minister of foreign affairs, said about democracy that "each nation has its own history, its own context and its own projects" and when he rejected the idea of "exporting models,"[30] he was expressing his belief in the viability of autonomous projects to be constructed according to schemes that are not universally applicable. His gradual isolation within PSOE and his departure from the government two years later showed the extent to which his ideas were alien to the official line of the party and of the government.

The "poliarchical" notion held by PSOE caused it to become close to parties or groups that, because of their situation in the political system of each country, either were playing a very active role in the process of democratic consolidation itself or were helping the system to work. In this manner, PSOE developed close relations with the Unión Civica Radical in Argentina, APRA in Perú (a consultative member of the SI), Izquierda Democrática in Ecuador, the Partido Colorado in Uruguay, the Alianza Democrática Chilena and the Partido Socialista (Nuñez-Arrata) that was part of it and even with the PRI in México. The refusal to give explicit support to the Partido de la Revolución Democrática in México or, in the case of Uruguay, to the Frente Amplio is an example of the pragmatism reigning in PSOE and making it value each associate according to its access to power and success in controlling internal polarizing tendencies (notably those caused by Communists). In other areas, PSOE has practiced a policy of "building bridges" between the various political actors. This allowed it to play a mediating role in situations of crisis where the road to negotiation appeared completely closed.

Strangely enough, the role finally played by PSOE in regard to the hottest Latin American political issues was authored by the most experienced social democratic parties of the region. The Costa Rican president and leader of the Partido de Liberación Nacional, Luis Alberto Monge, pointed out in February 1982 that the role of Spain was to "inject hope into the democratization processes of our continent."[31] Carlos Andrés Pérez, who was hostile to the Sandinistas, influenced the PSOE's decision not to send observers to the Nicaraguan elections of 1984.[32] Also, he gradually managed to erode the sympathy Spanish Socialists had initially felt toward the Nicaraguan Revolution to such an extent that in late 1984 Felipe González was having interviews with members of the anti-Sandinista opposition.

These perceptions were absorbed by the Socialist International, where PSOE was increasingly vocal regarding Latin American issues. Revolutionary change was being replaced by gradual support for processes of controlled democratization. In political analysis pragmatism replaced ideology. For example, in Central America, there was acceptance of the fact that international factors would determine its fate. It was acknowledged that, even though regional social and economic conditions had caused the conflict, the United States also had legitimate interests in the Caribbean and Central America.[33]

The executive bureau of the Socialist International met in October 1984 in Rio de Janeiro to discuss "peace and democracy for Latin America." It picked up the change of strategy (as to Central America, it urged the Sandinistas to start talks with the contras) that was ratified by the 17th Congress of the Socialist International held in June 1986 in Lima. The representatives of PSOE who attended this event were Elena Flores, Enrique Barón (who was then president of the European Parliament), and Ludolfo Paramio, director of the Pablo Iglesias Foundation. The tragic events in the Peruvian prisons at the time of the congress did not disturb the relationship between PSOE and APRA.

The Interest in Latin America

One important key to an understanding of PSOE's approach toward Latin America concerns its attempt to take from the Spanish political Right the flag of *hispanidad* that had been hoisted by the Franco regime as a symbol of unity of Spanish-speaking peoples. The connection was denounced because of its rhetoric, its mobilization of the most reactionary sectors in Latin America, its unilateral and unidirectional interpretation of the Spanish contribution to the formation of the new societies and its emphasis on the superiority of the Spanish cultural heritage as opposed to aboriginal or mestizo realities. In view of this situation, the term *Hispanoamérica* was erased from the official vocabulary, to be replaced by the word *Iberoamérica* or, more colloquially, *Latinoamérica*.

Once the excitement caused by the new trends toward democratization in Latin America had worn off, Spanish Socialists began to reorganize their priorities. The Second Encounter on Democracy: Europa-Iberoamérica, which took place in Madrid in November 1985, presented a drastic change compared to the agenda of the meeting held less than three years before. Latin America no longer appeared as an exclusive subject of Spanish action. The situation now had to be looked at from the viewpoint of the European Economic Community that Spain was soon to join. In adaptation to the new times and circumstances, the possibilities of "strengthening the lines of communication between the two continents" and of "defining areas of economic cooperation" now complemented the earlier democratic paradigm.[34]

In 1983, everything Latin American was regarded by the Socialist government with "special, priority interest." This was based on "the history of mutual enrichment" of the peoples on both sides of the Atlantic and on the fact that "Latin America has been a home, and even more than that, a land of promise to many Spaniards who have gone there to work, or for ideological or political reasons."[35] Only five years later, however, the Spanish minister of foreign affairs declared that "the priority of the Spanish presidency [of the EEC] is called Europe."[36] Both quotes sufficiently illustrate two different levels on which Spanish foreign policy had moved during the 1980s—on the one hand, projection toward Latin America; on the other, European integration. The Latin American challenge posed multiple possibilities: the exploitation close to 1992 (commemoration of Columbus's travel to America in 1492) of a topic that until then had been monopolized by the opposition, the reciprocation for the generous reception to exiled Spaniards, the assertion of moral leadership over societies experiencing an accelerated process of political change and the establishment of a community of Latin American peoples. The European connection, on the other hand, meant Spain's reintegration —after three centuries of isolation—in the area to which it historically and physically belongs. It signified a definite consolidation of the democratic system, economic prosperity and the modernization of the country.

The balance shows that, after eight years of Socialist government, the expectations have been sufficiently fulfilled on the European level, while on the Latin American side, this is not the case. The policy of the EEC toward Latin America, supported by Spain, shows serious weaknesses. This policy is to a certain degree an obsession of the Socialists and centers around their attempt to reconcile Latin America and Europe. In pursuit of this, Spanish socialism presented its actions within the EEC with the insistent justification that it was also acting for Latin America. It did its utmost to advertise the "Ibero American component" that—allegedly—had "strongly characterized" its foreign policy during the preceding few years.[37] Furthermore, it was pointed out that "an institutionalized political dialogue between the European communities and Latin America should lead to a fairer and more stable global system of economic relations."[38] It is obvious that Spain's joining the EEC generated a certain dynamism between the EEC and Latin America. The European Council meeting at The Hague in June 1986 approved policies explicitly directed toward a strengthening of the relationship. However, in political practice, European activity was confined to the area of political cooperation, encouraging the peace initiatives in Central America and supporting straightforward the democratization processes.[39] Little was accomplished in the improvement of economic relations between the EEC and Latin America. Even an attitude of "relative optimism" would not be justified in this area of Euro–Latin American relations.[40] After the events in Central and Eastern Europe during the last trimester of 1989, everything seems to indicate that Latin America will have an even lower priority on the agenda of the European

Economic Community. In spite of the lukewarm efforts of the Spanish Socialist government, Latin America has again become an object of rhetoric, without receiving support for concrete projects that could directly and significantly influence the life and welfare of its people. Two motions of Spanish diplomacy in late 1989 emphasized the solitary position of the Socialist government. The demand presented to the Salvadorian president, Alfredo Cristiani, concerning the investigation into the murders of more than six Jesuits and two other people at the Universidad Centroamericana in San Salvador and the vote of censure in the General Assembly of the United Nations to the North American invasion of Panamá remained isolated actions. They put in doubt the political cooperation between the EEC and Latin America, which until then had appeared to be a real achievement.

Final Considerations

It is interesting to remember that in Latin America, in reaction to the brutal and disheartening authoritarian processes of the 1970s, the efforts at democratization among the Left and other progressive sectors unexpectedly confronted with a European political situation in which social democracy had changed its position toward Latin America. A coincidence of interests developed that has benefited the Latin American political parties. PSOE played a notable role in this process, through which it found a way to affiliate itself internationally.

However, the importance of Latin America for the Socialist International, which had its highest moment in the mid-1980s, is clearly receding today. The sudden and rapid political changes that occurred in the "Socialist" countries of Eastern Europe have taken attention away from Latin America. The center of attention is again Europe. At the same time, the North American intervention in Panamá at the close of the 1980s has left a very narrow and limited space for a "third way." The military action on the isthmus has reinforced the position of the more rightist sectors in the area, who feel their actions are backed by the United States. Consequently, this blocks the social democratic program for Central America that was a fundamental item in the Latin American policy of the Socialist International. The assassination of the Salvadorian social democratic leader, Hector Oqueli, in Guatemala in 1990 is one indication of this. Another is the triumph of the Partido Nacional in the Honduran election of November 1989, as well as the January 1990 electoral success of the Social Christians in Costa Rica, after eight years of opposition.

The political success of the Latin American parties directly supported by the Socialist International has been rather small until now. The only new triumph has been the election of Rodrigo Borja in Ecuador. In other cases the failures in the opposition have been notorious. The independent batllista movement in Uruguay was defeated in the last elections, and in the Dominican Republic the Peña Gómez sector of the PRD, supported by the Socialist International, did not manage to defeat the candidacy of Juan Bosch. Even the policies of adjustment designed by Carlos Andrés Pérez in Venezuela during 1989 clash with the essentials of a social democratic project.

Spanish socialism has maintained a multifaceted policy, combining approaches that vary in time and in space. The former have to do with the internal political dynamics, defined by PSOE's role as opposition party until 1982 and as governing party since then and by uneasiness in its relations with labor and with the critical sectors within the party. The latter concern the different areas of interest in Latin America that also change as time goes on. The democratic transitions in the Southern Cone (1983–1985), the Central American crisis, the relations with Cuba and the Chilean transition represent different areas of interest. Good relations are maintained with the classic social democratic parties in the area, as demonstrated by the designation of one of the few "political" Spanish diplomats (Alberto de Armas, ex–secretary-general of the PSOE in the Canary Islands) as ambassador to Venezuela. All of this offers a kaleidoscopic view of Latin America.

If we analyze the dual challenge with which the PSOE administration is confronted in its foreign policy concerning relations with Europe and with Ibero America, we can confirm that Spain's Latin American policy is subordinated to that of the European Economic Community. The absence of any specific reference to Latin America in the Manifiesto del Programa 2000 and the reference to Europe as Spain's "world platform" is evidence of this.[41] In no case can both lines of policy be fully maintained. In fact they function as a zero-sum game: Whatever Europe gains, Latin America loses and vice versa.

Presently, the manoeuvering capacity of Spanish socialism and of the Socialist International is centred on the possibility of influencing Washington, which today, as in previous times, controls the keys of access to Latin America. The confirmation that the same basic objectives are shared with regard to Latin America (the extension of pluralistic democracy and the consolidation of respect for human rights)—with the only difference being in the means to achieve these things[42]—must give way to the conviction that the North American objectives should be modified gradually in order to come closer to other essential social democratic goals (development programs, elimination of social injustices, more equal distribution of income and wealth). Felipe González's visit with George Bush in October 1989 should be seen in this light. It showed a greater level of relaxation and a lessening of suspicion between the Socialist and Republican administrations. In spite of the official and declared Spanish opposition to the North American invasion of Panamá, President Bush acknowledged, during an informational press conference that took place after the operation, that he "had spoken twice during the last ten days with President González, a leader respected throughout the continent."[43]

The present situation in which there is only one superpower that is "hyperhegemonic" in the area,[44] together with the instability of Central and Eastern Europe, notably reduces the possibilities for European socialism to act or intercede in Latin America. However, it could stimulate PSOE's interest and actions in relation to Latin America.[45] This could result from the fact that the European crisis is alien to the inclinations and expectations of the Spanish party, which may force it to strengthen its Latin American policy in the pursuit of a difficult but convenient equilibrium in the internal power struggle within the Socialist International. The presence of the PSOE in Latin America, the only region outside the European Economic Community where it feels comfortable, would counterbalance the new situation in the social democratic world. Nevertheless, any action along this line has to be channeled through the foreign policy of the Spanish government, and it is impossible to bypass Washington in such matters.

Notes

1. Carlos Rico, "La Influencia de Factores Extraregionales en el Conflicto Centroamericano: El Socialismo Europeo, la Alianza Atlántica y Centroamérica: ¿Una Historia de Expectativas Frustradas?" in *Pensamiento Iberoamericano*, no. 13, 1988, p. 117.

2. Antonio Garcia Santesmases, "Evolución Ideológica del Socialismo en la España Actual," in *Sistema*, no. 68–69, 1985, pp. 61–77.

3. Joan Piñol i Rull, "Las Relaciones Españolas con Centroamérica en el Periodo de los Gobiernos Socialistas (1982–1989)," in *Las Relaciones Entre España y América Central (1976–1989)* (Barcelona: Cidob-Aieti, 1989), p. 62.

4. José Maria Maravall and Julián Santamaria, "Political Change in Spain and the Prospects of Democracy," in Guillermo O'Donnell, Philippe C. Schmitter and Laurence Whitehead, eds., *Transitions from Authoritarian Rule: Southern Europe* (Baltimore, Md.: The Johns Hopkins University Press, 1986), p. 71.

5. There is an extensive bibliography on the theme: See Pedro Luis Gomis, "Reflexiones Sobre las Relaciones entre la Comunidad Ampliada y América Latina," in *Cuadernos CIPIE*, Madrid, 1987, pp. 1–39; Gabriel Rosenzweig,

España y las Relaciones Entre las Comunidades Europeas y América Latina (Madrid: IRELA, 1987), pp. 1–39; Secretaria Permanente SELA, "Impacto Sobre América Latina de la Incorporación de España a la CEE," in *Capítulos del SELA*, Caracas, 1987, pp. 28–33; Alfonso Najera, "Europa y América: Un Lento Proceso de Acercamiento," in *Revista de Estudios Internacionales*, vol. 7, no. 2, 1986, pp. 473–499; Juan Pablo de Laiglesia, "Las Relaciones Entre la Europa de los Doce y América Latina: Un Proceso de Cambio Acelerado," in *Pensamiento Iberoamericano*, no. 13, 1988, pp. 137–160; and Marisa González de Oleaga, "¿Del Optimismo de la Volundad al Pesimismo de la Sinrazón?" in *Pensamiento Iberoamericano*, no. 13, 1988, pp. 280–285.

6. The participation of the union confederations in the collective bargaining of the big companies in the period 1985–1988 changed as follows: CCOO from 34.9 percent to 36.2 percent and UGT from 30.9 percent to 30.7 percent, according to *Anuario El País* (Madrid), 1986, p. 406, and 1989, p. 421.

7. This is according to the letter sent by Nicolás Redondo to the president of the PSOE, Ramón Rubila, published in *El País*, April 19, 1989.

8. Julián Ariza Rico, "Sobre el Sindicalismo y la Izquierda," in *El País*, April 14, 1989. Rico was a member of the secretariat of the CCOO.

9. Ignacio Sotelo even doubts the existence of a project that would merit that qualification. According to him, it would have to contain two essential elements: full employment and a strong unified union movement. Both are absent. See his article "Buenas Notas para Gobierno y Sindicatos," in *El País*, May 25, 1989.

10. See "La Negociación Posible," in *El País*, January 7, 1990.

11. Caterina Garcia i Segura, "La Política Exterior del PSOE Durante la Transición Política Española," in *Afers Internacionals*, no. 7, 1985, pp. 51–52.

12. Jean Grugel, "Spain's Socialist Government and Central America Dilemmas," in *International Affairs*, vol. 63, no. 4, 1987, p. 604.

13. Carlos Rico, "La Influencia de Factores Extraregionales," p. 126.

14. Graham Greene, *Descubriendo al General* (Barcelona: Plaza y Janés, 1985), p. 134.

15. *El País*, August 17, 1978.

16. Marcos Roitman, *La Política del PSOE en América Latina* (Madrid: Editorial Revolución, 1985), p. 132.

17. Carlos Rico, "La Influencia de Factores Extraregionales," p. 132.

18. Jean Grugel, "Spain's Socialist Government," pp. 611–612.

19. Ramón Cotarelo, *La Izquierda: Desengaño, Resignación y Utopia* (Madrid: Ediciones del Drac, 1989), p. 42.

20. *Afers Internacionals*, no. 6, 1985, pp. 146–148.

21. Cited by Carlos Rico, "La Influencia de Factores Extraregionales," p. 129.

22. "I have not sufficient information available to determine why the president decided that I had to leave. I was not against NATO and my relations with the allies were good." See Fernando Morán, *España en su Sitio* (Barcelona: Plaza y Janés/Cambio 16, 1990), p. 348.

23. See Marcos Roitman, La Política del PSOE, pp. 94–97.

24. Statement by Fidel Castro when Cuba was banned from a meeting with democratic countries. See El País, December 27, 1986.

25. José Maria Benegas, "El Papel de Europa en el Concierto de las Naciones," in *El Nuevo Compromiso Europeo: Jávea III* (Madrid: Editorial Sistema, 1987), p. 217.

26. Robert Barros, "The Left and Democracy: Recent Debates in Latin America," in *Telos*, no. 68, 1986, p. 52.

27. *El País*, May 20, 1978.

28. Speech by Alfonso Guerra, in *Europa-Iberoamérica: Encuentro en la Democracia* (Madrid: Ediciones Cultura Hispánica ICI, 1983), p. 30.

29. Intervention by Elena Flores in the proceedings of the colloquium "Democracy and Democratisation: A Dialogue Between Europe and Latin America," Strassburg, June 3–5, 1986 (Madrid: Irela 1986), p. 92.

30. Speech by Fernando Morán, in *Europa-Iberoamérica: Encuentro en la Democracia*, p. 15.

31. Interview with Luis Alberto Monge, *El País*, February 7, 1982.

32. Jean Grugel, "Spain's Socialist Government," p. 615.

33. Ibid., p. 615.

34. Speech by González, in *Europa-Iberoamérica: Encuentro en la Democracia* (Madrid: Ediciones Cultura Hispánica ICI, 1986), p. 185.

35. Speech by Alfonso Guerra, in *Europa-Iberoamérica: Encuentro en la Democracia*, pp. 22–23.

36. Statement by Francisco Fernández Ordóñez, minister of foreign affairs, *El País*, December 4, 1988.

37. Speech by Francisco Fernández Ordóñez commemorating this policy on October 12, 1989. Three objectives of the Spanish presidency of the EEC pertaining to Latin America were emphasized: consciousness-raising with regard to the debt question; the elaboration of a concrete program of cooperation with Central America, with support for the peace process; and a strengthening of the institutional dialogue.

38. Felipe González, "La Europa que Queremos," in *Leviatán*, no. 29–30, 1987, p. 13.

39. Joan Piñol i Rull, "Las Relaciones Españolas con Centroamérica," p. 55.

40. Thus defined by Elena Flores, in "Europa y América Latina: El Desafío de la Cooperación, in *Leviatán*, no. 27, 1987, p. 100.

41. PSOE, *Manifiesto del Programa 2000, Borrador para Debate, Enero 1990* (Madrid: Editorial Pablo Iglesias, 1989), p. 49. This document offers a synthesis of the new ideas and perspectives that have sprung up in Spanish socialism since 1985.

42. In the case of Panamá the SI had taken a critical attitude against Noriega and had suspended the membership of his party, PRD. The U.S. intervention was not condemned by the French Socialist government in the United Nations.

43. *El País*, January 6, 1990.

44. According to the concept developed by Carlos Rico, in "La Influencia de Factores Extraregionales," p. 113.

45. Luis Yañez, secretary for international cooperation in the Spanish government, when asked to comment on the possible decrease in interest regarding Latin America among European countries after the developments in Eastern

Europe, said the following: "It is true that Eastern Europe offers a profitable market for Western investments and the processes of democratization should be supported. I do not think that this will result in a weakening of the relations between the EEC and Latin America. These relations function at so low a level that they hardly can be reduced further. At any rate, Spain should not abide by what the EEC does or does not do, but should take action unilaterally." See *El País*, January 23, 1990.

PART THREE

Concrete Experiences, Possibilities and Limitations

6

The Crisis of the State and the Struggle for Democracy in Latin America

Pablo González Casanova

Today we are witnessing new struggles for democracy in Latin America. They come in the midst of a crisis of worldwide proportions. The novelty of the historical moment we are living in, the way the crisis affects us in each of our countries and its immediate and medium-term effects are all subjects demanding deep reflection.

Any crisis implies a sharpening of struggles and a reorganization of forces. In other words, any crisis presupposes a "concentration of contradictions," at both national and class levels. This is manifest in politics and the economy, ideologically and through repression.

Generally, crises end with the conquest and liberation of territories, with new forms of participation and power for some classes or factions at the expense of others and with the establishment of new political systems, be they more democratic or more authoritarian, more rooted in the people or in the oligarchy, more proletarian or more bourgeois. Crises give rise to expropriations, nationalizations and the socialization of capital or to a stronger presence of monopoly capital with privatization and denationalization measures. As intensified conflicts, crises give rise to new forms of hegemony in government and over the masses of people, together with a new discourse to justify it or the application of systematic repressive measures in de facto situations that can go on for years.

When, in the midst of this long crisis, we refer to the struggle for democracy, we are alluding directly to the struggle for a particular political system, a particular political regime. We are also alluding implicitly or explicitly to a particular state. Without going into the definitions different groups and classes have of democracy, it would seem necessary to begin with a relatively simple definition of the state. The definition must contribute to the clarification of today's struggles for democracy in Latin America and the practical definitions of political regimes.

The state is the power over the economy. That power can be based on persuasion, coercion or negotiation—that is to say, on hegemony or repression or a combination of the two. The state has institutions and systems of coercion, persuasion and negotiation. Behind it is an immense network of relationships among territories, nations and classes. Classes, particularly, are highly significant. Their ability to make decisions about the economic surplus and surplus value generated within a territory or nation and by an entire population is very profound. Their relationship with state apparatuses is national and transnational. They determine the conduct of the states themselves through the market, investment and financing. The big bourgeoisie, monopoly capital and the international corporations all have a decisive influence on rates of accumulation, rates of exploitation and the regional use of the surplus. Each country experiences concrete variations according to the power of national and foreign companies. The power of both contributes to the enlarging or shrinking of the state apparatus itself and influences its use of negotiation or repression.

Political systems are only part of the state, and therefore we must make a clear distinction between politics and power. A very significant part of the struggle over the economy occurs beyond the sphere of political regimes. The groups in power do not permit economic measures to go beyond the limits assigned to political systems. Though there may be interaction between the state, understood as the power to distribute the surplus, and the political system, as a limited and specifically circumscribed economic power, that interaction does not erase the differences. The distinction should always be made between the struggle for the state and the struggle to establish a political system, the crisis of the state and the crisis of a political system. From this difference arises an observation worthy of attention, one that was very clear in the case of Unidad Popular, which headed the Chilean government from 1970 to 1973: The struggle for a political system does not comprise the whole struggle, nor does the crisis of a political system necessarily entail a crisis of the state.

In the last analysis, political systems are determined by state structures, by the power relations that themselves determine patterns of generation, transfer and distribution of the surplus. The possibilities and limits of political systems are closely linked to the structures of surplus value, accumulated through exploitation and development. If this is the case *in the last analysis,* do political systems lose all significance? Far from it: I think that political systems are significant—and sometimes highly significant—in all circumstances. Taking them as a starting point, they can direct transformations of state structures and changes in the use of the surplus. What is more, political systems themselves encompass significant values for citizens and republics alike—values related to political representation and participation, to the renovation of leadership cadre, to the respect for ethnic and corporate autonomy (an example of this would be university or union autonomy), to religious, ideological and political pluralism, to social and individual rights, to collective bargaining and negotiations at the top and to national sovereignty. But to make these values a reality, political systems' strategies and models must not be divorced from the states' strategies and structures. Using a conception of the state as a starting point, a viable theory of political systems can be reached as long as the political system's logic is not subsumed in that of the state.

State and Political Systems:
Crises and Perspectives

In Latin America, the state experienced major crises around the years 1800, 1850, 1930, 1945, 1959, and most recently in approximately 1980, with the rise of neoliberalism. At these moments in history, the advent of different forms of the state can be distinguished. Around 1800, regional oligarchies and armies headed by caudillos established a state at their service. In the mid-nineteenth century, the weak, urban commercial bourgeoisie imposed their state, though with great difficulty. By 1880, the forging of the state of the oligarchies associated with nascent imperialism began; that was the time when the first professional armies were formed, which began to take control over national territories away from local strongmen and to protect foreign enclaves. In the midst of the 1930 crisis, grass-roots or populist leaders arose who established a sort of pact with the middle classes and even with the workers, a pact that little by little led to the rise of the national bourgeoisie and to its increasing link to monopoly capital. In that same period, military dictatorships, the result of oligarchic and imperialist intervention, triumphed in many countries.

After World War II, the pan-American superstate with its military, economic, educational, journalistic and workers' institutions, headed up by the OAS and the Pentagon, came into being. The U.S. State Department had its functions redefined and broadened as much as possible its participation in Latin American states, using all means within its reach and accusing those who opposed it of being Communist or Fascist. This situation lasted through the 1950s.

After the Cuban Revolution, to confront the revolutionary currents that proliferated in the 1960s, a new, authoritarian, military bureaucratic state arose. It corresponded to a new restructuring of transnational and transindustrial monopoly capital. By the end of the 1970s and in the 1980s, the military bureaucratic state gave rise to: (1) new forms of articulation of markets for goods, services and money, (2) appropriation and plunder of natural resources, (3) privatization and denationalization of state-owned businesses, (4) the refunctionalization of differential rates of surplus value and captive labor power, and (5) the domestic and international migration of manual and intellectual workers. The new transnational, associate state was created after an internal war in each country against the national liberation movements, many of which were revolutionary and Socialist. Politically, it eliminated nationalist and populist governments that were already caught up in grave contradictions. The broadening and renewal of this process was helped along by a policy of indebtedness and the states' reconversion to their minimal forms, their disintegration or their growing integration into the United States. The entire process seemed to point in the 1990s to the gestation of a multinational state in North America—headed by the United States and including Canada and Mexico—that threatens to extend itself to the rest of the Americas.

In all these cases, the crises and changes in the state responded to both national and class struggles. In all of them, there were diametrically opposed initiatives: those implemented by imperialism, the oligarchy and the great landowning and industrial bourgeoisie on the one hand and those promoted by the great peasant and middle-class movements on the other. In many of them, the workers' struggle to play a bigger part in the economy, politics and even power itself played a substantial role. From this point of view, the crisis and evolution of the state took a radical turn from the time that the Socialist revolution triumphed in Cuba. While previously there had been clashes between two social systems—albeit in an extremely incipient way—the crisis of the state had never been as profound in the terrain of social systems or the transition to a new social system. Generally it had been limited to proposals for restructuring property and surplus distribution within the same social system, giving more or less room to monopoly capital, the old landowning oligarchy, the local large bourgeoisie or grass-roots and populist political-military formations. But since Cuba, a crisis with a "concentration of contradictions" between the owners and nonowners of the means of production has been posed. That crisis, typical of the social system of a country on the periphery of capitalism, tended to reformulate the national struggle, the struggle for democracy and the struggle for socialism itself. All three struggles went on in the midst of imperialism's blockade, which continues even today.

At the opposite end of the Americas, in Chile, the brief experience along the political road to democratic socialism was canceled by an aggressive destabilization policy and a coup d'état that openly recognized U.S. government intervention. The end of the Unidad Popular meant not only the end of Chilean democracy based on strong workers' and peasants' groups but also the beginning of the model of the new state, already inaugurated in 1964, that would spread throughout the continent as the transnational associate state of the 1980s.

From 1979 on, the Sandinista revolution stood out because of its attempt to erect a state based on grass-roots support and a democracy of the people with religious, political and ideological pluralism, as well as a mixed economy with public, private and social property. After a long war, openly organized, armed and financed by the U.S. government, the Sandinista incumbent was democratically defeated in the elections when his group's position within a besieged, indebted state was no longer tenable.

For a time the crisis of the state in Latin America seemed to clearly exemplify the struggle between two classes and two types of nation. The working class and the Socialist or Socialist-oriented states confronted the bourgeoisie and oligarchies of capitalism's peripheral states. The two sides were supported by two major power blocs headed by the Soviet Union on the one hand and the United States on the other. With the crisis and fall of the Leninist project, the struggle between social systems tended to be mediated by a different conflict— between regimes of "limited democracy" and the repressive regimes that had begun to flower in the 1960s. Until now, this conflict has only led to the transformation of some political forms of the transnational associate state. While the rule of law and an electoral system took the place of states of emergency and military juntas, the rest of the state structures continued to operate through the same model of accumulation and extortion. The struggle for survival of a new social system and a new state—in which a grass-roots and workers' structure prevailed, rather than the private monopolistic transnational corporations—was limited practically to Cuba. In the rest of the Americas, the struggle against exploitation and marginalization—the class struggle—was mediated by "limited democracy" and in general was forced to change, on the basis of emerging ideas about a new democracy with grass-roots power. In this new discourse, the model of the new state—much less the view of a historical, geographic, national and worldwide transition to socialism—is not yet very clear.

In any case, the struggle for democracy, with power in the hands of the people, seems to continue to be, *in the last analysis*, a struggle for democratic socialism, while the struggle in defense of "limited democracy" (as it has been called since the Trilateral Conference) continues to be, *in the last analysis*, a struggle in favor of the empire of the transnational corporations and the amplified and conquering reproduction of capital that today rules the world. In the uncertain future, the goal of democracy for the social and national majority, as opposed to a democracy of the minorities or neoliberal and transnational political elites, seems to be a priority of the first order. Democracy's major objectives tend to summarize and reformulate the essential experiences of political systems and states in a new historic project, building both of them politically and socially.

The struggle for democracy in Latin America has been both linked to and separated from the struggles for independence, social justice and power—the struggle for the state. Today, it is important to evaluate how that has happened historically. It is necessary to review the links between the democratic project and the national, people's, social, Socialist and social democratic projects. It is also indispensable to review the *structure and movement* of blocs and alliances in relation to these projects, looking at all the problems of dissension, confrontation and fragmentation. We have to look at the negative effects and the factions, cliques and clans, as well as the obstacles blocking the unity of populist, Communist, social democratic, democratic and religious forces. If these obstacles can be overcome, the blocs where the interests of the majority prevail will be strengthened.

The study of broad, grass-roots movements is of utmost importance, particularly today when they generally seem to encompass the whole spectrum of struggles, including that between the social systems themselves. They also incorporate all sorts of currents and groupings, including religious movements that, though they clashed head on with lay and Marxist organizations in the past, today would seem to converge with them through liberation theology and a reformulation of their thinking to develop a less scholastic, more pluralistic viewpoint.

To clarify the problem of a new political system with a new form of power in the hands of the majority, the question of state power has to be brought into play. It is absolutely necessary to keep in mind the fact that when crises deepen, they give rise to different types of political systems and states. The changes are not limited simply to a restructuring of political struggle; they also extend to a qualitative change both in democracy and in the state, and they point the way to a change in the social system itself, often without consciously meaning to do so. This is what is new. It is clear that past crises of state restructuring within capitalism gave rise to different types of political systems within the same sort of state. And these are real first steps for a restructuring of the state within capitalism. From the Cuban Revolution to the crisis of the "Socialist" bloc headed up by the USSR, the fight for broadened political systems and the grass-roots and national struggles against dictatorships often became the first step in a fight for a *different* state and for a different society, a society of transition to socialism or capitalism. Today, the struggle for a broad, grass-roots democracy with ideological, religious and political pluralism immediately raises the question of restructuring state power. Without that restructuring, a social policy in favor of the majority would seem impossible; broad democracy would seem untenable. This makes it obligatory to take three dimensions into consideration when formulating any serious democratic project: the political system, the state and the social system itself. Certain general tendencies in today's world must of necessity be taken into account: what would seem to be an increased expansionism by the United States in Latin America, the historic change signified by the collapse of the Socialist bloc and growing, worldwide U.S. hegemony. While we must not be discouraged by these facts, neither should we exclude them from our analysis.

We are in the midst of one of the sharpest crises of the Latin American indebted state and underdeveloped, informal, underground society. We are witnessing a structural, systemic crisis of the capitalist world and the Socialist world themselves, a crisis that in all probability will sharpen even more in the next few years. In that context and with that prognosis, after many experiences of struggle, the mixed results of which have been well documented, an enormous number of grass-roots and revolutionary forces have put the struggle for democracy—and democracy with power—at the top of their list of priorities for Latin American politics.

What does that struggle mean? How can it be characterized? What have its most recent developments been? And what is its probable historical outcome? Above all, how can we keep it from turning into a new form of colonial democracy? These are some of the questions posed by all the forces that from a grass-roots, social democratic or revolutionary viewpoint see democracy in Latin America as their struggle.

The Struggle for Democracy:
Sense and Movement

The term *democracy* is extremely ambiguous. It is a flag that can be flown by the most contradictory of forces. Today, the ruling classes themselves, the very centers of imperialist hegemony, and even groups and individuals who are clearly authoritarian and repressive talk about democracy. The contradiction between their words and deeds is obvious, even blatant. But that is not the only contradiction. Their definition of democracy is different from that espoused by grass-roots and revolutionary forces. In fact, it is the exact opposite.

Moreover, grass-roots and revolutionary forces themselves have different concepts of democracy. That becomes clear if we examine their internal debates. One of the most significant debates has marked the difference between two major groups of Latin American Socialists: One broad grouping maintains that is necessary to fight for democracy to be able to fight for socialism, while the other contends that it is necessary to put the fight for socialism forward directly, to march straight toward the Socialist revolution. In this bitter debate, those who maintain the need for the direct march have come to the conclusion that the other position, the struggle for democracy, is predominantly a bourgeois perspective. They have quoted the texts of the Trilateral Conference and many documents, statements and democratic measures taken by the Latin American ruling classes or by spokespeople for liberalism, social democracy, Christian democracy and the new populist movements to prove the validity of their suspicion. The others have answered that it is necessary to include democracy as an integral part of their own struggle—an integral part of a long and complex battle for a new society, for a socialism with broad participation by the people in decisionmaking. Elucidating this problem has been one of the most important tasks in Latin American thought and social sciences in the last few decades, particularly over the last few years. Going into it deeply has meant dwelling on a plethora of points that democratic rhetoric usually ignores, making it more difficult to discern the differences between one kind of democracy and another. This leads to a repetition of the same debate over and over again, using the same words, in a kind of vicious circle. Some points have been clarified, but a more precise, rigorous definition is needed.

Imperialism and the ruling classes in Latin America do not have one policy; they have two or more policies that they apply simultaneously in different countries or alternately in the same one. One policy is associated with democracy, and the other with repression. One involves the restoration of constitutional regimes, human rights and electoral systems, and the other the use of violence. The use of violence is described as "conventional," or overt, and "nonconventional," or covert. Covert violence encompasses all varieties of what is known as state terrorism. It is wrong to think that the ruling classes have only one policy today, that of substituting military regimes with democratic ones. At the very minimum, U.S. administrations and those who support them and are supported by them in Latin America implement policies of limited democracy *and* selective and mass repression, both overt and covert, using both specialized and conventional armies and forces. That is why the Latin American Left is confronted with a very real problem: Whether it adopts a policy of limited democracy and tries to broaden it out or rejects a limited democracy policy by abstaining or implementing civil disobedience or other forms of resistance, sooner or later it will tend to clash with the state's repressive apparatus. A leftist movement that tries to adopt a double policy has great difficulties putting it into practice. There are some countries in which an organization has both a democratic policy and an armed wing. The organizations at war—for example, in El Salvador, Guatemala and Colombia—have a legal, peaceful wing that strives, along with other grass-roots, autonomous organizations, for new forms of creative diplomacy, social negotiation and pacification to force recognition of the people's power. Meanwhile, armed groups understand the need to continue with their two-pronged policy of negotiations and military actions, in search of a new kind of democracy with power in the hands of the people. Though this alternative is not being developed in many places at any one time, it seems destined to combine negotiated solutions of democracy and revolution. But in general, the Left continues to be divided between those tendencies in favor of legal political and union struggle and those who exist illegally, who are forced to struggle within that framework and who, ultimately, *choose* that option. Given the limits of the rule of law in many Latin American countries, the Left will probably continue to be divided, and it could even suffer sharp internal confrontations, ending only when one of the currents gains hegemony. Such was the case in Nicaragua with the Frente Sandinista de Liberación Nacional before it took power or with the Frente de Liberación Nacional Farabundo Martí in El Salvador today. In both these cases, the Left, rife with factionalism, achieved an exceptionally high degree of unity, first in Nicaragua and then in El Salvador. The problem is more difficult—or even impossible—to solve if Left insurgents practice terrorism or harassment against leftist militants themselves, as in the case of the Sendero Luminoso (SL) guerrillas in Perú.

Overall, if it is a mistake to think that the ruling classes have only one policy, it is equally unrealistic to think that the Left has only one tactic open to it. The concrete possibilities for democratic struggle in each country determine which will prevail: a legal political Left or a persecuted, illegal, repressed Left made up of those who opt to respond with revolutionary violence. It is not a question of calculating probabilities or possibilities. Each of the forces involved will make those calculations in the midst of their struggle: While participating in a legal struggle, they will tend to be more precise about legal possibilities and give less attention to the other ones; while participating in insurgent activities, they will barely note civic and political possibilities. In any case, they will break with the idea of having to choose between the false opposites, electoral or armed struggle, and they will try to discern and mobilize all the emerging sectors of the people. At times, one leftist movement will adopt the tactic of the other, as the Tupamaros did when joining the Frente Amplio or as the terceristas did in joining the Frente Sandinista. But generally, the Left will adopt both the electoral option and armed struggle, as well as one more option: mass action at the moment when systems and structures begin to collapse. Their polemical differences will reflect their structural and conjunctural differences, dictated by the legal situation and repression, as well as those schisms that may arise at those moments when the masses break into history and the vanguards both follow and guide them.

It could be argued that after the crisis of the Soviet bloc and the worldwide victory of capitalism, the possibility that these two different leftist movements with their divergent policies would continue to exist has diminished considerably. From a purely pragmatic point of view, we could say that this hypothesis is correct. But armed policies based on grass-roots organizations do not develop for purely pragmatic reasons. Pragmatic rationality, in the best of cases, is combined with the logic of the impossible. An armed revolution has never been made with the instigation or the support of the Soviet bloc. A belief that the Soviets might support them was not the determining reason that set the people's forces on the road to struggle. It *is* true that, today, the insurrectional ideology of the 1960s and 1970s has suffered hard blows that will be difficult to overcome in the short term. But while in many countries, civic and legal measures have tended to predominate in leftist movements, there are whole regions like Central America and the Andes where both types of struggle continue and, in some cases, intensify. In those countries where civic, peaceful movements predominate—like Uruguay, Brazil or Mexico—the possible victory over governments of limited democracy cannot mask the danger of new destabilization or intervention policies being used against such movements. These policies would once again pose the two options open to a Left confronted with terror: the civic struggle and the armed struggle.

It seems necessary to consider a second point: In the broadest, most general sense, how do grass-roots and revolutionary forces define the struggle for democracy? In this matter, we should distinguish the major groupings, which reflect the currents of opinion and correspond to formations and goals that lie at the root of any people's struggle for democracy. Three main categories can be identified.

First, there are people who fight *as citizens* for democracy with minimal goals, such as maintaining or regaining formal legality, constitutionality, human rights, systems of political parties and systems of universal suffrage. This is a very large group, and particularly significant when people are living under the terror of a dictatorship.

Second, there are people who struggle *as exploited and marginalized workers and shantytown dwellers*. Using the workplace or marginalized communities as their reference, they put forward problems related to union or community democracy, in defense of increased wages and fringe benefits, or for public services like water, sewage, electricity, schools, food and medicine. A many-sided grouping, made up of poor people and workers, it exerts pressure on the first, "citizens" category, and from that category, it attracts middle-class people who tend to support it with social democratic policies or policies from democratic and people's governments. This movement of the poor also has its own field of development, ranging from the workplace and the marginalized community—where their immediate interests lie—to broader, more general proposals that encompass structural changes in the state or changes in the social system (about which, since the collapse of so-called real socialism, there is only a very weak theoretical basis). However, the movements of the poor who fight for democracy today pose problems that threaten the present system of accumulation and the state. The response they encounter is not simply repression and marginalization: Rather, the transnational state basically combines exploitation, repression and exclusion with individual and collective co-optation. Not even the most severe austerity plans fail to contemplate the need to maintain control over the system as a whole and, therefore, the need to separate part of the poor from the rest of the poor, giving that part privileges in the form of jobs or *on* the job. They also try to separate as many leaders as possible from their rank and file. In order to reach these goals, the World Bank has designed the general framework of "solidarity" policies, the transnational corporate complex has perfected its policies of stratification and duality of the economy and society and the Trilateral Commission and its successors have perfected mechanisms to co-opt and alienate leaders and their clienteles, members of congress, senators, mayors and their social bases.

New democratic struggles by grass-roots forces are conditioned in different ways: with *selective policies* of wage hikes, fringe benefits and hiring; through *partial modernizing* of union negotiation guidelines or technological modernizing limited to some companies, departments or sections; through *limited structural changes* giving a broader participation to "informal" or "marginal" itinerant vendors and artisans or allowing part of the masses of people greater economic, political and cultural participation in the state. At the same time the crisis deepens and tends to accent and increase exploitation and exclusion of the vast majority. Under these circumstances, the new rules of the game do not eliminate the possibility of ever more desperate or radical grass-roots responses. But in all probability these responses will not prevail in the near future across most of the continent, and it is quite possible that they will continue to be disjointed and isolated for an unpredictable length of time. Meanwhile, the struggles by more specific social movements would seem to take the lead in most countries and serve to gather strength, even if the grass-roots democratic organizations are not really theoretically or practically clear about what they are experiencing.

Besides these broad, intertwining movements, the democratic front and the work front, there is a third and highly significant group of people who are struggling for *national independence,* for territory under the control of a sovereign people. Their movement, which originally expressed itself as a fight for the land—the struggle of the peasant for a piece of land and that of the population for a nation—is one of the oldest, but today it continues to be completely valid. However, it is increasingly complex and ineffectual, especially since neocolonialism came to dominate "national" territories through local intermediaries, both conservative and populist, with transnational economic, military, governmental and cultural policies of domination. The relative numerical reduction of the peasantry, the articulation among local and foreign ruling classes and the penetration of U.S. cultural models among the middle layers of society and the poorer classes themselves are all factors that have changed the characteristics of the national struggle, increasingly centred on the struggle for democracy and around cultural questions, particularly language. National liberation as defined today also embodies democratic liberation, encompassing a broader organic participation and practice of the people in the economy, in politics, in the culture and in the state. The national struggle is depicted as seeking more *relative independence* of the state from both foreign and domestic monopoly capital or as a *partial disconnection* from market mechanisms, at least in relation to some aspects of production and services. Today, the national liberation struggle does not seem to be defined mainly in terms of the struggle of the nation-state against the imperial nation-state. In that sense, it would also seem to be destined to be a process of accumulation of forces of peoples against their domestic and foreign exploiters and oppressors, all the while trying to structure and strengthen grass-roots organizations in different regions of any one country and in different countries, including the United States. Time and space are open to the world from the vista of immediate, local struggles of communities, of marginalized workers and of associated democratic, social democratic, reformist and revolutionary organizations. Perhaps someday there will be a sort of people's multinational, democratic, Socialist revolution that will eliminate or subordinate the transnational governments with their forces, companies and markets. That multinational revolution would organize the economy of transition of the majority through public and private social structures. It would have to happen in several parts of the world where people were capable of defending their territory, their new institutions and themselves. Today, this is just a vague dream.

Although the three main movements—the democratic one, the one of the workers and marginalized individuals and the nationalist one —have differing levels of profundity, they are obviously interrelated, be it because one tries to take on the struggle of the others or because several try to join together with a common goal. When one of the struggles is promoted without contemplating the others, the neglected movements inevitably appear on the scene. People then confront the need to join forces against a common enemy or to go their separate ways and even fight each other, dividing into the well-known factions of liberals, unionists, nationalists, social democrats, Socialists and Communists (when there are any of the latter left).

What should be emphasized here is that any struggle for democracy involves the other ones. Any struggle for democracy is defined in practice by singling out its opponents and supporters, both on the political plane and on the level of the class struggle, understood as the fight against domestic, foreign, national and transnational exploitation and for distribution of the surplus. But this has to be done without promoting the idea of a homogeneous working class (which is nonexistent today), without putting an absent industrial working class at the centre of the definition and while incorporating the great mass of underemployed, marginalized, often self-employed poor.

Democracy, according to the ruling classes today, is defined in various ways in relation to social and national problems. The prevalent—and most conservative—approach takes a few effective steps toward implementing democracy without the least intention of conceding anything at all in the workplace, much less in relation to property and the surplus. The neoliberal policy is applied without any regard whatsoever to democratic influences. Debtor nations continue to pay tribute through the payment of capital and the servicing of foreign debt. Industrial and agricultural production continues to be oriented toward the foreign market, while production of basic goods for the majority of the population continues to drop. Transnational corporations, with their high capital density and small number of jobs, continue to be the priority. The *maquiladoras*, or assembly plants, with their nonunion workers and absence of job security, have become the main new industries. The reduction in imports of capital goods is justified with the argument that this will lower the deficit in the balance of payments, and when there *is* an increase in capital goods imports, it is directed toward the transnational corporations and their associates. The dependence on the imports of foodstuffs and other basic consumer items, supposedly encouraged to take advantage of "relative international efficiency" and a larger marginal productivity of the great powers, are on the rise. The dollar is overvalued "to stimulate exports," adding external inflation to its internal effects. Social spending plummets with the excuse that it is a measure to "balance the budget." Companies are privatized and denationalized "to put an end to corruption and inefficiency in the public sector," "so the government can concentrate on its main tasks" or even "to use the proceeds from the sale to solve poverty-related problems." Direct and indirect wages drop sharply. "Limited democracy" carries out exactly the same social and economic policies as repressive dictatorships. Naturally, it "modernizes" and restructures not only work relations and the relationship with trade unions but also the dependent relationship of nation-states with financial centres such as the World Bank or the IMF or commercial, technological and military institutions, from the General Agreement on Tariffs and Trade (GATT) to the Pentagon. Its otherwise limited character has a certain importance and distinction with regard to repressive, unconstitutional regimes, but the superficiality of the political process and its ephemeral—or theatrically democratic—nature becomes even clearer as the social problems of the majority of the population sharpen, while imperialism and the transnational corporations and their associates expand.

Efforts to block or eliminate any alternative policy are characteristic of this kind of democracy. Any important measure for social justice and economic independence tends to be labeled subversive or Communist, replacing the previous epithets of populist and corrupt, old-fashioned and inefficient.

After World War II, precarious processes of democratization gave rise to the so-called cold war, during which any struggle for social justice and national independence was labeled Communist. Today, the intimidation goes even further. Confronted with any movement for a democracy that would solve a country's national and social problems by organizing the majority of the population and the lower classes, the trend is to try to eradicate the movement's identity and get it to internalize neoliberal, "free enterprise" values. In the workplace, from factories to universities, there is a functional propagation of latent values that pose social problems as individual ones. A new project of practical civilization presents the efficiency of private enterprise as the paradigm of human efficiency.

This is a grave limitation in the conservative-democratic project, which attempts to establish democracy without social justice and national liberation. But, as grave as that limitation is, it is not the only one. The neoconservative project goes so far as to put forward a democratic system in which it is not possible to choose an economic policy different from the neoliberal one, nor a democratic government with strong grass-roots support. It offers a "governable" democracy in which elections have the limited function of selecting which ruling-class groups—or which groups co-opted by the ruling classes—will get the most support in half-empty ballot boxes. It offers a democracy without options, in which a minority of citizens vote to make a selection from a tiny group of ideologically and programmatically indistinguishable professional politicians.

Today, there is a much bigger dearth of options than in the past. For most of the last fifty years in most countries, Communist and Socialist parties—but particularly Communist parties—have existed semi-legally or illegally. Many ultraconservative, Macarthyite democrats postulate a colossal idiocy: The real alternatives of our time should not be legally represented; they should not be embodied in legal parties; their supporters should not have the right to participate in elections for congress or other elected posts, but if they are allowed to participate and win, their victories should not be recognized. As a proposal for democracy it is most illusory: The citizenry should be prevented from choosing between Socialist or Communist parties and conservative and liberal parties, between grass-roots parties and parties of the oligarchy, between workers' parties and bourgeois parties, between nationalist and annexationist parties. What is incredible about this proposal is that in the 1980s, it became a reality that ran deeper than anti-Communist laws or counterrevolutionary violence. The working class lost its centrality; the Communists lost their identity; the nationalists lost their security; the populists lost their rhetoric. The political and ideological elimination of the alternative only *seems* to have given rise to an emerging alternative: democracy with power to the people. That new alternative encounters enormous obstacles, and its future is not clear. In general, conservatives deny the possibility of alternating positions in state power; what is more, they deny that conditions exist to permit it. Until today, it has only been possible in a few cities or countries or in relation to parliamentary seats. But there is a big difference between that and governing a nation—a difference that consists in the difficulty that the majority of the population has in electing its leaders and the difficulties the leaders have in implementing a policy in favor of the majority. Evidence to this effect abounds. Austerity policies define the limits of the politically and economically possible. Within these limits, what is good and functional for transnational corporations prevails. Any contrary measure will have undesirable secondary effects. Some of these are "natural" responses of the system; others are counterattacks by the banks, the U.S. State Department, local big business and neoliberal governments. If these very governments try to modify something, they do not have the power. Obviously, potential people's governments are threatened with natural and provoked destabilization similar to that suffered by other governments in the past, from that of Jacobo Arbenz, through Salvador Allende's and Maurice Bishop's. For them, what the system offers as possible is unacceptable, and what it deems impossible is insufficient.

All of these circumstances pose a grave problem for grass-roots, democratic forces. They cannot, as much as they might like, fight for a neoliberal democracy so completely limited in its social and national effects.

Democratic, grass-roots forces cannot interest themselves in a democracy that does not solve, at least partially, the social and national questions. If they did become captivated by it, they would be neither effective nor truly people's democratic forces. If they were elected by the people, they would not serve the people, who would soon abandon them, or they would be defeated by the oligarchy, imperialism and reaction, which would take advantage of popular unrest to implement destabilization measures against irresponsible, demagogic governments.

If all this is true—and everything would seem to point to that conclusion (starting with the econometric matrices of a transnationalized economy)—then democratic forces at the grass-roots and the working-class movement at a national level must have a project from the very start that includes all stages of struggle and the unification of or alliances among today's divided tendencies. Of course, to put together alliances or unifications, they will have to take into consideration universal experiences as well as the concrete conditions pertaining to fronts and classes. This is what is happening increasingly among a large number of community, union, national and revolutionary forces in Latin America that have put the fight for democracy in the forefront. They propose both an immediate and historic fight for democracy. This movement goes from politics to power, to social and national questions, finding ever more profound answers; strategically it is *defensive*, though tactically it sometimes takes the initiative instead of waiting to be attacked. It is a movement, a struggle, that supports: (1) the demand for respect for the vote and election results; (2) demands for public services and respect for social movements; (3) economic and democratic demands by industrial and farm workers in relation to their unions and organizations; (4) the demand for the people's participation in the state and the economy; (5) demands for direct, macroeconomic measures to ensure the production and distribution of nondurable consumer goods; (6) the demand for an increase in social property and the social product, in national property and the surplus, whereby people aim to change not only property relations but also the relations of domination and accumulation and exploitation and the use of the surplus for amplified reproduction and social spending; (7) the demand for financial, economic, political, military, communications and cultural autonomy; (8) proposals to ensure the existence of autonomous universities and centers for critical thinking and higher education, where intellectual discipline is not based on party discipline; (9) ever-greater demands for democratic workers' and people's power, with class autonomy as well as ideological, political, ethnic and religious autonomy and pluralism; (10) proposals by progressive parties that put the priority on fomenting centers of urban, rural, community, workers' and people's power, whether they are called councils, defense committees or something else. Very probably a new objective will be added: a program of public morality with political, democratic controls. Without public rectitude, any people's, revolutionary or democratic proposal is inexorably condemned to failure, a tenet proven from Russia to Nicaragua.

All these components are necessary, even inevitable. They are not proposed as a result of an ideology or a philosophical system. They appear in multiple variants. Perhaps this is because of their incipient character or because of the very nature of the movement's protagonists, who are heterogeneous. Or perhaps it is because of the grass-roots and social movements that organize the democratic struggle more on a *cultural* than on an *ideological* level, as though democracy does not concern a way of ordering society but rather a way of living, thinking and establishing a dialogue. At the same time, however, it continues to be very important to rethink the problem of grass-roots organizations, including their discipline and effectiveness.

Today, however, proposals for a democracy based on the people do not spring, fully grown, from the head of Zeus with precise objectives and norms, with ready-made calculations about how to achieve democracy and what obstacles and assistance are to be encountered nationally and internationally on the way. Extrapolated from isolated, scattered—even utopian or illusory—struggles, the proposals are valuable insofar as they are a starting point for broad people's organizations. Many semiabstract proposals seek to concretize themselves in the national organizations of social movements. In practice, these organizations will permit people to do the impossible and, what is more difficult to envision, perhaps even establish governable people's states.

It is true that when the question of governable democracies with people's power is raised, the international aspect must also of necessity be examined. The establishment of this sort of state and the implementation of new social, social democratic or Socialist and democratic policies without organized international support is inconceivable. But even today, many marginalized movement organizations foreshadow this possibility. Examples can be found in small countries like El Salvador and Haiti or in important regions of large countries, like Mexico, Brazil, Colombia, Ecuador and Perú. The emerging democracy involves those who are normally marginalized and excluded, and it implies a worldwide solidarity policy. It will not limit itself to one jurisdictional area or to one national territory, even though these may have been the places where it all started.

The point is that a people's struggle for democracy that does not include social justice and national independence is senseless. That is why such regimes can do nothing and are short lived. At the same time, it is highly likely that the fight for sovereign, independent democracy with social justice will become the new historical alternative, and for that reason it is persecuted.

The most perceptive grass-roots and democratic forces know that sooner or later political struggle will lead them to the question of the struggle for power and a policy of broad alliances will confront them with the class question. This does not mean, however, that a policy of broad alliances will disappear but rather that it will increasingly center on a struggle for democracy and liberation socially based, for the most part, on the working people, the marginalized, the "informal" workers and those excluded from society, with help from all the groups and organizations whose objectives are centered on a government by the people and a society where men and women work and participate without being exploited.

The move from a broad alliance to a class policy and from a class policy to one of broad class alliances is determined by (1) the concrete conditions of struggle against wage exploitation and the loss of fringe benefits and social services in the new transnational state; (2) the struggle against transfers of inflation and the foreign debt; and (3) the authoritarianism prevalent in the political formations of each country. It is also determined by the place given to legal activity in each country. Therefore, to the universal character of a policy (which in order to be a broad front must include a class policy and in order to be a class policy must embody aspects of a broad front), many particular variations can be added. These differ according to the articulation or disarticulation of parties and unions, the form and political practices of the state and the opposition, the form and economic practices of the state and monopoly capital and the weight of legality or illegality (that is to say, depending on the symbols and ideology of legal and illegal, electoral, parliamentary, union and religious political practice). Also, the whole of this enormous movement goes through changes that depend on the fight against direct and indirect, overt and covert, military and repressive interventions made by foreign armies and "security" forces and their local delegates.

All these and other elements make for enormous variations in the fight for democracy in a relatively homogeneous region, like Central America and Panamá. But the people's democratic forces confront a common enemy: the most reactionary circles of U.S. imperialism and the Latin American bourgeoisie. All the democratic people's forces confront a dynamic that of necessity poses questions on a policy of broad fronts, as well as on the struggle against exploitation and exclusion—questions that will continue to be the dynamic of both broad alliances and class needs and that will determine how far the process goes. This is what happened in Nicaragua and what will happen in the future in all of Latin America.

Social science, Latin American political science and the intellectual who is pledged to the fight for democracy, to working people and to liberation will lose all possibility of influencing the process through helping to make its history and movement clearer if they lose sight of the double dialectics of the broad political alliance and the struggle against exploitation with the concrete variants of each depending on country and historic moment. It is a difficult dialectic that is easily lost in illusory broad front alliances or in isolated classes if we lose sight of how to move from the logic of political unity among the grass-roots, people's forces to the logic of unity centered on working people and those citizens who live—or want to live—from their toil. For politicians, unifying forces means only unifying organizations. But this dynamic combines the unification of already organized forces with the great mass of people as yet unorganized, for whom it is necessary to link every action more closely with a practical and moral, political and ethical leadership that carries on a dialogue and is integrated with the people. Hegemony over the broad alliance is won in a fight to attract the unorganized masses; hegemony is lost if the organizations in the alliance make it their main task to rob members and authority from the other groups in the alliance. Increasing unity in the alliance is unity of the people previously divided and unorganized in a national or multinational front. This means that the triple struggle against exploitation and for democracy and liberation is transformed into one great force of the citizen, the worker and marginal sectors of society and the nation. Depending on concrete conditions, this force will advance toward new points of agreement and disagreement in a long, complex historical process that will ultimately lead to democracy in socialism—to democracy as a way of government and to socialism as a form of organizing production by a civil society no longer dominated by private monopolies and a state serving these monopolies or the bureaucrats.

Today, the struggle is taking its first steps. To be successful, it needs international solidarity, which is also only just beginning to build. That solidarity depends on the application from now on of three different dynamics: what Mikhail Gorbachev has deemed the "logic of survival," which has led to the new Soviet philosophy; the logic of reforms necessary to the social democracies; and the new logic of unity with the workers of the South that the United States has begun to consider. If applied, these dynamics can help to solve three basic problems. If they are not solved, neither global democracy nor the very survival of the world can be guaranteed. These three problems— which *can* be solved—consist of (1) canceling the Latin American and Third World foreign debt, charging it to military budgets and war; (2) reconverting the military-industrial complex to implement a policy of worldwide investment in the production of goods needed for the majority of the population and for preserving the environment; and (3) recognizing that hypocrisy is an epistemological, as well as a moral, phenomenon and that it simply is not possible to seriously propose democracy in a terribly exploited, impoverished Latin America. Nor is it possible to demand a peace-democracy in a republic like Cuba, which the United States has subjected to an economic, ideological, psychological and diplomatic blockade for more than thirty years. Along with putting an end to epistemological hypocrisy, an end must be put to the impoverishment, blockade and harassment of our peoples. This is the basis of any struggle for democracy.

7

The Left in South America: Politics as the Only Option

Marcelo Cavarozzi

In this chapter I will analyze the role of the Left in contemporary Latin American politics. The last decade has been one of changes more than of continuity. Therefore, my comments concern in particular the relations among these changes and the roles performed by the different actors belonging to the Left.

Latin America went through two coeval transitions during the 1980s.[1] One of these had to do with changes in the nature of political regimes: The majority of the authoritarian governments of the region were replaced by political democracies. Even those countries that still have not completed the transition to a full political democracy, such as Paraguay, have liberalized to a significant degree in the areas of human rights and guarantees for the effective formation of opposition parties. The other transition began in fact before 1980, in the mid-1970s. It was tied to a longer-term process. The state-centered model (SCM) that had been predominant since the Great Depression in Brazil, México, Argentina, Chile and Uruguay—and had emerged later in other countries, such as Columbia, Venezuela and Perú—was confronted with a multifaceted and irreversible crisis that led to its exhaustion. As a result, the two basic mechanisms of the model, which are the complementary relation between the market and state regulation, on the one hand, and a type of political society that was organized around the state, on the other, were irreparably disarticulated.

My observations concentrate on the countries of South America. However, on more than one occasion I also will refer to Latin America in general, and I hope that this will not confuse the reader. There are two closely related reasons for this. In the first place, one of the effects of the Cuban Revolution was the definition of a common political space for all of Latin America in which the events of Central America and the Caribbean had an unusual impact. Therefore, although I am concerned with South America, I prefer not to leave aside the effects of the "continentalization" of political conflicts on the actions of the Left and its adversaries. In the second place, the foreign policy of the United States in relation to Latin America has shown since 1959 an obsession with Cuba and produced a number of interventions, military and otherwise, in the conflicts of Central America and the Caribbean —especially in Cuba itself, in the Dominican Republic, in Nicaragua and in El Salvador. Although North American interventions and pressures in South America never reached the levels found in the Caribbean and its immediate periphery, until the last years of the 1980s they were fueled also by the East-West confrontation. To a considerable degree, the U.S. view of the general Latin American situation passed through the prism of this conflict. As is well known, in the Latin American context the strategic conflict was embodied in Fidel Castro's Cuba and, after 1979, in the Nicaragua of the Sandinistas. The international context within which the South American leftist organizations moved cannot be properly understood if we leave this hemispheric perspective aside.

I pointed out that this chapter explores the reactions and behaviors of *the* Latin American Left in general as it confronts change.[2] However, the process of internal differentiation within the Left has accelerated during the last decade. Consequently, I will refer to the various segments of the Left and the different manners in which each of these has reacted to the double transition. My central hypothesis is relatively straightforward. While the majority of the leftist organizations did not remain aloof from the transitions to democracy, they did not succeed in becoming protagonists of these changes either. Nevertheless, the traumatic experience of authoritarianism, together with what the Left learned through this transition, led to a revaluing of democracy. This revaluing has coincided, in good part accidentally, with the crises of "real socialism" and of the very idea of socialism itself. Consequently, the Latin American leftist organizations experienced a profound mutation during the 1980s that is still continuing and whose future course is difficult to foresee.

As I discuss in the following section, the exhaustion of the SCM was in part obscured by the transitions to democracy. Although it is true that this influenced all political and social actors, it greatly affected the perceptions of the Left. The Latin American leftist organizations were particularly disoriented by the progressive emergence of a new political-economic model. More concretely, this implied that:

1. After the Socialist utopia had been extinguished and state-directed development exhausted, leftist organizations have not come up with an alternative to free market capitalism;
2. The parties and other leftist political organizations still have not repositioned themselves in relation to the process of rearticulation of democratic institutions, civil society (that is to say, the diverse movements, organizations and groups, as well as the space within which they operate) and the state apparatus itself. This rearticulation is one of the results of the collapse (or at least the pronounced weakening) of the institutions and practices of political societies anchored in the state;
3. Leftist organizations have not succeeded in interpreting the behavioral changes of the various social sectors that, from the point of view of the Left itself, were the backbone of the Socialist project, that is, the workers, the peasants and the poor.

This chapter will limit itself to a schematic analysis of the characteristics of the double transition to which I have referred. I will examine them from the perspective of how these characteristics are entwined with the perceptions and strategies of the various leftist organizations. First, I will explore some general tendencies, and later, I will point out four methods of action that developed during the last few years. These modes of action were also common to various other segments within the political-ideological field of the Left. For this reason, the chapter concludes with a preliminary mapping of these segments, including an implicit proposal of criteria to analyze their specificity.

The Left Facing Democratization and the Economic and Political Crisis in the 1980s

As opposed to what had occurred in the past, the processes of political democratization, which took place during the 1980s in South America, have been characterized by the fact that until now there has been no regression to authoritarian rule. The risk of a return to this type of government has not been completely eliminated, but since 1978—when the armed forces of Ecuador transferred power to a constitutionally elected regime—the military, once it returned to the barracks, has not conducted any successful coups. After Ecuador's return to democracy, Perú, Bolivia, Argentina, Uruguay, Brazil, Chile and Paraguay were added to the list of political democracies that, at one point in the 1970s, had only included Colombia and Venezuela.

The greater (democratic) political stability in South America can be explained in several ways. Here I simply wish to emphasize that one of the factors that doubtlessly contributed to this increased stability has been a certain convergence of leftist and rightist groups. With some exceptions, groups on both sides have been progressively rejecting an appeal to the use of violence, and they have succeeded in increasing their tolerance for political adversaries. In this process, the majority of the leftist fringe groups have overcome the attraction they felt, beginning in the 1960s, for militarist currents. In a parallel development, the Right's fascination with authoritarian and repressive schemes has also diminished.

I would hesitate, nevertheless, to interpret this phenomenon as indicative of a consolidation of the emergent South American democracies. I believe, instead, that what has taken place in the last few years is a process of redefinition, probably irreversible, of the factors that affect the consolidation of democracy. It is the end of an era that in some cases had begun in the 1930s and in other cases in the postwar years. In this era, all the national political systems were organized, to a greater or lesser extent, by dealing with the interaction (real *and* imagined) between two fields of forces. Some of these forces, in one way or another, were threatening or were perceived as a threat to the continuity of the basic parameters of the economic and social order of capitalism. These forces belonged, almost without exception, to the Left or to national popular movements. Their opponents (that is, the military, the Right or at times simply the capitalists) gave priority to the defense of the prevailing order even at the cost of violating the rules of the democratic game. During this long era, the repeated disruptions of institutionality were the result of the conviction that the continuation of political democracy, whether total or limited, would produce, directly or indirectly, an intolerable threat to the capitalist order. In fact, in every single case, these disruptions were associated with military coups.

As stated earlier, the recent transitions toward democracy have coincided with the advent of a new era—inaugurated as a consequence of the progressive exhaustion of the predominant SCM. In this new era, the most serious threats to democracy *and to any stable political order* derive principally from the ungovernability of the economy. This ungovernability ultimately implies a situation under which any social order defined by collectively shared norms, whatever these norms happen to be, will probably collapse.

This change has had a profound but ambivalent influence over the way in which the Left involves itself in politics. In a way, it has contributed to legitimate the presence and the actions of the Left.

Nevertheless, it is still true that in most countries, a leftist electoral triumph and the Left's arrival to power represent an alternative whose effects over democratic stability are uncertain. What, for example, would have happened in Brazil if Luiz Inacio da Silva (*Lula*) had won the last presidential elections? Or, to cite a country with more solid democratic traditions, what would happen in Uruguay if the candidate of the Frente Amplio were to win the next elections? In both cases it is risky to guarantee the military's loyalty to constitutional norms. However, the example of Ecuador and Bolivia (where the current presidents were supported by leftist coalitions) and the even more surprising case of Paraguay (where in 1991 a military-influenced administration accepted the election of an independent leftist candidate in the municipal election in Asunción) indicate that a qualitative change has taken place. The acceptability of the Left has increased significantly even in countries where recalcitrantly authoritarian military and civil sectors still survive.

However, this greater acceptability has come with a price for the Left. Its involvement in nonexcluding political systems helps dissolve the association that, rhetorically or practically, the Left had established between the fact of its own exclusion (or the permanent threat of exclusion) and the existence of social sectors that were economically, politically and culturally excluded and oppressed. In the half century after the Great Depression, the Left was able to maintain with credibility that, really or potentially, it represented subordinated social sectors. Now, the argument that this is automatically the case is no longer valid. In other words, this previously natural link between excluded political actors and oppressed social sectors is now broken.

But this is not the complete extent of the transformation. The relationship between the Left and its adversaries has also changed. The creation, still in process, of a common political space for the Left, Right and Center has also worked in another direction. Leninist political projects had emphasized political-military dimensions, while Gramscian versions had underlined political-cultural confrontation. They all agreed, however, that the goal of the Left was to establish supremacy over bourgeois adversaries, either through their elimination or through their subordination to the political-cultural "proletarian project." The creation of a common arena in which the Left is accepted but is also expected to accept its opponents implies that leftists also have to change their points of view, which were, ultimately, equally totalitarian. In this respect the Gramscian approach toward politics was as antidemocratic as Vladimir Lenin's. Both are the opposite of strategies that give priority to political interaction between actors, who—while recognizing their conflicting interests—seek negotiation rather than the neutralization of their opponents.

At this point, I would like to emphasize that the practices and ideology of the majority of the leftist groups are out of step with the changes that have occurred in Latin American societies. It is true that they have condemned and abandoned militaristic visions of politics and are participating nonopportunistically in elections and the parliamentary game. In other words, the bulk of the Left perceives parliamentary democracy as something substantively different from a mere tactical springboard to power. But, on the other hand, when they concentrate their energy on the traditional theme of access to power, leftists have failed to perceive that the Latin America in which they and other actors had operated during half a century has changed dramatically.

In spite of the fact that the leftists continue to claim that theirs is the discourse of the future, the majority of their segments have remained bogged down in the past. As a consequence, during the decade of the 1980s, the Left lost the ideological leadership it had enjoyed during the five previous decades. Until the last decade, even under conditions of extremely severe repression and after having suffered catastrophic political and military defeats, the Left had retained the possibility of giving its struggles the progressive aura that had fueled both the enthusiasm of its members and sympathizers and the fear of its enemies. This tendency has been reversed dramatically during the last decade. For the first time since 1930 the Left found itself relegated to a defensive position and frequently anchored in the past.

This ideological debacle is intimately connected with the exhaustion of the SCM. The old model has crumbled and has taken with it the understanding of how politics work that had been thoroughly ingrained in leftist groups. The collapse of Latin American states involves more than the crisis of fiscal and monetary mechanisms and the fall of the productive and services apparatus. There has also been a serious weakening of the principles and practices that supported public authority. This has caused, in some extreme cases like that of Perú, the disarticulation of the (state-centered) rules that regulated daily interaction among people. An important part of this process is related to the partial disintegration of labor unions, neighborhood groups, popular organizations and associations of entrepreneurs, state managers, technocrats and other collective actors who had organized social conduct in the past. To a large extent, the organizations and informal groups, which were directly or indirectly oriented toward political action, have seen a drastic decrease in their capacity to control and/or channel the behaviors of their members and sympathizers. An additional correlative of this phenomenon has been the parallel disorganization of the patterns of interaction among collective actors, which has occurred because the formal and informal rules that governed these interactions have deteriorated. The new political-economic model that is emerging in Latin America, with a predominance of atomistic competition over organized competition, is connected to the structuring of more precarious societies in which the shared norms are extremely fragile.

These transformations of the patterns of social organization and of the functioning of the political system have especially harmed the popular sectors. In their case, the capacity for collective organization is a variable that very decisively affects their way of life and the possibilities of seeing their demands satisfied. Nevertheless, within the spectrum of Latin American political actors, the Left—which supposedly should be the closest to the popular sectors—has been the most inept at adapting itself to the new tendencies. That is why I have asserted that the transitions toward democracy have obscured, especially in the case of the leftist groups, the more general transformations that are occurring in Latin America.

It is true that segments of the old leftist groups as well as many new leftist parties and organizations have renovated their discourse and have swerved in the direction of an unambiguous compromise with political democracy. But these very same groups, as I have already pointed out, are strategically dislocated in relation to the new modalities of economic organization and to the redefined role played by politics, particularly by democratic institutions, in Latin American societies. The majority of the responses that have been articulated, as we will see in the next section, vary between an extreme of passive adaptation (in which the parties and organizations take refuge in styles of action from the past that are losing their relevance) and another extreme of a flight forward, associated with millenarian utopias. In these utopias, "proletarian violence" does not seek simply to eliminate the rich and other enemies but also to purify the poor, even if this entails exterminating them.

The ideological crisis of the Latin American Left has certainly intensified with the collapse of the Communist regimes of Eastern Europe and the Soviet Union. The Socialist economies of the East were transformed, quite a while ago, into a model that elicited no excess of enthusiasm. Nevertheless, their mere survival was enough to fuel illusions of replicating them in Latin America, purging them of their negative traits—that is, bureaucratic control and political totalitarianism—and preserving their relative egalitarianism. In this sense, the evaporation of the Communist regimes in Europe—and the confirmation of the fact that almost the entire population of these countries perceived these systems as oppressive and stagnant—has affected the credibility of the entire Latin American Left. Not only members and sympathizers of the minority orthodox Communist parties but also members of the majority of other leftist parties and organizations have suddenly found themselves in a devastated political space in which references to the utopias that had inspired their actions during the last six or seven decades have completely lost credibility. There are still some activists and ideologues who argue that there are still a thousand million Chinese living under a communist regime and that there is a remnant of virtue in the Vietnamese and Cuban regimes. But this can only be understood as the desperate search for a psychological refuge from the wreckage of the political and ideological parameters that had prevailed for seven decades.

From the perspective of leftist groups in Latin America, the collapse of the Communist regimes in Eastern Europe and the Soviet Union has only accelerated a process that remained determined, to a large extent, by internal factors. During the decade of the 1980s, the majority of the Left was embroiled in a battle, doomed from the beginning, in which, without shedding the rhetorical wrapping of Marxism, they clamored for a return to state-directed development and for the reconstitution of the heroic social actors of the past. Thus a new blindness obscured to the mythical visions that prevailed earlier and that assumed that the working class, the peasants and the poor would be the builders of socialism. The leftist groups have refused to understand that the patterns of collective action of the workers in particular and of the poor in general have been disintegrating precisely because they had been historically structured to relate to a tutelary state. Of all political actors, the Left has been the least successful in grasping the new types of behavior that have emerged among the oppressed and the excluded. These new behaviors range from the expansion of an informal economy and changes in the people's style of interaction with the public educational system and the mass communications media to a transformation in the patterns of popular religiosity and the emergence of novel manners of relating to politics.

The economic, political and cultural mutations of the last ten or fifteen years have affected all segments of the South American Left equally. However, diverse currents and traditions have reacted differently. Let us see what has occurred with the four segments to which I alluded earlier.

Old and New Leftist Groups

The Grass-roots Left

The organizations and movements of this current emerged in numerous countries in Latin America beginning in the 1970s. The majority of them were connected to processes of popular mobilization directed against military dictatorships and organizations under the state's hierarchical control or under the control of institutions such as the Catholic church and the labor unions. The earliest and perhaps the most significant example was that of the "new labor movement" that originally appeared in the industrial suburbs of São Paulo and later served as a foundation for the emergence of the Partido dos Trabalhadores (PT). The grass-roots Left also appeared in neighborhood organizations that were frequently sponsored or protected by the progressive sectors of Catholicism, the ecclesiastical base communities (CEBs).

One of the main characteristics of the grass-roots Left, even of groups like the Brazilian PT, is its intrinsic lack of trust in all mechanisms of political representation. Basically, the grass-roots Left perceives political representation, at its best, as a distortion of *true and real* democracy, which, from a leftist perspective, is associated with modalities of direct participation. At an extreme, this concept encourages a Manichean view of politics in which the state and its institutions, both authoritarian and democratic, are considered as inherently perverse, while civil society and the groups that function within it are viewed, symmetrically, as good.

When the grass-roots Left promotes the creation of political parties, such as the PT, these become ambivalent organizations during the processes of transition to democracy. Grass-roots parties necessarily function in the arena of representative democracy, and their members gain elective positions in government. In spite of this, they continue to maintain, at least rhetorically, that the adoption and expansion of the participatory mechanisms imbedded in civil society are the only true way to democratize Latin American societies. In practice, however, the grass-roots parties confront various dilemmas. On the one hand, while functioning in the political arena, they face opportunities and restrictions similar to those of other parties. Consequently, they are forced to negotiate and make compromises, even with oligarchical sectors, and at times resort to such traditional mechanisms as clientelism. Frequently, these compromises imply that grass-roots parties sacrifice, at least partially, the demands of their supporters.

On the other hand, as I already mentioned, the disorganization of the state has been accompanied by the weakening of civil society and its organizations. One of the effects of this weakening has been a sustained decrease in the level of participation of the popular sectors. Often, as a result of this phenomenon, the vibrant mobilizations of the popular sectors that, in some cases, had been associated with the upsurge of grass-roots activity are replaced by an increasingly virulent and self-referential assemblyism. The assemblies become the hunting ground of militants, who dispose of rhetorical resources, have more time and eventually drive away the popular participation they claim to promote. The most dramatic example of this has been the case of the Brazilian PT, where the partial dominance of Trotskyist elements has imbued the program and rhetoric of the party with a language that is alien to the popular and working sectors that it claims to represent. This has caused the people to become apathetic and to withdraw.

This dilemma is exacerbated when members of grass-roots groups occupy executive positions, generally at the local level, as happened in São Paulo, São Luis and other Brazilian municipalities and in the case of Izquierda Unida in Lima, Perú. The daily performance of the tasks of government during a time of acute economic crisis has transformed some of their electoral triumphs into Pyrrhic victories. As public officials, they have not been effective in solving the concrete problems of the general population, in selecting appropriate alternatives and in negotiating with generally hostile state and federal powers. Finally, these groups have failed to respond positively to the challenge of refraining from turning government institutions into new spaces for confrontation among their many subgroups.

Millenarian Violence

This new type of leftist militarism, of which Sendero Luminoso is the most representative example, has taken to an extreme—bordering on paroxysm—the insistence, characteristic of the Guevarist stage of the Cuban Revolution, on breaking with the past. The first break concerns the rejection of capitalism in all its variations. In this respect, in their attempt to replace the ideal image of the profit-maximizing bourgeois individual with the new Socialist man or woman, these groups go to the extreme of trying not only to exterminate the exploiters but also to forcibly reeducate the poor. To this end, they employ methods that include the most severe forms of punishment.

A second break is connected with the total eradication of the institutions of the bourgeois state and especially of those leftist organizations that compete with the millenarian movement. Some of their favorite targets are those organizations that operate within the popular sector and try to penetrate the political institutions in order to reform or influence them from within.

From the perspective of these new crusaders, their hegemonic goal excludes any compromise. It can only be reached through the extermination of the adversary. Consequently, the millennial movement is intrinsically militaristic since the attainment of hegemony entails a long moment of political-military confrontation with the main enemy: the armed forces of the bourgeois state. However—and this is a paradox that is not accidental in cases such as that of Sendero Luminoso and to a much lesser extent the Colombian Ejército de Liberación Nacional (ELN), in which extreme militaristic positions had a significant national impact—millenarian movements frequently resemble the antidemocratic and repressive armed forces. These latter also repudiate parliamentary democracy and reject elected officials. Both groups distrust those they propose to indoctrinate as much as they distrust their enemies. They have created a cross fire, and the common people are caught in the middle.

Militarist millenarianism is essentially authoritarian, politically as well as socioculturally. In addition to promoting modalities of hierarchical organizations, they also—particularly in the case of Sendero Luminoso—foment, at times even by force, puritanical, sexist and punitive behaviors. In this respect, instead of representing a change, Sendero Luminoso represents a double continuity: on the one hand, with the authoritarian traditions of the Left, and on the other, with patterns of community organization based on castelike hierarchies.

The millenarian violence is fed by a political context characterized by the deterioration of the state and by social fragmentation. The first of these variables has characterized, to a certain extent, contemporary Colombian politics; the ELN is an extremely minor part of the Left in that country. In Perú, on the contrary, a much graver combination of the two phenomena has caused the majority of the territory—and a substantial part of the population—to be embroiled in a war of all against all.

Though rhetorically they continue to refer to a Socialist future, advocates of millennial violence evoke images of redemption through a purifying withdrawal into a primitive, collectivist and authoritarian utopia.

Guerrilla Movements

During the 1970s the majority of Latin American guerrilla groups were annihilated by armed forces that did not hesitate to resort to whatever methods they could mobilize, whether legal or illegal. That "war without battles," as it was described by one of the characters in Hector Aguilar Camin's novel *La Guerra de Galio*,[3] exterminated all guerrillas, from Lucio Cabañas and his followers in the Mexican Guerrero mountain range to the urban guerrillas of the Southern Cone. In addition to an opponent that employed torture and systematic "disappearance," the guerrillas were faced with an even greater obstacle: the indifference of the masses. Confronted with the weakness or absence of ethnic and/or regional cleavages, on which they could have based some sort of subcultural legitimacy, the guerrillas were unable to devise except in the case of the Sandinistas, a definite political platform at the national level that would allow them to question effectively the democratic or nondemocratic nature of state institutions.

At the beginning of the 1970s, however, an alternative to complete extermination appeared. Teodoro Petkoff, one of the leaders of the Venezuelan guerrillas that had initially emerged in the left wing of Rómulo Betancourt's party, Acción Democrática, was its originator. He began negotiations for amnesty with the government. In exchange for giving up military action and terrorism, the amnesty negotiated by Petkoff allowed the ex-guerrillas to become a political party, Movimiento al Socialismo (MAS), and to aspire to elective offices. MAS became the third Venezuelan party, but it never went beyond having a minority position in relation to the major parties, AD and Comité Organización Político-Electoral Independiente (COPEI), and their splinter groups.

The most significant recent example of a process of negotiated reincorporation of guerrillas into parliamentary life has been taking place in Colombia for the last couple of years. During the 1980s this country experienced a resurgence of political and extrapolitical violence that led to the virtual extinction of the state. Political violence had not disappeared completely after the period of La Violencia (1948–1957) and the administrations of the Frente Nacional that lasted until 1974. In fact, the oldest and most powerful guerrilla group, Fuerzas Armadas Revolucionarias de Colombia (FARC), was a legacy of that period. During the 1970s and 1980s guerrilla groups multiplied; perhaps the most important one was M-19, which derived its name from the date of a presidential election characterized by fraud and by the suspicion (never completely eliminated) that the real winner had been the ex-dictator Gustavo Rojas Pinilla. The other organizations were the Ejército Popular de Liberación (EPL) and the Ejército de Liberación Nacional, both founded during the 1960s, and Quintín Lame, which succeeded in gaining the support of some sectors among the Indian population in the southwestern departments.

The explosion of violence at the end of the 1980s, however, was not solely due to the expansion of guerrilla activity. In fact, the most cruel and spectacular episodes of terrorist violence were orchestrated by the narcotraffickers, particularly the leaders of the Medellín cartel, and by paramilitary groups that were frequently promoted by the traffickers themselves. These latter groups entered upon a campaign to exterminate leftist leaders and activists, especially those who did not operate under the protection of the guerrillas. The failure of Conservative President Belisario Betancur's pacifying efforts (1982–1986) and the total war declared by his successor, Virgilio Barco, against the narcotraffickers unleashed a series of assassinations and terrorist acts that seemed to indicate that Colombia was sliding toward a total collapse of the state of law and even to the end of all political order. However, during the last year of the Barco administration and the beginning of the presidency of his successor, Cesar Gavíria, a process of negotiation at several levels led, on the one hand, to the integration of three guerrilla groups—M-19, EPL and Quintín Lame—into parliamentary life and, on the other hand, to a de facto armistice with the Medellín cartel. The main leader of M-19, Antonio Navarro Wolff, became a member of President Gavíria's cabinet as health minister and later led his party to a significant victory in the Constitutive Assembly election, where they obtained a plurality of votes. In practice, members of M-19 contributed considerably in the drafting of the new constitution, where they worked together with Gavíria's liberal faction and a sector of the conservatives.

The successful integration of M-19 and to a lesser extent of Quintín Lame persuaded the Coordinadora Guerrillera Simón Bolívar (formed by FARC, ELN and a dissident faction of EPL) that it was on a dead-end street and that it might behoove the group to negotiate with the government. This process began in mid-1991 and by the end of the year had reached a difficult impasse.

The Colombian case has a double relevance. First, though it is true that the outcome is still uncertain, experience appears to indicate that negotiation is an adequate way of overcoming extreme violence and preventing the collapse of the state of law. Second, the integration of the guerrillas into parliamentary life has not been unrelated to a process of democratization in this oligarchical and clientelist society.

The Colombian political map has been redesigned, not simply with the emergence of a third political force that is of a leftist persuasion but also with the modernization of the ruling Liberal Party. In this process, the regional bases of its powerful, clientelist barons have eroded considerably.

In Venezuela and Colombia the reintegration of the guerrillas into political life is connected to the processes of full democratization. In El Salvador, on the contrary, where there is a similar agreement between the administration of President Cristiani and the Frente Farabundo Martí para la Liberación Nacional (FMLN), complete democratization appears to be far away. The power of the military in El Salvador is almost unlimited since it is not subject to any civil authority. The most probable effect of the agreement will be that of extending civil rights (especially the right to life) to guerrillas and leftist leaders.

The Political Left

This is the most heterogeneous of the segments analyzed in this chapter. I distinguish three main currents that have one element in common: They have unequivocally chosen to participate in the parliamentary scene through political parties.

The first current I will label as *the opportunistic Left*. It includes the broad coalitions that have attained power in Bolivia and Ecuador. In both cases (but especially in the former), the springboard to power has been the agreements with opposing political forces, including the Right: that is, the pact between Paz Zamora's movement (MIR) and Banzerismo, which allowed Paz Zamora to become president in spite of his third-place showing in the presidential elections. Both Jaime Paz Zamora's movement and the Izquierda Democrática administration of Rodrigo Borja in Ecuador have been characterized by the absence of politics that would have meant an alternative to those implemented by the conservative governments that preceded them.

The lack of reformist projects in MIR and ID denotes a serious weakness. This suggests the failure of these groups to address the dominant theme of the end of the 1980s and the beginning of the 1990s: the measures with which to face the economic crisis. The passive adaptation to the courses laid out by their conservative predecessors, Víctor Paz Estenssoro and Febres Cordero, seems to indicate that the main goal of the previously reformist Andean leaders was simply that of gaining access to state resources and sinecures. At any rate, in the present context of economic crisis, opportunism does not seem to bear electoral fruit in the medium term: In Ecuador, the Left has practically been erased from the political scene. It has no prospects in the next presidential election. In Bolivia, MIR has become the second fiddle in a government coalition that lost votes in the 1991 election.

The second current includes groups that are still centered around the task of fully democratizing the political systems in which they operate. The most obvious case in South America is that of the independents in Paraguay. They achieved an important victory at the beginning of 1991, when they won the mayoralty in Asunción. This was unprecedented, both because it was the first electoral success of the Left in the country and because it was validated by General Andrés Rodriguez. However, the triumph of Mario Filissola was not repeated in the following election for the Constitutive Assembly that took place toward the end of the year; at that time, the independents lost in Asunción and did not do significantly better in the interior of the country. In more than one sense, outside South America, México's Partido de la Revolución Democrática is also an example of this *democratizing Left*. In any case, the division of the old PRI headed by Cuauthémoc Cárdenas combines, in difficult equilibrium, the new and the old. It combines demands for the effective democratization of Mexican politics—which in 1988 allowed it to attract one-third of the electorate—with a platform in which a certain facile populism ignored the dilemmas of economic adjustment and restructuration. Its methods of political action were not very innovative in comparison with those long practiced by the PRI.

The Chilean Left, especially the sector composed by the Partido Socialista and the Partido por la Democracia (PPD)—originally only an electoral mechanism—represents the most successful example of the third current, *the renewed Left*. Some portions of Uruguay's Frente Amplio and Nuevo Espacio share, incompletely, the main traits of this category. The Brazilian PSB is more decidedly renovated than that of its Uruguayan neighbors. However, its importance in its respective national scene is much less. The risk the moderate segments of the Sandinistas took in 1990 places them in this group, though their origins relate them more closely to the guerrilla Left.

The first characteristic of the renewed Left is its perception that, in the postauthoritarian era, one of the indispensable requirements for assuring the viability of a progressive alternative is the (re)construction and consolidation of a party system encompassing different political and ideological options. In Chile, as well as in most of Latin America, this means, above all, that the Right should unquestionably operate through parliamentary parties and renounce the authoritarian alternative. From this perspective, the construction of a system of parties could be construed as the unfolding of a "security net." This net would fulfill two essential functions in the process of democratic consolidation, as defined earlier. First, it would prevent a regression toward authoritarianism and second, it would provide an effective meshing of the main economic and social actors with a pluralistic system marked by the dominance of compromise and political exchange over violent confrontation. In the arena of political institutions, democratic consolidation requires the party system to provide an alternative way for the conservative forces to express themselves and gain access to power.

The second trait of the renewed Left is connected to the need to formulate a progressive alternative that can help avoid the dead end that is the result of the long cycle of growth associated with import-substituting industrialization and state intervention. This entails building social and political mechanisms that could help to recover the economic dynamism lost during the 1980s and to incorporate excluded sectors into the job and consumers markets. One of the challenges confronting the new South American democracies is that of using the state to create arenas in which to negotiate and elucidate divergent economic interests and orientations.

To a certain extent, the Left could be the greatest help in solving this problem. It is the only force that has the potential for recognizing it. The conservative parties uniformly preach the convenience of relying exclusively on the mechanism of the market—in which obviously naked economic power is the dominant currency. If this point of view prevails, as seems to be the case in several South American countries, the result could be an "emptying" or minimization of democracy, not its collapse. This would mean that the perspectives and ideas of those in government—one party or an alliance of several—and the manner in which they are elected—through free and competitive elections— could end up having little impact on the governing process and on the substance of government policies. In that case, the democratic election of high officials and a strict respect for the constitution and the law would not have any effect over the creation of public arenas for the definition and solution of significant collective concerns.

All this explains the somewhat exhortative title that I have given this chapter: The only option for the Left is to prevent politics from becoming an irrelevant process.

Notes

1. The most distinguishing characteristics of the double transition are described in Marcelo Cavarozzi, "Beyond Transitions to Democracy in Latin America," in *Journal of Latin American Studies* 24, no. 3 (1992): 665–684.

2. For a more extensive exposition on the segmentation of the Latin American Left, see my contribution in Jonathan Hartlyn, Lars Schoultz and Augusto Varas, eds., *United States–Latin American Relations in the 1990s* (Chapel Hill: University of North Carolina Press, forthcoming).

3. Hector Aguilar Camin, *La Guerra de Galio* (México, D.F.: Cal y Arena, 1991).

8

Internationalization and Social Democratization of Politics in Chile

Alex Fernández Jilberto

The crisis of the Keynesian models of industrial development, the failures of the neoliberal policies of economic restructuring applied in some countries of Latin America in the 1960s, the political genocide that preceded their implementation (in the cases of Argentina, Uruguay and Chile) and the complete support of the Socialist International for the political oppositions that confronted the neoliberal dictatorships have revived the question of the viability of a social democratic model in a period of democratic restoration. Indeed, a host of factors reinforce the need to examine this model in today's context. These include: the ideological influence of the debate on Eurocommunism, the social democratization of the "new democracies" of Southern Europe (Spain, Greece and Portugal), the political crisis of the Socialist countries of Eastern Europe, the "ideological renovation" of SI via the abandonment of its traditional anti-Communist Atlantism and of its Eurocentrist vision of international politics, the theoretical crisis of Marxism, the debate about "real socialism," democratizing political reforms, the economic reforms instituted in the Soviet Union by Mikhail Gorbachev and the partial reassessment of the mechanisms of the market in Socialist economies.

In general, there is too precipitous an association of the eventual political viability of social democratic actors with the existence of a third way of development. Under the experience known as populism, this third way had combined modernization and nationalism through models of self-supporting industrialization. The SI reassessment of social democracy in Latin America is taking place in a period of profound political crisis in European social democracy itself. This has resulted from what has been called the "crisis of Fordism," the crisis of the welfare state and the crisis of the Keynesian developmental policies carried out since World War II. These have provoked a neoliberal reconversion. The questions that this brings up refer to the possibilities and limitations of a social democratic alternative for a society like Chile. Chile is highly internationalized and has had a rigorous experience of neoliberal restructuring. At the moment it is going through a political process of democratic restoration. The study of this problem is the objective of the first part of this chapter.

The political experiences of countries like Argentina and Uruguay, which effected a transition toward democracy from the crises of the neoliberal, military dictatorships,[1] have brought up the issue of a restoration of populism. Because of the economic crisis, other populist governments such as those of the APRA of Alan García in Perú and of Carlos Andrés Pérez in Venezuela, have become defensive administrators of a political crisis in which they experienced complete failure. However, the expansion of the SI in Latin America has resulted not in the foundation of social democratic parties but rather in the reinforcing and/or assimilation of parties of populist origin. Consideration of an eventual social democratization of Chile suggests the need to delineate the historical, theoretical and conceptual differences between social democracy and populism. This will be the main goal of the second part of this chapter.

What is unique about Chile, when dealing with the issue of the viability of a social democratic alternative or of democratic socialism, is the legacy of neoliberal restructuring to which this society was subjected by the authoritarian state. This has generated radical changes in the social structure and in the relations between social classes that have basically altered the social context that had been the basis of both a moderate populist experience (Christian democracy, 1964 to 1970) and a radical one (Unidad Popular, 1970 to 1973). In addition to the external debt, this has caused an accelerated transfer of national sovereignty to the International Monetary Fund as well as a loss of political sovereignty by society since the population has to adjust its economic and social demands to the limits imposed by the IMF. The future impact of neoliberal restructuring on eventual social democratization is considered in the third part of this chapter. All this leads to the question concerning the characteristics of the national political actor that, in the period of transition toward democracy in Chile, could become the central element of social democratization. Thus, I have concentrated in the fourth part of this chapter on the Socialist Party and on its political transformation during the last decade as a consequence of the process of "Socialist renovation." Finally, I will offer conclusions and prospects regarding future redemocratization of the state and society in Chile.

Possibilities and Limitations of
Social Democratization in Chile

One of the most relevant political characteristics that can be observed in the prolonged effort to reestablish democracy is the marked internationalization of the Chilean political arena. The increasing political influence of international organizations (social democratic and social Christian) in Latin America that began in the mid-1970s and the political impact of the economic resources invested in grass-root social organizations by nongovernment organizations constitute a partial explanation of this phenomenon.[2] The greater orientation and adaptation of the internal structures of Chilean opposition parties toward international material resources and ideological demands constitute the other pole of a comprehensive explanation. Nongovernment organizations, with European financial support, have controlled the private institutes of social sciences. These institutes had consolidated their existence at the end of the 1970s, allowing the intellectual class to survive and assuring its preservation as a political class in a democratic state. On the other hand, the internationals, through their development aid, have assumed an influential role in their relations with social actors and national politicians. However, the fact that the internationalization of the political arena could stimulate a Socialist democratic alternative in the transition or consolidation of democracy in Chile depends on factors that are beyond the scope of this chapter.

The possibility of implementing a social democratic strategy that can make the idea of a third way a reality depends on the formulation of a model of economic development different from the ones applied during the last fifty years. This model is not free of problems or of ideological resistance from civil society. The first difficulty that comes up is the Messianic nature that historically characterizes the Chilean political elites.[3] Since the crisis of the 1920s, the idea that the successful implementation of development entails a re-creation or reconstruction of the nation has dominated the Chilean political arena. Reform, revolution, capitalism, socialism and noncapitalist development constitute the paradigmatic references around which social and political participants have articulated their ideas. The notion that society and the state are a social laboratory for the most varied ideas, all of which aim to produce a model thus far unknown, has dominated Chilean politics for the last half century. Demonstrations of this include the Chile Nuevo of the dictator Carlos Ibañez in 1927, the Revolución en Libertad of Christian democracy (1964–1970), the Via Chilena al Socialismo of Unidad Popular (1970–1973) and the Milagro Económico Chileno of the tyranny of Augusto Pinochet (1973–1990).[4] The people's skepticism regarding the supposed virtues of any new model (social democracy, third way and so on) has historical justification.

The second difficulty arises from the reassessment of the capacity of the state to intervene in social, political or economic problems. This is a hard task for a society that recently has been ideologically drowned in the antistate propaganda of neoliberalism and in the political Messianism of the military bureaucracy that has been controlling the state for the last fifteen years. But historically, Chile is a country in which state intervention and centralism have been inherent.[5] This has been exemplified by the replacement of the oligarchical state by a populist one after the crisis of the 1930s, as well as by the monetarist restructuring implemented by the military dictatorship since 1975. The neoliberal dictatorship interpreted the stagnation of industrialization as being a result of state intervention in economic development. It believed that between 1970 and 1973 the process had become one in which the state hindered and eliminated private enterprise.[6]

State capitalism, originating from import-substituting industrialization, was interpreted as a cause of the distortions in the functioning of the internal market, distortions that were made worse by the existence of protectionist policies. On the other hand, the relationship between industrialization and democracy, which resulted from the social program of the populist state, was considered to be the decisive political factor in economic stagnation. The democratic system created a legitimate space for the social actors to demand their rights, and this was considered to be negative for the process of capital accumulation. Democracy was presented as incompatible with the exigencies of development and economic growth.[7] To this was added the political radicalization of populism, which meant the crystallization of a Socialist political demand (1970–1973). This latter compromised not only the political stability of the populist state, since it subjected it to the political siege of a mass movement, but also the survival of the capitalist system. In this context, the military dictatorship established in 1973 attempted, through the state, to reverse forty years of development that had been characterized by the progressive inclusion of groups that had been excluded from enjoying of the benefits of development, by industrialization supported by the state and by the existence of a democratic system in a continuous process of refinement.[8]

The result was an effort at totally reshaping society by changing the state, the model of development and the manner in which the economy participated in the world market.

Another difficulty regarding the viability of an eventual model of social democratic development derives from the transformations undergone by the state, the social actors and the social classes as a result of the application of a neoliberal model of economic restructuring. The state lost the capacity to regulate the social inequalities generated by development. The reestablishment of this regulating function is indispensable to overcoming the social inequalities that have been aggravated by the transfer of this regulating function to the market.

The consolidation of power by the new bloc, which started to rule in 1973, was achieved through a process that undertook the reshaping of social classes and the structuring of an export economy. The bloc included a powerful front of businessmen who were also involved in the reorganization of the economy. This front was led by a group of financiers who gave cohesion to the bloc and had direct access to the international financial system. The bloc also included the armed forces, which in the same process had been transformed into a military bureaucracy with social, economic and political interests of their own. The two groups that form the bloc have a common origin, but their structure, interests and positions within the state are different, even though they both move toward the structuring of an export economy.[9]

The transformations in the structure and in the degree of influence of the social classes derive, to a large extent, from the new economic and political functions of the state.[10] These new functions, in turn, result from the fusion of the military bureaucracy and the neoliberal policy of economic restructuring. From this latter derives the substitution of the model of development founded on industrialization for one founded on agricultural exports. This would constitute the material basis for the changes in the structure of the social classes.

The changes in the structures, the relationships and the influence of the social classes radically altered the social basis of the populism that supported the process of industrialization with Keynesian economic policies.[11] This has a certain theoretical relevance concerning the possibilities of a social democratic policy in a period of restoration and consolidation of democracy in Chile, and it is especially important if one considers that populism is the political process that most resembles the European concept of social democracy.

Several studies indicate that the middle class is the one most directly affected by the transformation of the labor structure deriving

from the change of the economic functions of the state and the reduction in its size. The policies destined to reduce its influence were based
on the transfer of public sector companies and banks to the private sector. The decrease in the size of the state resulted in a significant reduction in public employment (nearly 25 percent) between 1973 and 1979. In
spite of the fact that this reduction was not compensated for by increased employment in the private sector, this process was called the
"privatization" of the middle class. This privatization and the expulsion of the middle class from the state apparatus (which had created
it during the long period of populism as a class of its own) deprived the
middle class of its capacity to exercise political pressure and reduced
its traditional role as the main modernizer of society.

The working class not only suffered the structural impact of the reduced role of the state as economic agent but also suffered the effects of
the unconditional opening of the economy to foreign trade, which stimulated the deindustrialization of the economy and reduced industrial
employment. The negative impact on industrial growth altered the influence of the working class on the rest of society.[12] This class then
found itself confronted with the fact that it had been reduced in numbers, had lost its strategic importance in the economy and had grown
less homogeneous. This compromised the classic image of a social
democratic movement supported by a powerful industrial working class
or by a union apparatus capable of decisively influencing economic policy. However, the working class's loss of its role as political protagonist was connected to a broader tendency toward less participation by
all wage earners in the secondary sector of the structure of
employment. This tendency started in the 1960s and has been noted by
several Latin American sociologists.[13] On the other hand, agricultural
workers were confronted with a series of transformations resulting in a
new agrarian structure. This process has been amply studied. It comes
down to the conjunction of three parallel processes.[14] The first has to
do with the changes occurring in agriculture as a result of the agrarian
reform initiated in the 1960s. The second process has to do with the
fact that plot owners created by the agrarian reform had some of the
best fertile land but were still poor peasants due to insufficient
working capital. In the third place, increasing impoverishment among
traditional small land owners and peasants occurred as a result of the
changing prices of agricultural products. The predominance of export
agriculture and its transformation into the main means of capital
accumulation has consolidated the restructuring not only of capital but
also of the working sectors. This is reflected in the cycles of activity
and passivity for the seasonal workers, whose jobs depend on the
changing volume of exports.

The main characteristic of this model of agricultural-export capitalism is the on-and-off quality of employment and the capacity of capital to reduce or enlarge the labor market according to the requirements of the international market. This is all done in a context of absolute job insecurity and complete lack of coherence between the period of work and the minimum subsistence needs of the members of the working class.[15]

Populism and Social Democratization

Several theoretical and political questions come up in the debates about the possibility of implementing a Socialist project as social democracy. These questions are linked to the characteristics of an economic policy limited by the neoliberal legacy of the Chilean dictatorship, and they are also connected with the possibility of a "neoliberal reconversion" of social democracy following the example of the new democracies of Southern Europe (Spain and Portugal).[16] These democracies have attempted to combine neoliberal policies with social protectionism and the selective intervention of the state in the economy. The difficulties in reestablishing Keynesian policies of reindustrialization,[17] in restoring the state role as developer (populism) and in maintaining the dynamic role of the modern exporting sector in the process of accumulating capital could lead to a reassessment of the economic policy followed by the social democracies of Southern Europe. This suggests that there is a need to reconsider the growing political influence of European social democracy in Latin America, which began in the middle of the 1960s.

In Latin America, the international process of political social democratization assumed characteristics that are notably different from the European ones. According to Michael Lowy,[18] this has neither regenerated truly social democratic parties of the past, nor created new ones. Also, there has not been a rapprochement between Communist parties and social democracy. What did take place was the linking of Latin American parties and movements, whose political natures could not be defined as social democratic, to the Socialist International. This includes populist currents as well as national parties and movements of an anti-imperialist and anticapitalist definition.

The diverse Latin American parties and movements that are members of the SI have their social and political origins in the development of national populism. They formed around peasant rebellions or around urban populism linked to projects of import-substituting industrialization in the period between 1930 and 1950.

They were organized as multiclass parties that considered themselves to be representative of the people on whom the national interest is based. They either lacked an ideological connection with socialism or had a marginal or merely rhetorical one. The middle class, the political class of the populist state, became the most dynamic actor in the modernization and industrialization of the economy. These parties articulated and combined the patronage, corporativism, bureaucratism and caudillismo of the political and social actors of society.

Populism had its origin in modernization based on industrialization that had been facilitated by international factors. Technologically, this industrialization was largely imported, and it aspired to replace and neutralize the effects of a dependent modernization by promoting development "from below" and "inwardly directed."[19] In order to limit the effects of national domination by international capital, an idea was developed—namely, that the objectives of development did not necessarily consist of increasing investment and the profitability of capital but rather of increasing participation in and integration of a society whose modernization threatened to increase its social heterogeneity. This understanding of the political actors, which in Latin America became assimilated into the concept of social democratic parties, contrasted with the political nature of the European social democracies. These latter were based on parties of working-class origin, directly linked with labor organizations. The parties adhered to a Socialist doctrine, were reformers of capitalism, had a Keynesian economic orientation and advocated the free world and Atlantism.

However, the convergence of the Latin American populist phenomenon and European social democratization arose from an ample conception of Western European socialism, when, in the capitalist democracies, it was identified with the application of Keynesian economic policies and with the utilization of state resources for the promotion of social egalitarianism. This is expressed in the aspirations for increased social welfare, for the redistribution of wealth and for state control of certain sectors of the economy. In this model, socialism does not go through either the stage of substituting capitalist relations of production or the stage of eliminating political domination by capital.[20] Without doubt, this model is closely related to the nationalist populism of Latin America and also to the most progressive versions, such as the "Chilean path to socialism" of Salvador Allende (1970–1973).

Several theoretical and political explanations have been offered regarding the internationalization of the SI and its expansion toward Latin America, which are discussed in Tilman Evers's contribution to this volume. This process took place in a context that abandoned the spirit of the cold war, Atlantism and the need to fight communism by means of North American policies in Latin America. The SI support for the political oppositions to the authoritarian states that were established in the 1970s sealed its political alliance with the democratic populisms of Latin America.

Social Democratization and Neoliberal Restructuring

The restoration of democracy and the reconstruction of the political arena in Chile will be conditioned by the legacy of the neoliberal restructuring of Chilean society. Politically, this restructuring consolidated the destruction of the Unidad Popular project (of the Socialist movement), which was characterized by its independence from both the SI and East European socialism. This restructuring also eradicated the anti-imperialist ideology from a significant segment of the Chilean intelligentsia. However, from the political point of view and with the prospect of an eventual social democratization of the political arena, the economic transformations have profound social consequences.

When regarding the impact of the economic transformations on the different social classes, particularly on the working class, we can distinguish two tendencies. The first emphasizes the loss of the "structural weight" of the working class,[21] expressed in the increase of its heterogeneity and in the lessening of its size and strategic economic importance. The political implication of this involves questioning of the role of the working class as a protagonist in the policies of social change. The second tendency rests on the idea of a restructuring of the working class as a result of the neoliberal transformations of the economy and, particularly, because of the dynamic role of the agro-exporting sector. This interpretation supports the moderate conceptions of the opposition,[22] which stress the idea of a "Socialist renovation" supported by a new realism, derived from the modernization of the economy. This seeks to combine the preservation of the efficiency of the export economy with "labor-union pragmatism" in order to prevent the disorganization of the economic model.

In spite of the polemic nature of both interpretations, the structural changes they describe are not contradictory. The political defeat of the dictatorship in the plebiscite of 1988 was based on an alignment of social forces that emerged from the transformation of the economy and the new relationships among the classes. The restructuring of capital and the accelerated internationalization of an economy based on agro-exporting capitalism has adapted the work force to the expansion and contraction of exports, through the restoration of seasonal work in agriculture. This "flexibilization" of the labor market has been the fundamental mechanism of capital for its adjustment to the international market. The source of this type of laborer is the rural population and the have-nots in the large cities. This use of the urban poor explains the political relevance of the urban social movement that depends on grass-root organizations for subsistence, housing and the search for political representation at the local and national levels—all of this in a country with five million poor people.[23] The poor have been a substantial part of the social resistance to the neoliberal regime and would be the main obstacle a democratic government would have to confront if it sought to continue these economic policies. The urban social movement combines the demands for subsistence with the search for a structural insertion in the productive process (and in employment) in opposition to the cyclical insertion offered by the economic policy.

The Social Democratization of Segments of the Opposition: The Socialist Renovation

At the end of the 1970s and beginning of the 1980s a new theoretical reasoning was articulated to take the place of the political paradigm that had been the foundation of leftist opposition to the authoritarian state.[24] It contained a double logic: the acknowledgment of the failure of the opposition in their attempt, since 1973, to substitute the dictatorship with a democratic regime and the ideological influence of the debates about Eurocommunism and about the real socialism in the countries of Eastern Europe. To this was added a crisis in and division of the Socialist Party, as well as a change of tactics by the Communist Party that replaced its policy of an anti-Fascist alliance (including the decisive participation of Christian democracy) with the tactic of "acute violence." This created a crisis in the political bloc of Unidad Popular that had supported the Allende administration and opened the way for an ample "revision," attempting two things: first, to bring under discussion the strategy this political bloc had used regarding the dictatorship and second, to replace the classical paradigm on which socialism in Chile was based and also to discuss the "democratic nature" of Marxism. These are two central tendencies of the leftist opposition that came together with the political defeat of the dictatorship in the plebiscite of 1988. The first of them, represented by the Socialist Party (Nuñez group), favored connection with Christian democracy and with political segments of the old Right. They were originally grouped together when Alianza

Democrática was formed in 1983, and they stimulated the regrouping of democratic socialism through the Socialist bloc. The main strategy of this tendency was to bring about the forced integration of the authoritarian regime and institutionalism. The second tendency initially gathered around Movimiento Democrático Popular, Izquierda Unida and el PAIS. Its political core was the Communist Party and the Fracción Almeyda of the Socialist Party. Their strategy of democratic restoration was based, beginning in 1980, on the policy of popular rebellion of the masses that included military resistance to the regime.

In the efforts among the Left toward renovation, there was ample consensus that the transformations carried out by the dictatorship have resulted in substantial changes in the social structure of society. The relevance of this to the Left came from the close relationship that it established between its political project and its social base of support. The economic transformations would affect its traditional base of support (the working class and the traditional sectors of the middle class). The classical paradigm departed from the assumption that socialism would be the logical result of the "universalization" of the interests of the working class. The increasing importance of this class—thought to be the historical bearer of the future of a society—depended on labor organization and on the role of the class party and its capacity to gain the support of the middle class for its project. This was based on the hypothesis of the continuous expansion of the political and economic influence of the working class as a result of the inevitable expansion of industrial development.

From the formal point of view, the political process of renovation or social democratization of the Socialist Party (Nuñez) started with the debates of the Ariccia (Italy) seminar in March 1979. The concept of renovation should be understood as an effort on the part of the Left and particularly on the part of sectors of the Socialist Party to reformulate and revise their program, the theoretical conceptualizations underlying their political practice, their means of action and their party apparatuses. The central topic of the seminar was "Chilean Socialism: History and Perspective." This seminar confirmed the presence in the social struggles of the last century of two great politico-ideological currents. The first of them was communism, identified with the Soviet version of Marxism and characterized by great doctrinal and organizational cohesion. The second one was socialism, whose relative ideological confusion and marked dispersion led to increasing political sterility. These characteristics had caused a political and ideological vacuum among the social forces, which were fighting the dictatorship and generated the need to seek a convergence. The need was also felt to create a theoretical basis serving the reconstruction of a Socialist area that would express the people's receptivity to the Socialist call and reestablish the party electoral capacity of the last five decades.[25]

The Socialist Party had, since 1964, been losing consensus and authority over the grass-roots support on which it had rested. This facilitated the appearance of other ideological groups of similar perspective. Examples are political organizations such as Movimiento de Izquierda Revolucionaria (MIR), Izquierda Cristiana (IC), and Unión Socialista Popular (USOPO). The adhesion of the Socialist Party to Marxism since its foundation never meant a connection to a codified set of immutable precepts. Now there was the need to come up with a new project of the Chilean popular movement capable of defeating the dictatorship and of attaining the complete democratization of the country, following Socialist principles. This democratizing project had to be an autonomous one, following the historical tradition of Chilean socialism's independence from the ideological influences of both the Soviet Union and the SI. It had to be based on the representation of the interests of not only the working class but also the middle class and workers in general. For this, social and political forces needed to be accumulated to facilitate the development of a "power of masses" inside and outside the "bourgeois state." This last objective was only to be attained in case of a gradual process of political and organic convergence of the constitutive organizations of the Socialist area. All of this was to create conditions favorable to the establishment of a political organization of a new type that would solve the insufficiencies of the traditional conceptions of the party and its relation with social movements.

Viewed in its totality, the debate about renovation was centered on the "historical separation between socialism and democracy." The resolution of this goes beyond the definition of democracy as space and boundary of the Socialist political action,[26] since it is the result of a popular political achievement rather than the simple concession of a decadent oligarchy or a generous bourgeoisie. The reassessment of democracy by the Left goes beyond its simple definition as "formal and bourgeois" and appears as the logical result of the experience of extermination lived through under the dictatorship.[27] It also entailed an interpretation of the experience of *Unidad Popular* and an attempt to identify the type of socialism to which it aspired. Its definition emerged from the consideration of two contradictory projects: the Marxist-Leninist one and the Chilean way to socialism, advocating democracy, pluralism and freedom. This allows us to advance to the conception that democracy is an uncertain arrangement of interests, it means advancing by negotiations, it is the frame for changing consensus, it is a system subject to uncertainty which, for this reason, does not tolerate irreversible gains, official truths or the immutable laws of history. Democracy, on the other hand, makes reforms possible even if they are major ones. It does not assure them, but it makes them attainable through the actions of the majority, through agreement and conflict, through effective persuasion.[28]

It is evident that such a conception of democracy amply acknowledges the right of capital to exercise political domination if it can achieve hegemony. This opens up the debate about the social democratization of the movement for social renovation.

The reconciliation of socialism and democracy and the abandonment of Leninism has suggested the need to have the movement for renovation, as well as the Socialist Party, identify with a process of social democratization. This identification is categorically rejected by both groups on the grounds that it corresponds to the historical experience of Western Europe. It is believed that the solution to the problems of Chilean society does not consist in transplanting models used in other places. It is argued that Chilean Socialists have been, from the very beginning, different from European social democracy and from the communists. They presented themselves as an original Chilean brand of revolutionary socialists. For others, the Socialist Party shares with European social democracy the idea of improving upon liberal democracy. However, "Chile is a Third-World country, a Latin American country, a country with an enormous socialist tradition that is very precise and very clear, posing radical transformations and changes."[29] It is important to remember that the third way (*tercera via*) in the Socialist Chilean tradition does not refer to an alternative between capitalism and socialism but rather to one between the Third and the Second International, that is, between East European socialism and social democracy. This also explains the systematic reluctance of this party to join the Socialist International. This latter group has to settle for the Partido Radical, which has only secondary significance in Chile. All of this leaves us with the question of what "radical changes" may mean and what really happens regarding the "revolutionary vocation" of Chilean socialism. The absence of a categorical answer is explained by the fact that in the view of the Socialist Party, the challenges of democracy have more than surpassed those of the revolution. The revolutionary content of socialism is equated to its capacity to transform social life. In this context democratic socialism refers specifically to the establishment of a political regime that abandons the idea of replacing the capitalist state.

The transcendence and the impact of the ideological transformation that the Socialist Party has undergone during this debate about renovation can be conveniently evaluated if we remember, for example, the Leninist political radicalism that this party utilized in 1974 to evaluate the causes of the defeat of the Unidad Popular administration. A document from the Dirección Interior, which survived the coup and was published in 1974,[30] stated that the defeat of Unidad Popular was an inevitable consequence of the inadequacies of a "vanguard" that was not capable of organizing the revolutionary potential of the mass movement. The lack of a "single proletarian direction" within the Socialist Party was said to be caused by the existence of "rightist deviations," "leftist snipers," "parliamentary cretinism" and "infantile extremism." The objective of a Socialist revolution aiming at the establishment of a "dictatorship of the proletariat" was reaffirmed. The debate on the Documento de Marzo and the conflict involving the internal and external departments of the party (in exile) were the origin of the future division of the party.

It is evident that the Socialist renovation movement is, to a large extent, the result of the ideological crisis of the Socialist Party that culminated with its division in 1979. There was a partial reunification later on (with the exception of the Almeyda party) and the recruiting of other minor parties, such as Movimiento de Acción Popular Unitaria (MAPU) and Movimiento de Acción Popular Unitaria Obrero y Campesino (MAPU-OC) that had gathered around the Movimiento de Convergencia Socialista and Bloque Socialista. The crisis had started with the conversion of the party to Marxism-Leninism during its XXII Congress (Chilean) in 1967. The "Bolshevizing" of the party was permanently resisted by its social democratic, populist and nationalist branches, which advocated an authentically Chilean party detached from international organizations. The confrontation between these groups continued even during the period of the administration of the Unidad Popular (1970–1973). During these years, the moderate or reformist political tendencies were not represented by the Socialist Party but rather by the Communist Party. The latter wholeheartedly defended the original spirit of the "Chilean way to socialism" expressed in the government program of the Unidad Popular. The content of this strategy was a model of social change that sought to transform the class character of the Chilean state without first destroying it. It also supported a radical process of democratization. The polemic between the "reformist" tendencies of the Communist Party and the "revolutionary" tendencies of the Socialist Party acquired the form of a debate about economic policy, particularly about the degree of state control of the economy. The so-called

Arrayan Agreements stressed the conflict between the two lines and studied in depth the tactical differences between the two parties at the core of the Unidad Popular. The Communist Party adopted the slogan "consolidation in order to advance" as an alternative to the economic crisis, implying that the mobilization of the masses hindered the control of the popular government. Luis Corvalán, secretary general of the Communist Party, stated:

> The main objective of the revolution is not the acquisition of power, but the transformation of society, the creation of a new economic, political, social and cultural order. To increase production, it is urgently necessary to improve the direction of the economy by giving the workers more participation, more power in the direction of the enterprise, thus producing a real change in the relations of production by having the workers understand that things have changed, that the increase of productivity is the basis of the continuous improvement of their situation, of enlarged industrial reproduction, and of the accumulation necessary for more investment and for social betterment.[31]

The Socialist Party, on the contrary, had the opposite thesis and denounced the bourgeois character of the state that justified the mobilization of the masses in an effort to gain complete political control.[32] The essential part of the economic policies of the last stage of the Unidad Popular administration was described by Minister Orlando Millas in the following terms:

> What is characteristic about this particular situation is that the relations among the different forces have changed to the detriment of the working class and of popular government. This has happened because of political errors that can be summarized by saying that they constitute transgressions of the program of *Unidad Popular*. It is fitting, then, to stress the defense of the popular government, its preservation, and the continuation of its work. It would be unfortunate to continue to increase the number of its enemies. On the contrary, it will be necessary to make concessions and, at least, neutralize the middle layers of society and certain other groups by correcting some tactical errors. Under these conditions, it is not helpful to the revolutionary process to publicly state what we will do in the future when there are more favorable conditions.[33]

The conflictive coexistence of the two strategic lines that was so obvious during the Unidad Popular administration has been a consistent element in the ideological history of the Socialist Party.

The division of 1979 and the ideological stability, no doubt transitory, that had been obtained by the Socialist Party (Nuñez) as a result of the process of renovation were not firsts in the political history of the party.[34] This did not have to do only with the "normal" internal conflicts of a party strongly affected by the political instability of society; its extreme adherence to ideology and the ambiguity and generality of these ideological principles also contributed. In 1933, for example, at the moment of its foundation, its connection to Marxism had a purely "methodological" character, that is, the party accepted Marxism, enriched and corrected by the scientific study of a constantly changing social reality, as a method for interpreting reality. Fifteen years later, at the National Program Convention of 1947, the pragmatic sense of the utilization of Marxism was reaffirmed when the party maintained that

> Socialist doctrine is not a set of static dogmas, but rather, a living conception, essentially dynamic, expressing in the realm of political ideas the creative tendencies of the modern proletariat. . . . Socialism does not formulate absolute principles of universal abstract value, nor does it rest on a metaphysical concept.[35]

However, in the real politics of the late 1930s and beginning of the 1940s, during the period of radical governments of the Popular Front, internal divisions abounded and resulted in the formation of the Partido Socialista Popular. This crisis had been preceded by the first division that occurred during the process of selecting presidential candidates in 1938. It began when some of the members of the group decided to support the dictator Carlos Ibañez. This led to the founding of Unión Socialista. The second division resulted in the creation of Partido Socialista de los Trabajadores. This occurred after the VI General Ordinary Congress in 1939 and issued from the debate over whether to continue to support the Frente Popular administration. The third division took place during the IX General Ordinary Congress, Rancagua, 1943. The new party, Partido Socialista Auténtico, was headed by Marmaduke Grove and José Domínguez and was determined to continue supporting the government of Frente Popular. In 1946 the presidential candidate of the party was defeated, having obtained a mere twelve thousand votes. At the XI Congress of the same year the direction of the party, in the hands of Bernardo Ibañez, was defeated and Raúl Ampuero became secretary general. The division of 1952 came about when the party decided to support the presidential candidacy of General Carlos Ibañez and those opposed to it formed the group Movimiento de Recuperación Socialista headed by Salvador Allende. This group united with Partido Socialista de Chile and formed the group called Partido Socialista. The latter, together with the

Communist Party, the Democratic Party and sectors from the Radical Party, organized the Frente del Pueblo, which selected Salvador Allende as the presidential candidate for 1952. This was the first experience of political alliance with the Communists that twenty years later, in 1970, would result in the electoral success of the Unidad Popular. General Ibañez included three Socialists in his cabinet; Clodomiro Almeyda, Felipe Herrera and Carlos Altamirano.[36] In 1957 the Congreso de Unidad de Partido united the majority of the members who had abandoned the party, and it was not until the XX General Ordinary Congress that the next split occurred. This time it was caused by the prestige of a militaristic ideology derived from the political impact of the Cuban Revolution and resulted in the creation of Movimiento de Izquierda Revolucionario. The division of 1967 made the expulsion of Raúl Ampuero definite, generated the Unión Socialista Liberal and was the last one before the Unidad Popular victory in the presidential elections of 1970.

Conclusion

When considering the possibilities of a third way based on a social democratic political project for Chile, the first surprising thing, from a European perspective, is the vast experience this country has in dealing with a strategy of this type. It is necessary to remember that the forty years that preceded the establishment of the neoliberal dictatorship of 1973 were characterized by the implementation of a third way model that was supported by the most varied political participants. In the development known as *arreglo democrático chileno* (the Chilean democratic agreement), national development was considered to be an objective shared by all the social actors. It was based on a Keynesian economic policy of industrialization supported by the state and directed toward a protected internal market. This economic policy was stimulated by the presence of a democratic political regime.

Since the era of the Frente Popular (1938–1947), the consensus regarding the need to industrialize the country was undermined by social tensions coming from two irreconcilable tendencies, expressed in the dilemma of "higher salaries or more accumulation." The incorporation of the working class into "official" political structures started during this period. The workers progressively replaced their initial Socialist orientation with a commitment to industrialization and modernization combined with income redistribution. The popular parties, on the other hand, set their goals beyond a more equitable redistribution of income to a consideration of the "historical illegitimacy of capitalism." Both explain the emphasis on democratic legality, as well as the social democratization adopted so early by the Chilean Left. The democratic character of the Chilean way to socialism in the 1970s is also explained. From 1958 to 1970, three administrations supported by different political coalitions, ranging from the Right to the Left, dealt with the accumulation-distribution dilemma. It was precisely the failure of the conservative government of Arturo Alessandri (1958–1964) that created the favorable political conditions for a radical project of capitalist modernization based on the increase of state intervention in the economy. Basic reforms had to be carried out in the agrarian sphere, and the mining export sector had to be nationalized. This view was shared by Christian democracy as well as by the leftist parties that later formed the Unidad Popular. The first supported the project as a "populist-reformist" policy of the "third way" or "revolution in freedom," the latter as a "Chilean way to socialism."

The restoration of a reformist strategy compatible with a social democratic model was hindered by the internationally proven inadequacy of the Keynesian development policies. At the same time, the legacy of neoliberal restructuring has been accepted as irreversible by the majority of the Center-Right and Center-Left opposition because of the booming export economy. Therefore, the restoration of democracy in Chile has been accompanied by the continuation of economic policies that were established by the authoritarian regime and that had left an accumulated "social debt." The parties forming Concertación por la Democracia had a program that established the solution of this problem as a priority. It demanded in fact the convergence of a neoliberal economic policy and political action of populist or social democratic leanings. This option is helped by the reconciliation of the Center-Left Chilean intelligentsia with the legitimacy of capitalism. At the same time, however, it will enable them to become a political elite in the new democratic state at the cost of its past political commitment to social change. The present political weakness of the Socialist Party—now subordinate to Christian democracy—is another factor compromising future possibilities of social democratization, particularly since Christian democracy has demonstrated in the past an enormous political capacity to implement progressive alternatives and even radical forms of social populism.

The political agreement that culminated in democracy and the election of President Patricio Aylwin in November 1989 facilitated the transition of the Socialist Party toward neoliberal positions. The same happened with the rest of the democratic opposition. The constitutional reforms approved in the July plebiscite completed the formulation of a political regime, confirming an ambiguous and dominant position for the armed forces that almost comes down to a "political cohabitation" of the military bureaucracy and the civilian regime. The victory of the parties of the Concertación por la Democracia in the parliamentary elections had included a strong showing from the Right and from the military regime sympathizers. This narrowed the room for maneuver of the democratic government in its attempts to modify the institutional bases established by the authoritarian regime.

The absence of a mass movement to restore civil and political rights after seventeen years of dictatorship can be explained, in part, by the political legitimacy of the new democracy. The neoliberal economic policy of the democratic government was supported by a categorical commitment to macroeconomic stability as the best formula for sustained economic growth, the increased internationalization of the economy and, finally, a growing effort to improve health, education, housing and social planning.

The Aylwin administration leaned on the political direction of the group of parties united in the Concertación por la Democracia. Within this coalition, the parties had a minimal political autonomy. This bred social passivity. This political stagnation also affected the parties of the Right and of the old regime. They remained associated with the maintenance of the military status quo and with the continuation of the economic policies defined by the dictatorship. This creates a serious problem in the present political conjuncture since it interferes with the institutional modifications that are necessary for the full democratization of the political system (municipal regime and two-party system). These modifications will be the result of difficult negotiations and will be limited by the need for political support of the military bureaucracy.

In addition, the neoliberalization of the democratic opposition— including the Socialist Party—should be considered. This phenomenon ended the situation of having two types of opposition to the military regime. Previously, the dividing line between the different sectors of the opposition was drawn by the type of political reference they made to the role of the state. For some the reestablishment of democracy meant the replacement of the authoritarian political regime and nothing more; others went beyond that and stressed the necessity to radically change the type of state that had been defined to design and implement neoliberal economic policies. The neoliberalization of the political forces that support the Aylwin administration places Chile's new democracy in a situation similar to that of the authoritarian regimes that characterized the conservative democratization of Argentina, Uruguay and Brazil. The search to reconcile neoliberalism and real democracy constitutes the central problem of the Chilean transition.

An important part of the neoliberalization and social democratization of the Chilean Left is explained by ideological changes among the Chilean intelligentsia itself. We see these changes reflected in the production of the private social science research institutes that had foreign financing (especially from European nongovernment organizations) and employed intellectuals who opposed the authoritarian regime. The studies of these institutes criticized the neoliberal economic policies of the military regime and its human rights violations, analyzed the "new social movements" and the conditions necessary for a future process of democratization and reviewed the consequences of the foreign debt. Such studies have a common focus. Studies of the dictatorship analyzed its repressive aspects, excluding all references to the ties between that policy and the economic and military elites of the United States and Western Europe. The violence of the state was studied only as a case of human rights violations expressing social domination. The central political concept characterizing these studies was that of a conflict between liberal democracy and military dictatorship. The role of the ruling classes was deliberately ignored, parting from an assumed autonomy of civil society. The studies on social movements were isolated from those on political class. The classes' heterogeneous internal social composition was emphasized that would make the participation of social movements in a common political project impossible. The idea of "social movement autonomy" was launched. It cut social movements loose from their ideological ties with most politically radical sectors. Only one viable option was stressed by the democratization studies: An agreement had to be reached between the democratic opposition and the civil/military conservative sectors. In practice this led to a type of democracy based on the acceptance of the viability and legitimacy of the neoliberal restructuring implemented by the authoritarian state. Considering the political deterioration of other redemocratization experiments (Brazil, Argentina and Perú), the accelerated neoliberal transmutation of the Chilean social democratic sectors could transform them into actor/managers of a political conformism in permanent search of a consensus with the authoritarian Right.

Notes

1. Philip O'Brien and Paul Cammack, eds., *Generals in Retreat: The Crisis of Military Rule in Latin America* (Manchester, England: Manchester University

Press, 1985); Alfred Stepan, *Rethinking Military Politics: Brazil and the Southern Cone* (Princeton, N.J.: Princeton University Press, 1988); James M. Malloy and Mitchell A. Seligson, eds., *Authoritarians and Democrats: Regime Transition in Latin America* (Pittsburgh, Penn.: University of Pittsburgh Press, 1987); Larry Diamond and Juan Linz, "Politics, Society and Democracy in Latin America," in Larry Diamond, Juan Linz and Seymour Martin Lipset, eds., *Democracy in Developing Countries* (Boulder, Colo.: Lynne Rienner, 1989); Guillermo O'Donnell, Philippe Schmitter and Laurence Whitehead, eds., *Transitions from Authoritarian Rule: Latin America* (Baltimore, Md.: Johns Hopkins University Press, 1986).

2. Franz Hinkelammert, "Socialdemocracia y Democracia Cristiana: Las Reformas Sociales y sus Limitaciones," in *Nueva Sociedad*, no. 3, 1981, pp. 155–170.

3. Javier Martínez, "Chile Nuevo: Une Fois Encore?" in *Chile: Une Project de Revolution Capitaliste, Special Issue of "Revue Amerique Latine,"* no. 6, 1981, pp. 27–29.

4. Barbara Stallings, *Class Conflict and Economic Development in Chile, 1958–1973* (Stanford, Calif.: Stanford University Press, 1978); James Petras, *Politics and Social Forces in Chilean Development* (Berkeley: University of California Press, 1969).

5. Mario Gongora, *Ensayo Histórico Sobre la Noción de Estado en Chile en los Siglos XIX y XX* (Santiago: Ediciones La Ciudad, 1981).

6. Humberto Vega and Jaime Ruiz-Tagle, *Capitalismo Autoritario y Desarrollo Económico: Chile 1973–1981* (Santiago: Academia de Humanismo Cristiano, 1983); Joseph Ramos, *Neoconservative Economics in the Southern Cone of Latin America, 1977–1983* (Baltimore, Md.: Johns Hopkins University Press, 1986); Alejandro Foxley, *Latin American Experiments in Neoconservative Economics* (Berkeley: University of California Press, 1983).

7. A. E. Fernández Jilberto, "Estado y Desarrollo," in *Nueva Sociedad*, no. 96, 1988, pp. 65–71.

8. Eugenio Tironi, *El Liberalismo Real* (Santiago: Ediciones SUR, 1986).

9. A. E. Fernández Jilberto, "Military Bureaucracy, Political Opposition and Democratic Transition," in *Latin American Perspectives*, vol. 18, no. 1, 1991, pp. 33–65.

10. Pilar Vergara, *Auge y Caida del Neoliberalismo en Chile: Un Estudio Sobre la Evolución Ideológica del Régimen Militar* (Santiago: FLACSO, 1986).

11. Javier Martínez and Eugenio Tironi, *Las Clases Sociales en Chile: Cambio y Estratificación, 1970–1980* (Santiago: Ediciones SUR, 1986); A. E. Fernández Jilberto and Fernando Polle, "Burocracia Militar y Transición a la Democracia en Chile," in *Boletín de Estudios Latinoamericanos y del Caribe*, no. 45, 1988, pp. 3–28; Guillermo Campero, *Los Gremios Empresariales en el Período 1970–1973: Comportamiento Sociopolítico y Orientaciones Ideológicas* (Santiago: Estudios ILET, 1984).

12. Javier Martínez and Eugenio Tironi, *Clase Obrera y Modelo Económico para América Latina: Un Estudio del Peso y la Estructura del Proletariado en Chile, 1973–1980* (Santiago: Ediciones SUR, 1983).

13. R. Slavonksky, "Los Cambios Estructurales del Empleo en el Desarrollo de America Latina," in *Boletín Económico para América Latina*, vol. 10, no. 2, 1965, pp. 76–87; F. H. Cardoso and José Luis Reyna, "Industrialización, Estructura Ocupacional y Estratificación Social en América Latina," in *Cuestiones de Sociología del Desarrollo* (Santiago: Editorial Universitaria, 1968).

14. L. Jarvis, *Chilean Agriculture Under Military Rule* (Berkeley: University of California Press, 1985); Jose Bengoa, *El Campesino Chileno Después de la Reforma Agraria* (Santiago: Ediciones SUR, 1984); S. Gómez, J. M. Arteaga and M. E. Cruz, eds., *Cambios Estructurales en el Campo y Migraciones en Chile* (Santiago: FLACSO, 1981).

15. James Petras, "The New Class Basis of Chilean Politics," in *New Left Review*, no. 172, 1989, pp. 18–27.

16. Otto Holman, "Felipismo or Failure of Neoliberalism in Spain," paper presented at the Annual Conference of the British Political Studies Association, University of Warwick, April 4–6, 1989; Rafael López Pintor, "Mass and Elite Perspectives in the Process of Transition to Democracy," in Enrique Baloyra, ed., *Comparing New Democracies* (Boulder, Colo.: Westview Press, 1987).

17. Raphael Kaplinsky, "The International Context for Industrialization in the Coming Decade," in Raphael Kaplinsky, ed., *Third World Industrialization in the 1980s: Open Economies in a Closing World* (London: Frank Cass, 1984); Carlos Ominami, "Désindustralisation et Restructuration Industrielle en Argentine, au Brásil et au Chili," in *Problemes D'Amerique Latine*, no. 89, 1987, pp. 27–37.

18. Michael Lowy, "Trayectoria de la Internacional Socialista en la América Latina," in Sofía Méndez, ed., *La Crisis Internacional y la América Latina* (México, D.F.: Fondo de Cultura Económica, 1984).

19. Alain Touraine, *Actores Sociales y Sistemas Políticos en América Latina* (Santiago: Ediciones PREALC/OIT, 1987).

20. David Slater, "Socialismo, Democracia y el Imperativo Territorial: Elementos para una Comparación de las Experiencias Cubana y Nicaraguense," in *Revista Estudios Sociales Centroamericanos*, no. 44, 1987, pp. 20–40.

21. Javier Martínez and Arturo León, *Clases y Clasificaciones Sociales* (Santiago: Ediciones SUR, 1987).

22. James Petras, "Transición, Política Electoral y Redefiniciones Políticas," in *Revista Andes*, no. 5, 1987, pp. 9–40.

23. Humberto Vega, "La Macroeconomia de la Pobreza en Chile," in *Revista Mensaje*, no. 369, 1988, pp. 17–21.

24. A. E. Fernández Jilberto, *Dictadura Militar y Oposición Política en Chile 1973–1981* (Amsterdam: CEDLA, 1985).

25. Leslio Basso, "Carta de Invitación al Seminario de Ariccia," and Raúl Ampuero, "Informe Introductorio (I) al Seminario de Ariccia," in A. E. Fernández Jilberto, ed., *Colección de Documentos para la Historia de la Oposición Política al Estado Autoritario en Chile* (Amsterdam: CEDLA, 1985), vol. 3.

26. Jorge Arrate, *La Fuerza Democrática de la Idea Socialista* (Santiago: Ediciones Documentas/Ornitorrinco, 1985).

27. Manuel Antonio Garretón, "Una Alternativa Socialista," in *Revista*

APSI, no. 53, 1985, p. 7; Tomás Moulian, *Democracia y Socialismo en Chile* (Santiago: Ediciones ASCO, 1983), pp. 6–9.

28. J. J. Brunner, "Una Propuesta Socialista," in *Revista Análisis*, no. 53, 1983, p. 11.

29. Carlos Briones and Jorge Arrate, cited by Ignacio Walker, "Un Nuevo Socialismo Democrático en Chile," in *Colección de Estudios Cieplan*, no. 24, 1988, pp. 14–15.

30. Partido Socialista de Chile, "Documento de Marzo," in A. E. Fernández Jilberto, ed., *Colección de Documentos para la Historia de la Oposición Política al Estado Autoritario en Chile* (Amsterdam: CEDLA, 1985), vol. 1.

31. Interview with Luis Corvalán, in *Chile Hoy*, no. 43, April 1972, p. 3.

32. Manuel Castells, *La Lucha de Clases en Chile* (México, D.F.: Siglo XXI Editores, 1975).

33. Orlando Millas, "La Clase Obrera en las Condiciones del Gobierno Popular," in *Revista Principios*, May–June 1972, pp. 13–24.

34. Fernando Murillo, "Dossier: La Crisis en el Socialismo Chileno," in *Revista Chile-América*, no. 54–55, 1979, pp. 3–22.

35. Carmelo Furci, *The Chilean Communist Party and the Road to Socialism* (London: Zed Books, 1984).

36. For the history of the Socialist Party, see Benny Pollak and Hernan Rosenkranz, *Revolutionary Social Democracy: The Chilean Socialist Party* (London: Frances Pinter, 1986); Paul Drake, *Socialism and Populism in Chile, 1932–52* (Chicago: University of Illinois Press, 1978); M. Hochwald, *Imagery in Politics: A Study of the Ideology of the Chilean Socialist Party* (Ann Arbor: University Microfilms International Michigan, 1981).

9

Venezuelan Social Democracy: From Populism to Pragmatism

Luis Gómez Calcaño

This chapter will deal with the evolution of Acción Democrática in recent years, the party that represents the social democratic option in Venezuela. Its doctrine and programs will be examined, as well as its policies during the administrations of Carlos Andrés Pérez (1974–1979), Jaime Lusinchi (1984–1989) and again Pérez, whose second presidency started in February 1989.

The analysis will be framed within the general operational tendencies of the Venezuelan political system and will, therefore, take into consideration the actions and programs of the other important actors: political parties and the organizations representing labor and business.

Acción Democrática has been redefining its interpretation of the social democratic creed in recent years, not unlike other parties of populist or reformist origin. It places less emphasis on those structural reforms that are directed by the state and that pursue income redistribution in favor of low- and middle-income groups. It increasingly embraces a "developmentalist" orientation instead, with a priority on economic growth that supposedly would create the conditions for improving the situation of low-income groups while avoiding the confrontations that could jeopardize social stability and the continuity of private investment.

However, this change of orientation is not adopted openly by the party or its leaders. The official language of the party reveals a strong tension arising from its attempts to maintain the "populist" identity in a situation where several of the fundamental postulates of the neoliberal approach are being accepted.

This tension is detectable in the economic policies of Pérez's present administration. They elicit as much or more criticism from within the party as from other political parties and interest groups. With the decreasing viability of the mechanisms of legitimation traditionally used in the interaction between the party leadership and the rank and file, internal disruption and division occur. The present crisis of Acción Democrática seems to express the difficulties of maintaining the promises of social democracy in the context of economic stagnation and a stifling of the external sector. Venezuela shares these phenomena with many other countries of the region. But beyond the purely economic aspects, the crisis shows the breakdown of relations between the state, the political parties and society.

Antecedents: Origins and Development of Acción Democrática

The fundamental doctrines of the present Venezuelan political system come from diverse sources. Its creed emphasizes modernization and development. Both notions are rooted in the positivism of the nineteenth century and were enriched by the modern theories of economic growth. At the political level, they include the ideas of secularization and universalism, which were used to justify a transference of power from the traditional oligarchies to new elites. The latter legitimate their position, referring to their association with modernity, innovation and advanced technologies but also to the popular will as expressed through universal suffrage. In Venezuela, these two dimensions of modernization seem to have been separated and in conflict for a long time.[1] The capacity, derived from oil revenues, to induce modernization without directly antagonizing the traditional dominant classes may have contributed to this. Actually, these classes found themselves benefiting from such modernization. All Venezuelan governments of the twentieth century, including the Gómez dictatorship, formulated and executed modernizing projects in different areas: public administration, infrastructure, the promotion and protection of industry, communications, basic services, housing, health and education. However, political "modernity," if we can apply the term retrospectively, was conceived in divergent and conflicting ways by the different political actors. The more conservative ones, while accepting in principle the universalist criteria of political representation and organization, demanded that these be applied gradually to avoid—as they saw it—the risk of handing excessive political power to demagogic manipulators of uneducated masses. The newcomers to the political arena associated the demand for political democracy without restrictions—defined above all by a universal suffrage that would include the illiterate—with the fight against socioeconomic inequalities. In this struggle, which was one between different versions of the same program rather than between truly antagonistic views, the "question" of Acción Democrática (that is, the question of the legitimacy of its access to power) played the role of synthesizing the political passions that existed from the foundation of the party in 1941 until well into the 1970s.

Acción Democrática has been considered one of the characteristic products of the modernizing process that I have mentioned. The suppression of the traditional parties carried out by the Gómez regime (1908–1935) favored the emergence, beginning in the 1920s, of movements and organizations unconnected to the party structures and doctrines of the nineteenth century. Arising from the urban middle class and from student movements against the Gómez regime, Acción Democrática was the expression of a reformist tendency within the movement of leftist opposition to the governments that succeeded the Gómez dictatorship. Its ideological roots combine elements of Marxism (since some of the founders had been members of organizations related to the Third International) with others of a modernizing character.[2]

The program and conception of the party have always been explicitly pluralistic and gradualist. The first government of Acción Democrática, sprung from the coup of October 18, 1945, promoted modernizing political and economic reforms and clearly established capitalist development as an inevitable stage to be carried through. The founder and principal source of AD's ideology, Rómulo Betancourt, was to say later:

> The Venezuelan political leaders of 1946 were—and still are—convinced that our country cannot skip the stage of capitalistic development. The situation we are going through requires a national-revolutionary transformation and not one adjusted to socialist or communist models.[3]

The main policies of this government included the realization of general suffrage, negotiations with the oil companies to increase the country's share of the revenues, the promotion of industry, support for workers' organizations and an increase in social spending.[4] In spite of its moderation in programs and in its policies, the first government of Acción Democrática was perceived by the greater part of the bourgeoisie as too impatient in its reformist strivings. They feared that its capacity to mobilize the masses would stimulate disorder and reduce productivity. The massive electoral support of AD caused opposing groups to suspect that the party would seek to monopolize power. The military, some of whom had associated themselves closely with Acción Democrática to carry out the 1945 coup, began to have second thoughts regarding the amount of control they would have. These tensions culminated in the coup that overthrew President Rómulo Gallegos in November 1948.

During the subsequent dictatorship and even after its fall in January 1958, the traditional leaders of Acción Democrática, headed by Rómulo Betancourt, concentrated on explaining the abandonment of the "revolutionary" character of their political program. This was confirmed by the agreement, signed before the elections of December 1958, to establish a coalition of the three main parties, explicitly excluding the Communist Party.

The first division of Acción Democrática then, in 1961, resulted in the exclusion of those sectors that had been most strongly influenced by revolutionary or Marxist ideas. The doubts regarding this position were dispelled by the confrontations with the radicalized and armed leftist movements during the 1960s.

Two subsequent divisions, in 1963 and 1968, helped to homogenize the party around a pragmatic identity that some have even defined as conservative.[5] The bureaucratization of the party cadres and their close relations with the state, especially during the periods when the party was in government, contributed to this pragmatism. The relationships between the local and sectorial leaders and their clientele were increasingly utilitarian rather than ideological.[6] Also, Acción Democrática has developed close relationships with business groups that finance its electoral campaigns and in exchange expect— and in many cases obtain—preferential treatment by the state. AD shares these characteristics with most other political organizations competing with it for power.

The Venezuelan Model of Development

Venezuelan democracy, redefined in 1958, was characterized by a relatively high degree of consensus among the participating actors. It was organized around a common program that attempted to synthesize the different modernizing currents. The basic principles of this program included a strategy of protected industrialization. Roles were clearly divided: The political parties ran a mediating and intervening state and integrated the basic organizations, especially the workers' unions. The military, for its part, agreed to submit to the civil authorities, while preserving privileges and areas of its own exclusive competence.[7] The bourgeoisie, in exchange for state protection, was to accept organized and politicized labor as a legitimate interlocutor, and it submitted itself to state intervention in several matters. This interventionism had a fundamental legal expression: "economic rights," such as the freedom to establish a business, to trade and to determine prices. These rights, even though they are included in the constitution of 1961, were suspended a few hours after their promulgation, and they remain suspended today. In recent years the business sector has been demanding the restitution of these rights.

This sociopolitical model had as its basic objective the creation of a modern welfare state.[8] But in spite of the privileged situation of Venezuela as an oil-producing country, the development attempted through this model has evinced certain insufficiencies and tensions since its beginning. The main problem concerned the difficulties encountered in decreasing the dependency on oil revenues. The attempt at import-substituting industrialization serving a protected internal market did not always create efficient enterprises. In addition, the limited size of the internal market increasingly restricted production and the creation of employment. In 1975, when the high level of oil prices in combination with the nationalization of the oil industry seemed to open paths to redirect the development of the country, the Fifth National Plan—produced during the first administration of Carlos Andrés Pérez—acknowledged the existence of these problems, which had remained unsolved and in some cases had even worsened. It mentioned the destruction of nonrenewable natural resources, the deterioration of the quality of life, the unequal distribution of income, the low growth rate of the sectors producing essential goods, the dependency on imported inputs with industry and the great inter-regional differences in development.[9]

In response to these problems the process of industrialization was deepened through investments in infrastructure and basic industries, which were to generate a better integrated production apparatus capable of producing a more diversified export package. But the attempt to realize this transformation within a few years created a huge foreign debt. Organizational problems caused the large investments in basic industry to be less productive than planned.

In this manner, the state changed from an actor with the greatest economic clout and relative autonomy to an investor besieged by debts and burdened with nonproductive companies. Similarly, the protection of industry strengthened economic concentration and generated a number of oligopolistic groups interconnected through activities in the most diverse sectors. Originally, these groups were rather modest in size and economic power in comparison with the resources controlled by the state. However, they gradually increased in magnitude and influence as the government accumulated failures. Apart from the oil industry and a few other isolated cases, the public sector has displayed a recurrent pattern of inefficiency in the bureaucratic-administrative sphere as well as in the production sector. Yet, it remained the dominant investor and probably will continue to be so for a long time to come. It ran up the greater part of the external debt in the process.

The loss of prestige and operational capability of the state resulted in growing difficulties while the basic political agreements of 1958 were carried out. Their implementation also depended on continuous economic growth, which in fact took place, with ups and downs, between 1963 and 1978. In the beginning of the 1980s, in the midst of the second rise in oil prices, the economy stagnated because of the continued failure to use the revenues properly and productively.[10] Economic stagnation was accompanied by much higher rates of inflation than the country had ever experienced, unleashing a struggle among the political actors in the area of income distribution.

The role of the political parties, especially of Acción Democrática as arbitrator between the demands of labor and those of management, became more difficult as the possibilities diminished to redistribute without affecting profits. Under the conditions prevailing until the end of the 1970s, public expenditure was the main agent of economic stimulus. Large government investments created a market for national and international companies that produced capital goods, developed technology and were involved in construction. Public employment strengthened the market for consumer goods. But the supply capacity of the national industry fell short, and the two oil booms fanned inflation.

The Social Christian government of Luis Herrera Campins (1979–1984) attempted a reorganization toward a market economy by trying to restore macroeconomic equilibria. However, reactions against his program were not long in coming, both from the workers who were hurt by the liberation of prices and from the employers whose protection had been decreased. The government restored price controls and accepted a law providing a general wage increase that had been pushed by the labor movement.[11]

The second rise in oil prices (1979–1981) did not reactivate the internal economy, and it resulted in an increase of imports, a worsening of the external debt and growing capital transfers abroad. When the oil prices came down in 1982 and 1983, the state entered into a financial crisis, culminating in the devaluation of the national currency and the establishment of a complex system of differential rates of currency exchange.

This system is in itself an expression of the types of social relations that had thus far been favored. The state would decide, according to socioeconomic and political criteria, the rates of exchange for the importation of different products and inputs for national production. In doing so, it controlled their prices, or more precisely, it subsidized them by granting scarce foreign currency at a preferential rate. The intention was to minimize the impact of the devaluation on the prices of basic goods and consequently to protect the situation of the lower-income groups. At the same time, the system of differential exchange rates gave the state considerable power to direct industrial production and investment through the selective assignment of foreign currency.

State intervention, which had been a characteristic feature of the sociopolitical model all along, intensified even more when practically all industrial production came to depend on the decisions of the government. Paradoxically, just at the moment when the economic capacity of the state was declining, its political and bureaucratic functions gave it the means to continue controlling society. The incompetent handling of the economy, as well as what was perceived as a lack of receptivity to public dialogue, contributed to the defeat of the Social Christian Party (COPEI) in the elections of December 1983, opening the way for the administration of Jaime Lusinchi, candidate of Acción Democrática.

The Administration of Jaime Lusinchi: The Transition Toward a New Model

The Social Pact: An Attempt to Respond to the Crisis

The administration of Jaime Lusinchi started with the promise of restoring concerted action, which had been severely limited in the previous administration. This was to be accompanied by a program designed to achieve social democracy. The VII National Plan, formulated in 1984, acknowledged that, ever since the establishment of democracy in the country, the workers had been postponing their socioeconomic demands to help ensure sociopolitical stability. Now the time had come to give democracy its true social meaning. Three major objectives were established: to restart economic growth, to accelerate social development and to create more freedom in society. The achievement of these objectives required two main conditions: the fashioning of a consensual political program, called the "social pact" and the reform of the state.[12]

In spite of these declared intentions, concerted action and social democracy encountered many obstacles, originating from the difficult economic situation and from the separation between government politics and the contents of its own program. The Confederation of

Venezuelan Workers (CTV) had proposed, since 1982, a law of costs, prices and wages. Its main instrument of implementation would be a commission including representatives of the executive branch, congress, management and labor. This commission would analyze the socioeconomic effects of any change in wages and prices, prior to approval by the government. Its functioning would offer the opportunity to put the concept of concerted action and the social pact to a test.

The law was approved in 1984 but in a modified form that left the final decisions concerning costs, wages and prices in the hands of the executive branch. It had been fiercely opposed by the business organizations. However, once the law had been decreed, the commission served for several months as an agency that legitimized price increases requested by business. When the CTV began to pressure for a discussion of the financial situation of the companies in order to view the possibilities of wage increases for the workers, the group representing the businesspeople (Federación de Cámaras, Fedecamaras) withdrew from the commission.

The failure of these attempts at concerted action led CTV to resort, once more, to the state as protector. Although CTV did not engage in mass mobilization nor in open confrontation with the government, the union leaders within Acción Democrática put pressure on the party in order to obtain some compensations.

The response of the administration, indebted as it was to the workers of the party (since their support had been decisive to the success of Lusinchi's candidacy), consisted of compensatory measures, such as subsidies and price controls on some basic products and moderate wage increases. However, these economic policies were being hindered by the difficulties in the renegotiation of the external public debt and by the fall of the oil prices in 1986. In February 1987 the government announced an agreement with the foreign lending institutions that improved upon the payment conditions agreed to in 1986. However, it was criticized both by members of the government itself as well as by the rank and file of the party and considered to be inferior to agreements reached by other countries with similar circumstances. In addition, it was believed to undermine possible collective strategies by the Latin American debtor countries.[13]

The attempt to maintain the policies of a sociopolitical model directed toward harmony and distribution had the opposite effect in practice. The Lusinchi administration was relatively successful in controlling inflation, and it even produced a moderate growth rate. But this had two important consequences. First, it caused the decline of the international currency reserves of the country to a point that made it impossible to avoid an arrangement with international financial organizations (especially the IMF). Second, the system of differential rates in currency exchange generated a huge network of corruption and official favors that affected the credibility and prestige of the political and business elites.

The Reform of the State: Attempts to Redefine the Model

The second essential element of Lusinchi's strategy was to designate, at the end of 1984, the Presidential Commission for the Reform of the State (COPRE), composed of high-ranking leaders in politics, business and other fields. After much discussion and consultation, the commission presented several plans in 1986. The proposed reform has been playing a central role in the political debate in Venezuela because it confronted the main actors with several of the most important dilemmas. The reform of the state was understood by the commission to be a basically political task, which should not be limited to a simple administrative reform. It should not leave the basic conventions of the political system untouched but renew them and make them more democratic and efficient. Among the recommendations made by COPRE, the crucial ones concern the model of development and the proposed political reforms.

The studies and proposals about the model of development produced by COPRE responded to its shortcomings, which have been demonstrated in the last few years. However, it has been extremely difficult to reach a consensus in this area. The debate has been influenced by the familiar themes in recent discussions about Latin American development. Two basic positions can be distinguished. First, there is the position that follows the neoliberal argument that a reform of the state should consist in a reduction of its excessive intervention in society, especially in economic life. The obstacle to overcome will be the populism that places an immediate distribution of income and wealth ahead of a strategy that promotes investments leading to higher productivity and greater benefits in the long term. Reforms will have to enlarge the role of market forces and reduce the role of the state, and they should include the restoration of economic freedoms, the privatization of some state-owned businesses and the rationalization of the state apparatus itself to reduce government spending.

The other position parts from the idea that the present problems of development originate in the elitist character of the political system, which tends to favor the most organized and economically powerful groups to the detriment of the majority. From this point of view, the central problem is not the magnitude and scope of government interference but rather its weakness in the face of pressure groups and the control and manipulation that the political leaders exercise over the organizations of the subordinate sectors.

The reform proposals that flow from this analysis concern a greater control by the electorate over the elected, the democratization of the internal structure of the political parties, the institutionalization of channels of participation for the autonomous organizations of civil society, the guarantee that the civil rights granted in the constitution be respected and in general the decentralization of power at all levels. For this program to succeed it is necessary to strengthen the state, making it more resistant to private pressures and supporting its leading role in development. Obviously, this approach appeals to those concerned about the weakness and not about the omnipotence of the state.

Between these two approaches COPRE had tried to find an intermediate path, which is reflected in a certain imprecision in its economic proposals. This can be seen in the discussion of two central problems of the model of development: the question of "economic freedoms" and the one about development strategies, especially where the role of the state is concerned.

In a document produced by a subcommission of COPRE in 1986, the significance and consequences of an eventual restoration of economic guarantees were evaluated. This was one of the demands made by several actors, in particular the businesspeople, during previous consultations. The document emphasizes that the Venezuelan constitution does not allow total economic freedom but rather establishes such restrictions as the prohibition of monopolies and the regulation of foreign investment. Furthermore, the same constitution dictates the general orientation of economic policy and establishes a mixed economy directed toward social justice. For this reason, the commission decided that no motive existed to justify the continued suspension of these guarantees and that their restoration would be an advance for the democratic process and would broaden the bases for the constitutional state.

The document was not approved by consensus of the full commission. On the contrary, it was opposed by those who felt that a full restoration of economic rights would lead to a further concentration of production and capital, disproportionately augmenting the already considerable political power of the wealthiest economic groups. However, until the present moment, neither the Lusinchi administration nor the Pérez administration have brought up the subject again.

In addition to the issue of economic rights, COPRE also dealt with the question of economic strategies. Several proposals for economic action at both the national and sectorial levels were elaborated. I will mention only the most general and most representative of the views of COPRE.[14] The document proposes as essential requirements that the strategy be a long-term one, be economically viable, serve a democratic society and maximize the welfare of the majority of the population. The principal points are:

- the gradual and selective opening of the economy, in accordance with the principle of comparative advantages;
- the redefinition of the role of the state in the economy;
- the articulation of economic and social policies;
- the subordination of the problem of the external debt and general financial policy to a strategy of growth.

Regarding the role of the state in the economy, the document proposed that state intervention be carried out more selectively and strategically and in a manner promoting respect for the rule of law in the economy. This implied the restitution of economic rights in such a way that state intervention would respect market criteria; promote democratization, deconcentration, and decentralization; and establish a flexible, competitive economy with high levels of scientific and technological development and producing according to internationally competitive standards.

This proposition reflects the influence of the topics introduced by neoliberalism in the discussions of the last decade regarding the need to favor the market and to redefine the role of the state. However, the tradition of a strong, interventionist, redistributive state remains present to the extent that social policies continue to play an important role, and the state is still being viewed as the only agency capable of leading the country with a strategy of growth.

This ambiguity can be found on a more operational level, as we shall see later, in the program and policies of the second administration of Carlos Andrés Pérez. But first, it is necessary to consider the proposals for political reform and the implications they have had for the Venezuelan political parties, especially for Acción Democrática.

Several analyses, carried out during the last few years, have agreed that two main problems of the Venezuelan political system have steadily worsened: the decreasing efficiency in the performance of its basic functions, and the growing concentration and centralization of power. Basically, the criticism centers around the gap between the promise to reduce social inequality, explicit in the democratic program of 1958, and the real progress made in this area. In addition a deterioration of the operational capacity of the state is diagnosed, which even hinders the performance of its minimal functions. These negative tendencies are reinforced by the fact that, due to the processes of political concentration and administrative centralization, the demands of the citizens meet with great obstacles on their way to the high levels of decisionmaking.[15]

The first proposals for political reform made by COPRE addressed these problems. The strategic principle underlying the proposals concerned vertical and horizontal democratization as part of an overall process. The main measures that were recommended refer to:

1. A further democratization of the political parties. To this end, among other things, the direct election of its leaders and of its local candidates, the periodic renovation of its mandate and the public supervision of internal elections was proposed;
2. Reforms of the Organic Law of Suffrage, to replace the system of closed tickets prearranged by the parties with a "nominal" system that permitted the selection of individual candidates;
3. Direct and secret election of state governors. This provision was part of the constitution of 1961 but had been suspended, and COPRE considered it one of the means to promote decentralization;
4. Reforms of the Organic Law of Municipal Government that had the objective of creating local agencies that would be more accessible to the citizens, would have more power and would be under the control of local organizations;
5. The financing of the political parties. The purpose was to establish partial public financing of the political parties, to reduce the cost and duration of the electoral campaigns and to introduce public control of the party finances.[16]

Acción Democrática and the Reform of the State

The idea of state reform was originally welcomed by all the political actors. The pluralistic composition of the commission, its political scope and high level of technical competence were equally applauded. However, from the very beginning, something paradoxical began to take place. The main opposition to the reform came from members of the ruling party itself. So the president of the party, Gonzalo Barrios, declared on his official appearance before COPRE in 1985 that what was needed was a massive educational campaign, as well as a reorientation of certain policies rather than a reform of the state.[17]

Upon publication, in 1986, of the proposal for immediate political reforms, the main leaders of Acción Democrática not belonging to COPRE were unwilling to accept the recommendations and, in some cases, even frankly opposed them. Manuel Peñalver, who was the general secretary, expressed his opposition to the direct election of governors and added that he would prefer to limit nominal elections to the municipal level. He summed up his position by remarking that "we Venezuelans are not Swiss," by which he meant that—in his opinion—the reforms were not the appropriate ones given the political culture of the country. Finally, even President Lusinchi began to distance himself from his own creation, accusing the commission, in a veiled manner, of attempting to deny the validity and legitimacy of the political parties.[18]

This resistance to the reforms can be interpreted, in part, as an expression of the internal struggle taking place in Acción Democrática. President Lusinchi had come to his office with strong party and national support. He obtained the greatest percentage of votes of any AD candidate since 1958. This gave impetus to his plan to remove Carlos Andrés Pérez from the leadership of the party. To this end, Lusinchi used the resources of the government apparatus as well as those of the party and the trade unions and succeeded in controlling the national convention of Acción Democrática in 1985. However, Lusinchi and his followers knew that the charismatic leadership of Carlos Andrés Pérez had remained a powerful factor with the rank and file of the party. Consequently, any attempt to broaden participation would benefit Pérez. In this context, the economic policies of subsidies, price control and wage increases would play a more important role in promoting the president's popularity. However, these initially successful economic policies quickly encountered their financial and political limits. The decrease in oil revenues in 1986 frustrated the hopes for solid economic recuperation. Unemployment and inflation remained at relatively high levels, fanning the dissatisfaction of the rank and file with the government, whose capacity to compensate them via patronage had decreased. Politically, President Lusinchi isolated himself from the party and surrounded himself with a group of close collaborators, many of whom were later accused of multiple instances of corruption and of improper use of their influence.

A favorable swing toward Carlos Andrés Pérez slowly gained momentum in Acción Democrática, so that, in the primaries of October 1987, Pérez defeated the candidate favored by the administration. Upon accepting the candidacy, Pérez declared his complete support for the proposals of COPRE. One of the first consequences of his success was the resignation of the general secretary, Manuel Peñalver, and the beginning of a readjustment in the balance of forces within the party.

The Resurgence of Carlos Andrés Pérez

At the moment of victory a complex redefinition process of ideological and organizational positions started. Pérez, who had become the symbol of a populist, spendthrift champion of the Third World during his first administration, now became the promoter of austere and technocratic policies of adjustment. Parallel to this, there was a change of image. Earlier, Pérez personified a personalist, charismatic, patronage-oriented leader. Now, he represented one interested in modernizing and democratizing the political structures. The antecedents of Pérez's Third World position are widely known. In an interview in 1981, he said:

> It is indispensable to start from the fact that today a progressive party in Latin America has to operate from a Third World platform, because it is here that we can find the possibilities, the sustenance for the political project of our times which is economic liberation and Latin American integration.[19]

His opposition to neoliberalism is equally well known:

> Well then, neoliberalism means handing over our economy again to big capital. In Venezuela a reconcentration of capital in the hands of a few is taking place. . . . Of course, the path is also being opened to allow the multinational companies to take over all of our basic economic sources, violating the norms set by the Andean Pact.[20]

The sociopolitical context of Pérez's second administration had a decisive impact on the reorientation of his plans. The 1980s were a decade in which neoliberal doctrines were being promoted worldwide, especially in Third World countries. Venezuela did not escape this trend, as is proven by the appearance, among the ruling elites as well as among the general public, of organizations devoted explicitly to the advancement of the neoliberal approach.

But other aspects of the Latin American sociopolitical process also had a profound influence: the failure of the populist governments, on the one hand, and the demands for the institutionalization of the political processes and structures, on the other. In fact, in some countries of Latin America during the 1980s, the attempts to make unorthodox adjustments that pursued both growth and redistribution resulted in failure. In some cases these had catastrophic consequences not only at the economic but also at the political level. Moreover, the transition toward democracy in the countries that had been governed by authoritarian regimes showed the need for strong and modern party and citizen organizations, capable of establishing stable mechanisms for concerted action. The dependence on a charismatic leader appeared to be an increasingly unstable foundation for political systems.

All of these factors should be taken into consideration when analyzing the electoral program of Carlos Andrés Pérez and the policies that were put into practice. The economic program had a strategy emphasizing a restructuring of industry that was to achieve greater productivity. The new definition of the role of the state in the economic sphere dictated an emphasis on market criteria, on efficiency and productivity and on a more competent use of the redistributive mechanisms. Finally, there was the plan to end financial restrictions through, among other things, a restructuring of the payments of the foreign debt. The specific policies were the liberation of the foreign exchange and interest rates, the gradual decrease of protection to industry, the liberation of most of the prices and a fiscal reform that would include the decrease and eventual elimination of subsidies, the restitution of economic rights and the privatization of nonstrategic public companies.[21]

This program included, though in a rather imprecise language, the main policies with which Pérez was to start his second administration.[22] In this sense, he cannot be accused of a sudden betrayal of populist promises. On the contrary, during his campaign he repeatedly warned that there was a need for great adjustments. And, as was made clear in later statements, the situation was worse than Pérez and his team had expected.

At the political level, the program reaffirmed the candidate's commitment to the main proposal of COPRE, such as nominal elections, the democratization of the political parties, the strengthening of municipal governments and diverse types of decentralization. Pérez was victorious in the elections of December 1988. He had a comfortable majority of the votes and broke the pendular movement between social democracy and Christian democracy, which had characterized the four preceding presidential elections. Now he had to face the task of carrying out an unpopular program of adjustments.

We Are Not Swiss: The Policies and the Reactions

The attempt to implement the economic program was to trigger the greatest expression of popular dissatisfaction since 1958. The decrease of the international currency reserves and the refusal of international banks to modify the conditions for the payment of the international debt forced the government to consider an agreement with the International Monetary Fund, which had been avoided by President

Lusinchi. The economic policies revealed to the country on February 16, 1989, and the letter of intent, handed to Washington on February 28, clearly followed the directives of the IMF.

The most important measures were: the elimination of differential exchange rates and their replacement by the market rate (at that moment, approximately two-and-a-half times higher than the preferential rate); an increase of interest rates; the liberation of most prices with a shortening of the list of (subsidized) foods included in the "basic basket"; an increase in the prices of fuel and of the main public services; and the elimination or reduction of the greater part of subsidies and of protective tariffs. To compensate for the effect of these policies, moderate wage increases for public employees (to a maximum of 30 percent), as well as a social program of aid to the poor, were announced.[23]

The proclamation of these policies produced tension among all political actors. Acción Democrática expressed reticence and doubts, and there was a demand for prompt implementation of the social programs to minimize the political effect of the package of economic measures. Some leaders demanded a general increase of wages and salaries, while others asked for a broadening of concerted action with other segments of society as well as for a consideration of the political consequences of the package in the next local and regional elections. The top representative of labor within Acción Democrática stated that CTV did not oppose the economic package but that it demanded compensations.[24]

Businesspeople also warned about the dangers of implementing the policies without compensations. The president of Fedecamaras expressed worries, on February 26, about "a strong popular reaction which could endanger the carrying out of the program."[25] There was an effort to engage in concerted action. CTV and Fedecamaras held meetings to try to determine the rate of wage increases for workers in the private sector. However, negotiations broke down when they failed to agree on the percentages.[26]

The first two policies to go into effect were the increase in the price of gasoline and the increase in fares for public transportation. The first went into effect on Sunday, February 26, and the second on Monday, February 27. The events that occurred in Caracas and other cities of Venezuela on February 27 and 28 started as a protest against the nonauthorized increase of fares in private transportation—taxis and small buses owned by their drivers. The protest spread to several areas of the city and eventually resulted in generalized looting, during which the security forces were overwhelmed. The ineffectualness and lack of coordination of the police, as well as the ample coverage given by the media to the looting, caused an increase in looting on Tuesday, February 28. It was then that the government suspended constitutional rights and increased repression. For the next few days, there were confrontations between military units and armed groups. The most important cities were virtually occupied by the military. The number of victims was very high.

The devaluation of the currency in 1983 symbolized the exhaustion of the model of development. The events of February 1989 are the equivalent for the model of political hegemony. In fact, these events demonstrated the ineffectuality of public organizations, especially the political parties. The state could not control the social protest through normal means and had to resort to military force.[27]

Once order was restored, President Pérez provoked strong reactions from the private business sector when he stated that the public protest had not been directed against the political parties but that it had been a protest of "the poor against the rich."[28] He also addressed the director of the IMF, reproaching the industrialized countries for their refusal to change the present conditions of exchange in the international market.[29]

In spite of this situation, CTV and Fedecamaras, perhaps driven by the events, managed to agree on a rate of wage increases for private workers, later extended to government employees as well. Had the events been consciously planned to obtain political objectives, these wage increases and the promises to accelerate the implementation of the social programs would have been their only accomplishments. Beyond the speeches and warnings, the response of the government can be synthesized in decrees 50 and 51 of March 1, 1989, which eliminated price controls with the sole exception of a "basic basket" that now had less than twenty food items. The program contained in the letter of intent to the IMF began to be carried out as if nothing had ever happened. The riots in fact demonstrated that the political parties had left civil society disorganized by not tolerating any organization other than those depending upon them. At the same time the tremendous capacity of the masses to destroy order through acts of disobedience was demonstrated.[30]

Slowly, the political actors began to abandon the passivity they had shown during the critical week and started to come up with responses to the situation. CTV called for a national strike to protest the economic package. This was a clear swing away from the initial position of the labor leadership within Acción Democrática, and it revealed the concern about their legitimacy among the masses who were being hurt by the economic policies, especially by the large increases in the prices of basic products that had been occurring since

March. Since the strike planned for May 18 seemed inevitable, the government decided not to oppose it. Acción Democrática maintained an ambiguous position since it did not officially support the action but granted its labor leaders freedom to carry it out.[31]

The action took place in a peaceful manner, except for a few isolated incidents between "discipline brigades" of CTV and small groups of nonunionized workers. But an evaluation of the effects of the strike on the economic and social policies does not allow for much optimism. The country was effectively paralysed on May 18, indicating that most of the workers were willing to protest. Nevertheless, the government seemed convinced of the validity of its policies and did not modify any of them. This attitude, rather than coming from a firmly neoliberal ideological position, seemed to derive from the pragmatic conviction that there were no alternatives to the program, especially since its application was one of the conditions for the renegotiation of the foreign debt and for the granting of new loans by international organizations.

Social Decay and the Crisis of Acción Democrática

The application of the economic policies had a more recessive effect than expected. The fall of demand, which came as a consequence of the price hikes and the increase of unemployment, aggravated the economic stagnation of the two previous years. This could have had especially serious consequences for Acción Democrática since at the end of 1989 there were to be municipal elections and for the first time— thanks to the approval of one of the proposals of COPRE—nominal elections of governors and mayors. This situation intensified the tensions between the groups that had been opposing each other since the previous administration. On the one hand, there were the people connected to the party apparatus who had managed to hold on to their high positions even after the defeat of their candidate. This group participated in the administration of ex-President Lusinchi, and it included a large number of leaders who were accused of corruption. The other group, gathered around Carlos Andrés Pérez, appeared more interested in modernization and democratization, and it took the struggle against corruption as its main objective. The first group tended to be more critical of the economic policies and opposed them within the party. The second group accepted the policies even though many of them did not share their ideological foundation. However, they were committed to Pérez's leadership, which led them to see the policies as inevitable.

The selection of candidates caused confrontations among different segments of the party. The consequence was that many members of Acción Democrática refrained from participating in the campaign and even in the actual elections. The results were surprising: In the first place, there was a 57 percent abstention rate, which was without precedent in electoral history since 1958. This was interpreted as a worrisome sign, especially considering that it was the first time that there was an opportunity for nominal elections of candidates for mayor and governor. Acción Democrática was able to maintain a relative majority, but it lost the governorships in nine of the twenty states, including the most highly populated, urbanized and industrialized ones in the country.

The defeat was interpreted along the lines of AD's internal division. For the group in control of the party, the result of the elections was fundamentally attributable to the economic policies; for the circles close to the government, the popular rejection was due to the corrupted image of the previous administration and in particular of several candidates who had been directly linked to it.

The general economic policies will likely continue to be directed toward adjustment and the restructuring of industry, in order to reinitiate growth. Under such conditions, there seems to be no viable means of attempting redistribution or advanced reforms. Acción Democrática is more and more steeped in an internal power struggle, and, in this strife, ideological questions are paid notably scant attention. Topics that have to do with the necessity to bring AD theoretically and programmatically up to date, with its position regarding neoliberalism and with the redefinition of the Venezuelan model of development occupy a minimum of space within the discourse of the main leaders of the party.

Conclusions

The coexistence of populist discourse and developmental policies has been consistent in Acción Democrática since its first administration. In this respect and in spite of the specific features of the Venezuelan situation, the hypotheses about the limitations of social democracy pointed out by numerous authors are applicable here.[32]

The effects of internal economic stagnation and of the crisis of the export sector add to these limitations. They further diminish the distributive capacity on which clientelist policies were based. Under these conditions, salvaging the legitimacy of the sociopolitical order would require a modernization of the state and of the political parties, in order to restructure their relationship to civil society. In fact, the ambitious program of state reform had attempted just that.

But, as we have seen, it is precisely the leadership of Acción Democrática that has most resisted the modernizing reforms. Some have been attained but only through the combined action of the most enlightened members of AD and other political parties and under the pressure of public dissatisfaction as expressed, among other ways, by the high percentage of abstentions in the last election.

It is also significant that the reform project did not originate from the core of the majority party but rather from a committee of notables who represented not the political parties but business, industry, academia, labor and even some radical leftist groups. This is one more indication of the transformation of Acción Democrática into a pragmatic political machine that has not been able, until now, to come up with a coherent program for dealing with the crisis. In fact, the economic and social policies of the Lusinchi administration were an attempt to preserve the model of state, party and society relationships that had been effective during the two previous decades but was collapsing under the new conditions. The policies of Carlos Andrés Pérez, as he himself admitted, followed the "technical" directives of the international financial organizations.

This incapacity for renovation has provoked the other political actors to respond in a way exemplifying the limits of the consensual model adopted in 1958. The neoliberal offensive intensified at every level, with a strategy designed to redirect the political culture of the country from state control and populism toward the market and individualism. The Socialist Left, on the other hand, has been moving closer to advanced social democratic positions that are difficult to distinguish from more orthodox versions. The low-income masses either belong to corporatist organizations controlled by the political parties or have remained unorganized. There are only a few autonomous, grass-root organizations seeking to develop political and cultural alternatives to the present order.[33]

A possible but not very probable result of this situation would be a division of Acción Democrática into an advanced group capable of promoting modernization and a conservative group. Such a development is hindered by the internal heterogeneity of each segment of the party, subdivided by individual and generational rivalries. At the same time, however, they are interconnected by a network of complicity of very long standing.

A more probable outcome is the electoral and political weakening of Acción Democrática, which would give way to options such as the one advanced by COPEI, intending to combine social Christian doctrine with elements of neoliberalism. The most optimistic hypothesis would be the renovation of all the political parties in such a way that they can recover public confidence and agree to play a less paternalistic role. However, the experiences of the last few years do not allow for much optimism. On the contrary, a swing toward an authoritarian regime cannot be ruled out if the deterioration of the prestige of the political elite and of the democratic system of government continues. Until now, Venezuelan social democracy has not been able to escape from the tendency toward pragmatism and the penetration by neoliberal ideas that has also influenced this movement in other countries.

Notes

1. Heinz Sonntag, "Estado y Desarrollo Sociopolítico en Venezuela," in *Cuadernos del CENDES*, no. 4, 1984, pp. 13–66.

2. Manuel Caballero, *La Internacional Comunista y América Latina: La Sección Venezolana* (México, D.F.: Ediciones Era, 1978).

3. Rómulo Betancourt, *Venezuela, Política y Petroleo* (Caracas: Senderos, 1969), p. 378.

4. Ibid., passim; Margarita López Maya, *Venezuela: Estado y Sociedad Política en Dos Epocas de Coyuntura* (Caracas: CENDES, 1986).

5. Caballero, *La Internacional Comunista*, passim.

6. Juan Carlos Rey, "El Futuro de la Democracia en Venezuela," in J. A. Silva Michelena, ed., *Venezuela Hacia el 2000* (Caracas: Nueva Sociedad-ILDIS-UNITAR/PROFAL), pp. 183–246.

7. Margarita López Maya and Luis Gómez Calcaño, "Desarrollo y Hegemonía en la Sociedad Venezolana, 1958–1985," in Margarita López Maya, Luis Gómez Calcaño and Thaís Maingón, eds., *De Punto Fijo al Pacto Social* (Caracas: Fondo Editorial Acta Científica Venezolana, 1989), pp. 35–62.

8. Ricardo Combellas, *La Democratización de la Democracia* (Caracas: IFEDEC, 1988).

9. López Maya and Gómez Calcaño, "Desarrollo y Hegemonía," p. 44.

10. Bernard Mommer, "El Petroleo en el Desarrollo Económico Venezolano," paper presented at the Second Congress of Engineers and Architects, Caracas, September 1986.

11. José Julian Hernández, *La Política de Liberación de Precios: Un Análisis Sociopolítico* (Caracas: CENDES, 1986); Thaís Maingón and Carlos Aponte, *La Ley de Aumento de Salarios de 1979: Un Análisis Sociopolítico* (Caracas: CENDES, 1989).

12. CORDIPLAN, *VII Plan de la Nación, 1984–1988: Lineamientos Generales* (Caracas: CORDIPLAN, 1984).

13. Luis Gómez Calcaño, "La Adaptación de un Sistema Distributivista Consensual Frente a la Crisis: El Caso Venezolano," in *Cuestiones Políticas*, no. 3, 1987, pp. 109–147.

14. Gerver Torres, "Lineamientos Generales de una Nueva Estrategia Económica para Venezuela," Committee on Economic Strategy of the Presidential Commission on State Reform, Caracas, 1987.

15. López Maya and Gómez Calcaño, "Desarrolla y Hegemonía," passim.

16. Comisión Presidential para la Reforma del Estado, *Propuestas para Reformas Políticas Inmediates: Folletos para la Discusión*, no. 1 (Caracas: Ediciones de la COPRE, 1986).

17. Ibid.

18. López Maya and Gómez Calcaño, "Desarrolla y Hegemonía," passim.

19. Carlos Andrés Pérez, "La Opción Socialdemócrata en América Latina," in *Nueva Sociedad*, no. 54, 1981, p. 120.

20. Ibid., p. 122.

21. Carlos Andrés Pérez, *Acción de Gobierno para una Venezuela Moderna* (Caracas: Ediciones de Acción Democrática, 1988).

22. Maria José Bello, *Los Cien Primeros Dias de Gobierno del Presidente Carlos Andrés Pérez* (Caracas: Escuela de Sociología UCV, 1989).

23. *El Universal*, January 17, 1989, and March 3, 1989.

24. *El Universal*, February 13, 1989.

25. *El Diario de Caracas*, February 26, 1989.

26. *El Diario de Caracas*, February 24, 1989.

27. For a description and analysis of the events, see *Cuadernos del CENDES*, no. 10, January–April, 1989.

28. *El Nacional*, March 4, 1989.

29. Carlos Andrés Pérez, "No Nos Permiten Rectificar Nuestros Errores: Carta-denuncia de Carlos Andrés Pérez al FMI," in *Nueva Sociedad*, no. 101, 1989, pp. 73–74.

30. Luis Gómez Calcaño, "La Vitrina Rota: Interrogantes Sobre la Democracia Venezolana," paper presented at the XV LASA International Congress, Miami, Fla., December 4–6, 1989; Luis Gómez Calcaño and Margarita López Maya, *El Tejido de Penélope: La Reforma del Estado en Venezuela, 1984–1988* (Caracas: CENDES, 1989).

31. *El Nacional*, May 13, 1989.

32. See, among others, Adam Przeworski, *Capitalismo y Socialdemocracia* (Madrid: Alianza, 1988), pp. 17–60.

33. Luis Gómez Calcaño, "Los Movimientos Sociales: Democracia Emergente en el Sistema Político Venezolano," in Silva Michelena, *Venezuela*, pp. 337–367.

10

Democracy and Political Disintegration in Perú

Julio Cotler

In 1980, after twelve years of military government, democracy was established in Perú, and elections took place in accordance with the constitution approved the previous year. Since then, there have been two general elections (1985 and 1990) and four municipal ones (1980, 1983, 1986 and 1989). Regional assemblies were instituted in 1990.

In 1985, three momentous events took place. To begin with, for the first time in forty years, one elected government succeeded another. Secondly, since universal suffrage guaranteed by the constitution allowed for the enfranchisement of illiterate people, most of whom were peasants of Indian origin, there was true mass participation in the elections. And finally, the results of the elections were accepted without argument.

These conventional indicators could lead the observer to the conclusion that Perú is consolidating its democratic regime. However, an entire decade of elections and of constitutional life has not succeeded in firmly establishing the democratic system. On the contrary, during this period the old problems have become worse, and new conflicts threaten national stability.

There are several indications of the seriousness of the situation. Economic and social problems have increased, making Perú the country with the largest number of poor people in Latin America. Close to 85 percent of the population lacks the means to satisfy their basic needs. The state apparatus has gone bankrupt. The uncontrollable growth of crime and drug-trafficking has affected the police, the judiciary and the economy. Subversive organizations have caused $18 billion in damage, a figure that comes close to that of the foreign debt. Twenty thousand people have been killed in the fighting between the army and the insurgents. The political control that the army maintains over half of the territory restricts democracy and results in numerous human rights violations. Perú is the country with the largest number of "missing" persons in Latin America. Insecurity and pessimism about the country's future have led many young people, professionals and businesspeople to emigrate.

In addition, the Peruvian government has come into conflict with the United States and with private banks concerning the foreign debt, drug-trafficking, subversion and human rights. Perú's international relations could get even more complicated soon. The effects of the social crisis and of terrorism may begin to be felt in neighboring countries and threaten the security of the entire region.[1]

In Perú, increased political participation has led, paradoxically, to clear signs of political disintegration that may have international repercussions. This chapter will analyze this situation and discuss some of the proposed solutions.

The establishment of democracy in 1980 was seen as the culmination of decades of struggle for political and social rights. It was hoped that these rights would reduce, if not eliminate, profound social, ethnic and regional differences and bring about the integration of Peruvian society.

However, the persistence of political structures inherited from the oligarchical past betrayed the expectations of the citizens. The type of democracy that has been practiced during the 1980s in Perú is one in which the political parties and the elected governments have not heeded the electoral mandate. In Perú, democracy has not been representative, and this has caused the appearance of antagonistic centrifugal forces that further erode the state's authority and legitimacy. However, there are efforts in the direction of altering this disastrous situation, and though these efforts may be based on necessity rather than conviction, they may lead, nevertheless, to the beginning of true democracy.

The Traditional Pattern of Political Behavior

The development of capitalism and the disintegration of the system of authoritarian domination during the first decades of this century and in the mid-1950s, led to the emergence of political parties. Alianza Popular Revolucionaria Americana (APRA), organized in the 1920s by Victor Raúl Haya de la Torre, claimed to be a nationalist, revolutionary party. The party gathered together workers and sectors of the middle class displaced from their traditional positions.

Beginning in 1931 and until the 1950s—with a brief hiatus between

1945 and 1948—the oligarchical bloc systematically repressed APRA and its social bases as a way of stifling their demands for change. Resistance to this repression made APRA, with its membership from the middle and lower classes of the provinces and the coast, a closed organization directly controlled by Haya de la Torre.

In the decade of the 1950s economic modernization resulted in social changes and demands to enfranchise the population. At this point, APRA allied itself with its opponents in order to have access to power within the framework of oligarchical legality. As a result, some of the new social actors rejected APRA, and a new party, Acción Popular (AP), led by Fernando Belaúnde Terry, appeared. AP had a reformist, distributive platform, and its members were mainly professionals, military and religious individuals and businesspeople interested in modernization through a method of "changing structures." The party also attracted elements of the lower and middle classes that APRA had neglected.

Both parties were closely controlled by their respective leader. They attempted to provide an opposition based on "all-encompassing" ideas and tried to provide a semblance of national unity by simply ignoring the plurality of the actors and demands.[2]

Hostility and distrust typified the relationships between the parties. These parties aimed at controlling the government and using their power to reorganize society according to their own postulates, seeking to benefit only their own members. This enmity between the political parties not only precluded political agreements but actually caused people to reject such agreements as immoral or perverse. Thus, APRA systematically opposed the AP administration (1963–1968), effectively blocking all attempts at reform. The result was governmental paralysis, a worsening of social and economic contradictions and a general spread of the climate of conflict.

Because the parties based their relations on patronage and had the tendency to propose their own specific interests as universal postulates, they negated one another, thereby assuring their political inefficiency, the paralysis of the state and the impossibility of establishing a pluralistic democracy. In response to this situation, new political actors emerged. They claimed to be the true spokespersons of all national interests, but they merely furthered the ongoing political fragmentation. Numerous ideologies such as Marxism, populism and the new ideas of the Catholic church became popular and helped deepen the differences between the "people" and the oligarchy.[3]

Under these circumstances, the military had no difficulty overthrowing the government in 1968. It established the Revolutionary Government of the Armed Forces under the leadership of Juan

Velasco Alvarado. The political parties countered by engaging in an exchange of mutual recriminations.

During its first phase (1968–1975) and contrary to what happened in countries like Chile and Argentina, the military government made important antioligarchical, nationalist reforms. It eliminated the dominant oligarchical class that had been the agent of foreign dependency, and it transformed the state (in place of the market) into the organizing and dynamizing agent of society. This was expected to achieve the anxiously awaited cohesion of society into an organic national entity.

In addition to property reforms, the government increased public expenditure and began a system of subsidies. It promoted social rights and organized the middle and lower classes. It also gave ample backing to businesspeople and entrepreneurs to expand the internal market in cooperation with an enlarged public sector. On the other hand, the military silenced the parties and their leaders, tried to control social organizations and denied them political representation. Using the classic argument that the parties expropriated society's power and threatened the organic cohesion of the "people," which only the army and its government could ensure, the military revolution pursued democracy in an authoritarian manner.[4]

This military government had created expectations that it found impossible to satisfy, and it found itself confronting the typical economic problems of populism.[5] There were clashes between different sectors of society and between society and the government, which were impossible to control. The political scene was inundated with irreconcilable ideologies and movements that stifled all possibility of political mediation.

The increasing radicalization of the popular movement and the divisions within the armed forces, at a time thought to be the eve of a war with Chile, caused the overthrow of Velasco Alvarado in 1975. He was replaced by General Francisco Morales Bermúdez.

However, Morales Bermúdez did not satisfy anyone. He failed to unite the armed forces and did not imitate the Argentinean style of suppressing popular demands, as many individuals in the military and business wanted. His government also failed to return to the socialism of the first phase, as many radical military men and other members of society wished. This unanimous dissatisfaction created a bellicose mood.

Increasing radicalization and strong pressure from multinational organizations, from the Carter administration, from businesspeople and from the political parties forced General Morales Bermúdez to prepare for political liberalization and the eventual transfer of power. He was also compelled to adopt an orthodox policy of economic stabilization, directed by technocrats and endorsed by the multinational organizations.

The political liberalization involved negotiations of the military with APRA and the Partido Popular Cristiano (PPC). The deposed President Belaúnde and the radicalized Left controlling the popular movement were ignored. Elections for the constitutive assembly were called for 1978, to be followed by another election to choose the president and legislators.

The new situation revitalized the parties and gave legal status to the semiclandestine leftist organizations. They now replaced the business and labor organizations that had been the main political actors until then. But the conditions underlying these changes asserted themselves once more.

The deposed President Belaúnde refused to participate in the elections for the constitutive assembly and to recognize the validity of the agreement made with the military. The leaders of the divided Left favored the continuation of revolutionary activities, but their constituents forced them to participate in the elections for the constitutive assembly. To advance their hegemonic goals, the leftists propitiated the political fragmentation of the masses. Because of their contempt for formal democracy and their belief that power should come from the barrel of a gun, they refrained from conceiving a viable political project. Instead, they turned the constitutive assembly into an arena in which to fight for the betterment of the masses and in which to oppose the economic policies of the government. They defined themselves as a semiloyal opposition.

Because of these circumstances, the new constitution was drawn up exclusively by APRA, represented by its chief executive, and by PPC, represented by Luís Bedoya Reyes. Caudillismo, social strife and antagonistic conceptions threatened to reproduce the classic inflexible opposition between APRA and anti-APRA forces. Bedoya Reyes criticized APRA and the Marxists and blamed them for the failure of the Belaúnde administration. He also reproached Belaúnde for his lack of firmness. His criticism extended to all who supported military reforms. Soon, he presented his own neoliberal proposals as the only valid alternative. Thus, since AP was not participating in the electoral scene, Bedoya Reyes's PPC (a splinter group of Christian democracy) became the neoliberal mouthpiece of the businesspeople and obtained the backing of the air force, the navy and the conservative sectors of the church. The Left failed to form a united front and resumed its competition for totalitarian, all-encompassing solutions to the country's problems.

APRA, on the contrary, was united behind its leader, Haya de la Torre. His unwonted moderation and appeal to the different social and political actors who were seeking to lay the basis for political reconciliation enabled him to gain a majority in the election. He was proclaimed president of the constitutional assembly and was given the status of national patriarch after fifty years of hatred and persecutions. APRA's surprising tolerance allowed for hitherto unheard of negotiations with the PPC and made the drafting and ratification of the constitution possible. APRA's abandonment of an excluding position and the new pluralistic image of Haya de la Torre seemed to ensure his election as president in 1980. His unfortunate death at this time provoked the embarrassing spectacle of a seditious struggle within APRA and the return of coercion. This, of course, revived old fears about APRA's intolerance.

In the meantime Belaúnde, back on the electoral scene and uncompromised by the vicissitudes of the transition, adopted the tolerant posture that had worked so well for Haya de la Torre. As a result, he obtained the majority of votes in the elections of 1980. He even had the support of one of the important leftist groups, which considered him a "lesser evil" than the APRA candidate or representatives of the Marxist-Leninist fringe.[6]

The response to Haya de la Torre and Belaúnde showed a significant change in the political attitudes of the majority of the voters. The public showed a preference for tolerant leaders who adopted pluralistic positions. But while in society at large political behavior was changing, this was not the case with the behavior of the political parties, as became obvious in the 1980s.

Democracy: Parties and Government Versus Society

The change of political regime occurred without modification to the system of party structures based on caudillos, oligarchies and clients. The parties continued to adhere to ideologies and interests that perpetuated their tendency to treat party membership as a privilege to be granted selectively. They also had no claim to any of the political achievements of the recent past since the collapse of the Peruvian oligarchical regime was brought about without the participation of the political parties. In addition, not all the parties believed in democracy itself but rather saw it as a means to gain power. In other words, the parties did not have the type of experience that would have allowed them to develop a tradition of negotiation and compromise. They adopted the facade of democracy without altering their traditional organization and behavior. The constitu-

tion, drafted by the parties, reflects this and grants broad discretionary powers to the president to distribute sinecures to particular
interests. The fact that there are no mechanisms of accountability
results in irresponsibility on the part of political leaders.[7]

The three administrations that have succeeded one another since
1980 started with ample citizen support. However, each of them
adopted policies that went against campaign promises and against the
interests of the groups that gave them electoral support. There was
nothing the voters could do to alter these policies since there were no
mechanisms for the enforcement of the electoral mandate. Thus, in
Perú, the Marxist contention that democracy is illusory and deceitful
has a glimmer of truth.

The events of the preceding twenty years in Perú raised the hope for
a more socially responsible and responsive way of doing politics. To
this end Belaúnde invited various parties to participate in his
administration. However, the divided and beaten APRA preferred to
take the position of "constructive opposition," while the leftist groups
ignored the invitation and accused the government of being the
representative of the "enemy class." But the government did gain the
support of the more compatible PPC, thus assuring the chief executive
a parliamentary majority. This parliamentary majority and the broad
powers given to the president by the constitution made it possible for
Belaúnde's and Bedoya Reyes's friends, relatives, technicians and
dependents to institute neoliberal policies. This had the approval of
multinational organizations and international banking. But while the
government contemptuously overwhelmed the parliamentary
minorities, ignored public opinion and betrayed the electoral mandate,
the masses resumed their position of intransigent struggle and became
increasingly radicalized.

The foreign debt crisis in 1982 and natural phenomena in 1983
produced a big drop in production, income and employment as well as a
blossoming of the "informal sector." This caused a state of crisis, said
to be the worst since the country's defeat in the War of the Pacific one
hundred years earlier. The lower and urban middle classes that were
already protesting were joined by manufacturers, regional interest
groups and the press. President Belaúnde's credibility reached a new
low, and, after three years, the paralysis of the government was
evident.

Once more, in accordance with the pattern established during the
1960s, political fluctuations and the repeated betrayal of the electoral
mandate caused the multiplication of political actors and their
greater radicalization, thus contributing to the increasing fragmentation of the political spectrum. It was under these conditions that the

Left was further divided, and one branch became legal while another resorted to armed insurgency.

The legal branch was formed after the elections of 1980 when the leftist groups organized a precarious association called Izquierda Unida under the leadership of Alfonso Barrantes. The leftist parties developed the same vices as the bourgeois parties. They were based on loyalty to a particular leader rather than on a political platform or set of principles, and they had "hegemonic" aspirations. However, IU achieved some success. Its participation in the legal process started an ambiguous and conflictive "reformist" process that allowed Barrantes to win the municipal elections in Lima in 1983 and to become the first Socialist mayor of a Latin American capital city.

A different type of leftist organization, Sendero Luminoso, appeared in Ayacucho in 1980. It was the product of years of preparation by intellectuals inspired by the Maoist cultural revolution. Ignored at first, the group conquered the imagination and loyalty of the youth of this archaic region and, in a few years, had consolidated itself in the central mountains. Based on Maoist-Stalinist ideology as interpreted by university professor Abimael Guzmán, SL owed its development primarily to the organization of teachers and students, who were later joined by peasants. Using coercion and assassination, Sendero Luminoso was able to supersede both the weak state and the fragile social organizations and to establish the bases of what it called "the republic of new democracy." SL also owed its success to the fact that the entire region had traditionally been exploited and/or neglected by the state. People in the central mountains are extremely impoverished and had been denied political representation.[8]

In 1983 groups disaffected from the Left and from APRA came together in *Movimiento Revolucionario Túpac Amarú* (MRTA). They were disenchanted with the existing political parties and with the manifest inefficiency of the democratic regime. MRTA was different from SL. Its members were mainly young people from the cities and the coast who were attracted to Castro rather than to Mao or Stalin. So we see that in Perú, the profound social fragmentation of the country was also reflected in its subversive organizations that were in bloody competition for revolutionary hegemony.

The establishment of a democratic system in Perú coincided with the increased importance of the drug trade. The jungle, where state presence was virtually nonexistent, became the center of cocaine production. It attracted tens of thousands of impoverished peasant families and rootless urban youths. Soon, the region had the largest demographic and economic growth in the country. SL and MRTA filled the vacuum left by the government. They competed with each other for control of the region. Both groups strove to protect the coca producers from U.S.-supported police repression and from the pillaging of the cocaine traffickers. The population accepted this protection, and, ever since then, the armed forces have had difficulties asserting state control over the area.[9]

These antistate phenomena are interpreted, in some cases justifiably so, as desperate reactions of the most impoverished segments of the population, particularly young people, against the exploitation of the democratic regime. This exploitation has been called "structural violence" by sectors of the church, and it has resulted in the unleashing of political violence. This is a situation that only a national consensus to change the course of Peruvian history could resolve.[10]

Even though Belaúnde first alluded to the insurrectional groups as simple cattle thieves and terrorists associated with foreign interests, he eventually had to recognize the political character of the rebellion. His response to the situation, however, was to hand the antisubversive struggle over to the armed forces and also to give them political control of the emergency zones. This meant that half of the country came under military rule. This political abdication, as it was termed by Amnesty International, produced innumerable unpunished human rights violations and has motivated countless protests in the country and overseas. The relationship between Belaúnde and the military was disturbed by the president's direct intervention in the military hierarchy as he made decisions about changes and promotions to assure himself the personal loyalties of the commanding officers. This is a practice, by the way, that was continued by Alan García and Alberto Fujimori. Besides restricting the autonomy of the military, civilian intervention has created divisions within the armed forces that, together with the insurrection, have curbed temptations to stage coups. But it has also caused disorientation and demoralization among the military. These conditions and the refusal of the government to satisfy the continuous financial demands of the armed forces have ensured the inefficiency of the antisubversive struggle.[11]

From the very beginning, the armed struggle has contributed to the political debacle by creating situations of irreconcilable opposition. Public disapproval of the rebels is equaled only by rejection of the governments that have ignored their electoral mandate and have instituted policies that increase poverty and accentuate the already abysmal social and economic differences. The public is also unhappy with the way the armed forces are carrying out their fight against the insurgents. The military leaders counter that they cannot achieve victory without the full support of society. They claim that, to defeat the rebels, they need to gain the allegiance of the people of the region. They need financial resources to reduce the poverty that is the main cause of the people's support for the rebels.

This abundance of problems eventually resulted in public demands for political conciliation and compromise. The two politicians who responded appropriately to these aspirations were Barrantes, who had increased his popularity as mayor of Lima, and García, who came to public attention when he implemented more democratic procedures within APRA and was instrumental in changing the party from an absolute monarchy to a democratic republic.

Both APRA and the leftist groups gained public support by vigorously opposing the notoriously inefficient AP-PPC administration. But while Barrantes had to contend with a divided Left, García could count on a disciplined party apparatus and on a platform that responded to a variety of national issues. The latter followed Haya de la Torre's and Belaúnde's examples of pluralism and established himself as a conciliatory, tolerant candidate. This gained him the support of diverse groups of voters in the elections of 1985, while Barrantes and Bedoya Reyes received limited support.

After García's election to the presidency, Perú presented a unique political situation. It had in government one of the oldest and most powerful political groups, APRA. It had IU, which gathered an important segment of the masses belonging to leftist organizations whose ideologies went from Marxism-Leninism to the ideas of the Catholic church. Perú also had Sendero Luminoso, an efficient insurrectional group. Businesspeople and the armed forces found themselves overwhelmed by this situation.

García's triumph and the fact that he had attracted voters from all segments of the political spectrum showed very clearly that the population had a will for democracy. This was a political defeat for the insurrectional groups. This triumph also made it very clear that candidates who transcended the limited political identities of their parties and sought to represent the interests of the population at large would win.

However, Alan García soon disappointed many hopes. Carried away by the euphoria of APRA's triumph after 55 years of defeat, he adopted the type of conduct traditionally displayed by the victor. Personal control of the governmental apparatus, based on his electoral success and on the resources of the presidency, allowed him to place people he trusted in key positions of the government and armed forces. His willfulness, his disinclination toward institutional mechanisms, his "heterodox" economic policies, his personal intervention in all executive functions and his use of direct communication with the masses made him resemble the traditional Latin American populist leader.

García limited payments on the foreign debt and boldly confronted the IMF to the country's unanimous approval. He subsidized industrial development and public consumption with measures reminiscent of those previously adopted by General Velasco Alvarado. He paid particular attention to the Andean region, where there is the greatest concentration of poverty in the country. His special program to provide jobs, designed to satisfy the much-delayed expectations of APRA's membership, resulted in an explosive growth of public employment.

The expectations were that these policies would win García the united backing of the members of IU and APRA (who accounted for 75 percent of the votes in the 1985 elections) and also attract businesspeople who were interested in the development of the internal market. This successful political integration would force the insurgent groups to lay down their arms and join the legal process.[12]

Significant economic recovery during the first year produced a honeymoon period during which García was unquestionably popular at home and internationally. He was able to assert his personal will above party and governmental institutions. However, the killing of 250 Sendero Luminoso prisoners in June 1986, for which the president was held responsible, together with the emergence of paramilitary groups, gained him acerbic criticism from various sectors of society. Leftist organizations broke with García, but their leader, Barrantes, negotiated with him behind the scenes. The Left criticized Barrantes's caudillo-like behavior to no avail. This brought about the paralysis of Izquierda Unida, culminating in its disintegration in 1989.

The rapid exhaustion of the scarce reserves accumulated by the Belaúnde administration, which had been financing García's heterodox economic policies, led to a sudden return of inflation and social protest, a situation aggravated by capital flight. Technocrats and leaders within APRA recommended a change of economic policy, which García willfully refused to heed. Instead, relying on the boost his orthodox economic policies had given him, he considered altering the constitution to permit his reelection. This led to complaints from elements within APRA and from the population in general.

In order to stifle some of the complaints, García decreed the state takeover of the banks in July 1987, blaming the bankers for the exportation of capital and for the state of the economy. After two years of governing, in which he had made close connections with the bankers to involve them in his endeavor, García decided that it was necessary to sacrifice them to advance his populist strategy. The hope was that García's attacks on the bankers, as representatives of the new oligarchy, would unite APRA, the leftist groups and the popular movement around him and fulfill his populist aspirations.

Instead, his betrayal of the bankers caused an incalculable upheaval that upset the political scene, demonstrating that the bankers were more capable of enforcing their electoral mandate than the parties and the people seemed to be. Government irresponsibility, it appeared, could be tolerated only when it affected the lower and middle classes. A "classist" grouping of businesspeople, the upper middle class, the media and the defeated AP and PCC hurled itself into a virulent campaign against the president that was reminiscent of the worst moments of antagonism against APRA. The moneyed classes wanted not only to annul García's initiative but also to prevent future dispossession. They also feared the establishment of a totalitarian regime like the one in México.

García's personal maneuvering, which placed the future of the party in jeopardy, caused anguish and dissidence among the leadership of APRA. The leftist groups supported him but in a confused and ambivalent manner. Within a few months, his political isolation became clear. The plan for state control of the financial sector, paralyzed in large part by the delaying tactics of APRA's majority in the senate, resulted in the government's loss of authority. However, the president did not give up his heterodox plans. This encouraged speculative activities that gave Perú one of the highest rates of inflation in the world.[13]

At the same time, García's reluctance to meet the demands of the multinational organizations and international banks caused Perú to be declared ineligible for any type of loan and to be isolated from the international financial community. Similarly, the administration's opposition to Washington's strategy against drug-traffickers and the systematic violation of human rights dangerously reinforced the isolation of the government and increased fears about its stability and that of the political regime.

Under these circumstances, unemployment and subemployment grew unstoppably, and nonunion labor became the rule.[14] Neither street demonstrations nor the unions could change this state of affairs. The previously powerful popular movement entered a period of paralysis, as did APRA and IU, which found themselves unable to channel social demands. Thus, the political parties could no longer fulfill their function of providing links between society and the state. The entire system—encompassing not just AP and PPC but also the other parties—was discredited.

Public rejection was very strong. Police officers, judges, teachers and physicians stoutly opposed the government, even at the risks of their jobs. The nation was coming apart at its seams as state and society grew increasingly separated. Meanwhile, insurgency expanded, changing the daily life of Lima and of other cities of the country. After two years in office, characterized by his personal willfulness, García had nothing left. His populism impeded the fulfillment of his conciliatory promises and culminated in state bankruptcy and social disorganization.

The opposition organized a forceful neoliberal assault led by Alvaro Vargas Llosa and inspired by the ideas of Hernando de Soto.[15] Vargas Llosa not only attacked, in a devastating manner, the capricious behavior of the president, he also extended his criticisms to the parties and their leadership for having tolerated and propitiated the development of nationalist and distributive ideologies. He also criticized the intellectuals for their support of totalitarian Communist regimes and the businesspeople for their attachment to business perks and "mercantilism," to use de Soto's term. He held these groups responsible for Perú's decadence and crisis.

Vargas Llosa accompanied his discrediting of the political parties with a defense of the democratic regime and a staunch opposition to the military coups that some bankers and politicians actively advocated. Through the application of fashionable neoliberal, antistate precepts, he hoped to achieve the modernization of the country using as his models Margaret Thatcher and Augusto Pinochet. His vibrant discourse revitalized the intellectual and political atmosphere. He advocated the ideas dominant in the Northern Hemisphere and provided an inflexible prescription for the problems of the country and the world. The evident disaster caused by populism and the crisis of Marxism helped validate his proposals.

In this manner, Vargas Llosa and his neoliberal message burst with great force onto the political scene and rapidly became the center of all political discussion. In addition to a categorical defense of the free market, the prestigious author made a demolishing attack on President García, on APRA and on the leftist groups. He made it possible for multiple and heterogeneous political and social groups to gather around him in the Frente Democrático (FREDEMO) and was expected to win the elections of 1990. Bankers, entrepreneurs, the upper and middle classes and technocrats, all with the support of the media, participated directly in politics, bypassing the political parties that had thus far failed them. When the reviled leaders of AP and PPC joined FREDEMO, they caused a state of internal competition that forced Vargas Llosa to act as arbiter.[16]

Vargas Llosa succeeded in gaining the support of the lower and middle classes, who were tired of the authoritarian and inefficient García administration as well as of the incessant infighting and public divisions of Izquierda Unida. But just when Vargas Llosa's electoral success began to be taken as a given and predicted in the public opinion polls, there was an unexpected reaction. APRA and the Left called attention to Vargas Llosa's radical neoliberal pronouncements against free education, social security, job stability and other social gains and to his declared intention to reduce public employment drastically and to apply an economic shock in order to reduce inflation.

The unconcealed association of Vargas Llosa and his retinue with the "rich," his reiterated and virulent attacks on his opponents and, in general, on those who did not align themselves with his platform as the only definitive solution to the problems of Perú and the world generated a sudden reaction against him. But this situation did not favor the discredited parties. The beneficiary was Alberto Fujimori, an obscure politician who led CAMBIO 90, one of many groups trying to break into the political process during election time.

With nothing to offer but criticism of the parties and the slogan "work, honesty and technology," he managed, in less than a month and through informal channels of communication, to capture dissimilar lower- and middle-class sectors of urban and rural areas who were disappointed with the traditional parties. Fujimori, the son of Japanese immigrants, had the support of the Protestant church, and he caused a political commotion that was not devoid of racist statements and religious animosities. This, however, did not impede his triumph against Vargas Llosa.

Instead of the wide majority he aspired to in order to implement his neoliberal program, Vargas Llosa obtained only 28 percent of the votes in the first round. His defeat was consolidated in the second round when many members of APRA and the Left turned against him, thus assuring Fujimori's success.

The results of the elections demonstrated beyond a doubt the fragmented character of the Vargas Llosa's public support and the speed with which political identities can change. The rich ("white"), who were traditionally associated with AP and PPC and had received the endorsement of the Catholic hierarchy, voted for Vargas Llosa; the poor, the migrants, the informal-sector workers and the peasants voted for Fujimori.[17]

Fujimori campaigned against shock measures and in favor of heterodox formulas based on consensus. However, he quickly changed his mind when he had to confront the legacy of hyperinflation and realized he would have national and international support only if he aligned himself with orthodox policies. Consequently, a few days after taking office, the chief executive requested extraordinary powers from congress as Belaúnde and García had done under similar circumstances. Thus armed, Fujimori initiated a policy of economic stabilization that had the approval of the defeated FREDEMO, multinational companies and the governments of the Northern Hemisphere. The citizens found themselves betrayed once more.

Since Belaúnde and García personally controlled the parliamentary majority, Fujimori's political base was precarious. He has tried to compensate for this by choosing as ministers well-known members of diverse political parties. He has also gained APRA's neutrality by remaining silent regarding the accusations about García and his administration.

On the other hand, Fujimori has used proven populist expedients to reduce popular disillusionment and protest and to free himself from the party requirements that limit his personal role. This style of government has provoked conflicts between the executive and the other branches of government since the president has interfered with both the judiciary and the legislative powers. There have also been problems with the parties and the local and regional governments. The entire situation tends to be additionally aggravated by the negative reaction to the neoliberal economic measures.

After he overcame the first obstacles in his fight against high inflation, Fujimori removed the ministers who overshadowed him or did not silently acquiesce to his personal schemes, and he turned to technocrats recommended by Hernando de Soto. These technocrats have taken decisive measures for the implementation of the neoliberal model proposed by Vargas Llosa and have gained the euphoric backing of the forces that the famous author had attracted. Another source of support is the military, to whom Fujimori has given complete freedom of action in their antisubversive struggle. In this way, Fujimori has established political alliances and objectives that are completely contrary to the ones that gained him the presidency, and, as in the past, the people have been unable to enforce their mandate.

The multiple conflicts that threaten to disintegrate the state apparatus have led several groups in congress to seriously criticize the president's abuse of the extraordinary powers granted to him. To improve the situation, Fujimori initiated negotiations with the legislative branch through the political parties' spokespeople. The purpose was to reach a "national agreement" that could eventually lead to regulated, interinstitutional negotiations.

To Make a Virtue of Necessity

National unity was a goal that the Morales Bermúdez administration tried in vain to achieve. This idea, which came out of academic-military circles, sought a gathering of "live forces" to solve the social, ethnic and regional conflicts and assure the governability and development of Perú. Alfonso Grados, labor minister in the Belaúnde administration, later formulated a similar idea. He proposed a pact between the state, businesspeople and the labor unions. However, this proposal received no support because, in the first place, it sounded like the corporative formulas promoted by the military, and in the second place, it included measures that were contrary to popular interests and demands.

However, social conditions have become increasingly precarious, popular organizations have lost their organizing capacities and terrorism and violations of human rights have increased to more threatening levels. In response, there have been diverse initiatives to pursue ways of reaching collective agreement, arrest the dominant dissociative tendencies and consolidate the democratic regime.

The situation has been educational. The crisis of Marxism, the democratization of Europe and Latin America and the emergence of different versions of neoliberal thinking[18] have encouraged the Left and the intellectuals to look at democracy in a new way. The political groups have reevaluated and revalued "formal" democracy and have developed the conviction that agreement and compromise are viable methods of bringing about social and national integration in Perú. This receptiveness to compromise and agreement extends to other organizations as well. Feminist groups, local and regional governments and neighborhood groups are all attempting to come up with rules and procedures conducive to the achievement of consensus. Human rights organizations and research centers have presented plans to promote political democratization and are trying to reach a national consensus with which to oppose the fundamentalist ideas of the past. Influenced by what is happening within the parties and the intellectual circles, labor unions and business groups are also arguing in favor of dialogue and agreement as necessary formulas for overcoming the crisis. The armed forces, aware of the fact that they need the consensus of society at all levels to succeed in the struggle against insurrection, have also formulated similar ideas.

While within the government itself there is a periodic revival of the rhetoric of consensus as a formula to ensure the governability of the country, the media and the intellectuals continue to criticize the "irresponsible" and caudillo-like behavior of the political class, as well as some of the administration's proposals to ensure greater democratization.[19]

It is under these conditions that representatives of contrasting social interests are coming together for the first time in an atmosphere of unprecedented tolerance. They are trying to overcome the fragmentation that until now has impeded dialogue and consensus.[20]

In response to the imminent danger of dissolution, there has appeared a new current of opinion that operates outside politics and the state. The goal is to establish communication among the many groups and to seek agreement and compromise as a way of bridging the differences that make the country so difficult to govern. If this also fails, the country will doubtless lapse into a war that could very well expand to other countries in the region.

Notes

1. As I write this, the danger that Perú poses to the entire region has increased, and it now includes matters of health. There is a cholera epidemic that has caused the death of over one thousand people and a loss of approximately $1 billion. This epidemic is directly attributable to the wretched living conditions of the population and to the persistent reduction of social spending during the last fifteen years. Perú is also a center of drug production (it produces 60 percent of the coca in the world market), and it has been instrumental in disseminating drugs to other Latin American countries. Regarding the threat of subversion, the government of Bolivia has expressed concern about the presence of some Sendero Luminoso members in the country. Vargas Llosa, in *La Historia de Mayta*, presents a scenario that anticipates a war between Perú and its neighbors in the case of an eventual Sendero Luminoso victory. In short, Perú is a threat to the entire hemisphere.

2. Giorgio Alberti, "Notes on a Framework for the Analysis of the Politics of Democratic Consolidation in Latin America," unpublished manuscript, 1990.

3. Julio Cotler, *Clases, Estado y Nación en el Perú* (Lima: Instituto de Estudios Peruanos, 1978).

4. There is an ample bibliography about the military government, including, among others, Carlos Franco, ed., *El Perú de Velasco* (Lima: Editorial Horizonte, 1983); Abraham F. Lowenthal, ed., *The Peruvian Experiment: Continuity and Change Under Military Rule* (Princeton, N.J.: Princeton University Press, 1975); Cynthia McClintock and Abraham F. Lowenthal, eds., *The Peruvian Experiment Reconsidered* (Princeton, N.J.: Princeton University Press, 1983); Alfred Stepan, *The State and Society: Perú in Comparative Perspective* (Princeton, N.J.: Princeton University Press, 1987).

5. On the economic policies of the military populism, see William Ascher, *Scheming for the Poor: The Politics of Redistribution in Latin America* (Cambridge, Mass.: Harvard University Press, 1984); John Sheahan, *Patterns of Development in Latin America* (Princeton, N.J.: Princeton University Press, 1978).

6. Julio Cotler, "Military Interventions and Transfer of Power to Civilians in Perú," in Guillermo O'Donnell, Philippe C. Schmitter and Laurence Whitehead, eds., *Transition from Authoritarian Rule: Prospects for Democracy* (Baltimore, Md.: Johns Hopkins University Press, 1986), part 2, pp. 148–172.

7. In Guillermo O'Donnell's unpublished manuscript, "Delegative Democracy?" (1990), these features are discussed as belonging to delegated rather than to representative democracy. See *SI*, no. 213, March 17–24, 1990, for a discussion of the excessive powers granted to the president and the critical response to this procedure. Hernando de Soto and his Instituto de Libertad y Democracia have criticized the irresponsibility of the political class and its "mercantilism." They have pointed out that the executive branch decrees about 26,000 administrative norms per year without establishing any means of control. They have proposed a program of democratization of government rules. See also Juan J. Linz, "The Virtues of Parliamentarism," in *Journal of Democracy*, Fall 1990, and Linz, "The Perils of Presidentialism," in *Journal of Democracy*, Winter 1990.

8. There is plenty of literature about this organization. See the publications of Carlos Iván Degregori: "Sendero Luminoso: Los Hondos y Mortales Desencuentros," in Eduardo Ballón, ed., *Movimientos Sociales y Crisis: El Caso Peruano* (Lima: Instituto de Estudios Peruanos, 1986), pp. 225–286; *Que Difícil es Ser Dios: Ideologia y Violencia Política en Sendero Luminoso* (Lima: El Zorro de Abajo Ediciones, 1989); and *Ayacucho 1969–1979, El Surgimiento de Sendero Luminoso* (Lima: Instituto de Estudio Peruanos, 1990).

9. For a Peruvian point of view on the production of coca and the drug traffic, see Diego García Sayan, ed., *Coca, Cocaína y Narcotráfico: Laberinto en los Andes* (Lima: Comisión Andina de Juristas, 1989).

10. *Violencia y Democracia* (Lima: Comisión por la Defensa de los Derechos de la Persona y Construcción de la Paz, 1988); Jeffrey Klaiber, ed., *Violencia y Crisis de Valores en el Perú* (Lima: Pontificia Universidad Católica del Perú, 1987).

11. Philip Mauceri, *Militares: Insurgencia y Democratización en el Perú 1980–1988* (Lima: Instituto de Estudios Peruanos, 1989); G. Gorriti Ellenbogen, *Sendero: Historia de la Guerra Milenaria en el Perú* (Lima: Editorial Apoyo, 1990).

12. Julio Cotler, "Los Partidos Políticos en la Democracia Peruana," in Luís Pásara and Jorge Parodi, eds., *Democracia, Sociedad y Gobierno en el Perú* (Lima: Cedys, 1988).

13. Rudiger Dornbusch and Sebastián Edwards, "Economic Crisis and the Macroeconomics of Populism in Latin America: Lessons from Chile and Perú," paper presented at the Second Meeting of IASE, Bogotá, March 30–April 1, 1989; Jeffrey D. Sachs, *Social Conflict and Populist Policies in Latin America* (Washington D.C.: National Bureau of Economic Research, 1989).

14. The last few years of the 1980s have been characterized by underemployment—only 20 percent of the active population is adequately employed—and by the destruction of the community organizations that, in one way or another, had established mechanisms of "competitive cooperation." These organizations have been replaced by a policy of each individual being on his or

her own. In addition, there has been an increase in Protestant churches, and many people appeal to quacks and false shamans in their attempts to regain some control of their social life. See the studies of Romeo Grompone, *De Marginales a Informales* (Lima: Desco, 1990), and *El Velero y el Viento: Actores Sociales y Política* (Lima: Instituto de Estudios Peruanos, 1991).

15. Hernando de Soto, *El Otro Sendero* (Lima: Institúto Libertad y Democracia, 1986). This celebrated book, which has been quoted by Reagan and Bush, was an early neoliberal indictment of the paternalistic state. It also provided the basis for the movement directed by Vargas Llosa and for the present neoliberal revolution.

16. Alvaro Vargas Llosa, *El Diablo en Campaña* (Madrid: El Pais, 1991).

17. On the campaign and its results, see Fernando Rospigliosi, "Polarización Social y Desprestigio de los Partidos Políticos: Los Sorprendentes Resultados de las Elecciones Peruanas de 1990," unpublished manuscript, 1990, and Carlos Iván Degregori and Romeo Grompone, *Elecciones 1990: Demonios y Redentores en el Nuevo Perú* (Lima: Instituto de Estudios Peruanos, 1990).

18. The process of democratization in Latin America has stimulated intellectual production and has helped broaden the themes of intellectual debate. This is a notable change that comes after 20 years of the intellectual and educational monopoly (in secondary schools and universities) of Marxism-Leninism. It has not yet been written about.

19. For the problems of modernity and the "Andean utopia," see Manuel Burga, *Nacimiento de una Utopía: Muerte y Resurrección de los Incas* (Lima: Instituto de Apoyo Agrario, 1988), and Alberto Flores Galindo, *Buscando un Inca: Identidad y Utopía en los Andes* (Lima: Instituto de Apoyo Agrario, 1987). The dissatisfaction with representative democracy has provoked proposals for "direct democracy." See Alberto Rocha, *Democracia Representativa y Democracia Directa: Una Via Posible de Democracia Mixta* (Lima: Instituto Peruano de Investigación Cientifica, 1991), and the much-disputed project of the Instituto Libertad y Democracia, *La Democratización de las Decisiones Gubernamentales* (Lima, 1991).

20. These meetings have resulted in books, such as Julio Cotler, ed., *Para Afirmar la Democracia* (Lima: Instituto de Estudios Peruanos, 1987) and *Estrategias para el Desarrollo de la Democracia en el Perú y la América Latina* (Lima: Instituto de Estudios Peruanos, 1990). They have also contributed to the creation of Inter Centers, organizations that group the main research institutes devoted to the creation of new mechanisms for reaching political consensus.

11

Social Democracy in Ecuador

Agustín Cueva

Ecuador was the first country in South America to establish a democratic regime after the wave of dictatorial governments of the 1960s and 1970s.[1] This happened on August 10, 1979, after three dictatorships: (1) the civilian dictatorship of José Maria Velasco Ibarra (1970–1972), a caudillo who had been president for five different terms, the last beginning in 1968; (2) the military dictatorship of Guillermo Rodriguez Lara (1972–1976); and (3) the military dictatorship headed by Vice Admiral Alfredo Poveda Burbano (1976–1979).

The return to constitutional life was easier in Ecuador than in other South American countries due to two interrelated facts. On the one hand, the military dictatorships had been relatively mild—if such a term can be used about dictatorships—when compared to similar regimes in other countries of the region (by sheer luck, Ecuador has not been subjected to truly cruel dictatorships in this century). The administration of Rodriguez Lara, for example, was characterized by its nationalistic, reformist tendencies, and, paradoxically, the civilian dictatorship of Velasco Ibarra was the most repressive of the three mentioned earlier. On the other hand, higher oil prices beginning in 1972, just at the time Rodriguez Lara was starting his presidency, diminished many sociopolitical tensions and, above all, awakened new hope.

In the elections of April 1979 (in the second round, as demanded by the Ecuadorian constitution, closely resembling the French system of "ballottage"), the winning ticket was that of the lawyer Jaime Roldós Aguilera, president, and Dr. Osvaldo Hurtado, vice president. Roldós Aguilera was a member of the Concentración de Fuerzas Populares (CFP), and Hurtado a member of Democracia Popular (the Christian democratic party in Ecuador). They defeated, by an overwhelming majority, the candidate of a right-wing coalition, Sixto Durán Ballán.

227

It is a sign of the times that, even though Roldós Aguilera was a member of CFP, a populist party, his attitude as president and his vision of the world placed him close to social democratic positions, which were then new in Latin America. This political evolution (to which we can add the struggle for hegemony between Roldós and his relative and sponsor, Assad Bucaram, the highest ranking leader of CFP) resulted in a constant fight between the legislative power, headed by Assad, and the executive power. This fight obstructed many of the progressive social initiatives of Roldós Aguilera. A division began to appear between traditional populism, on the one hand, and a certain social democratic manner of making policies, on the other. These kinds of social democratic tendencies began to emerge from the very core of populism, just as they had in many other South American countries. They were not to prosper, in the long run, due to the superior organic and ideological consistency of Izquierda Democrática and to certain regional differences and conflicts between the mountain areas (La Sierra) and the coastal ones—a topic that greatly exceeds the scope of this chapter.

On May 24, 1981, Jaime Roldós Aguilera perished in a strange plane crash, the circumstances of which have not yet been clarified; it was very reminiscent of that other air "accident" in which the victim was the nationalist Panamanian leader, General Omar Torrijos. Jaime Roldós Aguilera was replaced in the presidency, in accordance with constitutional previsions, by Osvaldo Hurtado, who remained in the post until 1984. Congress elected the economist León Roldós Aguilera, brother of Jaime Roldós Aguilera, as vice president.

Hurtado had to deal with the harsh economic crisis that, in Ecuador, started earlier than in the rest of Latin America due to the war with Perú at the beginning of 1981. This was really a "miniwar," but it constituted a real burden for the less than solid Ecuadorian economy, which became worse in 1982 with the generalized downturn of the Latin American economies. To this were added natural catastrophes in 1982 and 1983, such as serious droughts followed by great floods.

Hurtado and his party (founded in 1964 under the name Partido Demócrata Cristiano and renamed Democracia Popular after its fusion with a group from the Partido Conservador) did not have a solid popular base. The "Christian" element, which they claimed as their own, was really controlled by the conservative parties, and the "democratic" element, which was middle of the road, was virtually preempted by social democratic tendencies. The austerity policies that the president had to apply made him even less popular, and because of this, he inaugurated a bastardized form of legitimation that would become prevalent in the new and shining South American democracies: to govern not according to the wishes and hopes of the electorate or to the programs the people voted for but, rather, according to the concept of the lesser of two evils. For example, if there was danger of a general strike, the negotiations between the unions and the government would inevitably come to the point where the president or one of the ministers would warn the labor leaders that a successful strike could bring a military coup. This finally amounted to a "take it or leave it" situation. Under these conditions, the opposition to Hurtado came to be united by the engineer León Febres Cordero, a dynamic representative of the new Right. He led a radical opposition made possible by the fact that he had nothing to lose since if a coup occurred, it would be launched by the Right rather than the Left. Thanks to this device, Febres Cordero was able to win the presidential elections of 1984, even though he had only a narrow majority: 1,381,000 to the 1,299,084 obtained by Dr. Rodrigo Borja Cevallos, leader of Izquierda Democrática. The latter political movement had been founded in 1970 by Dr. Borja Cevallos, bringing together dissidents from the Partido Liberal, some independent groups and some ex-members of Socialist groups, and it had developed a great electoral appeal. It had only obtained 165,258 votes in the first electoral round of 1978 (the second round took place in 1979), with the same candidate that now received almost eight times as many votes.

Ecuador was the first South American country that returned to democracy. At the same time it was first in getting a civilian government of neoliberal orientation. The Latin American "new Right" prefers not to be reminded of this episode. The government of Febres Cordero was a true failure in the economic area, and—worse—it practiced an extreme authoritarianism. It was in fact more repressive than any of the dictatorships that I mentioned in the beginning. It was the first time that contemporary Ecuador lived in constant fear of a repression that was carefully directly and measured out by the state.[2]

In a historical paradox, the military insurrections led by Air Force General Frank Vargas Pazzos in March 1986 (which started by denouncing illegal activities of the government and ended by challenging its authoritarianism and arbitrariness) were the movements capable of checking the dominance of Febres Cordero. In any case, they were able to destroy the image of a new invulnerable Right against which little could be done without risk of precipitating a coup led by Febres Cordero himself. This hypothesis was absurd, if only because in the 1980s no armed forces in Latin America were ready to lead a coup in favor of a civilian. But a large part of the population believed this hypothesis because they had been frightened by a government that presented itself as almighty.

In January 1986, Febres Cordero called a plebiscite on an issue that appeared to guarantee him an easy victory. This, of course, would be interpreted as a vote of confidence in his government. What was being weighed was whether independent citizens—that is, those not belonging to any political party—had the right to run for office, a right that was not and is not permitted under Ecuadorian law. Febres Cordero's predictions of victory were not completely mistaken, because the majority of Ecuadorians remained outside the parties and because the government had complete control of the political situation. But the insurrections of March destroyed his image of complete dominance and undermined the political role of fear. The negative votes prevailed overwhelmingly in the June plebiscite. This constituted a virtual vote of censure against the Febres Cordero administration. An important thing to remember is that the hesitation of a large portion of the opposition was so great that ID, for example, did not officially support the no vote until May, when the outcome was already assured.

Febres Cordero ended up by playing the role of sorcerer's apprentice, but even then he did not learn from events. He continued engaging in all sorts of arbitrary actions, going over the heads of parliament and the judiciary, until one of his outrages had grotesque, although understandable, consequences. Febres Cordero refused to accept the amnesty granted by congress to General Vargas Pazzos. This transgression provoked the anger of the leader of Taura, the most important air force base in Ecuador. They kidnapped the president in January 1987 and forced him to free Vargas Pazzos. The decline of the government had reached its lowest point, and the way was paved for the triumph of the opposition in 1988.

The Time for Social Democracy

Given his political trajectory, as well as the conditions of his party (without any doubt the best organized in the country), Rodrigo Borja Cevallos began to appear, beginning in 1987, as the logical successor to Febres Cordero. However, Febres Cordero was determined to prevent this and, with that in mind, allowed Abdalá Bucaram, leader of the Partido Roldosista Ecuatoriano (PRE), to return from exile in Panamá. It was to be a complex game plan in which Bucaram would challenge Rodrigo Borja Cevallos and defeat him on the Center-Left of the political spectrum, while the Right, united around the candidacy of Sixto Durán Ballán, would get enough votes to go to the second round against Bucaram. Once more, Febres Cordero played the role of sorcerer's apprentice. In fact, for reasons we cannot examine here, Bucaram actually ended up taking votes from Sixto Durán, which was relegated to third place. The decisive election was, then, between Rodrigo Borja Cevallos, who got 744,409 votes, and Abdalá Bucaram, who had 535,482 in this first round.[3]

What political tendencies did each one of the contenders have? If historians would have only Bucaram's statement published under the title *Las Verdades de Abdalá* and Rodrigo Borja's essay entitled *Socialismo Democrático* at their disposal, they would doubtlessly arrive at peculiar conclusions. In fact, Bucaram defines himself as an "advance-guard social democrat, without following the Socialist International because that creates dependence." As far as Rodrigo Borja Cevallos is concerned, he emphasizes that neither he nor his party are social democrats but are democratic Socialists, "so that it will not be believed that it is possible to transplant social democracy to the Latin American tropical jungles, as some naive and misguided people suppose."[4]

The populist caudillo Abdalá Bucaram, a man who was equally lavish in his admiration for Adolph Hitler as for the liberator Simón Bolívar, managed, through his incongruent, haughty and brazen discourse, to mobilize the passions and frustrations of the inhabitants of suburban Guayaquil, while at the same time sowing terror in the taciturn Andean areas. His opponent in the May 1988 election, Dr. Rodrigo Borja Cevallos, is difficult to place outside of the social democratic spectrum, in spite of the "clarification" quoted earlier. Borja Cevallos won with an ample margin: 1,700,648 votes in his favor, compared to 1,448,498 for his opponent.

Was this the success of a sufficiently coherent and relatively universal programmatic conception as opposed to an inorganic, regional and mildly circuslike discourse? The answer is yes and no. "Better gray than red" was the title with which *Newsweek* commented on the triumph of Borja Cevallos over Bucaram. Bucaram was right in saying that

> there was only one protagonist in this political campaign. The Ecuadorian people did not vote for Borja. The Ecuadorian people voted for Bucaram or against Bucaram, since the great mass of votes that Borja had in the Andes [la Sierra] were not the product of any sympathy for Dr. Borja. They were the product of antipathy for the lawyer, Bucaram, in the Ecuadorian mountains.[5]

There is some truth to this. It also explained the efforts Bucaram made after the elections of 1988 to present a more peaceable countenance, that is, a social democratic one. On the other hand, we must not undervalue the solid implantation of the democratic Left, especially in the mountainous area. Nor must we neglect the dogged labor of Dr. Borja Cevallos, who was even able to enlist the support of an important group of leftist intellectuals who had thus far belonged to Marxist parties or at least gravitated toward them.[6] Besides, there was another phenomenon that we cannot skip: the multinationalization of the Latin American political spectrum, in which the social democratic, Christian democratic, and neoconservative tendencies penetrate more and more, creating "culture" paths that are already part of the national political being.

The Administration of Rodrigo Borja Cevallos

As far as foreign policy is concerned, the government of Dr. Borja Cevallos started with great dynamism at the very moment of its inauguration. There was a lot to do in that area. The previous administration had managed to isolate Ecuador from the international community through a series of clumsy actions. The first was the break of diplomatic relations with Nicaragua. Instead of placing the Sandinista government in quarantine (as Febres Cordero intended), this move ended up by keeping Ecuador out of a group of mediators who, in one way or another, interpreted the situation in Central and South America with a great deal more subtlety than Febres Cordero and were trying to act accordingly. In addition, Febres Cordero did not have a fellow politician in the government of any Central or South American country who was thinking along the same lines. There was one in the Caribbean, the Jamaican Edward Seaga, but neither Seaga nor even a pat on the back by the Reagan administration managed to break the isolation. In his desire to ingratiate himself with the North American president, Febres Cordero went so far as to attack OPEC, of which Ecuador is a member.

Rodrigo Borja Cevallos, on the other hand, started by reestablishing diplomatic relations with Nicaragua. This was done so quickly that President Daniel Ortega arrived almost immediately after the inauguration, which, by the way, was attended by Fidel Castro (back on South American soil after nearly 17 years) and by the secretary of state of the United States, George Shultz (who did not fail to protest the fact that a mural in the Legislative Palace of Quito depicted a member of the CIA wearing a Nazi helmet). There were also countless social democratic heads of state and others of similar persuasion who had come to celebrate the inauguration of the first truly social democratic government in Ecuador.

From this point forward, Ecuadorian diplomacy, under the direction of chancellor Diego Cordovez (who had gained worldwide renown through his mediating efforts in the Afghanistan war), continued to be very active, although it was not always successful. For example, Ecuador was not able to join on time the "Rio group of eight" of the SI, in part, this was because President Borja Cevallos refused to be a scab when his Colombian colleague Virgilio Barco suggested that he occupy the place of Panamá, whose membership to the group had been "suspended." But another reason for the lack of success was that the "Rio group" did not want to provide an opening through which many other countries could have entered. Theirs was a policy of prudence designed to prevent the group from becoming a sort of OAS without the United States. This, of course, would have been very good for the region, but it would not have failed to profoundly irritate the neighbor to the north, who was already planning to reactivate the OAS in accordance with the document known as Santa Fe II.[7]

In any case, Ecuador has continued to participate with decorum in multiple international gatherings and forums, although without great tangible results due to the country's lack of clout in a world scene in which the Third World itself matters less and less all the time.

In most conflict situations, the position of the social democratic Ecuadorian government has been a moderate or low-profile one. During the crisis preceding the invasion of Panamá, for example, Ecuador's diplomacy did not offer itself as a battering ram for U.S. policy, as the social democratic governments of Carlos Andrés Pérez (Venezuela) and of Michael Manley (Jamaica) had done. As a member of the OAS commission that traveled to Panamá as mediators, the chancellor of Ecuador, Diego Cordovez, consistently maintained a correct and independent attitude that did not fail to exasperate the members of so-called civil crusade. However, once Panamá was invaded, the government of Rodrigo Borja Cevallos did not protest with any energy, as did, for example, Alan García from Perú, who subsequently was isolated within the realm of Latin American social democracy.

One issue on which the external policy of Borja Cevallos did not pass its trial by fire involved the organization of a Latin American association of debtors. In the political program of Izquierda Democrática, there had been reference to "a union of the countries with foreign debt." However, in a statement issued to the U.S. press after his election, Borja Cevallos took this back and argued that "each country should seek its own solutions to its own problems."[8] It is obvious that this sudden change of mind was influenced not only by warnings from the United States (always containing a threat) but also by the evident determination of international social democracy not to open up this area of confrontation with the United States. In the 1970s and early 1980s social democracy appeared as a third option for Latin America, as distant from Soviet-style communism as from the imperialistic capitalism of the United States. By the end of the 1980s this alternative was encountering severe problems. At about the same time that Dr. Borja Cevallos was issuing the postelection statement, Spanish Prime Minister Felipe González summed up very accurately the new social democratic position by saying "it is stupid not to acknowledge that the United States is the world leader, especially in Latin America."[9] In domestic policy, Rodrigo Borja Cevallos's administration made the sensible decision, from his inauguration on August 10, 1988, to create a climate of civilized coexistence. This was in great contrast with the tense atmosphere that prevailed during the long period of Febres Cordero's administration, and the sense of relative security instilled by the Borja Cevallos government was also very distant from the leap into the abyss that the triumph of Bucaram would have signified. There was an end to threats and insults, and adversaries were no longer considered enemies. Offensive personal remarks and arrogance disappeared (temporarily, at least). Concerted action was encouraged, even at the social level, although, for reasons I will discuss later, it did not bear fruit. Political dialogue between the government and guerrilla groups such as Alfaro Vive took place with better results. Alfaro Vive agreed to desist from violent action and to join the constitutional life of the country.

In the midst of this renovated and improved climate, a very progressive group from the Ministry of Education planned what eventually came to be the most successful cultural (and probably social) effort of the Borja administration. I am referring to the national campaign for literacy, denominated Monseñor Leonidas Proaña. This campaign took place between June and September 1989, and it had highly satisfactory results. Two hundred thousand Ecuadorians of different ages and from different areas of the country were taught to read and write by about 70,000 young, secondary-school students. This was not just a teaching-learning process, as the saying goes, but something a great deal more important. It was a frolic of fraternity and mutual discovery, without the barriers of age, sex, social class and geographical origin. The number of people directly or indirectly involved in this experience is very high, if we take in consideration that the total population of Ecuador barely comes close to 11 million inhabitants.[10]

In dealing with the economy, the administration of Rodrigo Borja Cevallos has put a great deal of emphasis on the fact that, in a situation of crisis like the one Latin America is undergoing, there are only two options: a policy of shock, widely known and carrying with it an implacable social cost, and a policy of gradualism, which, as the word indicates, consists in applying the necessary policies of readjustment in a slow way. The adjustments, incidentally, are not significantly different from those recommended (not to say imposed) by the International Monetary Fund: increases in domestic price levels without adequate compensation in wages and salaries, reduction of government expenditures, elimination of subsidies on consumer goods and public services, devaluation of the national currency and so forth. What is different with gradualism is the rhythm at which this is done and, therefore, the intensity of the application of these measures.

An important difference between the Ecuadorian model and those applied in México, Brazil or Argentina concerned the absence in Ecuador of a policy of massive privatization of state-owned companies. When asked whether the preservation of these companies by the state does not go against the historical trend, Borja Cevallos replied that, in his opinion, the solution to the problem is not to reduce state property to its minimum but to make it more flexible and efficient.

Was this social democratic policy in Ecuador "original," or were there no pressures to yield to due to the fact that the country does not have "attractive" prospects for multinational capital? The latter facilitated the former. In fact, the only known external pressure was the statement issued by U.S. Ambassador Richard Holwil in November 1989 asking for the privatization of the seventeen companies of the Dirección de Industrias del Ejército (DINE), whose net sales in 1989 came close to $100 million—a high figure for Ecuador but modest internationally. The ambassador however, was not very felicitous in his selection of targets and managed to elicit angry replies from both the armed forces and the chief executive.

The Rodrigo Borja administration did not come up with any original initiatives in regard to the Ecuadorian foreign debt, which surpasses $11 billion (more than $1,000 per inhabitant). Instead, it allowed inertia to set in, convinced, and not without reason, that the international banks have bigger fish to fry. Some payments were made, but the country remained behind. Interest for 1987 and 1988, for example, was still owed. In spite of this, the only confrontation with the international lending institutions occurred when City Bank retained $80 million that the Banco Central de Ecuador had deposited in its New York agency. This arbitrary gesture did not cause political complications even though the sum was not a small one for Ecuador. Actually, it exactly equaled the total amount of foreign investment made in Ecuador in 1988 and 1989.

What have the results of Borja Cevallos's gradualist economic policy been? His first two years in office were not too successful. In 1989, the GNP—as a general macroeconomic indicator—increased only 0.9 percent. This implies a decrease of per capita income of about 2 percent since the rate of population growth in Ecuador is 2.8 percent per year. The government had planned to reach an economic growth rate of 3.5 percent by 1990, in spite of negative indications that suggested that the best that could be hoped for was economic growth equal to the birthrate, meaning no growth per capita. The Persian Gulf crisis and the subsequent increase in the price of oil, Ecuador's main export, contributed to make the goal reachable in addition to a solid growth of 4.4 percent in 1991, although it was not realized in the manner in which it had been planned. Also, it helped that the international lending agencies did not force the government to use the unexpected windfall toward the payment of the foreign debt.

Inflation, which in 1988 came close to 100 percent, was reduced to about 50 percent in 1991, a figure that, compared to what Ecuador has been accustomed to, was still extremely high.

Finally—and this is the main problem of the economic model of social democracy in Ecuador—the deterioration of real wages has been rather pronounced, oscillating between 10 and 25 percent, depending on which factors are taken into consideration. But regardless of which figure one claims, most observers agree that during the last year and a half there has been an acute deterioration of the standard of living for the working classes.

As expected, this situation had serious political consequences for the Borja Cevallos administration, whose image was palpably tarnished. The Frente Unico de Trabajadores (FUT) directed three rather successful national strikes: on November 24, 1988, on July 14, 1989, and on July 11, 1990. Also, the number of local conflicts that evolved into strikes almost doubled during the first two years under Borja Cevallos.

The less than popular economic policies of the government were also the reason for the breakup of the parliamentary alliance of the Izquierda Democrática and Democracia Popular parties in November 1989, when leaders of Democracia Popular decided that they did not want to continue to appear as coauthors of something that was bound to hurt them in the legislative elections of June 1990.

As it turned out, those elections resulted in a clear vote of censure for the economic and social policies of the Borja Cevallos administration. According to the official count, Izquierda Democrática dropped to third place nationally, being surpassed by Partido Social Cristiano (PSC) (to which ex-President Febres Cordero belongs) and also by PRE

(Abdal Bucaram's group). From 30 legislators in 1988, Izquierda Democrática went down to only 13 in 1990. The presidency of congress landed in the hands of the opposition. One of the traditional Ecuadorian power struggles between the executive and the legislative branches appeared on the horizon once again. This time, the judiciary also became involved since congress decided to reorganize it, in order, it was claimed, to free it from government control.

But here is something even more ominous: As the government has found itself losing popularity, it has turned less flexible and less respectful of its adversaries, and arrogance has come to overtake presidential discourse. For example, in June 1990, shortly before the elections, there was an important, totally peaceful Indian demonstration. The Indians wanted solutions for problems concerning their land and requested legal recognition of the ethnocultural and multinational nature of the country, as well as respect for the dignity of aboriginal peoples. The president refused to talk to them, even though they were a group of more than 200,000 Indians from the Ecuadorian high plateau and had the support of the Catholic church.

In the months following the demonstration, Borja Cevallos's attitude toward the Indian movement became even more rigid. The president, as well as his spokespersons and the leadership of the armed forces, began to use language similar to that used by the Febres Cordero Right. They began to talk about a lack of patriotism that could divide the people of Ecuador, of extremists trained overseas to promote subversion in the country and of other such things. It was as though the social democratic government had completely forgotten its initial democratic steps and its own public acknowledgment of the fact that Ecuador is a multiethnic, plurinational country—an idea that does not imply a lack of patriotism or the presence of subversive intentions. It seemed that the president had no desire to accept the fact that the cold war had ended—not the ideal way to solve the country's problems.

Conclusion

As I have pointed out in other works, one of the tragedies of Latin America is that social democracy has come to the continent without a *social* dimension. In present times it has been unable to define and implement an economic model that could be an alternative to the one produced by the International Monetary Fund (and the great interests that operate behind it). It has also been unable (except in the Perú of Alan García) to carry out a policy that, if not in frank opposition to, at least is independent of the United States. Thus, social democracy has certainly contributed a great deal to help Latin America get rid of the dictatorial regimes and to institute political democracy, which is of great value, but it has done little or nothing in regard to social justice and the economic development of the region and even less in the defense of national sovereignty. Because of this, the four elements (political democracy, economic development, social justice and national sovereignty) that in European social democracies historically occur together have separated traumatically in Latin America.

Within this general picture, one must acknowledge that the Ecuadorian social democratic government represented a more or less moderate version of what has been described previously. It promoted a climate of political liberty (in spite of a few lapses), and, although in a very limited way, it made the country move ahead in the direction of social justice and economic progress. Moreover, it did not adhere to a brutal shock policy or a policy of handing state wealth to monopolistic capital. It did not engage in struggles or promote initiatives designed to regain the much-diminished Latin American sovereignty, but neither did it take up arms in favor of the hegemonic center. That is a lot to say these days.

Notes

1. See Agustín Cueva, *El Proceso de Dominación Política en el Ecuador* (Quito: Editorial Planeta, 1989, 2d ed.) for an analysis of the sociopolitical situation in those decades.

2. This episode was analyzed by Osvaldo Hurtado in *La Dictadura Civil* (Quito: Fundación Ecuatoriana de Estudios Sociales, 1988).

3. Oscar Ayerve, *¿ Quien Gana la Segunda Vuelta?* (Quito: Taski Editora, 1988).

4. Abdalá Bucaram, *Las Verdades de Abdalá* (Quito: Editorial El Duende, 1990); Rodrigo Borja, *Socialismo Democrático* (Guayaquil: Editora Democrática, 1984, 2d ed.).

5. *Newsweek*, May 23, 1988.

6. For the political developments in these years, see the works by Alfredo Mancero Samás, *Ecuador: Coyuntura 1988–1989*, and *Ecuador: Coyuntura 1989–1990* (Quito: Coordinación de Estudios para el Desarrollo, 1989 and 1990); Tribunal Supremo Electoral, *Elecciones y Democracia en el Ecuador* (Quito: Corporación Editora Nacional, 1989), 2 vol.; and the 1988, 1989 and 1990 volumes of the journals *Nueva*, published in Quito, and *Vistazo*, published in Guayaquil.

7. Subsequently the "group of eight" was amplified, and Ecuador joined; at that time, however, the influence of the group in the Latin American political arena had evaporated.

8. *Newsweek*, May 30, 1988.

9. *Newsweek*, May 23, 1988.

10. Maria Rosa Torres, *El Nombre de Ramona Cuji: Reportajes de la Campaña Nacional de Alfabetización "Monseñor Leonidas Proaña"* (Quito: Editorial El Conejo, 1990).

11. The 1992 elections—won by Center-Right candidate Sixto Durán Ballán—promises to bring Ecuador more in line with the neoliberal economic policies practised in the rest of Latin America. This will mean privatization of state-owned businesses, cutting bureaucracy, combating inflation through drastic means, lowering tariffs and promoting free trade. See *The Economist*, July 11, 1992.

12

Personalities, Ideologies and Circumstances: Social Democracy in Central America

Edelberto Torres-Rivas

Once again, we must analyze a European phenomenon—this time social democracy—that as it moves into societies of dependent-capitalist development, seems to change their constitutive elements. But as soon as we approach the topic of the nature of social democracy in conditions of underdevelopment, we are confronted with an important contradiction: In Latin America social democracy does not represent an advanced form of the workers' movement attempting to overcome capitalism through reforms. However, the tendency toward Eurocentrism, which is almost instinctively Latin American because it is an integral part of that region's cultural deformation, makes it possible for us to coordinate diverse and even contradictory situations.

In order to place these differences or similarities in their proper context, it is important to remember two theoretical points that are at the root of this phenomenon that forms an ultimate part of European political culture: first, the conviction that capitalism, whose expansion has notably increased the wealth of this society, could be reformed and second, the belief that the working class was the only group that could effect this reform for the general benefit. All of this was to change during the postwar period.

Capitalism and democracy underwent profound transformations in Europe in the second half of the nineteenth century. The different perceptions of these changes and the varied notions of how to best use them in favor of the working class resulted in a political, ideological and cultural contradiction between reform and revolution, between communism and social democracy. The theoretical force of this dichotomy had significant political, social and even emotional consequences, and it created a situation that led to a permanent split within the European Left and the political life in which it participated. Soviet Marxism contributed to the consolidation and spread of this division in the Left by proclaiming the truth of world revolution.

Reformism succeeded in creating political support later. It grew rapidly during the second decade of this century, when a whole generation of social activists realized that the capitalist system had not gone bankrupt, was not about to do so and had also failed to produce a much-predicted proletarian majority. In addition, the capitalist system created political institutions in which it was possible to participate, and that participation became an irresistible means of working toward change. It also became the death potion of the revolution.

It is not necessary to recall, even briefly, the situations confronted at the beginning of this century by Bernstein within the core of orthodox social democracy in Germany and by Karl Kautsky in the midst of the Second International, where the ferocious polemic with Lenin became the legacy of the workers' movement and of progressive intellectuals. The debate was no longer limited to questions on what to do with capitalism but on what to do within it. The deliberation within social democracy between the options of participation and the option of not lending itself to a game between classes continued in Europe until 1930.[1]

Democratic forces in Central America, heirs without inheritance to this European tradition, were also divided into reformist and revolutionary groups. But the historical significance of this division was profoundly different in societies whose economic and political development were alien to European ways. The division only appeared and made sense after World War II, when social movements saw, for the first time, a real possibility of changing the political order by modifying both the rural bases on which it rested and the ideology that justified it and gave it impetus. The objective of replacing the capitalist system with a different one appeared rather late. The political forces that included this goal in their programs were mainly the Communist parties and the revolutionary guerrillas in the 1960s radicalized by the Cuban revolutionary experience. Democratic ideals and the reasoned option of economic development with the state as a promoter of change (the formula elaborated under Raúl Prebish at the Economic Commission for Latin America [ECLA] in Santiago, Chile) made their (rather incomplete) appearance in Central America in the 1950s. These ideas were immediately seized as ideological opposition to the old oligarchical dominance. There was an intellectual renovation that was expressed, in all the countries of the area, in the belief that it was finally necessary to have a rule of law. The efforts to attain this goal, postponed for such a long time in the region, were originally limited to reiterated attempts to go beyond the neoliberalism of the coffee-producing republic. Thus the struggle for political democracy was carried out by denouncing the big landowners and their excessive wealth and by seeking symbolical expression for cultural and nationalistic aspirations. The programs to modernize society and the state put together by youthful, provincial and inexperienced leftist groups never questioned the advantages of capitalism. What these groups were fighting against were social and economic backwardness, dictatorship, violence and the arbitrary ways of the great landlords, all of which were expressions of the absence of true capitalism.

Arbenz and Figueres

There is, then, no social democratic tradition in Central America with the ideological and political form it originally had in Europe. What emerged, at the core of the political struggle initiated after 1945, were reformist and revolutionary projects in the form of ideologies, methods and discourses produced within leftist groups. Communists and liberal democrats shared the eagerness to bring about the modernization of (1) the state, (2) the ways in which power was exercised, (3) the economy, (4) culture and so forth. The burden of political backwardness reduced the split between reformists and revolutionaries to a family quarrel that was, as family quarrels tend to be, bitter and spiteful. In Central America the aim was not to reform capitalism but to develop it. Neither was the goal to expand democracy but to establish it. There was, however, an ideological break with previous history, with the liberal ideology and with its concrete results.

During the postwar period two unique attempts in Costa Rica and Guatemala represented opposite approaches to the same end of reforming the system. Two important historical figures devoted themselves to the fundamental task of critically confronting the backwardness of the agro-export society. Jacobo Arbenz and José Figueres made headstrong political efforts to democratize and modernize society and to find paths toward social justice. They worked toward similar goals but used different methods and arrived at contrasting points. Both individuals were so different from each other that the failure of one and the long-term success of the other places them in opposition to one another in contemporary history. In fact, however, what was significantly different was the types of society from which they emerged and in which they worked.

Revolutionary Arbenz and reformist Figueres are the best representatives of that Latin American tradition of progressive thought and action that takes the opposition to oligarchy as its point of departure. Arbenz represented Jacobinic thinking taken to its limits. He advocated an advanced form of radical democracy, characterized by the impatience that was the inevitable result of having emerged from an Indian society in which most people were illiterate and had no land. This was a society in which peasants were permanently discriminated against by an agrarian bourgeoisie devoid of social consciousness and holding, since colonial times, a monopoly on power, wealth and pride. It is my hypothesis that in Guatemala, the social and political structure produces radicalism of the Right as well as of the Left. The violence that permeates social life fuels revolutionary sentiment constantly.

Arbenz transformed revolutionary conviction into economic policy and applied it without hesitation. This is exemplified in the rigour and directness of his agrarian reform. The basic goal of the reform was to transform the country from a colonial, dependent one into an independent nation, from a semifeudal economy into a modern capitalist society, in order to assure a substantial improvement in the living conditions of the population.[2] Arbenz was revolutionary in his antioligarchical discourse, in his unblemished nationalism and in his belief that capitalist development would destroy authoritarianism and peasant servitude. He was also a revolutionary in the methods he employed. The agrarian reform, which assigned land to about 100,000 peasants, was based on the mobilization of these individuals. In addition, to complete the revolutionary character of that movement, there were the anti-imperialist language, the haste to achieve change here and now, the exclusive confidence in popular forces, the placing of conflicts on an ideological plane and the exacerbated voluntarism of the leadership.

Figueres, on the other hand, had a slower ideological and practical evolution. Perhaps this was because he had more time at his disposal.[3] He also was temperamentally suited for a life of action.[4] He started differently, and, even though it appears that originally he just had electioneering goals in mind, he became the representative of successful reformism. Success came slowly and was occasionally ambiguous, but it had great scope and duration. His achievements included the nationalization of the banks; the reform of the state, encompassing nothing less than the actual elimination of the army; the modernization of agriculture through the renovation of coffee plantations; and the institutionalization of the electoral system (forcing agrocapitalists to change their oligarchical ways). *Figuer-*

ismo is a movement based on the reform of the state as a way of reforming society, and it promotes a type of capitalism that is politically protected by a decidedly active state.

The modernization of Costa Rica after 1950 is not the accomplishment of just one man, and it is certainly a generalization to attribute to Figueres an attainment that is the result of a series of favorable circumstances. But if we accept this generalization, Figueres represents a reformism that was victorious because of the extraordinary role assigned to the public sector. There is no reformism in Central America that does not have an antioligarchical objective. At the same time, there are no great landlords willing to change on their own. *Figuerismo*, which eventually identified itself with social democracy, is a movement that earned, from the very beginning, the hatred of the Costa Rican oligarchy.

Arbenz and Figueres did their work under very similar circumstances. Both of them were the heirs of the most important democratic and progressive governments in the history of Central America— Juan Arávalo's in Guatemala (1945–1951) and Rafael Ángel Calderón Guardia's in Costa Rica (1940–1944). Without the reforms of these predecessors, the similar favorable circumstances that Arbenz and Figueres inherited would not have existed. Another legacy the two leaders shared was that of the cold war, and to this they responded in drastically different manners. Figueres was profoundly anti-Communist and pro–North American. During his administration he weakened the labor movement and allowed the peasants to organize only to form cooperatives of production. His rhetoric was very much in line with the exigencies of the cold war. Arbenz's reaction to the cold war was the opposite of Figueres's, and the consequences of this are well known. Arbenz's national-revolutionary tenure was of very short duration and ended with the violent defeat of the popular movement by an alliance—of the military, the agrarian bourgeoisie, and North American interests—that is only now beginning to break up. Conversely, Figueres's success was long lasting, and it was a victorious experience for the small and middle bourgeoisie, in a situation of a debilitated labor movement and the open sympathy of the United States. A good part of the modernization of Costa Rican society is due to Figueres's leadership, inspiration and willpower.

The course of the modernization of Central America was set during the 1950s. It got tangled up with antirevolutionary and anti-insurgent activities in Guatemala and El Salvador, and it failed to combine democracy and development in Honduras and Nicaragua. Only Costa Rica was an exception.

Ortega and Arias

The political storm that was unleashed during the 1970s was favorable to reformist and revolutionary strategies. Revolutionary action did not derive so much from the presence and inspiration of the Communist parties as from the political-military movements of the times. Reform was benefited by the proliferation of political movements calling themselves social democratic.

But times have changed. The evolution of per capita income indicates that during the decade of the 1980s four of the five Central American countries lost the economic and social advances they had achieved during the previous twenty-five years.[5] During these years there was a deep crisis in which the most prominent feature was the use of extreme political violence in the competition for power. The cause of this is the historical failure of the oligarchy as a leading force. I refer to the bourgeoisie for whom the ownership of large estates to which they owe their original wealth is more important in explaining their actions than their light industrial investments or their financial and commercial speculation.

Nowhere in Latin America were there expressions of discontent as radical as those occurring in Central America during the 1980s. The political imprisonment within stagnant authoritarian societies developed, in diverse ways and in groups thus far rather dissimilar, the taste for armed struggle with mass support, as happened in Nicaragua after 1974–1975, in Guatemala after 1978–1979, and in El Salvador after 1979–1980. The simultaneous way in which these events took place plunged the entire region into a social crisis in which all of society's constitutive elements have been affected.

The crisis contributed to lend new vigor to the revolutionary movement while, at the same time, the revolution aggravated the crisis by impeding possible reforms.[6] An example of this are the reforms attempted by the civilian-military administrations in El Salvador between 1979 and 1981. The situation of the revolutionary movement, in the three countries where it flourished, became more difficult during the 1980s due to local and international causes. By the end of the decade, it had become impossible from every angle.

The most conspicuous of these revolutionary movements was the one in Nicaragua, and it is of interest to take a brief look at this case. The original, historical, revolutionary program of the Sandinistas dates from 1961. But even if this program had not existed, the circumstances of the long Somoza dictatorship and the way in which it was eventually overthrown placed Nicaraguan society on the threshold of revolution. The execution of the original program was mainly the work of the terceristas headed by Daniel Ortega, who became the representative figure of the drive toward change. Tercerismo meant not a third movement to compete with capitalism and socialism but a third force in opposition to the "proletarian" current (doctrinary Marxism) and to the prolonged popular war current (Maoism). It was one of the branches into which the Sandinista Front was divided at the beginning of the 1970s. The main strategy of tercerismo was flexible in its alliances and had as its immediate goal the struggle against dictatorship. Terceristas were quick to capitalize on the bitterness generated by the Somoza government. The so-called group of twelve—an alliance of the trading bourgeoisie, intellectuals and radical democrats—was formed with the terceristas. The movement also attracted members of the Catholic church, including the Jesuits. In addition, the terceristas established solid contacts with Figueres in Costa Rica, Torrijos in Panamá and, especially, with Carlos Andrés Pérez in Venezuela. The other subdivision of the Sandinista Front— the prolonged popular war movement— headed by Tomás Borge, had the support of Fidel Castro and Cuba. When the FSLN was united in 1979, the terceristas were the ones who facilitated the contacts with the Socialist International and with international social democracy. Today, there are debates as to whether there was really a revolution in Nicaragua. The Sandinistas intended to implement drastic reforms that would open up the path for socialism. The quality of these reforms was determined by the fact that they were being instituted at a moment of extraordinary increase of the popular movement and profound crisis in the dominant forces.[7] Thus Ortega represents a frustrated revolutionary destiny that underwent ideological changes and, finally, at the beginning of the 1990s relied on a successful reformist practice. The strength of the historical circumstances—the so-called conjuncture—and Ortega's political personality blended to produce a situation in which there was the opportunity for reformism to issue from revolution.

In Costa Rica the reformist impulse has deep historical roots. Costa Rican society gained political stability and democracy relatively easily because it was not deeply polarized and had a consensual culture that was not inclined toward conflict. This is all obvious. Figueres and the National Liberation Party acted accordingly during the 1950s when they implemented their program of development and democracy. They modernized society gradually and always with the support of the middle class—and the United States. We have already seen how programs of capitalist modernization that advocated anti-imperialism failed because they were perceived as direct threats to the anti-Communist conception of national security.

The Social Democratic Party appeared in Costa Rica in 1945. From it and also from other groups, the Partido de Liberación Nacional was founded in October 1951 with a program that naturally resembled those of similar political movements in other Latin American countries during the postwar period.[8] Its intellectual leader believed that economic development was feasible and would be followed by political democracy. They were sensible enough to recognize the increased importance of the "social question" and the role of the masses in a democratic system. José Luis Romero has noted that the new social phenomena started as movements of liberal origins that gradually modified their fundamental tenets in response to their encounter with the urban masses and to their own increasingly sharp consciousness of the urgency of the social problems that had to be handled.[9] This is the thinking and sensibility of the members of the liberationist generation who contributed to the secularization of social life in Costa Rica. They called themselves social democrats, because of their reformism, a long time before the Socialist International became active in the region.

The events of the 1980s debilitated the will and perhaps even the imagination of the reformist forces in Costa Rica. There was a political turn toward pragmatism in the treatment of social issues, opportunism prevailed and electoral realism dictated the course to follow. Gradually, there came a loss of direction, of programmatic discourse and of the spirit of renovation. Only electoral aims were important. Oscar Arias assumed the presidency in this situation, which is also accompanied by harsh economic and social problems arising from the reordering of international forces. It is all the consequence of the move toward the political Right in the West that later became universal.

The end of the crisis resulted in a paradox. Oscar Arias, who came from a social democratic tradition, implemented neoliberal policies and brought about, during his administration in 1986–1990, the end of a long period of modernizing reformism. Of course, the conservative slide had begun with Luis Alberto Monge, but, in my opinion, it was Arias who consciously pursued this end. Daniel Ortega, a revolutionary, headed a government that in 1988 began to apply policies that were clearly antipopular in their class orientation. International factors and the narrow limits that the economy in crisis set determined electoral results. Tercerista realism now turned Ortega into a left-wing social democrat.

The traditional reform/revolution dichotomy became mired during the terrible decade of the 1980s. Revolutionary leaders became reformist, and social democratic leaders turned neoliberal. This did not mean the end of ideology but rather its transmutation. Once more, as had happened at the beginning of this century, the development of capital altered political conviction and the ideological motivation of social change. The Russian Revolution, an interval of extraordinary experiences animated by a utopian hope for social justice, is now over. European social democrats now accept the upsurge of the market and the ineffectiveness of politics. Their original goal of overcoming capitalism is discarded, and, to survive, they have to consent to just administering it. The revolutionary forces are left without choice in this situation.

The Present Definition of Social Democracy

The political crisis in Central America during these years of violence both created and destroyed the political center, the middle-of-the-road possibilities. Social polarization does not explain everything. However, it did serve as the foundation of the ideological extremes on the Left and the Right that culminated in bloodshed. In Guatemala, El Salvador and Nicaragua, Christian democracy and social democracy have attempted to occupy the ideological center, motivated at times by electoral alliances and disputes. In the 1980s, the Christian democrats were finally elected. They had been establishing strong popular organizations since the 1970s. This is something social democratic forces did not do.

The Movimiento Nacional Revolucionario was founded in El Salvador in 1967 as a group of intellectuals led by Guillermo Manuel Ungo. It adhered, according to one of the founders, to a revolutionary, nationalistic, social democratic ideology.[10] In Guatemala two groups identified themselves as social democratic: the Unión Revolucionaria Democrático, which later became Frente Unido de la Revolución and was led by Manuel Colom Argueta, and the Partido Socialista Democrático, led by Alberto Fuentes Mohr. Both parties were affiliated with the Socialist International, the latter being a full member since the XV Congress (held in Caracas in 1980).[11]

The social democracy that emerged in these two countries was clearly of the leftist democratic type. In the midst of the crisis, their leaders sought to find a political solution, even if they did have a utopian/eschatological rhetoric. They were decimated by homicidal intransigence.[12] They were both assassinated by the armed forces at the beginning of the 1980s, when one of them had just registered his party and the other was about to do so. These deaths indicate that political accommodation was extremely difficult and that the crisis had led to rampant extremism.

The difference in receptivity to social democratic ideas in Central

America is due to the diverse composition of these societies. In Honduras, there were failed attempts to end the bipartisan system by creating a social democratic group, in reality an exercise in political travesty. Something similar happened in Nicaragua in 1981 when a small social democratic group tried to take its place in opposition to the Sandinistas. However, in spite of the difficulties, we are now witnessing a recovery of democratic and Socialist principles in a conservative milieu, where the issues of reform or revolution seem to be postponed forever and the fear of a return to the worst kind of authoritarianism is pervasive. All energy is devoted to the struggle for democracy, understood as a program of affirmation and respect of human rights. Demands for social and economic change are presented once more. This period of electoral democratization in Central America is favorable to projects to modernize the system. This is extremely important since the frustration of that modernization is what unleashed the storm. However, the economic crisis makes it difficult to concentrate on programs that could strengthen democratic legitimacy. At the present time, it is essential to have democracy accompanied by development, social justice and participation. These goals seem to be part of the social democratic strategy for the 1990s. Could social democracy become the renovated face of the Central American Left? This seems to be very much like the struggles of the postwar period. And the goals resemble those that were pursued almost forty years ago and were never accomplished. Now, like then, there is an urgency to reform the system.

The policies of structural adjustment reform the system in an adverse manner. These policies have accentuated behavioral changes in producers and consumers that the crisis had already provoked. The results have been an increase in speculation, a weakening of social solidarity and, above all and as a consequence of all this, greater disparity in the patterns of the distribution of income and wealth. Now, more than ever, there is a need for ideological and political forces to consolidate political democracy by giving it a social basis. Universal suffrage and ideological pluralism do not go well with poverty and the concentration of well-being in just one group. Political democracy requires *social* democracy. However, the Central American Left, which could achieve this objective, was defeated in the Costa Rican elections, is politically isolated in Honduras and is negotiating its legal political participation in El Salvador and Guatemala. In other words, the Left is extraordinarily debilitated, except in Nicaragua.

The so-called antinomy of modernization—that is, the conflict between political rationality and freedom of the market, between economic growth and democratic participation—can only be confronted and resolved if there is a departure from the liberal perspective in which it has been viewed. This will only be achieved within the political terrain, with democratic ways and an absence of violence and arbitrary actions. Political realism should not become political opportunism. There are tendencies toward ideological travesty.

What should be the content of social and democratic policy at this difficult moment, which is exacerbated by an "every-man-for-himself" individualism? The stakes are greater than ever before. This time it is the entire society that has to be rescued rather than just some of its privileged parts. The choice between contractual freedom and rational direction can be made if we realize that only society can solve its own problems by instituting changes that, at the moment, can only be reformist. These issues can be the object of debate, negotiation and struggles that would hopefully transcend the selfishness of the self-satisfied who are promoting an ideology of conformism. It is necessary to embrace the values of solidarity, of community, of struggle on behalf of those who have not been able to solve any of their problems, thereby laying the foundations of a political democracy based on a social one. A bit of hope is indispensable at this time.

Notes

1. Adam Przeworski's essay on "Social Democracy as a Historical Phenomenon," in his *Capitalismo y Socialdemocracia* (Madrid: Alianza, 1988), pp. 17–59, is a well-documented study of this important issue.

2. This is almost an exact quotation of one of the basic arguments of Decree #900, *Ley de Reforma Agraria*, May 1992. A well-documented description of this process, of Arbenz's personality and of the ideologies of the moment is contained in Piero Gleijeses's *Shattered Hope: The Guatemalan Revolution and the U.S.A., 1944–54* (Princeton, N.J.: Princeton University Press, 1990).

3. Figueres said that "social changes [occurred] slowly. The struggle to abolish slavery was prolonged for over two centuries." Speech delivered to UNCTAD I, cited in Tomás Guerra, *José Figueres, Una Vida por la Justicia Social* (San José: Cedal, 1977), p. 245. Figueres would reiterate this point on several occasions.

4. There are several biographies of Figueres. One of the best, Guerra's *José Figueres*, contains a bibliography of the leader's speeches and papers, but it is incomplete. José Figueres' *Essays and Speeches 1942 to 1962* (San Jose: Editorial Costa Rica, 1986) is a superb study of his ideological development. The "autobiography" entitled *José Figueres: El Espíritu del 48* (San José: Editorial Costa Rica, 1987), although written in the first person, was actually prepared by Figueres's intellectual collaborators.

5. FLACSO, *Centroamérica en Cifras* (San José: FLACSO-IICA, 1990), pp. 45 and 67.

6. What differentiates revolutionary projects from reformist ones is not the actual reforms but the manner in which they are applied. The efficacy of an anticapitalist measure is not evaluated according to the program that inspired it but according to the final results.

7. Among other events that exemplified the critical situation were the strikes and lockouts of the first semester of 1979, the combination of turmoil in the main cities and guerrilla war in the countryside and the general strike of 1979, as well as the fight of Somoza and his generals and the anecdote of Urcuyo.

8. From the ample literature about PLN, I suggest one of the first works: Carlos Araya Pochet's *Historia de los Partidos Políticos: Liberación Nacional* (San José: Editorial Costa Rica, 1968). I also recommend what is perhaps the most recent study: Alberto Salom Echeverría's *Los Orígenes del Partido de Liberación Nacional y la Socialdemocracia* (San José: Editorial Porvenir-Cedal, 1991). This contains a good interpretation of class, ideology and the origins of social democracy in Costa Rica.

9. José Luis Romero, *Latinoamérica: Situaciones e Ideologías* (Buenos Aires: Editorial El Candil, 1985), p. 65.

10. Italo López Vallecillos, "Fuerzas Sociales y Cambios Sociales en El Salvador," in *Estudios Centro-Americanos*, July–August 1979, p. 568.

11. Fuentes Mohr pointed out that "the main objective of democratic socialism is the establishment and consolidation of political, social and economic democracy. To this end, [democratic socialism] employs methods that lead to the transformation of capitalist society or to its replacement by a socialist system." Cited in Mario Solórzano, *Guatemala: Autoritarismo y Democracia* (San José: FLACSO-EDUCA, 1987), p. 107.

12. Mario Solórzano, in several of the essays in *Guatemala: Autoritarismo y Democracia*, refers to the role of Christian democracy and social democracy in Central America's politics. See his chapter "Centroamerica en la Encrucijada."

13

Social Democracy and Populism in México

Jaime Tamayo

Social democracy has a long trajectory in México, but this has not always been openly recognized. This is perhaps due to the fact that, since the Mexican Revolution, social democracy has been closely related to populism. Like socialism and social democracy, populism is one of the political currents through which subordinate classes express their interests. It is true that populist policies can be used to legitimize a rightist regime or one that represents the interests of the dominant classes, but as a means of political expression, populism always has a popular basis whose concerns it generally voices.[1]

In Latin America, populism has been the dominant means for the political expression of popular interests. The Mexican Revolution and those regimes most closely identified with it contained a strong dose of populism and had a clearly social democratic orientation. This is the case with the governments of Alvaro Obregón, Lázaro Cárdenas and Luis Echeverría. Mexican populism rose with the revolution and has deep historical roots. It made the social pact possible, incorporated the lower classes in the national development effort and gave it social significance. In the final analysis, the project of *social* democracy established in article three of the constitution is directly related to the proposals of social democracy, but it has its roots in Mexican social Jacobinism, which, in turn, is the immediate ancestor of Mexican populism.

In México, as in the rest of the world, neoliberalism has triumphed over socialism, social democracy and populism—three great forces that, according to Pablo González Casanova, seem to have lost the present battle but will nevertheless be the bases of a new civilization. As a consequence of this political development, the state that emerged from the Mexican Revolution is being dismantled. The neoliberal ideas, which are hegemonic today, place great emphasis on taking apart the state institutions and structures erected by the Obregón administration, consolidated by Cárdenas and expanded and revitalized by Echeverría. Social democracy and populism, ruling political currents until recently, now operate as forces of opposition resisting the dismantling of the Mexican state forged by the revolution.

Historical Roots of Social Democracy in México in the Nineteenth Century

Reformist socialism took root in México after the success of the liberal reform led by Benito Juárez in the second half of the nineteenth century.[2] It established itself particularly through workers' groups and newspapers such as *El Socialista*,[3] *El Hijo del Trabajo, El Pueblo*,[4] *La Internacional*[5] and others.[6] These first manifestations of socialism, especially the ones identified with the reformist wing of international socialism, were warmly received by the liberals in power. The government of Benito Juárez was sympathetic to and even subsidized some workers' organizations.[7] But it was during the administration of Miguel Lerdo de Tejada that the links became so close that some of the most important liberal intellectuals, such as Ignacio Altamirano, Ignacio Ramírez, Justo Sierra and Guillermo Prieto, collaborated with *El Socialista*. At this time even the Cuban hero José Martí[8] wrote for this newspaper, "advocating Mexican socialism and its social and moral reforms such as education, the establishment of cooperative workshops, political and social rights, equitable military service, and other measures proposed by the manifesto of the Workers' Congress." [9]

Contrary to the policies of anarchist groups, Mexican reformist Socialists maintained close connections with the liberal government. They also participated openly in the political process, joining, for example, the campaign to reelect Lerdo de Tejada and influencing his policies. This active Socialist participation ended abruptly during the administration of Porfirio Díaz. In July 1878 the Partido Socialista Mexicano was founded in Puebla with the goal of "legally conquering political power in order to establish the rule of the people."[10] This, however, was an anomaly; only a few groups calling themselves Socialist continued to operate under Díaz's administration, and they did so as mere appendixes of the dictatorship. During the revolution, in August 1911, the German Pablo Zierold founded the *Partido Socialista Obrero*, modeled after the Spanish Socialist Party. Its influence was brief and not very broad, but the party did spread Socialist thinking, and it promoted the observance of International Workers' Day in México by celebrating it for the first time on May 1, 1912.[11]

Populism, the State and
Social Democracy, Mexican Style

The Mexican Revolution meant, among other things, the destruction of the old oligarchical state and its replacement by a new, essentially capitalist state. However, because of the circumstances of its origin, this new state had a congenital social-popular content that expressed the class interests of workers and peasants and included them, though in a subordinate manner, in the national project (even before the appearance of the so-called welfare state).

In fact, with the success of the Jacobin positions in the *Constituyente* (constitutional assembly) of 1917 and during the administrations that followed this congress, in particular those of Obregón and Cárdenas, the popular masses participated directly in the political processes of the moment and saw their demands included in the national project.

After Porfirio Díaz's resignation and Victoriano Huerta's defeat, there was political space for the creation of a new state. The collapse of the liberal or authoritarian oligarchies of the nineteenth century, together with the crisis of European and U.S. colonialism, opened new possibilities for the reorganization of the state apparatus, that is, of the state as a national society.[12]

After the success of the constitutionalist movement, which represented the rising revolutionary bourgeoisie, there was the necessity and possibility of structuring a new state in accordance with the requirements of the economic bases of society. Despite the antiquated liberalism of the head of the constitutionalists, Venustiano Carranza, this new state apparatus began to take shape in the decree of December 12, 1914, which reformed the Plan de Guadalupe. There was a commitment to implement laws and measures designed to satisfy the economic, political and social needs of the country and also to put into practice the reforms demanded by public opinion regarding the establishment of a democratic regime, protection of small property holdings and improvement in the conditions of the working class.[13]

This new order, which was promoted by the *Obregonistas*, was consolidated by the agreement made in the Casa del Obrero Mundial and by the law of January 6, 1915. The law regulated agrarian reform, encouraged and furthered the goals of the peasants and laid the bases for the populist reformism that led the Obregonistas to power. They supported the most important resolutions of the Constituyente of 1917, which were numbers 3, 27, 123 and 130.[14] They addressed the need to create a government that could serve as arbitrator of the class struggle and that could derive its strength and power of decision from the ability to establish a class alliance as the very basis of the state.

While the legal bases of the new political structure were laid during the Carranza administration, it was during the government of Alvaro Obregón (1920–1924) that the modern Mexican state began to take shape. Carranza, after defeating the peasant group and the most reactionary sectors of the bourgeoisie, had also plunged into conflict with the small and middle bourgeoisie. Thus, he had shown his inability to realize that it was necessary to unite the diverse social forces that participated in the revolution as the only way to strengthen his government. This crisis was resolved during the Obregón administration when the process of centralization and concentration of political power was started. Some important elements of the process were Obregón's populist policies, undiluted caudillismo that seemed to go further than the charismatic leadership characteristic of populism and a certain "Bonapartism," due perhaps to the power vacuum left by the revolutionary movement.

The social pact on which Obregón's regime was based included workers, peasants, and members of the middle class who participated in the process either through political parties such as Partido Laborista Mexicano, Nacional Agrarista, Social del Sureste and Nacional Cooperatista; through social organizations such as Confederación Regional Obrera Mexicana (CROM), Confederación Nacional Agraria, and Ligas Campesinas; or through regional caudillos, supporters of Obregón, such as José Guadalupe Zuno in Jalisco, Adalberto Tejeda in Veracruz, Felipe Carillo Puerto in Yucatán and Emilio Portes Gil in Tamaulipas.

The social project that was structured through these alliances radicalized the lukewarm proposals that Obregón had made during his campaign and resulted in the most polished version of Mexican socialism thus far. It is not without reason that the two most important Latin American Marxist theorists of the moment maintained that the Mexican Revolution was on the path to socialism during the Obregón administration. In addition, his government was used as a model by Haya de la Torre for his proposal of a social democratic party with continental aspirations: Alianza Popular Revolucionaria Americana (APRA).

Julio Antonio Mella came to the conclusion that the most radical articles of the Mexican constitution "establish principles which, more broadly developed, could lead directly to communism in its scientific, Marxist conception."[15] José Carlos Mariategui stated that

> Obregón increased the state's robustness after the revolution by refining and consolidating its solidarity with the different social groups. During his administration the state was proclaimed to be, and was perceived to be, at the service of the people. Its performance, it was hoped, no longer depended on the personal prestige of the leader, but rather on the interests and desires of the masses. The stability of the Obregón government rested on a very ample social basis. He did not rule for a party but for a large concentration of revolutionary groups whose demands were transformed into a program.[16]

Haya de la Torre, on pointing out that the five themes of APRA had been formulated for the first time in México in 1924,[17] remarked that

> The Mexican Revolution would have been the most advanced of the times if it hadn't collided with imperialist pressure. México has not stalled because of a lack of revolutionary élan, but because it did not have enough material force to implement totally the gains of the revolution.[18]

For a while, it looked as though the social democratic current of the revolution would prevail. At least, this is what the leaders of the Confederación Regional Obrera Mexicana foresaw when, on the occasion of the inauguration of President Plutarco Elias Calles, CROM's sixth convention predicted that Calles's government would be a Socialist one.[19] However, during his administration there was a great concentration of power in the executive office, and social movements began to be integrated into corporatist structures. This process was consolidated during the *Maximato* (the period between 1928 and 1934 dominated by the authority of the then ex-president Calles), when political power and expression were institutionalized through a state party, the Partido Nacional Revolucionario (PNR), as were social relations (such as the issuing of the new federal labor code).

Cardenism was a synthesis of the process in which the revolution culminated. The state recovered features of importance for the national objective, such as a policy directed toward the popular masses and the affirmation of presidential (centralized) power. The rallying call for the populist alliance in those years was social justice. Thus, the actions and discourse of this government justified its being considered a Socialist one.

During the Cárdenas administration, the Mexican revolutionary state was consolidated. In subsequent years it became the main promoter of the economic development of the country. The well-known policies of industrialization and import substitution, which formed part of the so-called model of stabilizing development, relied on state stimulus and protection of capital and jeopardized, to a considerable extent, the alliance with the subordinate classes.

In the late 1960s, the system entered a period of crisis. On the one hand, the response of the Gustavo Díaz Ordaz administration to the student movement of 1968 marked a break between the state and civil society, at least the parts of it that had not been squeezed into corporatist structures; on the other hand, the model of stabilizing development and the political system itself became anachronistic and ceased to offer viable alternatives.

Echeverrismo: A Last Attempt to
Revitalize the Revolutionary State

It was within this context that Luis Echeverría became president. His government initiated a new policy that restored, in great measure, the changes implemented by Obregón and Cárdenas. It attempted to recover the basic principles of the state that arose from the revolution. The social, political and economic crisis that the system was undergoing could be confronted in various ways. Díaz Ordaz had already started using authoritarian-repressive means. The new government, however, sought to gain the consensus of the subordinate classes through the revitalized historical alliance with the state, now called Alianza Popular Revolucionaria. It reenfranchised the intellectuals and the opposition parties, created a climate of democratic openness and reestablished the connections between the state and the university on the bases of a commitment to search for a political solution to the problems and to cease political repression. In addition, workers were allowed to create their own independent organizations.

Economically, there was an attempt to replace the stabilizing model, already in crisis, with one of "shared development" that would end economic stagnation and promote the redistribution of wealth through greater public expense subsidized by the private sector. This project went beyond the merely economic and into the political and social realms. It provided an indirect income increase to the workers and broadened the welfare state. It enhanced the government's leading role as protector of the civil, economic and social rights of the subordinate classes and was thus an important source of legitimation for the modern Mexican state. In this sense, shared development was the cornerstone of what the Echeverría administration, recovering the constitutional proposals and assuming its relationship with social democracy, was to call *social* democracy.

In this context, nationalism was a fourth ingredient of Echeverría's program. It was expressed in foreign policies that went beyond the traditional Mexican principles in the international scene by attempting to modify the international order in favor of countries whose situations were similar to México's.

Echeverrismo was the last effort to revitalize the state produced by the Mexican Revolution, and its most important ingredients were four reforms that would give shape to the new state. The first, the social reform expressed through the Alianza Popular Revolucionaria, was intended to recover and rearticulate the social pact by reasserting the validity of social justice. The second, the political reform, replaced the policies of repression and exclusion with policies in which dialogue and negotiation were the dominant means of relating. This new "democratic aperture" ensured the free expression and participation of political parties and political and social groups that had been excluded by the traditional political system. It also established new ways of responding to the universities and the intellectuals and made room for independent social organizations. The third reform addressed the economy and tried to replace the stabilizing model with the model of shared development. It strengthened the state and allowed it direct intervention in the economy as the provider of social well-being to the subordinate classes and as the redistributor of wealth. The purpose was not to create an obese state, as neoliberals now claim, but to create a strong one that could concern itself equally with economic and social issues. The last reform, nationalism, was the basis of a very active foreign policy, placing México in a position of leadership in the struggle to assure and defend the rights of Third World countries and in the promotion of a new international economic order.

The policies and actions of the Echeverría administration had positive effects in México. The most important consequence was that the government was able to confront the crisis without resorting to force, even though there were scattered incidents of violence in the population. The revitalization of the revolutionary state made it strong enough to protect its own increasingly threatened logic and validity, even when dealing with internal and external questioning and when defending itself against the systematic attacks of the hegemonic neoliberalism that was seeking to dismantle it.

Regarding civil society, independent unions still exist and retain some negotiating power in spite of the new neoliberal policies of "flexibilization" of the labor market. This is due, in great part, to the labor policies of the Echeverría administration, which allowed the unions to become so strong that neoliberalism has not been able to effect their total destruction. However, it is also true that the belligerence displayed by the private sector in their dealings with the state, as well as the appearance of autonomous business organizations, are also results of these policies.

Echeverría's nationalistic policy was expressed so actively at the international level that it became crucial as the promoting force for a front of Third World countries that began to struggle for the recognition and defense of their particular interests. In this manner, México's traditional anti-imperialist policy became international, and what was originally a bilateral issue became a collective demand. The bases of the new international order, particularly in regard to economics, were contributed by Echeverría's foreign policy.

As could be expected, these policies did not suit the Mexican bourgeoisie, national and international capital, the imperialist countries and some sectors of political and labor organizations. They all launched a campaign designed to vilify the Echeverría administration and its achievements. In addition, leftist groups that had been driven into clandestine activities by Díaz Ordaz's repression were not receptive to Echeverría's efforts to create the bases for working together. Instead, they responded with their usual dogmatism and messianism. They declared war against all "reformism" and attacked Echeverría more viciously than the capitalists had attacked the populism that was so inimical to their interests. During the six years of his administration, there was a proliferation of rural and urban armed groups; leftist political organizations, such as the Communist Party, violently opposed all reforms on the grounds that their only objective was to delay the revolution.

The Echeverría administration began to identify itself more formally with social democracy. A meeting of social democratic leaders from Europe and Latin America took place in México in May 1976. Its slogan was "justice in liberty." On this occasion, Echeverría enumerated those characteristics of the Mexican state that coincided with the principles of social democracy and added, "It is very important that the lucid minds of our times persist in their quest for ways to achieve justice within a system of liberty. This is the Mexican purpose, it is the doctrine of our revolution."[20] After a cordial rebuke to social democratic parties that had abstained or voted against the United Nations resolution on the economic rights and duties of countries, Echeverría expressed his satisfaction with their "coming to Latin America—first to Caracas and now to México—to tell us that they also want a new international economic order."[21] He pointed out that these "meetings of international majority parties and high European officials with Third World leaders reveal the emergence of a new type of consciousness" and emphasized the shared belief in all-encompassing development: economic, social and political. He went on to remark that "it was extremely stimulating to anticipate the development of a new Latin American political consciousness that would militantly favor democracy."[22]

The president of the Partido Revolucionario Institucional, Porfirio Muñoz Ledo, stated that the common purpose was that "each party should, to the best of its ability and without compromising its own freedom and autonomy, endeavor to further the attainment of those common goals which provide links of compatibility among all." The leader of the ruling party concluded by saying, "The common purposes, and the concerted action of all involved, could create world social democracy."[23] This was an indication that, even though the PRI was not formally joining the Socialist International, it was willing to become part of social democracy explicitly. In fact, the social democratic meeting took place in the midst of the electoral campaign in México, and this served to reinforce the social democratic image of PRI's presidential candidate, José López Portillo, who freely expressed his faith in social democracy. He defined it as "not just a guarantee of equal opportunity, but also of equal protection against the fundamental risks of life: hunger, ignorance, poor health and lack of happiness."[24] But when López Portillo was eventually elected, his government started to depart from the social democratic project.

At the end of his presidential term, Echeverría found himself surrounded by a general repudiation of his policies. The diverse groups that were affected by his populism orchestrated a campaign designed to end the application of his despised policies. They monopolized public opinion and enlisted the support of the middle class, which had previously backed the government. The middle class was not only dissatisfied with its lack of upper mobility but also felt that its social situation was jeopardized by some populist measures. As had been the case with other populist regimes, the alterations in workers' wages and salaries was placing the middle class in a situation of relative inferiority. The salary increases of industrial workers were, indirectly, leading to the proletarization of large sectors of the middle class. Inflation also vigorously contributed to bring about this change.[25] Industrial workers were keeping up with inflation better than the middle class.

The failure of Echeverría's economic model, evident at the end of the six-year presidential period, accelerated the disintegration of the populist coalition. What happened was that, from the very moment that the generation of new wealth ceased, it became obvious that the only way to satisfy the demands of the masses was by redistributing the existent assets. At that instant the coalition began to collapse because the middle classes, seeing their standard of living threatened by a process that affected them predominantly, concluded that wealth redistribution was a subversive thing.[26]

Neoliberalism Versus Populism and Social Democracy

A new development has helped to transform Mexican politics in the last few years. During the López Portillo administration (1976–1982) something occurred that was described by Porfirio Muñoz Ledo as "a coup within the government party." He was referring to the ascent to power, within the PRI, of a group of foreign-educated technocrats who were neoliberals concealed under the camouflage of Mexican revolutionary discourse. These technocrats quickly displaced the previously hegemonic leadership. During the next administration, headed by Miguel de la Madrid, and under the excuse of ending administrative inefficiency, the gradual and systematic dismantling of the revolutionary state began.

In fact, the ruling neoliberals, together with a considerable portion of the democratic opposition, maintain that it is necessary to reduce the size of the state (to "slim it down") in order not to distract the state from its obligation to protect all the interests of society. They claim, in addition, that the reduction of the state is indispensable for the enlargement of civil society and for the broadening of democratic life. The problem is, as González Casanova would say, that when the neoliberals talk about "slimming down," it is very difficult to know what it is that they are talking about. Alan Wolfe has stated that

> those who advocate lower government expenditure on social programs know what they are doing since, given the fact that the state has a function of accumulation, the only way that government activity can be reduced is by attacking social welfare which is the most democratic aspect of it. What is at play here is not an abstraction called "expenditure" or "politics" but the social needs of real people. Consequently, the most immediate political strategy of the common people would have to direct itself toward the preservation and expansion of government services.[27]

Evidently, the neoliberal project in México does not contemplate, at least thus far, the possibility of really reducing the margins of power of the state. As a matter of fact, the tendency toward greater concentration and centralization of political power has not yet reached its limit, and when I refer to the state I am essentially talking about political power. I find then that, through the very agencies of the state, a thorough process of self-dismantling is being carried out. This process has the explicit aim of obliterating the populist, welfare state inherited from the revolution by limiting its traditional means of legitimation, but it is not designed to reduce the quasi-absolutist power the state has traditionally claimed for itself. On the contrary, the process has tended to strengthen this power and to increase the state's leanings toward authoritarianism. The supposed enlargement of civil society, at the same time, resembles a sort of "Balkanization" of the social subjects through various agreements. In other words, the quasi-absolutist character of the Mexican state is not being questioned by the regime since this would imply the existence of a state of law. This, paradoxically, would not necessarily result in a combination of democracy and neoliberal policies since, as Daniel Bell has noted, "although historically capitalism and democracy have appeared together and have used philosophical liberalism to justify themselves, there is nothing, theoretically or practically, requiring them to be thus tied to the same yoke."[28]

A dissident current appeared in PRI to oppose the neoliberal policies of the government of Miguel de la Madrid (1982–1988) and its attempts to destroy the revolutionary state. The group was led by a small number of distinguished members of the party. The most prominent among them was Cuauhtémoc Cárdenas, ex-governor of Michoacán, son and political heir of Lázaro Cárdenas and leading figure of the Cardenista faction within PRI. There was also Porfirio Muñoz Ledo, labor minister and president of the PRI during the Echeverría administration, ex-secretary in the United Nations, main promoter of close links between the PRI and the Socialist International and the most conspicuous representative of social democracy in México. Another outstanding dissident was Ifigenia Martinez, ex-director of the Department of Economics at the National University and leader of the group of nationalist economists within the party.

The first demand made by the dissidents was the democratization of the PRI and the abandonment of the corporativism that had assured the ruling party a virtual monopoly of mass political activities. They also advocated a nationalist stand and readopted the project that had been questioned by the ruling technocrats. In their first document, the dissidents called for a reestablishment of national alliances, reform to allow the party bases direct participation in the decisionmaking process and "a defense of the integrity and unity of the nation carried out with the participation of all social forces."[29] In their second document, the democratic current ratified its conviction that "nationalism and democracy are concurrent objectives of the same struggle."[30]

The "democratic proposal" made public after the announcement of the PRI's presidential candidate and after Cárdenas's group had broken with the PRI included a program that appropriated the revolutionary project and emphasized the need to democratize the country and recognize the political pluralism in society.[31]

The nomination of Carlos Salinas de Gortari as the official candidate not only precipitated the separation of the democratic current from the PRI but also led to the nomination of the dissidents' own presidential candidate. The candidacy of Cuauhtémoc Cárdenas created great expectations among the Mexican political opposition and among many sectors of civil society. Even though the high-ranking dissidents were few, the PRI's split had serious implications at the lower levels of the party and among the masses. The dissident group became the gravitational center of the Mexican Left, and Cárdenas's candidacy provided the centripetal force for popular opposition to the PRI.

Neo-Cardenism: Social Democracy as Opposition and Democratizing Populism

After the dismantling of the welfare state there was an attempt to replace it with a charitable state that retained populist policies of social justice but carried them out in a limited and excluding manner (as in the case of the Programa Nacional de Solidaridad). Populism, displaced from its former position, managed to recover social consensus and, from its place in the opposition, became the sentinel for the defense of the revolutionary state. Paradoxically, populism's role in the opposition transformed it into the main promoter of democratic reform in México. This paradox was most noticeable in populism's efforts to eliminate the state apparatus of the authoritarian social control that it had helped create when it was in power.

Neo-Cardenism was the political expression of a revitalized populism, the main vehicle for processing the antagonism felt for the neoliberal ideology and the articulator of the demands for pluralistic democracy. In this manner, it became the most important factor in the effort to effect a transition to democracy in México. The choice of the moment was between "a reformist nationalism based on populist democracy, and a technocratic dictatorship based on a broad agreement with foreign sectors."[32] The specific characteristics of the

Mexican state and the neoliberal policies implemented by Miguel de la Madrid made it possible for neo-Cardenism to become the nucleus of an ample Center-Left alliance. This alliance included four registered parties, several unregistered ones, numerous social organizations and a large number of nonorganized citizens. Neo-Cardenism attracted these groups by advocating legality, democracy and nationalism and by seriously questioning the system and the direction in which it was heading.

The issue around which the alliance was formed was opposition to a common enemy: the neoliberal administration. This is what made it possible for so many diverse social and political organizations and movements to join hands in the electoral process. This gathering of people opposed to the neoliberal policies of exclusion and privatization also attracted citizens and emergent sectors that were not represented in the Mexican political system and were seeking to exercise the right to participate.

The alliance's most urgent objectives were preventive ones. Members of this group sought to impede the loss of the social gains attained through a benevolent, intervening and regulating state. These gains included generous social expenditure, the policy of subsidies, intervention to stabilize "factors of production" and the mediation of demands and conflicts that minimized class struggle. They were also determined to prevent political denationalization arising from the country's abdication of its own political sovereignty and economic denationalization resulting from reprivatization and the indiscriminate receptiveness to multinational capital.

The movement was successful in enlisting new members because there was a general demand for a state of law that had not existed until then. It attracted people who deplored the existence of a juridical structure that grants discretional powers to the quasi-absolutist state, thus allowing it to place itself above the law and to become a power that may consent to negotiate but is not obliged to follow any rules.[33] The diverse political forces and social sectors that opposed the government or were unhappy with its neoliberal orientation were able to go beyond their own partial goals and demands and join in the struggle for the legality and democratization of their sectors, the political system and the society at large. The acquisition and expansion of all sorts of democratic space began to gain an importance it never had before. Nationalism was also a strong link among these groups. This was in keeping with a historical tradition of national autonomy and with what befits any movement that pursues a state of law. In this manner, a symbiotic relationship developed between the Frente Democrático Nacional and the popular movements. This opened up the possibility of forming a national movement, capable of confronting the state more assertively and headed by a charismatic leader.

In accordance with the historical tradition of all Mexican revolts, revolutions, and mass movements, neo-Cardenism is characterized by caudillismo. In regard to this tendency of political movements to become personalized—to be embodied in a particular leader—Jorge Alonso has remarked:

> The personality of the leader magnetizes the movement in such a way that it gives it his or her own name and comes to characterize it. Such is the strength of the personality in this process, that if it were to disappear the movement would be in danger of dying.[34]

In October 1988, as a result of a proposal drafted by Cuauhtémoc Cárdenas while in the midst of the campaign to defend universal suffrage that was being conducted by the Frente Democrático Nacional, a committee was formed to pursue the creation of Partido de la Revolución Democrática (PRD). The point of departure was a document prepared by Cárdenas and signed by all the participants. It emphasized the need to create "an organization that would be representative of the times, to create a party that would pursue democracy, constitutionality, the Mexican Revolution, and the dignity and progress of the people."[35] The new party was described as a "citizen's organization endowed with the decision-making powers and acting capacity of a political party, and with the flexibility, inventiveness and autonomy of the different groups of which it was composed."[36]

The groups that welcomed Cárdenas's proposal were Corriente Democrática, Partido Mexicano Socialista (PMS), Fuerzas Progresistas, Consejo Nacional Obrero y Campesino de México (CNOC), Organización Revolucionaria Punto Crítico (ORPC), Partido Liberal, Movimiento al Socialismo, Grupo Poliforum, Asamblea de Barrios, Asociación Cívica Nacional Revolucionaria (ACNR), Convergencia Democrática, Consejo Nacional Cardenista, Partido Verde and Organización de Izquierda Revolucionaria-Linea de Masas (OIR-LM).[37]

Not all these organizations remained within the fold of PRD, but others have stayed even though they are simultaneously members of other organizations. This is the case, for example, with the last three of the organizations mentioned, which also belong to OIR-LM. The ample spectrum of political persuasions and the diversity of interests represented in the group can cause a buildup of tensions that are usually resolved by Cárdenas. Exercising his caudillo prerogatives, he tries to make a common endeavor out of political persuasions that go from social liberalism through social democracy to the radical Left.[38]

During the first PRD congress the radical Left won an ample majority of the executive positions in the party, and the so-called trisecta (formed by ultraleftists coming from PMS and by ACNR) was overrepresented. The groups favoring reform and dialogue, such as Movimiento de Acción Popular (MAP), and some members of the Communist Party were excluded from positions of power. However, the reformists have made a recovery lately, especially after the meeting of Porfirio Muñoz Ledo and President Salinas. On this occasion, the dialogue concerned "the need to improve substantially the democratic process in the country as the only true guarantee of preserving national sovereignty."[39] This move toward recovery will be benefited by the fact that PRD has applied to the Socialist International for membership. Should the response be positive, it would prop up the social democratic positions within PRD.[40]

Social Democracy: Perspectives

Although it is true that social democracy mainly seeks to work its way in México first within PRD and then through PRD to the nation, there are two other channels. The first one is the Partido Socialdemócrata, a small party issued from Grupo Acción Comunitaria (AC) in 1981. It participated in the 1982 elections and subsequently lost its registration due to low electoral results. However, it continues to operate in opposition, is openly anti-PRI and supports the National Agreement for Democracy proposed by Cárdenas. The second channel is the PRI itself. Within the party, there are social democratic tendencies that could conceivably try to model the regime after some European governments in which social democracy appears to be a hybrid of neoliberalism and social justice.

In support of this possibility one can cite two measures of the Salinas regime that depart from neoliberalism. There has been an increase of social spending beginning with the 1991 budget, and there is also the Programa Nacional de Solidaridad (PRONASOL) that, even though it is somewhat limited since it is aimed at reducing extreme poverty rather than at redistributing the wealth, is founded on the same idea on which Echeverría based his law concerning the Sociedades de Solidaridad Social. In a strategic but neat revindication of populism, Salinas maintained during a meeting with solidarity committees in Tlaxcala that "there is a rapprochement between government and citizens, between the people and the state. We are building the state together.

This is a nation whose system of government is the product of a great popular revolution, of a mass movement. For a long time in our country, mass policies ceased, and today we are trying to rescue that great tradition."[41] The theoreticians of neoliberalism argue that in order to redistribute wealth, it has to be generated first. They have suggested that after three years of policies designed to modernize and strengthen the economy there can be new expectations regarding social justice. The PRI in its XIV Assembly, which took place in September 1991, ratified its social democratic slogan, "democracy and social justice," and accepted "the obligation to promote the transformation of the economic structures in order to eliminate the grave social differences which exist in the country and to assist the millions of Mexicans who have been left behind economically." The party also expressed its conviction that "social justice is an irreplaceable value which is the essence of the national project of the Mexican Revolution."[42]

In the last instance, the PRI is facing a dilemma. It has to decide whether to adopt pragmatic neoliberalism completely or whether to pick up the struggle for social justice and follow the example of some European social democracies that have adapted the principles of democratic socialism to situations where the market, capital and neoliberalism reign.

Although the Mexican state will not go back to what it used to be, it is also true that the neoliberal project is not the best political "offer" for the Mexican social "market," since the recovery of consensus requires democratization and social justice. Nevertheless and despite PRONASOL, the dominant leaning of the Mexican government is toward those who, as Willy Brandt aptly put it, "cynically want to reduce welfare to charity, nationally and internationally, and wish to apply Thatcherism all over the globe."[43]

Notes

1. In *Política e Ideología en la Teoría Marxista* (México, D.F.: Siglo XXI Editores, 1988), pp. 203–204, Ernesto Laclau has noted that "populism is the presentation of popular-democratic appeals as antagonistic to the dominant ideology," which makes it possible for it to be used by the dominant and the dominated classes. The revolutionary potential of the appeals continues to be present since "the popular traditions represent the ideological crystallization of the general resistance to coercion." Finally, it becomes a mass movement that develops the antagonistic potential of popular appeals, in spite of the risks of incurring manipulation by some faction of the dominant group, as happened for example under Nazism. Moreover, successful Socialist movements unequivocally adopt a populistic character in order to expand the hegemony of the working class over the other "popular" sectors.

2. Gastón García Cantú, *Socialism in México* (México, D.F.: Editorial Era, 1974), pp. 11, 12, 101; Manuel Díaz Ramírez, *Apuntes Sobre el Movimiento Obrero y Campesino de México* (México, D.F.: Cultura Popular, 1974), pp. 54–118.

3. *Historia Obrera*, vol. 1, December 1974.

4. *La Voz de los Trabajadores, Periodicos y Obreros del Siglo XIX* (México, D.F.: CEHSMO, 1975), vol. 1.

5. Ibid., vol. 3.

6. Ibid., vol. 2.

7. Díaz Ramírez, *Apuntes*, pp. 61–62, 71.

8. Paul Estrade, "Un Socialista Mexicano: José Martí," in *Casa de las Americas*, no. 82, January–February 1974, pp. 40–50.

9. Ibid., p. 74.

10. Díaz Ramírez, *Apuntes*, p. 124.

11. García Cantú, *Socialism*, pp. 130–131.

12. Octavio Ianni, *La Formación del Estado Populista en América Latina* (México, D.F.: Editorial Era, 1975), p. 17.

13. Arnaldo Cordova, *The Ideology of the Mexican Revolution* (México, D.F.: Editorial Era, 1972), p. 200.

14. Narciso Bassols Batalla, *El Pensamiento de Alvaro Oregón* (México, D.F.: Nuestro Tiempo, 1967), p. 22.

15. Jaime Tamayo. "Julio Antonio Mella y el Marxismo en el Movimiento Obrero Jalisciense," in *Dialectica*, no. 18, September 18, 1986, p. 62.

16. José Carlos Mariategui, "Obregón y la Revolución Mexicana," in *Temas de Nuestra América* (Lima: Editora Amauta, 1975), pp. 49–52.

17. Victor Haya de la Torre, *El Imperialismo y el APRA* (Lima: Fundación Navidad del Niño del Pueblo, 1986), pp. 1–13.

18. Ibid., p. 49.

19. Tamayo, "Julio Antonio Mella," p. 93.

20. Luis Echeverría Alvarez, "Nacimiento de una Nueva Conciencia," in *Justicia en la Libertad* (México, D.F.: Secretaria de la Presidencia, 1976), p. 11.

21. Ibid.

22. Ibid., p. 12.

23. Porfirio Muñoz Ledo, "Solidaridad Para Avanzar," in *Justicia en la Libertad*, p. 36.

24. José López Portillo, "Cambio Social Conforme a la Constitución," in *Justicia en la Libertad*, p. 57.

25. Octavio Ianni, *El Colapso del Populismo en Brasil* (México, D.F.: UNAM, 1974), pp. 136–137.

26. Helio Jaguaribe, *Sociedad y Política en la Actualidad Brasileña* (Buenos Aires: Grupo Editor Latinoamericano, 1985), pp. 26–27.

27. Alan Wolfe, *Los Límites de la Legitimidad: Contradicciones Políticas del Capitalismo Contemporaneo* (México, D.F.: Siglo XXI Editores, 1980), pp. 369–370.

28. Daniel Bell, *The Cultural Contradictions of Capitalism* (New York: Basic Books, 1976), p. 14.

29. Documento de Trabajo Número Uno de la Corriente Democrática, Morelia, Mich., October, 1986.

30. Documento de Trabajo Número Dos de la Corriente Democrática, Chihuahua, May 6, 1987.

31. Propuesta Democrática de la Corriente Democrática, México, D.F., September 9, 1987.

32. Ianni, El Colapso, p. 18.

33. The discretionary powers of the executive branch are truly enormous. For example, it created a National Commission of Human Rights that, theoretically, had only advisory power but that, nevertheless, was able to make changes that the judiciary had never been able to put through.

34. Jorge Alonso, La Tendencia al Enmascaramiento de los Movimientos Políticos (México, D.F.: Collección Miguel Othón, CIESAS, 1985), p. 35.

35. "Llamamiento al Pueblo Mexicano," convocation proposed by Cuauthémoc Cárdenas and signed by many citizens, México, D.F., October 1988, mimeographed, pp. 1–2.

36. Ibid., p. 4.

37. Cuauthémoc Cárdenas speech delivered to the Committee to Promote PRD, México, D.F., October 1988, mimeographed.

38. Jaime Tamayo, "Neoliberalism Encounters Neo-Cardenism," in Joe Foweraker and Ann L. Craig, Popular Movements and Political Change in México (Boulder, Colo.: Lynne Rienner, 1990), p. 121.

39. "Comunicado a la Presidencia de la República," in La Jornada, February 12, 1991, p. 16.

40. Rudolf Dresler announced in La Jornada, July 3, 1991, that there is already a consensus within the SI to accept the PRD as full member.

41. El Nacional, November 22, 1990.

42. "Tribuna Nacional Sobre Declaración de Principios," in El Partido en el Poder (México, D.F.: IEPES-PRI, 1990), p. 404.

43. Willy Brandt. "La Internacional Socialista ante el Nuevo Milenio," in Nueva Sociedad, no. 103, 1989, p. 84.

PART FOUR

General Perspectives from Latin America and from Europe

14

The Challenges of Social Democracy in Latin America

Fernando Henrique Cardoso

Recently Albert Hirschman gave a talk on reactionary rhetoric in which, with his characteristic insight, he synthesized reactionary prophesies in what he called "two hundred years of reactionary rhetoric: the case of the perverse effect."[1] Basically, these are pessimistic with regard to the positive consequences of any transformation: *Plus ça change, plus c'est la même chose.* Of course, not all reactionary rhetoric is that simplistic. It is more sophisticated but indeed almost always ends up "demonstrating" that well-intentioned reforms always have unexpected consequences that eventually undermine good intentions and reinforce preexisting tendencies. Thus, for example, reactionaries counterattacked the first Poor Laws in England, trying to demonstrate their contribution to indolence and crime. It is the same today in the United States: Conservatives criticize social welfare measures, such as food stamps and unemployment insurance, saying that they generate abuses and laziness and intensify social problems.

Hirschman delighted his audience by demonstrating that the pessimism of the thesis of perverse effects—that "good" intentions of reform measures always result in regression—exhibits continuity with what he called the "thesis of futility"—that attempts to change are always abortive, useless, illusory and incapable of changing structures. The most popular version of this is the one presented by the prince of Lampeduse in "Il Gattopardo," when he affirms that "everything should change in order to remain the same." A third dimension of reactionary rhetoric mentioned by Hirschman is labeled by him the "jeopardy thesis," that is, any new reform puts in risk previous reforms. The "cost-benefit" calculation of innovation is always evaluated with reservation, in name of the positive result previously achieved.

What does this have to do with social democracy in Latin America? The answer is, a great deal, as it does with any reformist proposal. Hirschman himself discussed the reactionary theses in relation to the damage that the welfare state—according to these theses—may inflict on progress created by previous advances. Thus, reactionaries believe that it will endanger individual rights made effective by the extension of suffrage and respect for human rights (á la T. H. Marshall and his "development of citizenship") generated by the "democratic revolution." It may even undermine democratic government. In other words, the welfare state, with its emphasis on social policies and the regulating role of public power, may end up counteracting the great conquests of the liberal-bourgeois revolution.

I will not continue in the fascinating line of the history of ideas traced by Hirschman, which, as he himself wrote, hopefully will at least serve to "elevate the level of the discussion." However, I want to recall that functionalist sociology, with Robert Merton,[2] made a contribution to this debate that may not have operated in the line of "progress" and of the enlightenment but did avoid the terror of the "romantic" effect of retrogression. In his well-known essay on the serendipity effect, Merton treated the unexpected, the unforeseen events not so much as an inevitable disrupting phenomenon that impedes the realization of good intentions but as something that, although not imagined beforehand, ends up permitting a breakthrough in the comprehension of phenomena.

While forcing the interpretation—as Merton did not refer to the evolution or retrogression of real social processes but of unexpected scientific discoveries—I would say that in the case of Latin America, the chances of and motivation for social democracy are better evaluated through "unforeseen results" of the previous historical situation than through a reformist project that—by the force of things, as the reactionaries say—ends up getting lost. I share, therefore, Hirschman's position, rejecting the metaphysical pessimism, as well as the opportunism, of the reactionaries, but I will use other arguments to defend the possibility of reform.

The Supremacy of the Market and Social Democracy

Curiously enough, the social democratic élan in Latin America emerged at a time when elsewhere—and to a certain point also in Latin America—we watched the triumph of free market economy and liberalism.

The decade of the 1980s, with Thatcher and Reagan, constituted the apogee of "deregulation," the unshakable belief in the "gospel of the market," in the supremacy of private interest as the engine of progress. It was as if Adam Smith, with his "invisible hand"—which secularized the thesis of Divine Providence or, in the popular version, that "God works in mysterious ways"—had been reborn. Today economic thought follows on the idea that "the less state the better." And up to a certain point possessive individualism returns to center stage. To the misfortune of social democrats, the reconstruction of some mechanisms of the market economy in Eastern Europe and, in particular, in the Soviet Union is seen as "proof" that modernity depends on competition, private interest, liberty of initiative and so on.

It is therefore a future promising the triumph of liberalism and the supremacy of the free market as the prime regulator of the economy that discourages social democracy in Latin America. But social democracy does not only confront the difficulties derived from the prestige of liberal capitalism. It also has to deal with the unexpected effects brought about by the transformations in the Soviet world. Interpretations of what happened in Eastern Europe emphasizing the negative effects of state planning and presenting social democracy as a defender of state authoritarianism are deadly.

Contemporary social democracy will survive only if it is capable of recovering the line of thought and action of, among others, the Austrian social democrats of the beginning of this century. It should be a critic of the liberalism that restricts itself to deifying the market whose unexpected effects are, for reactionaries, always beneficial, as well as of Bolshevik socialism. The latter saw centralizing authoritarianism as an ersatz invisible hand, acting as intermediary for a pagan god (the party) capable of foreseeing and providing the daily needs of peoples through state planning, perhaps more inspired by Auguste Comte than by the dialectic.

It is in this ideological context that the Latin American social democratic challenge is presented, besieged by apparently triumphant neoliberalism and weakened by the criticism and death of real socialism. If that, nevertheless, were the only difficulty for the social democratic alternative, things would be relatively simple. Apart from the challenges of that ideological battle, social democracy struggles in Latin America with a political tradition that is unfavorable to it, and it confronts the emergence of a new democratic practice that is frequently confused with the success of liberalism. This all happens in a context of economic stagnation (the decade of the 1980s is considered, from this point of view, a lost decade) and increasing social inequality.

The National-Populist Tradition

Before returning to the challenges of the future, I want to review, if only briefly, the characteristics of the historical situation weighing upon the social democratic alternative. Urbanization and industrialization, with the emergence of the middle classes and the modern business class, strengthened in Latin America the belief that the central question, from the point of view of popular interests and the national interest, was that of sustaining policies of economic development that would substitute the previous practices focused on economic growth through the so called agro-export model.

The crisis of this model, so well described in the 1950s by the Economic Commission of Latin America (ECLA) and, in particular, by José Medina Echevarría,[3] corresponds in the social history of the continent to the crisis of the European "old regime." The landed estate (*fazenda* or *hacienda*) as the basic productive unit and nucleus for ordering social and political relations entered into crisis as the urban industrial economy expanded. Likewise, the patrimonial state, to utilize the Weberian typology, with its traditional clienteles and control by the "notables," was eroded by the pressure of the urban masses, the middle classes and the industrialists.

Basing his ideas on the experiences of the country in which the modernization of society had advanced most, Argentina, Gino Germani best characterized the formation of a type of unruly citizenry.[4] It was formed by multitudes of *descamisados* and *cabecitas negros* more than by individuals claiming rights and anxious to see them respected by the law. The urban crowds besieged the "traditional power." The state fortress, meanwhile, instead of collapsing upon hearing the trumpet of the "new barbarians"—as in the 1960s a frightened Father Rogier Vekemans, desirous of neutralizing them as a political force, used to call the "marginals"—resisted and transformed itself into the bulwark of those hoping for "development with income redistribution."

In this way, the passage from the "hacienda economy" to the urban-industrial economy occurred without a complete break with the previous political structures of domination. In Brazil, for example, the change from a slave social order to a free labor one had taken place without a civil war and without crushing the old elites.

All of that must be taken *cum grano salis*. In México, the revolution inherited an enlightened state—at the time supported by agro-export interests—but decimated the traditional ruling class. In Perú, APRA's attempts to modernize the social order and the state were repeatedly frustrated by the military. In Colombia, the "transition pact" cost tens of thousands, if not hundreds of thousands, of lives. In Venezuela, the death rattle of the "old regime" with the personalist dictatorships as its caricature was heard at the first signs of revolt, and so on. For better or for worse, nevertheless, the passage from the old regime to the bourgeois-democratic order concerned a transformation of the state, through an alliance of sectors of the traditional society with emergent social groups—urban middle classes and businesspeople—and with representatives, although more symbolic than effective, of the "popular masses" (*populacho, turba, populo minuto*), rather than a revolutionary rupture of the preexisting order.

The makeup of this new alliance varied from country to country. More than twenty years ago I wrote that, in general, in countries characterized by enclave economies, the passage referred to earlier reinforced the "revolutionary" character of the emergent middle classes, with a strong anti-imperialist tone. Bolivia with the MNR, Perú through APRA and other organizations, Chile with the Popular Front and the formation of a more Europeanized party system, Venezuela with Acción Democrática and Central America and the Caribbean with the Cuban and Nicaraguan revolutions are examples of this.[5]

In contrast, in the countries in which there was greater economic development, the passage occurred through nationalist-populist policies and with relative autonomy from representatives of the old regime, instead of through revolutionary explosions or the strengthening of parties representing the new interests. The bibliography on populism is ample and the phenomenon is sufficiently well known.[6] I do not want to occupy the reader's time with a repetition of its characteristics. I only want to call attention to the strengthening of the state with a rupture of the traditional order through either of the two basic developments indicated earlier. In the history of *all* of Latin America, however, from the 1930s on and with great continuity in the years after World War II, the emergence of the state as the central agent, promoting economic development and policies of income distribution and improvement of the people's living conditions, stands out as a remarkable phenomenon. The central agency that rationalized that role of the Latin American state was ECLA. It placed in circulation the great themes of Latin American progressivism. Industrialization, the end of deteriorating terms of trade, structural reforms in industry as well as in agriculture and income redistribution formed the central elements of social criticism. The expectations concerning a reorientation of the dependent economies of Latin America focused on these issues. As articulator of this process, the state came to be seen not as the expression of class domination (à la

Marx) but as a point of encounter between national and popular interests, without contradicting the interests of the "new producers." Those contradictions that occurred were with "imperialism," "great landholders" and other "nefarious characters" of the old regime. In this way, a theoretical blessing was given to national-populism and to middle-class revolutionism without criticizing the "redistribution without *real* redistribution" and, in the political realm, the "symbolic participation" without *real* democratic representation. Not that the theoreticians of development and dependency (and I include myself among them, although with distaste when one sees the mechanistic character into which dependency fell) were responsible for populism or its precursors or for petty bourgeois radicalism (which later strengthened in large part "foci" revolutionism). The Perón of his first period (1943–1955), Getulio Vargas and APRA preceded all of them. The Mexican Revolution—a deviant case within the evolution of the continent—was a contemporary of the Russian Revolution.

But in present Latin American history, the idea of progress did not emerge from the struggle of the popular classes against "bourgeois domination," nor from the efforts to perfect the mechanisms of political representation (electoral systems and parties), nor from a heightened love of human and civil rights. These ideas began to emerge forcefully in progressive thought more recently and after the political transformation to which I briefly referred.

Thus, in Europe criticism of the insufficiencies of formal democracy emerged *after* it—with universal suffrage and the rest—had become firmly rooted in political practice. In Latin America the demand for social rights—through populism—and the search for greater opportunities for economic development—through anti-imperialism— emerged *before* serious democratization and, up to a certain point, with disdain for it. Various factors contributed to this disdain. Among the Left, the criticism of the existing order was carried out through two great currents. Both minimized the "formal aspects" of democracy in the face of the necessity to combat the "substantial" causes of inequality: poverty and colonialist or imperialist exploitation. There, progressive developmentalism's criticism coincided with that of the Left, including the Communist Left. For them imperialism and its allies on the national level were the "immediate enemy."

Among the developmentalists, who did not all necessarily take a position on the Left, the defense of the rule of law was not a priority in the face of the challenge of industrialization and economic development. The so-called progressive bourgeoisie was more statist and nationalist than liberal-democratic. Therefore, the forces that could have been expected to criticize clientelism and patrimonialism in the name of democracy and the extension of human and political rights, until the mid-1970s, emphasized the "efficiency of the state." A strong state, in their view, would serve the accumulation process and, eventually, better the living conditions of the masses. Direct social action by the state, even for more critical progressives, had precedence over questions of democracy, autonomy of class movements and direct political representation. In this way, the idea of social well-being was intimately tied to the defense of state action. This, if not a welfare state, was seen as a demiurge, as the "developmentalist state" that, for that reason, was situated on the *bon côté* of Latin American progressivism.

In Europe social democracy, at a certain point, accepted the challenge of universal suffrage as an instrument to gain power. Its adherents believed that a reorientation of state policies and public expenditures—with fiscal and income policies permitting leveling actions on society—could be achieved within the context of a market economy without the need to substitute it for one based on the collective ownership of the means of production. The Latin American "proto" social democrats followed another path: They disdained the chances—perhaps because they were more remote—of taking over the state via "workers'" parties and preferred to participate in progressive fronts. These fronts, organised in general by the Communists, were much more interested in the growth of GNP and the formation of an autonomous national productive base than in redistributive policies and democratic control of the state or, even, of production.

This original sin of Latin American progressivism made it much more statist than democratic. It leaned toward corporatism and distributive action, focusing on the demands of the organized segments of society more than on those of the general population. There was a greater belief in the ability of the state to distribute income—at times perversely and inversely, as happens with inflation—than in the generalization of well-being through an economic rationality that would seek an optimization of investments, technological progress and competitiveness.

Therefore, curiously enough, progressive thought assumed as main theses those that in principle were supported by the bourgeoisie and had to do with economic growth, provided that it was "anti-imperialist." At the same time it enrolled itself in the defense of the state as the means to promote the common interest. Questions of welfare policies in the long term or of democratic control of decisionmaking and state government disappeared into the background. Not by chance a few Latin American populist dictatorships were admired by progressives, even when they overstepped individual liberties and affected political personalities and segments rooted in progressivism.

On the other hand, thought fluctuated, on the Right, between a strong defense of the virtues of *laissez-faire*—in general, at that time, prejudicial for the industrializing forces—and a ferocious criticism of the state, as the enemy of the people and suppressor of liberties. These liberties, it should also be recognised, had a rather abstract nature for the masses, like the Peronist descamisados or Vargas's *queremistas*. For them, legislation guaranteeing a minimum wage and the organisation of unions that—although linked to the state—ensured a worker presence in the concerns of the country's leaders, seemed better than the defense of the vote that, in Vargas's words, "does not fill bellies." Urban masses preferred "indirect political representation" through personalities identified symbolically with them to the struggle for autonomous political representation of the popular classes, the creation of "true parties" and stable rules for selecting officeholders. This preference was maintained, provided that the system allowed greater employment, some influence in the leadership's decisionmaking and salaries that mitigated poverty.

Times of Autocracy and Modernization

After the mid-1960s and, above all, during the 1970s, various Latin American countries of economic and demographic importance experienced a crisis in the populist and developmentalist model of economic growth. They also had to confront the challenges that the internationalization of the economy presented to the old beliefs of autonomous nationalism. In addition, progressivism had spread in the region and had even reached socially reactionary sectors.

There is insufficient space in this chapter to discuss the emergence of the new authoritarianism that strengthened the state, militarized it, created regimes that Guillermo O'Donnell termed "bureaucratic-authoritarian" and diverged from the previous developmentalist paradigm.[7] We can mention Argentina, Brazil, Chile, Uruguay and even, up to a point, Perú, next to the traditional dictatorships in Paraguay and, intermittently, in other countries of the continent. It is not that those regimes did not desire development. They wanted it and in a few cases, such as Brazil, pursued it with some success. But the military-authoritarian developmentalist phase emphasized an accumulation process that did not correspond to the rhetoric and social results that populist nationalism propounded.

Accumulation and investment became absolute priorities, to the detriment of income redistribution and also, to a lesser degree, national-statist interests. The internationalization of the productive system affected the more developed countries of the region in varying degrees, through formulas that ranged from Peter Evans's "triple alliance of dependent-associated development,"[8] which included the state, multinational corporations and national businessmen—as in Brazil—to the most pure "integration into the new international division of labor" with less concern for relatively autonomous industrial development, as in Chile.

The results of the militarization of the state in some countries and the fascination of governments almost everywhere with the new liberal mania (of Reaganomics and Thatcherism) resulted, in a few cases, in successful developmentalist performances and the expansion of exports. At first, after the oil shock and the recycling of financial surpluses of the oil trade through Eurodollars, as much external capital moved directly toward local economies as it did indirectly through the international financial system, then enjoying big dollar surpluses. From that point on, in the 1970s and, above all, in the decade of the 1980s, the price of that first attempt of the Latin American economies to adjust to the internationalization of production was the growth of the external debt. Paying it became the great headache of the continent.

Whatever the relative success of industrialization and/or integration into the world market, what really grew was the weight of the debt on economies that needed to accumulate capital to expand. They became exporters of liquid capital, instead of receiving external resources for investment and financing expansion. Internally, social and economic conditions declined: Inflation and low salaries worsened even more the already terrible distribution of income in Latin America.

In this panorama, repressive practices of the state hardened because of (1) a direct political struggle involving guerrillas and their subsequent repression, (2) an excessive authoritarianism restricting popular organizations and the liberties of nearly everyone, (3) agrarian struggles that were often bloodily repressed or (4) the emergence of a new nightmare in countries such as Bolivia, Perú and Colombia: the drug trade. In this context a rupture occurred between the state, the *mauvais côté*, and civil society that became the *bon côté* of ideological Manichaeism.

So, instead of the perverse effect of *plus ça change, plus c'est la même chose*, what occurred on the ideological level was more of an "unexpected effect." Instead of the inevitable, we had the unexpected in our Latin American serendipity: The state, the good guy in the beginning of the history of development, became the villain as a consequence of economic development or, better yet, of the type of development that prevailed. This "demonization" of the state occurred with greater stridency in the countries that had military governments. In these, the subjects of human rights and democracy resulted in criticism of the oppressive state. The state bureaucracy, especially its military-repressive segment, became the bête noire of the story.

Meanwhile, even in the countries in which state power remained under civilian control, the antistatist surge grew. The reasons had to do with the massive, worldwide liberal wave, which in the militarized countries also reinforced the criticism of statism. The events in Eastern Europe further supported this offensive of liberalism and helped transform the relationship of state versus market into the fundamental contradiction used to distinguish between good and bad.

In this way the criticism of statism got mixed up with the criticism of populism. The old theses of Latin American developmentalism and structuralism seem to have become obsolete. The new wave values private initiative, the market and deregulation as the pivots of economic development. And social development, as in the old theories that maintained the unilinearity of history, is supposed to be the by-product of economic growth. The old trickle-down effect, described by the liberal theoreticians of development via successive stages—like W. W. Rostow[9]—enjoys new popularity. It means the demise of the thesis that emphasizes efforts at structural reform as a precondition for development or if not that, for avoiding "bad development"—as Ignacy Sachs characterizes it.[10]

The Status of Social Democracy

The references made in this chapter to Latin American sociopolitical processes are sufficient to demonstrate that the criticism of the type of development that prevails in the continent are made under very different conditions from those in Europe, where socialism criticizes capitalist development. This applies to the realm of economics—privatism versus statism—as well as to the areas of politics—human rights versus state repression—and social conditions—distortions in income distribution as a consequence of a structure of privileges and bureaucratic-corporatist regulations assured by the state.

The choice for "reform instead of revolution" (that is, to accept the electoral process as an instrument to achieve governmental power and from there—through fiscal and social policies—to redistribute income) was made in Europe while recognizing the value of democracy. This choice made by the social democrats, in contrast to the path chosen by the Communists—one-party system, dictatorship of the proletariat, against pluralism and concessions under pressure by the dominant classes—was influenced by the social democratic theoreticians' criticism of the bureaucratization of centrally planned economies and the authoritarianism that one-party control of the state provoked.

As far as valuing party pluralism and the electoral process is concerned—and in concordance with the argument of Adam Przeworski on the transformation of social democratic parties from one-class to multiclass bases in order to obtain better electoral results[11]—a certain correspondence existed between the trajectories of European and Latin American social democracy.[12]

The armed struggle was tried by the Communist Left in Latin America, although without the heroism of the Soviet myth and the romanticism of the revolutionary seizure of power and also without entering into the debate about "socialism in one country." Meanwhile, with the exception of Cuba—whose revolution was in the beginning more democratic than social-revolutionary—it was not successful in fighting the military dictatorships and had no viable project for a new society.

Perhaps the analogies stop there. Instead of the capitalist *patrón*, the target of the new wave of liberalism in Latin America was the repressive state, while the market and free enterprise—read the businesspeople, the bourgeoisie—profited from the decisiveness of those who fought for more democracy and for better social conditions. The struggle for wage increases and betterment in social conditions came wrapped up in the populist practices of the workers' parties, the *Peronistas, the apristas* and even the PRI, with the well-known trade-off between more social improvements for some and more power for others, especially those linked to the elites. In contrast, the current idea of "progress with rationality" does not even save that "social populist"—and corporatist—dimension of the Latin American Left.

This is not to say that the emerging social democracy in Latin America should passively accept this unhinging of history: I am referring to ideology and not to real processes. Any effective proposal for change should begin with an ideological critique. This, as we know, will eventually lead us to the real, although a slight distortion may occur.

The perspectives for social democracy in Latin America will become clearer if we take today's politico-doctrinal battle into account. It is essential to realize that the traditional social democratic strategy of basing its force on criticism of the inequalities provoked by the workings of the free market economy (through exploitation of the work force and the unhindered accumulation of capital), which should be corrected by social and fiscal policies, collides with the triumphant neoliberal wave. In this context, it is not sufficient to reaffirm values without criticizing the Latin American "progressivism" of the past. To reduce the role of the state and to substitute the liberal thesis of the "minimal state" with the "socially necessary state" requires a criticism of the state as it really is and, from this perspective, also a criticism of liberalism, demonstrating its limitations and distortions. Likewise, while defending the workers' and salaried employees' points of view, one needs to recognize the necessity to restrict corporatism and respect the requirements of production in terms of efficiency, productivity and the necessary link between distribution and production.

This preoccupation differentiates social democracy under Latin American conditions as much from European social democracy as from the populism of the past. In Latin America income redistribution through corporatist pressures had much more negative effects than in Europe. Thatcher-style criticisms of the welfare state and the crisis of some European social democratic governments had to do with the weight of the social security guarantees and basic provisions of the welfare state on all of society and on the economy.[13] Corporatism and even trade unionism may have made a few European economies less competitive in a world economic context and may have set them back in the race for higher levels of productivity. It is unlikely, however, that the relative advantages of one group of workers will have meant losses for another group.

In Latin America, by contrast, given the enormous inequalities not only between the rich and the poor and between capitalists and wage earners but also between organized social sectors (which include important segments of the working and middle classes and sectors not organized, comprising not only those "marginal" to production but, *idem ibidem*, also people belonging to the working and middle classes) corporative pressures constitute impediments to the *universalization* of social conquests. This applies to wages, social security, retirement benefits, access to education, health care and so on.

On the shoulders of Latin American social democracy falls the difficult task of distinguishing itself from corporatist populism, in the name of the universalization of social improvements, without transforming itself into an obstacle for advances that a few isolated sectors can and should obtain. The liberal Right criticizes any and all claims for betterment in wages and working conditions as *partial* and benefiting only a limited number of sectors. Therefore they prefer the struggle of the free market that, without distortions of politics and state action, would assure equality in the long run. In the Latin American case, as we know, this almost always boils down to an equality to not possess. The populists accept as valid any demand *from those down below* and do not ask about the medium-term effects on society. Social democracy should oppose the liberal Right and the populists with different arguments but with equal firmness.

I mentioned the question of production. It is unlikely that this problem has played a role as important in the debates of European social democrats as in Latin America. Heirs of the philosophy of progress and reason, Latin American leftists have had to address the question of development, and therefore of production as a prerequisite for social welfare. It has been this way all through the age of "structural-developmentalist" thought from World War II until the crisis of contemporary authoritarianism.

On the other hand—and again there is the effect of the unexpected and not of the perverse, together with the valuing of "civil society" and of human rights—a novelty emerged on the Latin American political scene: the new Catholic social thought. This new Christian thought goes from liberation theology to theses emphasizing the importance of distribution to the detriment of production and capitalist prosperity. It has been important in disseminating a consciousness of rights and the spirit to claim these autonomously, apart from the state and traditional leaders. In this respect, the generally positive effect of liberation theology on the oppressed masses of Latin America is undeniable. In many instances, it is indeed liberating, as the name indicates. Equally, recuperation of the *ethical dimension* in life and in politics (without having resorted to Bernstein) constitutes an important contribution to the thought and practice of the Latin American Left. Liberation theology's criticism of instrumentalist theories, of the thesis that the ends justify the means and of conditions of alienation have become a fundamental part of the contemporary heritage of Latin American progressivism.

But, together with these positive aspects, there are elements in Catholic socialism's criticism of the idea of wealth that contain grains of regression. It is as if, following the Christian reactionary thought of the writer Gustavo Corçao, one would want to create a world of small independent producers, of equal wealth and opportunities, with little attention given to large-scale production and accumulation. The difficulty of this egalitarian utopia of Christian origins and with precapitalist characteristics lies with its underestimation of the rational aspects of accumulation, productivity and investment, to the benefit of pure and simple distribution. It is as if one acts from the naive belief that the existing wealth will provide enough for everyone. The only thing that remains to be done is to apply the principles of social justice, and the happiness and well-being of all will be guaranteed.

These aspects of Christian thought indirectly constitute a challenge to be confronted by social democracy. They have become integrated with two different but at the same time complementary forces: populism and state patrimonialism. It is clear that Christian socialism in itself opposes populism, as this is, in general, alienating and does not value the autonomous organization of the popular classes. The same can be said about the politics of favors, the clientelism and corporatism of state structures. But at one point they converge: They tend to say yes to all popular demands, demands that as such are almost always just in societies as unjust and unequal as those in Latin America.

Here social democracy returns to the problem mentioned before. It needs to oppose, in the name of economic growth and medium-term rationality, demands that, as just as they may be, will interrupt the continuity in the provision of desired benefits in the future. This is another dimension of the contradiction already discussed between the advantages for a specific group and a universalisation of benefits. There is more to these advantages than the simple gains for a professional category. General measures that, as such, can be considered just ones—for example, wage increases—may be unsustainable over time and/or may cost more than they benefit in the present.

Going further, social democracy will have failed if, in the existing situation of poverty and inequality in Latin America, it cannot combine economic prosperity with income redistribution. It is a critical posture toward the present type of development—combined with responsible positions concerning the necessity of accumulation and economic growth, added to its qualities as a moral and concrete political force in favor of income redistribution and social welfare policies—that will distinguish Latin American social democracy from populism, national-statism and renovated liberalism.

The Challenges of Social Democracy

Social Democracy and the State

It may seem superfluous to repeat what we all know and what I have explained in this chapter, but it is important. Social democracy, even in its blandest forms, does not accept the basic idea of liberalism—that the market, in itself, is the superior instrument to produce the best allocation of resources and that income redistribution is a subproduct of laissez-faire. I believe that the state versus private sector dilemma is fallacious. The question cannot be reduced to simply returning portions of the state to the private sector or to nationalizing the economy and the society even more.

The real question for contemporary social democracy concerns knowing how to increase economic competitiveness—leading to increases in productivity and the rationalization of the economy—and how to make the vital decisions concerning investment and consumption increasingly public ones, that is, how to make them transparent and controllable in society by consumers, producers, managers, workers and public opinion in general, not only by impersonal bureaucracies of the state or the private sector.

Nevertheless, under the present conditions in Latin America, where the external debt and inflation corrode the capacity of national states to accumulate, the key modernizing objective has been to privatize the state. There are especially strong pressures to privatize the state productive sector. In this situation, any objective analysis must begin to identity in this sector those companies that, by the well-known mechanism of "the socialization of losses," were turned over to the government because they were going bankrupt. In those cases the option is not between keeping such businesses in the hands of the state or privatizing them. One should establish whether they have any economic future or should be closed. In case they are useful and competitive, why not reprivatize them?

This is not to say that the state should not act to promote development, through state financial institutions and through investing directly in strategic or pioneering areas, even if they are potentially productive and lucrative. Nevertheless, in the past, many businesses became owned by the state simply because there was not sufficient private capital available to finance them. This happened, in general, with companies that need a long time to mature and to create a profit. Many of them represent phases in the struggle for economic development and possess strong symbolic value. In these cases the reaction of social democracy should be pragmatic: Does private capital really have the desire and the opportunity to invest in the purchase of these firms? If this is so, privatization should be done in a manner that promotes public interests, going beyond strictly market criteria in their sale. Above all, one should be certain that the firms concerned will function in situations of competition and not as private monopolies. Their operation in a bureaucratic-corporatist context would be at least as harmful socially as state monopolies. Yet, in social democratic politics symbolic elements of the struggle for economic development cannot be treated as irrelevant. In general, oil companies, some steel companies and others have such a strong symbolic connotation that a politico-economic cost/benefit analysis of their privatization would yield negative results.

I touched in passing on one of the essential elements in the social democratic discussion on modernity: the defense of competitiveness. The question of the state versus private sector dichotomy put in realistic terms is another element. Public interest requires that the economy be based on competitive firms, capable of absorbing modern technology, in order for their effects on society to be positive. The question becomes clear by viewing the role of competition in forcing the adoption of the results of technical progress in production, thereby increasing productivity. Without that increase the battle between investment and consumption, capital and labor becomes unmanageable, as in a zero-sum game in which a gain for one means a loss for the other.

Social democracy therefore changes the axis of the option between state and private sector from the ideological plane (the private sector would always be good and the state always bad for the economy) to an objective plane: The *conditions* that should be created in order for the economy to function well are important. Patrimonialist, predatory management and corruption can exist in both the private and the public sectors. Their presence is to be condemned in both. The competitive market is the antidote for these ills.

It is not easy to defeat, on the one hand, a neoliberalism that condemns all public administration and, on the other, a national statism that confuses the interests of the state and the people with a continued state ownership of firms, even when these are inefficient and supported by the treasury—that is, by everyone who pays taxes.

I would add a last word on the question of the state, as viewed from a social democratic perspective. It is true that in Europe there have been social democratic governments that privatized (that of Felipe González, in Spain) or rarely nationalized (as in Sweden) and others that nationalized productive firms and even financial intermediaries—the banks—such as the English Labour Party and French Socialists (although in a few cases, these reprivatized). All of this demonstrates that this question does not define the social democratic quality of public administration.

Privatization of the state, which occurs in Latin America in great proportions, is unacceptable. It entails, through alliances—which in other circumstances I have called "bureaucratic rings"—the feudalization of parts of the state bureaucracy, in its productive sector as well as in actual direct administration, to private interests. Many of the state firms operate with deficits because they follow pricing polices benefiting the private sector that consumes their products (steel, for example). The links between the state bureaucracy and private interests are enormous and frequently function to the detriment of the public interest. Likewise, even essentially public services, such as education, health and transport end up sheltering private interests in their spending decisions. The complacency that exists is simply scandalous, as is the fact that, in a few areas, state administration and private interests are in bed together.

What is the use of privatizing in these cases? First, democratic control in state administration should be increased in order to make the state more sensitive to public interest. It is obvious that there are sectors of the state—those connected with social welfare—whose function is not to *make a profit* but to *serve*. This is how they should be understood, and therefore they should remain in the state sphere.

Social Democracy and Nationalism

If the debate on state enterprise versus privatization were the key point in the battle between social democracy, neoliberalism and populist-nationalism, there would still be plenty of room for differentiation and political struggle. But there is another question, larger and more encompassing than the question of statism—a question that provokes strong value reactions. I refer to nationalism.

The roads traveled by the European Left were distinct from those traversed in Latin America. In Europe the workers' movement began under the aegis of internationalism. True, the bourgeoisie was "nationalist." It was only after the Third International and because of the existence of national interests in the Soviet Union (presented as interests of the proletariat and the revolution) that, given the menace of imperialism, there was an opening in the Left for nationalist banners.

In Latin America the nationalist flag was almost totally carried by the leftists, although they were not the only supporters. The reason for their adherence to nationalism is understandable: Popular and workers' movements in Latin America were born almost simultaneously with the anti-imperialist struggles. On the other hand, Latin American "progressivism" was almost always "developmentalist" and, therefore, made the question of national interest a key factor in promoting industrialization. It could not be any other way: In order to create jobs and improve the population's standard of living, it was necessary to invest, absorb technology, widen the internal market and reform archaic structures, above all in the countryside. In other words, the continuation of the process of capitalist revolution, in the economic and social plane, presupposed a struggle in favor of the internal market and the reversal of colonial export economies. Therefore, whatever the label, it postulated an anti-imperialist attitude.

One more time the twist of history caught the ideologists with their pants down. The internationalization of the productive process, the new international division of labor based on multinational companies, in a phrase, the "globalization of the economy"—now also reaching the countries of the East—made old positions obsolete. They had transformed imperialism or the interests of foreign capital into allies of the traditional agrarian economy and important obstacles to industrialization.

Protectionist policies had been defended against laissez-faire by the Left and by progressivism since the eighteenth century, when England appeared as the springboard of international exploration. The protecting umbrella of the state permitted—through tariff policies—the development of national industries. These policies were attacked by the Right as being "artificial."[14] Rare were arguments of the Left that opposed protectionism. Perhaps the most notable exception was the insistent opposition by Argentine Socialists, in the beginning of the century, in efforts to protect the consumers: The prosperity of the agro-export economy was such that the local Socialists could afford the luxury of avoiding the hard path of industrialization and could speak for the workers as consumers. But, apart from these extreme situations, Latin America still had to create consumers. Protectionism, like forced capital accumulation, was accepted by progressives as a historical contingency, the same contingency that led the Communist parties to propose the alliance between the bourgeoisie and the masses against imperialism and the landed estate. As the decades passed, various Latin American countries industrialized, local businesspeople became part of the style of development that twenty years earlier was called "associated-dependent," the urban masses became consumers (ample rural and urban sectors, in truth, are subconsumers) and a good part of Latin American progressivism continued to be purely and simply protectionist, defending the internal market.

Also in this case, we confront a false dichotomy. It even tempts one to imitate the reasoning of the famous essay by Rodolfo Stavenhagen on "Seven Fallacies on Development" in a section on "The False Dichotomies." Currently, as social democracy indicates, the important point is not to reject the external market and base economic growth on internal consumption but to diminish the differences between what is produced and what is consumed internally and externally. To the extent, however, that there is an emphasis on exports (to pay the external debt, for example) based on an extensive exploitation of labor or when the exporting economy functions through enclaves, isolated from the internal market, an anachronistic model of development is being sustained that is damaging to the interests of the majority of the population.

The struggle for economic autarchy and the search for complete autonomy—even in the technological field—rather than serving popular interests, are values that have more to do with "the policies of a great power"—so well-liked by the military governments—and with an ideal of isolation that runs against the universalizing tendencies of modern science and production. Does this mean that Latin American social democrats should simply support liberalization or the opening up of national economies? It does not, but they should, once again, affirm the criteria of competitiveness and of absorption and production of modern technologies that allow gains in productivity, as the touchstones of economic policies designed to increase the well-being of the population. That is the desideratum of social democracy. It affirms that the effort to promote economic growth is a precondition for social welfare. It recognizes that certain protectionist practices can be useful to create internal conditions of competitiveness. However, when these conditions permitting accumulation and competitiveness are already present, monopolistic and oligopolistic practices should be condemned, even if maintained in the name of defending the internal market. It is a question, therefore, of a differentiated and selective choice among alternative policies that, in combination, assure realization of the fundamental objective: the public interest. There obviously exists a national interest for social democracy. But this is only entitled to support when filtered through the interests of the people—through the public interest.

The Argentine Socialists of the beginning of the century who opposed protectionism were ideological prisoners of laissez-faire and, in that sense, were operating anachronistically. The current progressives are nothing better when—without taking account of the transformation of the local economies and of the processes of economic globalization—they continue defending protectionism, for its own sake, and national production as coinciding automatically with the general interests of the country and of the working population. Here, they become victims of conservative thought and they—the progressives—in the face of the transformation of the real say, *plus ça change, plus c'est la même chose.*

Social democrats must, without adhering to neoliberalism, discuss, case by case, the steps and methods by which the Latin American economies should open up. The basic criterion will be equality, in income, in technology and in consumption, between the exporting productive sector and the internal market. In neither case does social democracy accept debasing the value of labor as the price of progress.

Social Democracy and the Democratic Regime

In Europe social democratic parties obtained power when society was already, in a manner of speaking, "democratized." The rapid growth of the SPD in Germany and of the social democratic parties in the Scandinavian countries, in Belgium, and in Holland until World War I occurred as universal suffrage was achieved. Following the distinction made by León Blum, if the social democrats did not, during the interbellum period, conquer power, they at least exercised it. While in power they found Keynes's ideas to be the key to a cohabitation with private ownership of the means of production. They "nationalized" consumption, increased wages and used the state to construct what, after World War II, became the trademark of social democratic Europe, the welfare state.

In some ways, social democrats adopted liberalism's conquests in the political sphere of liberalism and, in a way of all democrats, obtained concrete improvements in the condition of workers, of salaried employees and of small property owners through parliamentary democracy. Leaving aside the heated discussion of reform or revolution, there remain no doubts that the objective of improving the living conditions of the masses was being achieved by social democratic parties. Moreover, after totalitarian experiences like Nazism—which extended its stain beyond Germany—Francoism and the diverse authoritarianisms that thrived after the 1930s, the retaking of democracy was supported by the idea that liberties also lead to prosperity.

Recently José Maria Maravall wrote an essay on "Democratic Values and Political Practice,"[15] in which he explained how it was possible for a "democratic culture" to take root in Spain. The Socialists were successful in this feat and managed to keep majority support for their party because they improved people's lives. That occurred, among other reasons, because social reforms were realized (including the democratization of education), economic development materialized and institutions were created that increased participatory democracy.

It was not only in Spain that this amalgam of democracy, economic development and strengthening of social democratic parties occurred. In the various countries in which social democracy has weight (with strong unions and corrective state action) and where, therefore, redistributive measures were taken, there was *a greater rate of economic growth* compared to the countries without a strong social democratic presence. Maravall demonstrated that this tendency is not only consistent in the long run. Even after the crisis of the 1970s, often attributed to the ultra-"welfarism" and a consequent loss of competitiveness, countries with social democratic influences presented more favorable indicators of economic performance.[16]

Leaving aside the defense of the advantages of European social democracy, the drama of its Latin American equivalent is that its prospects were reborn along with the redemocratization of the continent but at a time, principally in the 1980s, when the economic performance of the countries reached its worst levels. This constitutes a difficulty not only for social democracy but also for a democratic culture taking root. Vargas's famous phrase (already cited: "the vote does not fill bellies") may become a dramatic perspective adopted by the Latin American masses. Social democracy in this continent should insist on democracy as an objective in itself (in the past, something done only by liberals) and, at the same time, dedicate itself to the institutionalization of practices of liberty, creating the arenas where reforms can be decided and implemented.

As far as the forms of government are concerned, Latin American social democracy, confronted with an overinflated state and the hypertrophy of the executive, is inclined toward parliamentarism. The tradition of the strong executive, for which U.S. democracy served as an example, degenerated in Latin America. Clientelism, the fragility of parties and of the legislature and the lack of a judiciary independent from the executive (capable of opposing the president and not being only the guardian of the constitution but also its creative interpreter) undermined presidentialism. This resulted in multiple authoritarian experiences, both civilian and military.

Social democracy will not find the path to modernity through the defense of parliamentary government alone. The participatory dimension should be added to representative democracy. On this point Christian social thought, the efforts at consciousness-raising and the organization of popular demands by the ecclesiastical base communities, inspired by liberation theology, play an important and constructive role. Valuing the participation of the people in the control of public administration requires, nevertheless, more than simple words. It is there that social democracy can and should distinguish itself from other political currents that identify with it in its effort to amplify the forms of participation. There is an important political force on the Left, often also oriented by Christian thought, that reduces popular participation to movementism or assemblyism. The enormous strength of the so-called popular movements—of undeniable democratic character and consequences—frequently is not being used to support those who try to define the institutional mechanisms that permit a regular pressure for social demands. It is in this politico-institutional engineering that social democracy, accepting the premises and objectives of expanding the participatory forms of democracy, should concentrate and differentiate itself from the merely basist action that characterizes a good part of Latin American popular progressivism.

The character that social democratic parties assume in Latin America, in terms of their social base of support and organization, remains to be discussed. In the past, in Europe, the acceptance of free elections and universal suffrage, added to the relative decrease in numbers of the working class, changed the one-class, revolutionary character of social democratic parties. The same happens in Latin America and in an even stronger sense. With the internationalization of the market and the new industrial revolution, provoked by developments in the high-tech sectors (informatics, genetic engineering, robotization, changes in business company structure, and so on), the very structure of societies, including those in Latin America, suffers rapid transformations. Social democracy continues to represent the point of view of the majority (of wage earners and of those who confront capital), and in this sense it belongs to the Left—despite the Fukuyamas who surge every twenty years decreeing the end of history and ideologies. But there is no intention of forming a one-class movement, nor of becoming a privileged instrument of history—the one and only party capable of bringing about changes.

Accepting party pluralism and the convergence in given situations of producer, consumer and worker interests—and therein deriving its emphasis on increasing productivity and investment—social democracy continues seeking to base itself on the working and middle classes. All this must occur without exclusivism and, above all, without assuming the arrogance of believing itself to be the repository of the future, rejecting philosophies of history that believe they have detected a thread of consistency that carries humanity to a pre-determined destiny.

Instead of believing in an eternal repetition of history (the conservative position) or in the inevitability of the redeeming revolution (a utopia that is not always "progressive"), social democracy prefers, more modestly, to believe in progressive changes that can bring about transformations favorable to the masses.

Notes

1. Albert Hirschman, "Two Hundred Years of Reactionary Rhetoric: The Case of the Perverse Effect," Tanner Lectures on Human Values, University of Michigan, Ann-Arbor, Michigan, 1990.

2. Robert K. Merton, *Social Theory and Social Structure* (Glencoe, Ill.: Free Press, 1951), chap. 3, pp. 98–102.

3. José Medina Echevarría, *Aspectos Sociales del Desarrollo Económico* (Santiago: Editorial Andrés Bello, 1959), reedited by ECLA in 1973, and especially *El Desarrollo Social de América Latina en el Pós Guerra* (Buenos Aires: Solar-Hachette, 1963).

4. Gino Germani, *Política y Sociedad en una Epoca de Transición* (Buenos Aires: Paidos, 1966) and *Sociología de la Modernización* (Buenos Aires: Paidos, 1969).

5. See Fernando Henrique Cardoso and Enzo Faletto, *Dependencia y Desarrollo en América Latina* (México D.F.: Siglo XXI, 1969).

6. See especially Francisco Weffort, *O Populismo na Política Brasileira* (Rio de Janeiro: Paz e Terra, 1978), especially chapter 1 "Política de Massas," originally published in 1963; Octavio Ianni, *O Colapse do Populismo no Brasil* (Rio de Janeiro: Civilização Brasileira, 1968). See also Torcuato di Tella, *Classes Sociales y Estructuras Políticas* (Buenos Aires: Paidos, 1974).

7. Guillermo O'Donnell, *Modernization and Bureaucratic Authoritarianism: Studies in South American Politics* (Berkeley: Institute of International Studies, University of California, 1973).

8. Peter Evans, *Dependent Development: The Alliance of Multinational, State and Local Capital in Brazil* (Princeton, N.J.: Princeton University Press, 1979).

9. W. W. Rostow, *The Stages of Economic Growth: A Non-Communist Manifesto* (Cambridge: Cambridge University Press, 1960).

10. Ignacy Sachs, "Environment and Styles of Development," in W. Matheur, ed., *Outer Limits and Human Needs* (Uppsala, Sweden: Dag Hammarskjöld Foundation, 1973).

11. Adam Przeworski, *Capitalism and Social Democracy* (Cambridge: Cambridge University Press, 1985).

12. To examine synthetically the transformations that occurred in European social democratic policies and also to see the differences with the developments in Latin America, see Ignacio Walter, "Socialismo y Democrácia: Algunas Experiencias Europeas," in *Cieplan, Colección Estudios*, Santiago, no. 21, June 1987, pp. 23–48.

13. E. Oyen, *Comparing Welfare States and Their Futures* (Aldershot: Gower, 1986).

14. See Nicia V. Luz, *A Luta Industrialização do Brasil* (São Paulo: Difusão Europeia de Livros, 1961).

15. J. M. Maravall, "Valores Democráticos y Prácticas Políticas," in *Leviatán*, no. 37, Autumn 1989, pp. 5–24.

16. In another article, "Las Razones del Reformismo: Democracia y Política Social," in *Leviatán*, no. 35, Spring 1989, pp. 27–50, Maravall takes apart the structure of public spending to demonstrate that its level was maintained in the

advanced democracies even when conservatives governed. Social spending, in spite of economic crises, expanded substantially more in social democratic countries. Maravall's article defends state intervention to protect rights, including social ones, and to create effective conditions of equality of opportunity. He shows that there is ample room for reformist policies consistent with economic development. The figures on "fiscal pressure" as a percentage of GNP in European countries are significant. They vary from 33.6 percent in Spain to 51.9 percent in Denmark, with an average of 42.8 percent in the European Common Market. It is sufficient to compare these levels with the low 22 percent of Brazil.

15

Latin America:
From Populism Toward
Social Democracy

Alain Touraine

Social democracy, as its name indicates, is defined by the predominance of social categories over political categories. A social democratic party is above all a labor party, in the sense in which the term has been used up to now in the Swedish political vocabulary, where the distinction between labor party and bourgeois parties still is made. To speak of social democracy in Latin America seems at first incongruous. Latin American political life is defined by the predominance of political categories over social categories.[1] Those countries that have known social democratic parties and governments represent class societies. The greater part of the population is integrated in relationships of production typical of an industrial society. Latin American societies, however, are hardly integrated along such lines, as shown by so many classic studies on what Aníbal Pinto has called *la heterogeneidad estructural*.[2] How can one fail to notice the weakness, the near absence of Socialist parties on the continent? The major exception, the Chilean Socialist party, has operated, since its foundation, on the radical left of the political spectrum. It has always been more populist revolutionary than social reformist. The Communist parties had a greater importance, not only in Chile but also in other countries and especially in Brazil, right after World War II. There, the Communists choose to support the queremista, or populist movement, rather than to lead class action. Almost everywhere in Latin America, political life has been dominated by the distributive state that created a large urban middle class and incorporated many unionized workers, aided by the resources that a strong protectionism and the exportation of raw materials provided.

In short, social democratic countries are nations of industrial production—societies of classes where the leftist movement is strongly supported by workers' unions and often depends on them. In Latin American countries, on the other hand, politics is dedicated to redistribution, society is segmented and even sometimes has a multiple structure and the unions and other social movements are generally weaker than the political mobilization around a nationalist and populist party. Examples are the PRI in México, the APRA in Perú, Acción Democrática in Venezuela, the MNR in Bolivia, Justicialismo in Argentina and the Colorado party in Uruguay. Central America and the Caribbean, Brazil, Colombia, and Chile are not included in this list, for different reasons. The first-mentioned countries conform even less to the model of Northern and Western Europe than the rest of the continent, with the very notable exception of Costa Rica; Brazil has always been directed by a strong state, but its Bismarckian rather than populist nature brought it closer to European situations; Colombia had its national populist movement, which had triumphed there in the 1930s, destroyed by the assassination of Gaitán in 1948; and Chile came by far the closest to the European model of representative democracy, embodying the relationship between political parties and social forces. It is the only country on the continent where traditionally the real presence of social democracy can be discussed. These observations are so obvious that they seem to make any other commentary superfluous. However, they are insufficient and mask what connects Latin America as a whole to a number of European countries.

The definition of social democracy given at the beginning of this chapter, though accurate, is incomplete. Social democracy is in opposition to "pure" socialism, which always has been more a political than a social force, rooted in the struggles against preindustrial society and the power of the church and the state. Social democratic countries industrialized rather late. They were ruled by a mobilizing state rather than by a national bourgeoisie. Was not Germany the locus classicus of social democracy, the country in which it has known its greatest strength and its deepest divisions—before the Russian Social Democratic Party was torn by the struggles between Mensheviks and Bolsheviks—and the country from which social democracy has penetrated in Northern Europe? The developments in Germany were strongly influenced by the defeat of the Frankfort bourgeoisie in 1848, before Otto von Bismarck. Was not Sweden, which appeared as the model of social democracy after the last war, a country of very late industrialization and for a long time even of emigration? It maintained at the same time a strongly hierarchized society and a repressive Protestant culture that resisted industrialization. One might even add, with the necessary caution, that the late industrializing countries, where social democracy has developed, are also those where the strongest political force against social democracy—national socialism—emerged in various degrees. In many aspects this is its exact opposite and even its negation. This indicates that the two political models have elements in common. Among these we find the central role of the state in a voluntarist modernization process, which puts them in opposition to the belief of liberalism, and on emphasis on the dynamic functions of rationalization, technology, education, the market forces and communications.

Social democracy, if one brings together the two apparently antagonistic elements that form it, that is, the important role of the labor unions on the Left and the emphasis on state intervention, is therefore halfway between liberal countries where political life and social life are widely separated and where the labor movement is more a social than a political force (as in the United States) and the countries still influenced by the Socialist revolutionary tradition, like France, Spain and even Italy, notwithstanding the rapid and long-time domination by authoritarian regimes in the last two cases. The English Labour Party occupies a middle position between an independent labor movement, as it was defined by the Fabians and that remained for a long time a business unionism, and a social democratic party, subordinated to the TUC.

These two components of European social democracy led in political practice to two different positions. To assert the autonomy of the social actor leads to the insertion of class action into a more general political model, that of democracy. Such is the English concept of industrial democracy, which spread to Northern Europe before it took the very subdued shape of a social market economy in Germany. On the other hand, to insist on the role of the state produces a more radical brand of political action, which runs through Rosa Luxembourg up until the Soviet revolution. In Germany, during the Weimar Republic, some hoped to create a democratisation of industry; others wanted an industrial democracy, a more limited concept closer to the English model. The first-mentioned movement represented a more political force that could become revolutionary. For many theoreticians of socialism, these two movements could and should have come together in the ideas of workers' councils, soviets or workers' self-management. All of these would be the result of the political victory of a class identified with the destruction of the bourgeois state, and they would assert the priority of class action at the bottom over political action at the top. This trend of thought—which dominated the discussion from Anton Pannekoek to Antonio Gramsci, in republican Spain, among the workers' councils of Budapest in 1956, in Prague in 1968 and in Gdansk in 1980—nevertheless does not have a historical importance comparable to state socialism or to industrial democracy. These two form in fact the major dimensions of social democracy, which underlines this movement's vulnerability. Both principles are equally prominent. However, they are more contradictory than complementary.

In Latin America, the central role of the working class is rare, except in mining countries such as Chile and Bolivia and, to some extent, Perú and México. The intervention of the state in economic and social modernization, however, is a constant factor. Its redistributive function is often related to its *desarrollista* or *desenvolvimentista* role. This makes the social democratic and the national populist regimes very different from each other but comparable in the area of political mobilization through the intervention of social forces. The common ground for these two types of regimes is located between the United States and France, between a country animated by economic actors and another dominated by political ones or, in more global terms, between the East and the West. Latin America is not located in the world's center. It occupies an intermediary position between the West, the East and the South. Argentina has been almost entirely Western-oriented; México was profoundly influenced by the Soviet revolutionary model; and the Andean countries and Central America belong more clearly to the South.

Both European social democracy and the Latin American national populist regimes correspond to intermediary historical situations, which makes them unstable and fragile. Social democracy does not aim to create a Socialist society, that is, a society in which the state owns the means of production; it merely seeks to create a greater socioeconomic equality on the basis of a vigorous, sometimes even radical, redistribution of income by the state. If it succeeds in doing so and realizes modernization, the social classes will free themselves from the state's tutelage and directly bargain between themselves, with the business sector and the labor organizations taking a central role. The state will concentrate on the introduction of active social policies for urban life, education, health and the problem of unemployment.

The natural fate of social democracies appears to be an approximation to the model of the advanced industrialized societies under Keynesian influence, where a liberal management of the economy is complemented by strong social redistribution policies. The national populist regimes are doomed because they tend to reinforce the role of the state while weakening the formation of autonomous social actors, among business or labor. The result, almost inevitably, is a structural crisis of the kind that became apparent during the second phase of the Peronist regime (between 1950 and 1955), in the beginning of the 1960s in Brazil and in the year 1960 in México. Military dictatorships or a serious political crisis then replaced national populist regimes when the influx of foreign capital diminished and an excessive protectionism weakened the competitiveness of national producers.

The major deficiency of national populist regimes has indeed always been that they are more distributivist than desarrollista. This had to do with the abundance of resources for export that was so great for a long time, in particular during World War II and also during the period of the 1970s when triumphing liberalism led to a certain deindustrialization of Argentina, Chile and Venezuela. In those years, industrialized Europe increasingly related the problem of modernization to the politics of redistribution, creating systems of national collective bargaining. This was done in the spirit of British industrial democracy, in the spirit of the social rights introduced in France after 1945 or by following the model created by the Swedes in Saltjöbaden in 1938. Latin America followed an opposite path: The modernization of the economy was accompanied by increasing socioeconomic inequalities. The state intervened more in favor of the creation of an urban middle class than of the rapprochement of the rich with the poor. These groups, on the contrary, are moving farther away from each other.

That is why a current analysis of the various paths open to Latin America—among which the various forms of social democracy have to be assigned their places—must begin recognizing that the road leading to national populist solutions is definitely closed. This is most certainly the case at a moment when the continent has become a net exporter of capital and has experienced an entire decade of impoverishment and decline. The disarticulation of the economy and politics, made doubly worse by the impact of ideology, cannot go on. Surely, in a crisis situation, the social actors are looking more than ever to the state. Their own bargaining strength is diminishing, especially in times of high inflation. A distributive policy, however, can only accelerate the further decomposition of the economic and social system, when the internal deficit has taken on gigantic proportions and the state fiscal resources have weakened. The populist temptation is present everywhere in Latin America. In Argentina it assured Menem's victory, first over Cafiero within Justicialismo and then over the radical candidate Eduardo Angeloz in the national elections. It gave victory to Collor over Lula in Brazil. It explains the narrow and contested victory of Salinas de Gortari over Cuauthémoc Cárdenas in México, Alan García's triumph in Perú and, more recently, Fujimori's victory in June 1990. But there is no chance of success for a populist solution. The victories of Menem and Collor more than anything else meant the carrying out of policies bent on ending hyperinflation, analogous to those implemented in Bolivia under Paz Estenssoro. Populism is no more than the most efficient political discourse covering policies that break away from hyperinflation and either move toward liberalism and an extremely export-oriented economic model or, in a more complex and less predictable manner, toward a course that will allow internal economic forces and national business enterprises to restart a growth that had solid grounding but was destroyed by hyperinflation. This is probably the case in Brazil.

If one sets aside the wrong populist solution, three major paths open up for Latin American countries. The first, which is the opposite of any social democracy, will mean a partial incorporation into the world economy. The industrialized countries have embarked on a course of technological innovation that produces more inequalities than any development since the 1973 oil crisis, which hit Japan, Western Europe and the United States so violently. It increasingly impairs the industrial competitiveness of intermediary countries among themselves and vis-à-vis the new industrial countries that have installed advanced technologies, often at the price of very harsh social policies. This trend is the most visible one. Everywhere the incorporation into the world market and the search for comparative advantages are being discussed. In a country like México, this concerns an incorporation into the U.S. economy, like Canada, rather than into the world economy. In Chile, these policies, which yielded very negative results at the end of the 1970s, have been successful since 1985 due to the development of new exports of raw materials and the rise in the price of copper on the world market. These exports are the result of true modernization. In the production and export of fruit, fish and wood products, dynamic modern enterprises have come into existence. This development remains precarious, however, because it produces vast socioeconomic inequalities and rests on fiscal privileges to business, in particular in the fruit industry.

The second path is one of chaos, the result of neopopulist politics or of the resistance by the old populist model to new liberal solutions. Bolivia under the Hernán Siles Suazo government and in the period when the national mining enterprise was managed by the trade union confederation together with the government, sank into chaos. The same has happened with Perú where the state presence in many areas has almost ceased to exist and popular organizations have taken over. This *desborde popular*, so ably described by José Matos Mar, makes marginality the rule, and the armed struggle triggered by Sendero Luminoso creates risks of utter chaos.[3] Or consider Argentina: Despite the strength of the democratic restoration at the beginning of the Alfonsin presidency, it ended up in a state of chaos. Hunger riots dramatically revealed the collapse of the standard of living for the masses and the poverty of a large segment of low-income workers.

A third path remains, which Latin America calls social democracy. It must be studied attentively in order to determine if indeed it belongs to political regimes and societies similar to those of European countries. This path is defined, like all types of social democracy, as a voluntary action by the state—supported by at least a part of the popular classes—against the increasing dualism of society, in favor of a redistribution of income and a reduction of inequalities. But this definition is too general to differentiate such policies from the old national populist ones or from European social democratic policies. What sets present Latin American politics apart from the old populisms is above all the recognition of the separation between a logic of economic management and a logic of political action. The old national populist regimes desarticulated the economy and politics and initially combined the dependency of the economy in relation to foreign centers of decisionmaking with a direct interventionist policy in the whole of social life. Under these regimes, however, the state started, as Cárdenas did in México, a program of economic liberation and national integration. By contrast, national states now accept the market mechanism and international competition. This does not exclude protectionist measures, but it clearly aims at constructing and/or consolidating a competitive economy. This indeed marks a fundamental turnaround. In general, economic activity and especially economic policies of the government must conform to strictly economic criteria: The country must have one currency, not several, or be "dollarized"; prices must correspond to the best possible allocation of resources; and, more precisely, state enterprises must be run according to criteria of profitability and rationality. This means entering in the world that Max Weber described as modernity: differentiation of functions, triumph of economic rationality and bureaucracy as a rational organization of the state. Why is this transformation so important? It is because this liberation, this autonomization of the economic system, is the first condition for imposing a logic of functioning of the social system through which social actors will emerge. In the national popular regimes like those in the Communist or nationalist regimes of the Third World, the major logic was one of development, of voluntary change of the society by the state rather than by society itself.

This first transformation leads to a second one: Moves toward income redistribution must be led not entirely from inside the state but, in a large measure at least, by political agents representing the actors and social categories directly involved, especially unions and political parties. Finally, this change in perspective leads to a redefinition of the state as an agent of integration for two very different logics: an economic logic dominated by the world market and a social logic imposed by social movements or interest groups in the name of citizenship, liberty and equality.

These reminders allow us to formulate more precisely the possibility of a social democratic solution in Latin America. While international competitiveness and hence the domination of new technologies assert themselves as criteria of economic management, are there social actors emerging who claim to represent popular classes? Is the state a mediator inspired by a precise concept of national integration? In the light of what has been said about the increasing dualism of Latin American societies, if we are to answer these questions positively, difficult conditions must be met. The liberal solution more naturally calls for a repression of popular demands and a state identified with the most favored sector of the economy. It will leave the poor aside. Among them social movements, sometimes of a religious nature, will emerge. More often they will try to find individual solutions to their problems or end up in social disorganization. Is not the most salient trait of Latin America today the weakness of collective action, while a social democratic solution, as already said, is defined primarily by the priority and hence the strength of collective action? Socially and politically, Latin America is still very close to a situation that conforms to the national populist model—even though the latter is in its terminal phase of decomposition—while the state of its economy seems to push it almost inevitably toward liberal solutions. This contradiction is so extreme that it threatens to tear society apart, to intensify its dualism and hence to take Latin America farther away from social democratic models.

The term *social democracy* is, then, used in Latin America today in many senses, more often negative than positive. The term especially expresses the rejection of an absolute liberalism. This is the case in Ecuador where the social democratic government is in opposition to the politics of the economic power groups of Guayaquil and to those of the *narcotráfico* lords. In México, also, the PRI often defines itself as a social democratic party to the extent to which the union of the state and the party is dissolving and the Mexican perestroika materializes. But can the PRI be considered as an expression of an autonomous popular force? And is it not directed by a logic that, above all, corresponds to the end of the national populist system rather than to the construction of a new mode of democratic state intervention?

These experiences are so inconclusive that one is tempted to conclude that social democracy can only be realized within the framework of liberalism. This obviously would confirm the experience of the Western industrial countries: first, the triumph of capitalism; second, the formation of an entrepreneurial class; and then finally, the emergence of a labor movement forcing state intervention and the establishment of an industrial democracy. One country seems to be advancing on this road and even at great speed: Chile. After a series of "shocks," the economy was redirected with success toward the external market. An entrepreneurial class constituted itself, supported by a repressive state. The result came quickly enough to create room for an effective democratization. It made the ruling elites accept a certain rise in real wages, which had become extremely low, and tolerate a new fiscal law that will noticeably increase the tax burden. Chile would then take a shortcut that would bring it closer to the newly industrialized countries and even to European countries by avoiding the winding courses of social democracy, entering directly into a market-based social economy like the German or Dutch ones. In fact, today, the evolution of the Chilean situation is increasingly being commented upon in favorable terms. The weakening of the labor movement after 1984 has come to a halt, collective bargaining is being instituted and the state, ruled by Christian democrats with the collaboration of moderate Socialists, appears to follow a policy that reconciles a sustained growth *hacia afuera* with a reduction of the internal inequalities that had increased greatly during the military dictatorship. The Chilean model—if this expression can be used at this time—would be closer to the present welfare state than to the social democracy of the first half of the century. The economy is progressing faster than the political system. The latter reestablishes itself even before the social actors have become organized. Basically, this conforms to the definition of a liberal process of development. The question remains—and it may be too soon to answer it—to what extent does this development (which goes from the economic to the social, passing through the political) really fit the situation of a country and a continent where social inequalities are still increasing, where poverty is rampant and where the heritage of the authoritarian regimes cannot be eliminated in a few months? The difficulties that the young Chilean democracy will encounter in creating a social market economy should not be underestimated. It has the great merit of openly recognizing the priority of the market. However, in order for this economic realism to be combined with a substantial redistribution of income and the establishment of a true welfare state, the strength of popular pressure needs to increase. At the same time, a national policy should be followed that closely combines economic goals with social objectives. This will include an opposition to the unproductive endeavors of the privileged classes. The imbalances that have arisen or worsened during the military regime are so great that it is hard to see how they could be corrected other than by an increasing cooperation between the union movement and the state. This is the way European social democracy proceeded. This presupposes, however, the growth of an economic consciousness among the unions, while the state develops a capability to resist pressures from the dominant economic interest groups and the army.

The Chilean form of social democracy would have to be situated, if it does succeed, on the "Right" of the European experience in this area. There it would join the Center-Right or Center-Left regimes that, in Europe, have long combined an emphasis on economic modernization with policies of social redistribution, managed by a state apparatus that came to consume almost half of the gross domestic product. However, Chile's economic development is still in the intermediary phase, and it carries the weight of a long dictatorship. One hesitates to believe that it could instantly skip the stages that Northern European countries passed through over a long period of time and with much difficulty.

That is why other forms of social democracy may appear on the continent. In Brazil, in particular, economic modernization and the organization of social and political forces have reached a point where the return to economic truths should be combined with a redistribution of income. This would mean remaking a nation, segmented by extreme economic and social distances between the rich and the poor. The most recent presidential campaign has shown the strength of the popular movements. At the same time, however, they were unable to dispel the doubts about their ability to manage the economy. On the other hand, Collor de Melo obtained a victory that few predicted, but it was not accompanied by references to a populist or even liberal discourse. On the contrary, he constantly called for social democratic support. The distance remains great between the popular vote and the intentions of a new president and between yesterday's political opponents. But who does not recognize that in Brazil no solution exists other than their rapprochement, difficult as it may be? This gives a strategically central—and at the same time politically delicate—position to the Brazilian social democratic party and to its leaders, Fernando Henrique Cardoso, Mario Covas and José Serra, partisans of both realistic economic policies based on market criteria and deep social transformations. The combined realization of economic and social objectives seems too easy to be very solid in the Chile of 1990; it appears almost impossible in a Brazil that is not even guaranteed to survive the financial, economic and social shock that had been imposed in order to end the situation of hyperinflation. But the experience of the last twenty years calls for difficult rather than easy solutions. In any case, all countries need to combine strong action in the social field with the search for economic efficiency. This requires policies of social redistribution and, hence, a rise in the general level of political and social mobilization.

How is the present situation of Latin America to be defined? First, it is characterized by the complete exhaustion of the national populist model. Disorientation in politics is so great today because this model, which has dominated fifty years of the continent's history, is a spent force. The continent sees itself invaded by a neoliberalism that seems to be the inevitable ending stage of all politics, even when they are presented as antiliberal and populist. Some countries are ravaged by a most brutal form of extreme liberalism, identified with narcotráfico. In recent years we have witnessed the financial collapse of Argentina and Brazil, following the large-scale riots and massive repression that disrupted Venezuela. Latin America has now left the populist cycle. Many believed this was accomplished, for better or for worse, by military coups d'etat, rather than by the return of democracy. In reality, the military coups were antipopulist in orientation, and the return to democracy often runs the risk of deviating toward a neopopulism. It is exactly at the present moment that the decisive choices for the future will be made; a return to the past is now blocked. The state, in several cases, succeeded in stopping the further decline of the economy by taking action. Brazil had to resort to extreme measures after the successive failure of three plans for economic recovery. Argentina called for liberal policies in order to end the hyperinflation that threw the Alfonsin government into a precipice in a few months. Everyday Perú appears more dangerously threatened by the disintegration that Bolivia managed to evade a few years ago. Venezuela has been paralyzed since the Caracas riots and their repression. All this demonstrates the double impossibility of both pursuing populist policies and breaking away from them.

This consciousness of the necessary and at the same time almost impossible rupture with the past may be more important for Latin America than the search for individual solutions. In addition, we may assume that Latin America's options are not limited to either a savage capitalism or an extreme leveling and planning socialism. Latin America confronts its problems, its necessary transformation, at a time when the great ideological models have disappeared and when the optimism of the defenders of a liberal modernization seems absurd in the light of the increasing distance separating North from South and, in the South, rich from poor. That is why the hypothesis that is apparently most removed from present reality at the same time seems to me to be the most probable one: Latin American countries, if they do not sink into chaos, will rediscover a third path. This is the path that they already call social democracy and that, in effect, will transform the old national populist systems, developing new ways of participation by social and political forces in order to balance again an economic model directed toward the external market. Latin America's increasing dependence, caused by the external debt and the necessity to export in order to service it, creates new pressures on the state to act but this time less in favor of policies that have to do with the distribution of external resources than of those that deal with the immediate reduction of internal inequalities. The struggle these socioeconomic inequalities, what the International Labor Organization's regional employment program for Latin America and the Caribbean (PREALC) has called *la deuda social*, is the absolute priority in Latin America at the same time that the increase of exports is also an urgent everyday necessity.[4] We tend to believe that this economic liberalism and these advanced social policies are incompatible, but it is precisely their association that will create the variant of social democracy that Latin America is developing, as we see in Brazil and perhaps in México where the PRI pretends to be social democratic while Salinas leads a policy of integration into the entire North American economic community. And what represents the Chilean democratic government other than a pact between the defenders of the liberal option— continuing the policies of the years between 1985 and 1990—and those advocating policies of income redistribution demanded by the defenders of democracy? The danger of chaos increases: An extreme liberalism, reinforcing inequalities, has a great chance of ending in turmoil through the revolt of the popular and middle classes as a result of the elimination of the modern sector and their subsequent decline into marginality. Realizing the possibilities for catastrophes to happen in the near future certainly is not enough to prevent them from taking place. The room for positive solutions has become extremely narrow. Therefore, the threat of chaos rather than a project or coherent and strongly integrated program has the best chance to pressure a great part of the continent toward a mixture—apparently contradictory but realistic—of economic liberalism *hacia afuera* and a policy of important internal social transformation. This new social democracy appears delicate and constantly threatens to fall into pieces even before it has the chance to really constitute itself, but it is more than ever the only solution to a situation that does not sustain either old populism or new liberalism. Latin America has only one real choice: between chaos and a reduction of social inequalities, without which the indispensable search for economic competitiveness will also lead to chaos.

Notes

1. For an analysis of the general issues on Latin American political life dealt with in this chapter, see Alain Touraine, *Le Parole et le Sang: Politique et Société en Amerique Latine* (Paris: Editions Odile Jacob, 1988).

2. Aníbal Pinto, "Naturaleza e Implicaciones de la Heterogeneidad Estructural de la América Latina," in *El Trimestre Económico*, vol. 36, no. 1, 1970, pp. 34–67.

3. José Matos Mar, *Desborde Popular y Crisis del Estado* (Lima: Concytec, 1984).

4. PREALC, *Ajuste y Deuda Social* (Santiago: Oficina Internacional del Trabajo, 1987).

About the Book

In Western Europe the practice of social democracy has allowed governments to pursue equity as well as economic competitiveness. In this book, leading Latin American and European scholars examine the political crisis in Latin America and review the prospects for economic and social transformation using the European model. They begin by discussing the experience of social democracy in various European countries, drawing out lessons for Latin America. Next, they offer an analysis of social democratic theory, evaluating whether it can be applied consistently under differing conditions and whether the economic component is as significant as the political one. Finally, in a number of country and regional case studies, contributors examine what the social democratic alternative has to offer, given the margins for reformism, and analyze specific social democratic policies, including basic needs provision, income redistribution, and structural transformation.

About the Contributors

Manuel Alcántara Sáez, professor of political science at the Complutense University in Madrid, Spain, is the author of several books on Latin American politics, including *Sistemas Políticos de América Latina*, 2 vols. (1990).

Paul Cammack is a senior lecturer at the Department of Government, University of Manchester, England. He has published extensively on the problems of democratization in Latin America.

Fernando Henrique Cardoso, former director of the Brazilian Center for Research and Planning (CEBRAP) in São Paulo, is presently a member of the Brazilian Parliament and a senator for the social democratic party PSDB. He has published numerous works on Latin American development, including *Dependency and Development in Latin America* (1979, with Enzo Faletto).

Marcelo Cavarozzi, senior researcher at the Center for the Study of State and Society (CEDES) in Argentina and professor of political science at the University of Buenos Aires, has published widely on political development in the countries of the Southern Cone. His works include *Autoritarismo y Democracia* (1983).

Julio Cotler is a professor of anthropology at San Marcos University and a researcher at the Institute of Peruvian Studies (IEP), both in Lima, Perú. He has authored and edited numerous books and articles on social and political development in Perú and other Andean countries, including *Clases, Estado y Nación en el Perú* (1978).

Agustín Cueva died in 1992. In life he was professor of sociology at the Center for Latin American Studies (CELA) of the National University of Mexico (UNAM), has published widely on the general topics of dependence and development in Latin America and in his native country, Ecuador. His works include *El Desarrollo del Capitalismo en América Latina* (1977) and *The Process of Political Domination in Ecuador* (1982).

Tilman Evers, senior lecturer in political science at Free University in Berlin and at the Evangelical Institute in Hofgeismar, Germany, is the author of numerous articles on political development, the state and social movements in Latin America. His works include *El Estado en la Periferia Capitalista* (1979).

Alex Fernández Jilberto, senior lecturer in political science at the University of Amsterdam, The Netherlands, is the author of *Dictadura Militar y Oposición Política en Chile, 1973–1981* (1985) and of many articles on the state, the military and democratization in Chile.

Luís Gómez Calcaño, director of the Center for Development Studies (CENDES) of the Central University of Venezuela in Caracas has published many articles and research reports on sociopolitical development in Venezuela.

Pablo González Casanova, director of the Center for Interdisciplinary Research in the Humanities at the National University of Mexico (UNAM), is the author and editor of numerous books and articles on Latin American and, in particular, Mexican development. His most famous works include *Sociología de la Explotación* (1969) and *La Democracia en México* (1965).

Kenneth Hermele is a research fellow of the Center for the Study of Development Strategies in the Third World (AKUT) at Uppsala University, Sweden. His many publications focus on the social and political impact of economic reform programs in African and Latin American countries.

Jaime Tamayo, senior researcher at the Center for the Study of Social Movements (CISMOS) at the University of Guadalajara, Mexico, has published widely in the areas of politics and social movements in Mexico.

Edelberto Torres-Rivas is the director of the Latin American Social Sciences Faculty (FLACSO) in San José, Costa Rica. He has authored and edited numerous books and articles on Central American development, including *Repression and Resistance: The Struggle for Democracy in Central America* (1989).

Alain Touraine, professor of sociology at the École des Hautes Études en Sciences Sociales in Paris, France, has authored a great number of articles and books in the areas of the sociology of work and social movements, including most recently *La Parole et le Sang: Politique et Société en Amerique Latine* (1988).

Menno Vellinga is a senior lecturer at the Center for Caribbean and Latin American Studies (CARLAS), University of Utrecht, The Netherlands. He is the author and editor of many books and articles on sociopolitical aspects of development in Latin America, including *Industrialización, Burguesía y Clase Obrera en México* (1980) and *Burguesía e Industria en América Latina y Europa Meridional* (1988, with Mario Cerutti).

Index